THE RITSCHLIAN THEOLOGY

PRINTED BY MORRISON AND GIBB LIMITED

FOR

T. & T. CLARK, EDINBURGH.

LONDON : SIMPKIN, MARSHALL, HAMILTON, KENT, AND CO. LIMITED.
NEW YORK : CHARLES SCRIBNER'S SONS.
TORONTO : FLEMING H. REVELL COMPANY.

THE

RITSCHLIAN THEOLOGY

CRITICAL AND CONSTRUCTIVE

AN EXPOSITION AND AN ESTIMATE

BY

ALFRED E. GARVIE

M.A. (OXON.), B.D. (GLAS.)

EDINBURGH
T. & T. CLARK, 38 GEORGE STREET
1899

THIS BOOK IS DEDICATED

TO THE

REV. A. M. FAIRBAIRN, M.A., D.D., LL.D.,

PRINCIPAL OF MANSFIELD COLLEGE, OXFORD,

IN SINCERE GRATITUDE

FOR INSTRUCTION AND INSPIRATION IN THEOLOGICAL STUDY,

RECEIVED BY THE WRITER IN STUDENT DAYS,

AND

FOR WISE COUNSEL AND KIND ENCOURAGEMENT, IMPARTED

SINCE IN THE WORK OF THE CHRISTIAN MINISTRY;

AND IN CORDIAL ADMIRATION

OF THE

CONSPICUOUS ABILITIES DISPLAYED, AND THE VALUABLE

SERVICES RENDERED TO SACRED LEARNING AND

CHRISTIAN TRUTH IN HIS WRITINGS.

iv

PREFACE

THE writer asks the indulgence of the reader on the threshold of his book for a few words of explanation regarding its occasion, purpose, limits, method, and spirit.

(1) Dr. Fairbairn, to whom the writer is conscious of having but imperfectly expressed his obligations in the dedication of his book, proposed that the writer should deliver a course of lectures in Mansfield College, Oxford, during his absence in India ; and of several subjects submitted to him, selected the Ritschlian Theology as the theme of the proposed course of lectures. By the considerate and generous kindness of the writer's church in Montrose, for which he now desires heartily to express his gratitude, he was enabled to spend last November in Oxford, delivering his lectures. As the students of Mansfield College proved so appreciative and sympathetic an audience, he felt constrained to comply with their unanimous request that his lectures should be published. Conscious, however, of the inadequacy and imperfection of his treatment of the subject, he has revised, corrected, expanded, and, so far as he could, improved the lectures ; and now he publishes them in regular book-form, with chapters instead of lectures, in the hope that the wider public of theological readers may accord his labours the same generous recognition as was given by the students whom it was his privilege and pleasure for a short time to teach.

v

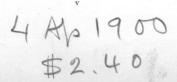

(2) The occasion of this book has defined its purpose. It is not intended, firstly, for the theological scholars, whose knowledge of the German language is sufficient to enable them to study the original literature, but for those students of Christian thought who either do not know German at all, or do not know it well enough to do altogether without such help in their study as one with a better knowledge can afford them. It is not intended, secondly, to give an exhaustive or a systematic account of the Ritschlian Theology; because, in the first place, that could not even be attempted in the bounds of one volume; and because, in the second place, those to whom the book is specially addressed neither require nor desire so full and thorough a knowledge, but will be more benefited by a treatment in which the attention is not dissipated over a multitude of details, but is concentrated on the few distinctive features and dominant factors of this theological school. Its significance and value, its importance and influence, can be estimated with sufficient truth and justice without so elaborate a discussion, as would tend to confuse and obscure instead of distinguishing and exhibiting the real, vital issues.

(3) This purpose determines the limits. Although none of Ritschl's writings, except one historical volume, which does not exhibit clearly or fully his distinctive position, has as yet been translated into English, yet it was impossible, even though the book is intended for English readers, to disregard his teaching. Most attention has been given, however, to the contents of a volume, which is being even now translated, and will be published in the course of a year. It is hoped that when this appears, Chapters IX., X., XI. especially of this present work will prove a useful guide in the study of it. Of the other Ritschlian writers, Herrmann, Kaftan, and Harnack are the only ones who have been dealt with, not only

because these are the recognised leaders of the school, but especially because their names are already familiar to English readers, as translations of some of their works have already appeared. The discussion of their teachings, however, has not been confined to their translated works, as a study of their untranslated works is often necessary for a clear and full understanding of those already translated. The writer's reading, it is needless to add, has not been subject to the same limitation.

(4) The purpose not only determines the limits, but also prescribes the method of the book. As far as possible, the writer has allowed Ritschl and his followers to speak for themselves. Instead of giving merely his own generalisations, he has endeavoured in the exposition of the more distinctive writings to let each Ritschlian present not only his own conclusions, but in his own way. It is this desire not to come between the Ritschlian school and the English reader, which explains both the quantity of the quotations and the quality of the translations. It would often have been easier for the writer to give his interpretation of a Ritschlian statement in his own words, but he preferred to quote, so that the reader might be able to judge for himself whether the interpretations given were correct or not. The translations do not pretend to be always in literary or even idiomatic English; but elegance of style has been sacrificed to fidelity of rendering. To do an obscure or difficult passage of German into plain and simple English is, as a rule, to interpret as well as to translate; and for his purpose it was important to separate translation and interpretation. Further, it does seem desirable that the English reader should know not only what the Ritschlians think, but also how they write, so that he may appreciate the difficulties of the interpreter.

(5) As the writer is convinced that English theological thought can only gain by the hospitable entertainment of

the religious teaching of other lands, and as the Ritschlian
school has as yet not received a cordial welcome in Britain,
he has sought to present his subject in as generous and
sympathetic a spirit as he can.   Although he has striven
to recognise fully the claims of truth and justice, yet he
would rather be charged with partiality than with prejudice, even though he cherishes the hope that he has not
afforded ground for either of the accusations.   As the
Ritschlian theology seeks, honestly if imperfectly, to win
men beset by doubt for Christian faith, it deserves to be
kindly as well as justly and truly treated.   May this
exposition and estimate of it in some measure serve the
same sacred cause.

MONTROSE,
21st September 1899.

TABLE OF CONTENTS

———◆———

CHAPTER I

THE PROBLEM NEEDING SOLUTION : HISTORICAL INTRODUCTION

A.—CRITICAL

CHAPTER II

THE EXCLUSION OF METAPHYSICS FROM THEOLOGY

I. (1) The inconsistency of Ritschl's position on the relation of
      metaphysics to theology, due to his aversion to philosophy,
      shows itself (2) in his insistence at one time on, and his
      denial at another time of, the necessity of an epistemology
      to theology   39–41

II. (1) After stating the theories of knowledge of Plato, Kant,
      and Lotze, (2) he rejects the first and second, but accepts
      the third. (3) He does not, however, correctly state any
      of them, not even that which he accepts, but (4) the
      epistemology he intends is *vulgar realism*, (5) which shows
      his philosophical incapacity, although it affords him a
      justification for his empirical theological method. (6)

CHAPTER III

THE REJECTION OF SPECULATIVE THEISM

I. (1) Inconsistent in his statements about the relation of metaphysics to theology, (2) Ritschl nevertheless is always

CHAPTER IV

THE CONDEMNATION OF ECCLESIASTICAL DOGMA

CHAPTER V

THE ANTAGONISM TO RELIGIOUS MYSTICISM

B.—CONSTRUCTIVE

CHAPTER VI

THE VALUE-JUDGMENTS OF RELIGION

b

CHAPTER VIII

THE REGULATIVE USE OF THE IDEA OF THE KINGDOM
OF GOD

CHAPTER IX

THE DOCTRINE OF THE PERSON AND THE WORK OF CHRIST

CHAPTER X

THE DOCTRINE OF SIN AND SALVATION

CHAPTER XI

THE DOCTRINE OF THE CHURCH AND THE KINGDOM

I. (1) The Christian life, according to Ritschl, has as its sphere the
Church, or the worshipping community, and the *kingdom*,
or the moral community, which are mutually dependent
and reciprocally serviceable; but in this description he

CHAPTER XII

CRITICAL ESTIMATE : THE SOLUTION OFFERED

THE RITSCHLIAN THEOLOGY

—◆—

CHAPTER I

THE PROBLEM NEEDING SOLUTION: HISTORICAL INTRODUCTION

I

(1) THEOLOGY, in spite of its claims, as its advocates believe, or its boast, as its assailants would maintain, to be the queen of the sciences, seems to have fallen on evil days. Not only is its right to so lofty a title challenged, but even the lowliest place within the realm of man's knowledge is refused to it by many. Comte has declared that man's knowledge passes through three stages—the theological, the metaphysical, and the scientific. Accordingly, as man advances from savagery to civilisation he leaves theology behind him as a worn-out superstition.[1] Spencer

---

[1] Comte's *System of Positive Polity,* vol. iii. Eng. trans. p. 23: "Seen in its full completeness the fundamental law of the Intellectual Evolution consists in the necessary passage of all human theories through three successive stages—first, the Theological or fictitious, which is provisional; secondly, the Metaphysical or abstract, which is transitional; and thirdly, the Positive or scientific, which alone is definitive." Caird's *The Social Philosophy and Religion of Comte,* p. 63: "While neither theology nor metaphysics can be regarded as forms of real knowledge, both must be regarded as necessary stages in the process by which real knowledge is attained. They are, in short, transitory forms of thought which now survive only as stages in the culture of childhood and youth, or as prejudices in the minds of those who have not yet been awakened to the spirit of their time."

has shown greater regard for the feelings of his country-
men; but he too claims the whole realm of knowledge
for science, although with amazing condescension and
surprising generosity he leaves to religion, of which theology
is the intellectual interpreter, the vast region of the
Unknowable.[1]   Kant seeks all the meaning and the
whole worth of Christian theology in the ethical principles
to which it gives a partial but inadequate expression.[2]
Hegel even gives to religious beliefs, with which theology
is concerned, a [lower place than to speculative ideas;
and assigns to philosophy the task of translating the
representations of religion into the *notions* of specula-

[1] Herbert Spencer's *First Principles*: "A critical examination
(of ultimate religious ideas) will prove not only that no current
hypothesis is tenable, but also that no tenable hypothesis can be
framed" (p. 30).   "If Religion and Science are to be reconciled, the
basis of reconciliation must be this deepest, widest, and most certain of
all facts, that the Power which the Universe manifests to us is utterly
inscrutable" (p. 46).   "It is alike our highest wisdom and our highest
duty to regard that through which all things exist as the Unknowable"
(p. 113).   "Not only is the omnipresence of something which passes
comprehension that most abstract belief which is common to all
religions, which becomes the more distinct as they develop, and
which remains after their discordant elements have been mutually
cancelled, but it is that belief which the most unsparing criticism of
each leaves unquestionable, or rather makes it ever clearer" (p. 45).

[2] Kant's *Religion within the Limits of Pure Reason* (Third Part,
vi.): "The faith of the Church has as its highest interpreter the pure
religious faith."   "In order to combine with such an empirical faith the
foundation of a moral faith, for this purpose there is demanded an
exposition of the revelation which has come to our hands, that is, a continuous interpretation of the same in a sense which accords with the
universal practical rules of a pure religion of reason.   For the theoretical
in the faith of the Church cannot interest us morally, if it does not work
for the fulfilment of all human duties as divine commands (which con-
stitutes what is essential in every religion).   This interpretation may
often appear to us forced in consideration of the text (of the revelation),
often actually be forced, and yet when it is only possible for the text to
receive such an interpretation, it must be preferred to a literal one,
which either does not contain anything at all for morality, or with
its motives works against morality."   See Pfleiderer's *The Philosophy of
Religion*, Eng. trans. i. p. 185.

tion.[1] Other instances might be given, but these are the most noteworthy.

(2) Along with this depreciation of theology there goes, however, an appreciation of religion. The science of religions, which collects, arranges, and compares the facts of man's religious consciousness and history, and the philosophy of religion, which interprets the significance, and estimates the value of these facts, are receiving ever closer attention, and are commanding ever better service. The necessity of religion for, and the contribution of religion to, social progress are now more commonly recognised facts. What Comte was compelled to admit, and did admit in fantastic form in his religion of humanity [2] is being acknowledged more soberly by more recent scientific thinkers. Huxley admits that the scientific interpretation of nature does not afford a basis for morals; [3] and Kidd

---

[1] *Studies in Hegel's Philosophy of Religion* by Sterrett : "The religious knowledge of ordinary thought is strained through finite images and materialised conceptions—is representative, figurate, and consequently inadequate. Even in the higher form of systematic theology it is one-sided and inadequate, because passed through the sieve of a narrow and rationalising logic. This narrow logic let free plays havoc with dogmas, exaggerating differences instead of giving unity. There must then be a higher method of knowing the content of religion, of grasping the manifold elements of divine truth so that they shall be seen as correlated members of an *organic whole.* Nature, man, God, these—their *reality* and *unity*—can only be rationally conceived of and held under the form of an *organic unity*, which is the Speculative Idea of Religion. There is an essential necessity, then, for thought to translate the content of the religious relation out of these inadequate forms into the Speculative Idea of Religion" (p. 115). "The spiritual import of the Revealed or Christian Religion is the same as that of the Speculative Philosophy, only that it is expressed there in the mode of conception, in the form of a history, here in the mode of the notion." Schwegler's *History of Philosophy,* p. 343. See also Pfleiderer's *Philosophy of Religion,* Eng. trans. ii. pp. 78–114. Caird's *Introduction to the Philosophy of Religion,* pp. 151–176. Caird's *Hegel,* pp. 211–218.

[2] See Caird's *The Social Philosophy of Comte,* pp. 23–33.

[3] Kidd's *Social Evolution,* p. 3 : "The negative and helpless position of science is fairly exemplified in England by Professor Huxley,

argues that religion has been the most potent factor in human progress.[1] The conviction is growing and spreading that religion is worth saving and keeping, if not for its own sake, yet at least on account of the services it has rendered, and may yet be expected to render, to mankind in its moral and social progress. Those to whom religion is the most precious possession and the most glorious distinction of humanity cannot but regard this gradual recognition of its meaning and worth with satisfaction and gratitude to God.

(3) Theology as the intellectual interpreter of religion is being now called to a difficult but distinguished task, the faithful discharge of which will alone guarantee its own claims. The sacred interests of religion are intrusted to its guardianship. The solemn obligation is laid upon it, not to prove the moral and social utility of religion, for that is commonly acknowledged, but to show, what is far harder, because more generally and confidently denied, the truth of religious ideas, and their necessity to and value for

who in some of his recent writings has devoted himself to reducing the aims of the two conflicting parties of the day—individualists and socialists—to absurdity and impossibility respectively. These efforts are not, however, to be regarded as preliminary to an attempt to inspire us with any clear idea as to where our duty lies in the circumstances. After this onslaught, his own faith in the future grows obscure, and he sends his readers on their way with, for guiding principle, no particular faith or hope in anything." See Huxley's *Evolution and Ethics*, the Romanes Lecture, 1893.

[1] Kidd's *Social Evolution*, pp. 107, 108 : "The central feature of human history, the meaning of which neither science nor philosophy has hitherto fully recognised is, apparently, the struggle which man throughout the whole period of his social development has carried on to effect the subordination of his own reason. The motive power in this struggle has undoubtedly been supplied by his religious beliefs. The conclusion towards which we seem to be carried is, therefore, that the function of these beliefs in human evolution must be to provide a *super-rational* sanction for that large class of conduct in the individual, necessary to the maintenance of the development which is proceeding, and for which there can never be, in the nature of things, any *rational* sanction."

human thought. It must be admitted that the intellectual situation of the present day makes this a task of the greatest difficulty; and only the inspiration, which is given to sincere and earnest piety, can afford the needed wisdom and courage.

(4) Only one who is ignorant of the complexity of all historical phenomena could cherish the delusion that he could give an exhaustive and adequate account, or a final and authoritative estimate, of the intellectual situation of any age. But the more prominent features may be viewed more or less clearly, and the more potent factors may be measured more or less justly; and we may at least attempt to gain the more rather than the less clearness of vision, and the more rather than the less justness of measure. Four of the features and factors of the present intellectual situation here claim special attention—the distrust of philosophy, the confidence in science, the activity of historical criticism, and the prominence of the social problem.

II

(1) The aim of Kant, with whom the latest era in philosophy opens, was twofold; on the one hand, he sought to vindicate the claims of science against the scepticism of Hume, but, on the other, he strove to rebuke the pretensions of rationalism as represented by Wolff specially, and the German Enlightenment generally. His analysis of the process of human knowledge was intended to show both the objective validity and the subjective limitation of that knowledge. Philosophy as it spoke through his lips was confident, yet modest in tone.[1] The philosophical move-

[1] Pfleiderer's *Development of Theology*, p. 4: "Kant is no less opposed to the complacent vanity of the German popular philosophers, who thought that they already possessed *Aufklaerung*—the truth in religion and morals—than he is to the radicalism of the French party of progress, who imagined that they could reach the goal by means of revolution, by abjuring in theory and practice all existing beliefs and institutions."

ment that ended in Hegel was very much more confident and
very much less modest. Human speculation seemed to be
practically identified with the Absolute Thought, from, in, and
unto whom, or perhaps we should more correctly say which,
are all things.[1] But here "vaulting ambition o'erleaps itself";
and the Idealistic development from Kant to Hegel was
followed by a return to the critical position of Kant, and even
by a reaction to a sceptical attitude towards all philosophy.[2]
Of this backward movement science, growing daily more
confident of its results and methods, was a potent factor.

(2) This idealism stood in a very close relation to
Christianity. It claimed to be a more adequate interpretation of the Christian religion than that which Christian
theology had hitherto been able to offer. Edward Caird,
the greatest and best English exponent of Hegelianism,
tells us that Hegel was led to his absolute idealism by the
study of Christian ideas, and that he found "a key to the
difficulties of ethics, a reconciliation of hedonism and
asceticism, in the great Christian aphorism that 'he who

---

[1] Hegel's *Philosophie der Religion*, i. pp. 199–201, quoted in Sterrett's
Studies in Hegel's Philosophy of Religion, p. 153: "The object which
the Absolute Spirit knows is himself. He is only Absolute Spirit
as knowing nothing but himself. Finiteness of consciousness is the
result of spirit distinguishing itself from its object. But this is a
real element of spirit. It is the spirit itself which makes this distinction, or posits itself as determined by its object. It is only by
this mediation (through consciousness or finite spirit) by which it
finitises itself, that it comes to knowledge of itself or to self-consciousness. Thus *religion is the knowledge which the Divine Spirit has of
himself*, through the mediation of the finite spirit." Schwegler's *History
of Philosophy*, p. 343: "With abstraction from the form of religious
conception, we have the position of the *Absolute Philosophy*, of thought
that knows itself as all truth, that reproduces from itself the entire
natural and spiritual universe—that thought the evolution of which is
precisely the system of Philosophy—a sphere of spheres self-closed."

[2] Pfleiderer's *The Philosophy of Religion*, ii. p. 161: "The Neo-
Kantians adhere only to the empiricist and sceptical side of Kant's
philosophy, the empiricism predominating at one time and the scepticism
at another; but in general the one passes immediately into the other,
as the nature of the case would lead us to expect."

loseth his life alone can save it.'"[1] There can be no
doubt that Hegel was himself sincerely convinced that he
was not only defending but advancing Christian truth by
translating the inadequate images of the religious consciousness into the perfect ideas of the speculative reason. With
the same honesty and earnestness of purpose, a school of
theology set itself to display Hegelianism as latent in
Christianity.[2] This attempt, however well meant, resulted
in giving the impression that the merit of Jesus lay
exclusively in His discovery of a metaphysical principle,
the essential unity of God and man, and of an ethical rule,
" dying to live," of both of which, however, Hegel has been
the first to make consistent and successful application.
Strauss' " mythical " theory of the life of Christ,[3] and Baur's

---

[1] Caird's *Hegel*, p. 218 : " What Christianity teaches is only that the
law of the life of spirit—the law of self-realisation through self-abnegation
—holds good for God as for man, and, indeed, that the Spirit that works
in man to 'die to live' is the Spirit of God. For Hegel such a doctrine
was the demonstrated result of the whole idealistic movement which is
summed up in his *Logic*. So far, then, as Christianity means this, it was
not in any spirit of external accommodation that he tried to connect his
doctrine with it. Rather it was the discovery of this as the essential
meaning of Christianity which first enabled him to recognise it as the
ultimate lesson of the idealistic movement of thought in Kant, Fichte,
and Schelling."

[2] Fisher's *History of Christian Doctrine*, pp. 532, 533 : " Hegel and
his followers professed to find an equivalent for the objects of Christian
faith and the propositions of orthodox theology in the dogmas of their
system. Christianity presents in a popular form that which philosophy
exhibits in the form of naked truth. The substantial contents of both
are averred to be identical. The Trinity is made to designate the
triplicity in the notion of the Absolute : first, the Absolute in itself ;
secondly, as developed in the intelligible world, corresponding to the
Son ; and, thirdly, in the philosophy in which the Absolute comes back
to itself. The sense of estrangement in man is sin, a necessary phase
in his spiritual progress, which gives way to a consciousness of unity
with the Absolute. Christ is a man who is conscious of being one with
the Infinite Being, and represents in this respect what every man is in
idea. That which is predicated of Him specifically is true literally of
humanity as a whole."

[3] Fairbairn's *Christ in Modern Theology*, pp. 236, 237 : " The speculative basis on which Strauss built was simply the Hegelian doctrine of

" tendency " theory of the history of the early Church,[1] both
claiming to be applications of Hegelian principles and
methods, were scarcely needed to confirm the suspicions of
many Christian thinkers, that the Christian Church would
look in vain to Hegelianism for a true interpretation and a
sure defence of its faith and its life.   However admirable in
many respects Caird's *Evolution of Religion*,[2] and Pfleiderer's
Philosophy and Development of Religion[3] are, yet the
teachers and the leaders of the Christian Churches in Great
Britain are generally agreed, not from inveterate prejudice,

the Absolute specifically developed and applied.   The disciple narrowed
ideas that the master had made large and indefinite.   Hegel meant his
philosophy to explain what had been and is : Strauss used it to determine what must be or have been."—" His speculative end was also
given him by the Hegelian philosophy.   The evangelical facts expressed
in the sensuous form truths which he wished to translate into the
notional.   He did not see why men should be satisfied with the lower
when they could by a critico-speculative process reach the higher form.
So he considered his work a real service to Christianity—at least the
ideal and absolute Christianity of the learned."

[1] *Op. cit.* pp. 261, 262.   Baur "was soon caught in the fine yet strong
network of the Hegelian dialectic, and it became to him at once a
philosophy of history and of religion, and an historical method.   In
harmony with it he construed history as the development and the
explication of the Idea.   Thought stood where God or Providence
used to stand ; instead of an order created by a personal will we had
the successions and relations of a dialectical movement.   Facts, events,
persons were but bearers of the idea, factors in its unfolding and
articulation."

[2] Fairbairn in *Critical Review*, iii. p. 199 : " From this fundamental
attitude of thought comes one of the main defects of the book—a law of
mind or logic is made to govern the development of religion and the
course of history, with the result that we have an inner and dialectical
process made the formula or framework for an outer and actual.   The
theory controls the history ; the history does not suggest and verify the
theory.   Thus particular instances which happen to illustrate the
philosophical principle are raised to the dignity of universal laws."

[3] Somerville in *Critical Review*, iv. p. 256 : " It may be doubted
whether the spiritual life will continue to be nourished, at least in
ordinary persons, by ideal representations, to which nothing corresponds
in the world of objective reality, and after the historic basis on which
these have rested has been cut away by the hand of a remorseless
criticism."

but for well-grounded reasons, that Christian truth cannot be assured of any safety or promised any advancement from philosophical idealism, as represented at least by these foremost thinkers. This growing distrust of philosophy, which seems to many more dangerous when it offers to defend than when it chooses to attack theology, finds literary expression in Balfour's *Foundations of Belief*,[1] the surprising popularity of which shows how prominent a feature of, and how potent a factor, in the present intellectual situation is this distrust of philosophy.

III

(1) In very marked contrast to this distrust of philosophy is the confidence in science. Science, the independence of which was successfully asserted by Bacon,[2]

---

[1] Fairbairn's *Catholicism, Roman and Anglican*, p. 368. Mr. Balfour "dismisses, by a searching critical process, our current philosophies, empirical and transcendental ; then confesses he has no effectual substitute to offer ; and finally offers a provisional theory for the unification of beliefs which throws into the most startling relief all the sceptical elements in his own criticicism."

[2] Bacon's *Advancement of Learning*, I. i. 3 : " Let no man upon a weak conceit of sobriety or an ill-applied moderation think or maintain that a man can search too far, or be too well studied in the book of God's word, or in the book of God's works, divinity or philosophy ; but rather let men endeavour an endless progress or proficience in both ; only let men beware that they apply both to charity, and not to swelling ; to use, and not to ostentation ; and again, that they do not unwisely mingle or confound these learnings together." In the last clause Bacon separates in mutual independence divinity and philosophy, in which he includes science. In the following sentence he distinguishes metaphysic and physic (II. vii. 4): " Physic (taking it according to the derivation, and not according to our idiom for medicine) is situate in a middle term or distance between natural history and metaphysic. For natural history describeth the variety of things : physic, the causes, but variable or respective causes ; and metaphysic the fixed and constant causes."—(5): " For metaphysic, we have assigned unto it the inquiry of formal and final causes."—" Physic doth make inquiry and take consideration of the same natures. But how ? Only as to the material and efficient causes of them."

has within three centuries made truly marvellous progress, and its discoveries and inventions in this century have quite surpassed in number, variety, and importance the intellectual achievements of any former age.   Success begets confidence; so great a success has bred over-confidence.   It seems as if there were no secret of nature that science could not discover, and no force of nature that science could not bring under control.   This insight into and power over nature has given to science the conviction that its methods and principles are universally valid ; that to its results every interest of man must be subordinated.[1]   The effect on Christian theology of such an attitude on the part of science cannot but be dangerous.

(2) The difference between the record of Creation given in Genesis and the report of the process of evolution which modern science gives is to be regarded altogether as a question of secondary importance and subordinate interest in this connection.   It is true that there are men of science who are Christian believers, and there are Christian theologians who cannot altogether ignore the results of science, by whom attempt after attempt has been made to reconcile Genesis and Science ; but it is coming to be more and more generally recognised that such a reconciliation is not necessary either in the interests of science, or in the

[1] Huxley's *Hume*, p. 51 : " On whatever ground we term physiology, science, psychology is entitled to the same appellation ; and the method of investigation which elucidates the true relations of the one set of phenomena will discover those of the other.   Hence, as philosophy is, in great measure, the exponent of the logical consequences of certain data established by psychology, and as psychology itself differs from physical science only in the nature of its subject-matter, and not in its method of investigation, it would seem to be an obvious conclusion that philosophers are likely to be successful in their inquiries, in proportion as they are familiar with the application of scientific method to less abstruse subjects ; just as it seems to require no elaborate demonstration, that an astronomer who wishes to comprehend the solar system, would do well to acquire a preliminary acquaintance with the elements of physics."

defence of religion; for, on the one hand, the religious value of the story of Creation in Genesis is altogether independent of its scientific accuracy, and, on the other hand, no legitimate conclusions of science can come in conflict with the theological affirmations of Genesis.[1]

(3) What has a threatening aspect for theology is the tendency of mind, which devotion to science often nourishes and fosters, to apply the category of causality and the principle of the uniformity of nature to all objects of human knowledge, and to deny reality to all events which cannot be explained by this category, or subordinated to this principle.[2] Those who are accustomed to find in all natural phenomena an exact equivalence between antecedents and consequents, when they turn to

[1] Driver in *Expositor*, Fifth Series, vii. p. 468 : "I cannot well abridge the trenchant and detailed criticisms by which President Morton exposes, one after another, the unreality of all these schemes of reconciliation (Professor Guyot's, Professor Dana's, Sir J. W. Dawson's, Mr. Gladstone's); but, speaking generally, the rock upon which each in turn is wrecked is the extreme and incredible violence done to the text of Genesis, for the purpose of forcing its statements into harmony with what is taught by science."—"And he considers the true solution of the problem presented by the cosmogony of Genesis to have been found by those scholars who read it in the light of the age in which it was written, and who, while not forgetful of the spiritual teaching of which it is made the vehicle, interpret it, on its material side, in accordance with the place which it holds in the history of Semitic cosmological speculation."

[2] Mill's *System of Logic*, VI. i. § 2 : "At the threshold of this inquiry we are met by an objection, which, if not removed, would be fatal to the attempt to treat human conduct as a subject of science. Are the actions of human beings, like all other natural events, subject to invariable laws? Does that constancy of causation, which is the foundation of every scientific theory of successive phenomena, really obtain among them? This is often denied; and for the sake of systematic completeness, if not from any urgent practical necessity, the question should receive a deliberate answer in this place."—(ii. § 4) : "With the corrections and explanations now given, the doctrine of the causation of our volitions by motives, and of motives by the desirable objects offered to us, combined with our particular susceptibilities of desire, may be considered, I hope, as sufficiently established for the purposes of this treatise."

history, in which life, mind, spirit, personality, genius are the ruling forces, fail to recognise that the change of the objects of knowledge demands a difference in the categories and principles of interpretation.   Although the attempt is made, personality cannot be explained by heredity and organism and environment.   The progress of the race cannot be accounted for by the uniformity of nature, although there are still some thinkers who dream of a science of history, using the same methods as the sciences of nature.   What is true of history generally is still more true of religion, which is the most distinctively human element in history, and expresses man at his furthest remove from nature, as science knows it.   Least capable of explanation by the ordinary methods of science, religion has come to be very generally suspected by men of science as an illusion, and theology with its claim to be science also as an impostor.

(4) There are many now who have been so deeply impressed by the success of science in gaining a knowledge of and a command over nature that to them scientific methods alone seem universally valid, and scientific results alone absolutely infallible; and accordingly the Universe, as they conceive it, is rigidly bound in all its parts in the fetters of causality, and is despotically ruled by uniform law.[1]   To such a habit of mind the

---

[1] Sabatier's *Esquisse d'une Philosophie de la Religion*, p. v. ("Sketch of a Philosophy of Religion") : "Our young people, it seems to me, are pushing forward bravely, marching between two high walls : on the one side, modern science and its severe methods, which it is no longer possible to renounce ; on the other, the dogmas and practices of the religious institution, on which their infancy was nourished, and to which they would be willing, but are not able, sincerely to return. The wise men who have hitherto led them show them the blind alley in which they have been brought to a stand, and invite them to take a side ; either to be for science against religion, or with religion against science. With reason they hesitate before this terrible alternative. Must one choose between pious ignorance and brutal knowledge?

distinctive ideas of Christian theology must appear altogether false and hurtful. Inspiration, grace, miracle, incarnation, all that reaches beyond and rises above the unity and uniformity of nature as thus conceived, must be dismissed as unreal and deceptive. While there are not a few eminent men of science who are also confessedly Christians, yet, on the other hand, it cannot be denied that the influence of science on very many minds is to make religious belief more and more difficult, if not altogether impossible. Theology is bound to recognise one of its strongest opponents in confident science.

IV

(1) At first sight it may seem as if theology were too weak to meet its foes without, because wounded in the house of its friends. Historical criticism has been very busy with the record of the Revelation, which for Christian theology is the final court of appeal.[1] A severe and searching analysis of the literary sources of this history

Ought we to continue to live by a morality which contradicts our science, or build up a theory of the world which our conscience condemns. Has the narrow and sombre valley in which our troubled youth advances no outlet at all?"

[1] *Lux Mundi*, Preface to Tenth Edition, iii.: "Our traditional belief in the Bible is at the present time confronted with a body of critical literature, which claims to overthrow a great many of the accepted opinions about the Old Testament Scriptures. The criticism is at least grave and important enough to claim attention, to necessitate that we should come to a more or less clear understanding of the relation in which our faith stands towards it. . . . The writer wrote 'in the mind of those who have felt the trouble in the air'; he wrote to succour a faith distressed by the problems criticism is raising. That faith is very widely distressed by them, and that not merely in academic circles, does not admit of question."

Faith and Criticism, Preface: "The writers of these Essays have been drawn together and led to issue this volume by a strong desire to help those very numerous seekers after truth whose minds have been disturbed by the work of criticism in Biblical and Theological questions."

has resulted in at least discrediting, if not altogether dis-
proving, the traditional assumptions regarding date and
authorship of some of these writings, on which their credi-
bility and authority appeared to depend. The evidence
for the supernatural events, doctrines, and persons now
seems exposed to a doubt hitherto unknown. There are
not a few inquiring persons who have " the will to believe,"
but cannot satisfy themselves of the sufficiency of the
evidence for the objects of their belief. The intellectual
process, by means of which the certainty of the truth of
the Christian religion can be reached, has become much
more complex and difficult; and to some sincere and
earnest minds it appears quite beyond their reach. It
would be impossible to estimate how many there are
among us who are under the impression that the certainty
of faith could be gained by them only at the too high
price of a sacrifice of their intellectual integrity.[1]

(2) But historical criticism has for very many not only
brought into doubt the literary evidence for the supernatural
facts which Christian faith accepts, it has excited a prejudice against even the presence of the supernatural element
in history. For some scholars the task of history is, not
only to record events, but also as exhaustively and
adequately as can be to explain them by what has gone
before. The category of causality, or rather the category
of development, is accepted as a guiding idea for historical
inquiry.[2] All the factors of the intellectual, moral, social,

[1] Mrs. Humphry Ward's *Robert Elsmere*, chap. xxvi.: " In other
men it might be right and possible that they should live on in the
ministry of the Church, doing the humane and charitable work of the
Church, while refusing assent to the intellectual and dogmatic framework on which the Church system rests ; but for himself it would be
neither right nor wrong, but simply impossible." The treatment of
such a psychological problem in a popular novel is a clear and strong
proof of how widespread and far-reaching is this state of mind.

[2] Pfleiderer's *Philosophy and Development of Religion*, ii. p. 1 : "To
investigate a history means to trace out the connection of its causes

or religious development are sought within itself; if the existence of any new elements is admitted at all, they are reduced to the smallest possible proportions. Such a view of history must lead evidently to a suspicion of all that claims to be supernatural in the record of Revelation ; a suspicion so strong that even the clearest evidence that can ordinarily be produced for any event whatever will not be likely to remove it. This intellectual habit, which the practice of historical criticism tends to produce, and having produced, to confirm, must be seriously reckoned with. When a scholar finds that so many complex historical movements can be resolved into their component factors, he will not be inclined to admit that there may be historical events, the most potent elements in which can escape his discovery by the same methods as he has elsewhere so successfully used.

(3) Any theologian who imagines that his doctrine of the inspiration of the Scriptures secures him against any dangerous assaults from historical criticism is simply deceiving himself; for of all the Christian doctrines it is just this doctrine which is most seriously affected by the methods and the results of historical criticism.[1] Only by a man who has a marvellous capacity for *intellectual insulation* can the theories of the verbal inspiration and the absolute inerrancy of the Scriptures be maintained.

and effects, and to make it intelligible to our understanding. This presupposes that in what once happened there exists such a connection of causes and effects as is analogous to our general experience of what happens among men and in men, and is therefore intelligible to our understanding."—"The appearing of a heavenly being for an episodic stay upon our earth breaks the connection of events in space and time upon which all our experience rests, and therefore it undoes the conception of history from the bottom" (pp. 2, 3).

[1] Stewart on "Bible," *Dictionary of the Bible*, i. p. 299 : "It is probable that no theory of inspiration will ever solve all these difficulties or be regarded as entirely satisfactory." The fact that such an admission should be made in such a place shows convincingly what the theological position is generally recognised to be in this matter.

It must be frankly confessed that the Christian Church has no doctrine of inspiration, universally or even generally accepted, which would enable it with invariable success to meet the difficulties for faith due to the activity of historical criticism.

V

(1) In view of these three prominent features and potent factors of the present intellectual situation, the perilous position of theology may be thus described. From philosophy, the efforts of which have resulted in disappointment, it cannot expect any effective assistance as an ally; from science, which has been made confident by its successes, it may anticipate serious attack; its own capacity for independence on the one hand, and for resistance on the other, appears greatly lessened by the activity of historical criticism. It must depend more and more exclusively on the inherent vitality and the inexhaustible vigour of religion.

(2) In religion itself, however, there has been a change, if not of content, yet of emphasis. Religion cannot but be receptive of, and responsive to, the dominant interests and the potent influences of any age. Surely it will be generally admitted that one of the most characteristic features of our own age is the prominence of the social question.[1] The French Revolution not only destroyed the existing order of society in France, but disturbed all the traditional and conventional ideas by which European society had

[1] Mackenzie's *Introduction to Social Philosophy*, p. 6: "There are a number of special circumstances which have caused social questions to assume a peculiar prominence in recent times, and have made it more than ever necessary to have clear ideas with regard to the principles on which their solution rests."—(P. 7): "We are now engaged in groping our way to something new; and whether the new light is to be better than the old will depend mainly on the thoroughness with which we set ourselves to discover what is ultimately true and what is ultimately desirable with reference to social affairs."

till then been ruled. It not only brought a fresh scene before the sight of men, but it even gave new eyes with which to look on it. The external revolution was even less significant than the internal transformation. The inventions of science, the developments of industry, the extensions of commerce, have brought about, if not so swiftly, yet more surely, a still greater change in the social conditions.[1] The material changes have been so many and so great, that the necessary moral and mental changes corresponding thereto have been unduly delayed. The intelligence and the conscience of society have not yet been thoroughly adjusted to the new social organism, which in turn is less sound and strong than it ought to be, just on account of this maladjustment. In our large cities, which are one of the most direct results of this social revolution, and in which, therefore, the pressure of the problem which it involves is most keenly felt, the minds of thoughtful and earnest men are very largely occupied with these social questions.

(3) A new demand is thus made upon religion. Can it not only assure a man of his individual salvation, but also secure for mankind its social regeneration?[2] The answer that the Christian Churches seem inclined to give, that it is

[1] Kidd's *Social Evolution*, p. 7 : " Amongst the advanced nations, the great wave of industrial expansion which follows in the wake of science is slowly but inevitably submerging the old landmarks of society, and preparing for us a world where the old things, material and social as well as political, have passed away, and in which the experience of the past is no longer a reliable guide."

[2] *Op. cit.* p. 14 : " Within the Churches one of the signs of this change is visible in a growing tendency to assert that religion is concerned with man's actual state in the world as well as with his possible state in the next."—" We are beginning to hear from many quarters that the social question is at bottom a religious question, and that to its solution it behoves the Churches in the interests of society to address themselves."—" We have the note sounded in varying keys that, after all, Christianity was intended to save not only men, but man, and that its mission should be to teach us not only how to die as individuals, but how to live as members of society."

2

only by individual salvation that social regeneration can be reached, is received by very many with evident impatience. Are there no Christian ideas which can be used as organising principles, are there no Christian motives that may be applied as formative forces in bringing about the social changes that are so urgently needed? This question is being pressed upon Christian theology; and if it is not satisfactorily answered, the social enthusiasm of the age, which might thus be brought into alliance with religious devotion, may in its disappointment and disgust separate itself from, and oppose itself to, religion. The task which the prominence of the social question sets to theology in the present day seems to be this, Christianity must be shown to be, not only in its truth but also in its life, a social community under God as well as an individual communion with God.[1]

VI

(1) Such, then, is the intellectual situation in which Christian theology is called to its sacred and solemn work. This situation has its decided defects as well as its evident excellences. The distrust of philosophy has been carried far farther than its mistakes and failures in the past even justified, and the confident conviction may be cherished that a genuinely Christian philosophy is possible, nay even that such a philosophy must needs be a corrected idealism. The confidence of science is without due warrant, as the categories and principles of science are assumptions, the investigation of which would show that their sphere is limited by, even as their application is

---

[1] Andrews' *Christianity and the Labour Conflict*, p. 5 : " The Christian faith on its social side has stood almost disregarded by the world. The time has now come to prove that faith in the wider fields of social life. The very despair and helplessness of men in the face of self-interest and self-seeking should show that the Christian victory is near."

necessary for, human thought. The activity of criticism need not be feared, as the Christian faith is quite capable of maintaining and defending the supernatural objects, which are necessary to its vitality and vigour. The prominence of the social question should be heartily welcomed, as Christian theology and piety alike need be saved from a onesided individualism by a return to, and a recovery of, the social ideas and laws of the Christian gospel.

(2) Whatever may be our individual judgment of this intellectual situation, one fact is beyond all doubt or question. The Christian gospel needs a restatement in which all these tendencies will find their due recognition, their justification where that is possible, or their correction where that is necessary.[1] Such a restatement is a work of very great delicacy and difficulty ; for, on the one hand, there must be no impoverishment of the " faith once delivered to the saints," and, on the other hand, this age must not be spoken to in a foreign tongue. How to do justice alike to the permanent elements and to the temporary expressions of the Christian faith, is a question which an open-minded, true-hearted man will find it by no means easy to answer. Accordingly there must be great patience and keen sympathy with any school of theologians who frankly and freely face our present position ; and who, being unable to find intellectual satisfaction in traditional forms

[1] Rashdall's *Doctrine and Development*, Preface, xii : " The restatement—let us say frankly the reconstruction—of Christian doctrine is the great intellectual task upon which the Church of our day is just entering, and with which it must go on boldly if Christianity is to retain its hold on the intellect as well as the sentiment and the social activities of our time." This writer, it may be remarked, refers to the Ritschlian theology. " This idea," he says, "that the Christian knowledge of God is based not upon speculative reasoning but upon the conviction wrought in the soul by personal experience of the moral effects of Christ's life, is the fundamental idea of the theology of Ritschl." While he commends this position, he disassociates himself from " other Ritschlian tendencies."

of faith, and being also anxious to help others in the same condition, essay such a restatement of Christian theology as will secure for the Christian religion its due place and its full influence in the thought and life of our time.

(3) It is in this spirit that the writer now invites the reader to study the Ritschlian Theology. As will be made abundantly evident in the discussions that follow, the methods and the principles of this theology appear to him to be open to serious objection, its results as a restatement of the Christian faith he cannot but regard as disappointing ; but, on the other hand, its critics in this country, he is persuaded, have sometimes misunderstood its positions, and so misjudged its intentions, and at least it has a claim to more sympathy and generosity than it has generally received,[1] for it does recognise and respond to the intellectual situation. It seeks to save theology from any entangling alliance with philosophy or any threatening assault from science by maintaining it in isolation in the realm of value judgments, which is distinguished from the sphere of theoretical judgments, to which science and philosophy belong. It strives so to conceive the objects of Christian faith, as shall allow it to be practically indifferent to the results of historical criticism. It lays such stress on the evangelical idea of the kingdom of God, as will enable the Church to meet the social demand made upon it.

VII

(1) The distinctive features of Ritschlianism are largely due to the religious individuality and the intellectual

---

[1] Somerville's *St. Paul's Conception of Christ*, ix : "It is deeply to be regretted, I think, that this great theologian (Albrecht Ritschl) has been for the most part introduced to this country in a way that hinders the appreciation of his real work in theology, and that his name has been made familiar to students chiefly in connection with errors he is supposed to have taught."

development of Ritschl himself.   While intensely absorbed
in the study of theological problems, he was exceedingly
reticent in intercourse as regards his religious beliefs.
When he did speak his words were few, and he was
careful not to betray the strength of his feelings.[1]   He
hated all pious sentimentality, and laid great stress on
practical morality as an expression of the religious life.
He showed no understanding of, and no sympathy with,
types of piety other than his own.[2]   In his intellectual
development, however, he showed himself receptive of,
and responsive to, many influences.   He came into contact
with, and received instruction and stimulus from, nearly
all the great thinkers of his time.   For a short time he
was won for Hegelianism by Erdmann at Halle, and
professed himself a disciple of Baur at Tübingen.   Even
orthodoxy in its more or less rigid types attracted him.
The strongest influence on his thought was exercised,
however, by Kant and Schleiermacher, and afterwards by

[1] Herrmann's *Der Evangelische Glaube und die Theologie Albrecht
Ritschls* (" The Evangelical Faith and the Theology of Albrecht
Ritschl "), pp. 7, 8 : " In religious intercourse Ritschl observed an
extraordinary severity towards himself.   How he lived in the world
of thought of the Christian faith, certainly was made so clear in his conversation, that a less powerful disposition could be wearied thereby.   In
his house and here in Marburg I have been whole days together with
him, without his having ever interrupted our occupation with the
highest things by a longer conversation of lighter content.   Herein
appeared his being deeply possessed by the subject.   But seldom did
this impel a feeble emotional word ; but he spoke austerely and severely
about what moved his heart."

[2] Ecke's *Die Theologische Schule Albrecht Ritschls und die
evangelische Kirche der Gegenwart* (" The Theological School of
Albrecht Ritschl and the Evangelical Church of the Present "), i. pp.
21–24.   " Ritschl was often incapable of sympathising with what was
justified in the tendency combated by him ; guided by his solid but
onesided and individually conditioned veracity, he struck in sharp controversy along with the aberrations also the approximate appearances
of a healthy Christian piety, for which he had no understanding, and he
without any necessity thus provoked greater opposition than the question
warranted " (p. 22).

Lotze.[1]   But as a profound scholar and learned theologian he drew the elements of his system and method from many sources.   His indebtedness to others did not, however, lessen his originality, as he used what he borrowed with great freedom, and combined his materials with thorough independence.[2]   It must be admitted, however, that foreign elements are allowed to remain even when he is thereby involved in inconsistency.   Ritschl cannot be understood unless his theology is traced to its historical origins.   By such a study of the organism of his thought in its intellectual environment we are enabled to explain its difficulties, account for its contradictions, as well as discover the reason for its success.[3]   It is because Ritschl in himself reproduced the tendencies of his age that he was able to meet its necessities.

[1] Orr's *The Ritschlian Theology and the Evangelical Faith*, p. 4 ; also " Albrecht Ritschl " in *Expository Times*, v. p. 534.   " He passed through and incorporated in himself all the important phases of thought in his generation " (p. 4).—" At Bonn he came under the powerful spell of Nitzsch, and even for a time venerated Hengstenberg. He was won to Hegelianism at Halle by Erdmann.   He was on friendly terms with Tholuck and Julius Müller, though he afterwards spoke of them in highly disparaging terms.   He sat for six months at the feet of the speculative Rothe.   Thereafter we find him an enthusiastic and convinced disciple of Baur at Tübingen.   At a later period we find him deserting Baur for Kant and Lotze " (p. 534).

[2] Ecke, *op. cit.* pp. 14, 15.   " Repeatedly has it been asserted from various standpoints that Ritschl borrowed nearly everything from others " (p. 14).—" In these remarks there is much in particulars correct." —" Nevertheless *the way in which Ritschl formulated* these principles and *combined* them is an altogether *original* one " (p. 15).—" What we have to regard as the distinctively *original* element in his *systematic contribution* is the *ability* to *carry out new* great *combinations* " (p. 14).

[3] Schoen's *Origines Historiques de la Theologie de Ritschl* (" Historical Origins of the Theology of Ritschl "), pp. 153, 154 : " As long as one had forgotten to study the organic evolution of the system its contradictions remained inexplicable.   When one had severed all the bonds that bound back the dogmatics of Ritschl to previous works, the reason for his influence remained a mystery.   On the other hand, regarded as a living organism, put back into its historical environment, this theology interests us for two reasons ; first of all as a crisis in the evolution of religious thought in Germany, then as the expression of the religious needs of a great part of our contemporaries."

The theology of Ritschl answered to the needs of his generation, and therefore it proved so " living and fruitful." [1]

(2) Because he spoke as a living man to living men in the speech all could understand he was not left alone, but slowly gathered around him a band of disciples, who, while ready to acknowledge their indebtedness to him,[2] are yet so prone to assert their independence by criticism alike of their master as of one another, that the question has been seriously asked whether we have a right to speak of a Ritschlian school at all.[3] But whatever the differences may be, yet there is enough common ground among a number of theologians in Germany to entitle us to speak of them as the school of Ritschl. The distinctive features of this school,[4] expressed as briefly as can be, are : [1] the

[1] Sabatier, quoted in Schoen, p. 155 : "To satisfy the expectation and the quest of spirits *at the very moment* living and troubled, to give them the means of justifying to themselves their faith and their hope . . . behold the principal merit and the supreme praise of every genuine theology. It is in the measure in which that of Ritschl answers to the needs of the present generation that it is living and fruitful."

[2] Herrmann's *Der Evangelische Glaube und die Theologie Albrecht Ritschls* ("The Evangelical Faith and the Theology of Albrecht Ritschl"), p. 6 ; and *Die Gewissheit des Glaubens und die Freiheit der Theologie* ("The Certainty of Faith and the Freedom of Theology"), pp. 16, 17 : "In the evening of his life he had drawn a small number of academical theologians into his circle" (p. 6).—"What secures for the theology of *Ritschl* so hostile an attention is, above all, the circumstance that among the theological products of the present it is the only figure full of character about which, in short, much can be said. Besides, it has been in a position to bring a small group of theologians to such an agreement in their fundamental ideas as is not met with anywhere else with so great a number " (pp. 16, 17).

[3] Pfleiderer's *Die Ritschl'sche Theologie* (" The Ritschlian Theology "), p. 77 : "Do not their opinions now already differ in so many ways that it appears perilous to bring them together under a common label?"

[4] Orr's "The School of Ritschl" in *Expository Times*, vi. p. 253 : "Among the generic features which bind together the Ritschlian party are . . . the strong contrast they all draw between religious and theoretic knowledge ; the desire to free theology from all association with, and dependence on, metaphysics ; the insisting on the positive revela-

exclusion of metaphysics from theology; [2] the rejection
consequently of speculative theism; [3] the condemnation
of ecclesiastical dogma as an illegitimate mixture of theology
and metaphysics; [4] the antagonism shown to religious
mysticism as a metaphysical type of piety; [5] the practical
conception of religion; [6] the consequent contrast between
religious and theoretical knowledge; [7] the emphasis laid
on the historical revelation of God in Christ as opposed to
any natural revelation; [8] the use of the idea of the
kingdom of God as the regulative principle of Christian
dogmatics; [9] the tendency to limit theological investigation to the contents of the religious consciousness. To
this school belong Herrmann, Kaftan, Harnack, Wendt,
Schultz, Bornemann, and others less noted. The differences
in the school, which are as marked as the agreements, will
claim our attention in the subsequent discussion.

(3) Ritschl and his school have enjoyed very great
popularity in Germany, and no other theological tendency
can compare with the Ritschlian as regards activity and
influence in the present day.[1] This is undoubtedly due to
its adaptation to the age, for it meets many needs, enlists

tion in Christ as the one source of true religious knowledge; the central
position they all assign to the doctrine of the kingdom of God, and their
making of this conception determinative of every other notion in theology, *e.g.* of that of God, of sin, of the Person of Christ, of redemption;
the vigorous exclusion from theology of everything which lies outside
the earthly manifestation of Christ (*e.g.* pre-existence, eschatology);
and, finally, the distrust of, and antagonism to, everything of the nature
of mysticism in religion. Partial exception must be made in the case
of individuals."

[1] Prefatory Note by R. Flint in Kaftan's *The Truth of the Christian
Religion*, i. pp. v, vi: "This theology has been dominant in Germany
during the last fifteen years, and is still gaining adherents and growing
in influence. In fact, no other German theological school or movement
can at present compare with it in strength and vitality." "It claims to
be thoroughly evangelical and Lutheran. It aims steadily at the pro-
motion of piety, the satisfaction of spiritual wants, and the furtherance of the practical work of the Church. It is intensely sincere and
alive."

many interests, and removes many difficulties.[1] But it has not been greeted with a chorus of approval alone. The opposition it has met with is as great as its popularity. Ritschl's controversial methods, in which he has unfortunately been followed by some of his disciples, were somewhat lacking in consideration and courtesy for his critics, and consequently the conflict is very keen and bitter. The narrowest orthodoxy is found in alliance with the broadest theological liberalism in denouncing and resisting this "new" theology, which condemns and rejects alike the confessional positions of the one and the philosophical principles of the other.[2]

[1] Schoen's *Les Origines Historiques de la Theologie de Ritschl* ("The Historical Origins of the Theology of Ritschl"), pp. 8, 9 : "To those who are disheartened by the attacks of criticism, it affirms that faith and salvation are independent of the results of our historical researches. To theologians weary of dogmatic controversies it presents a Christianity freed from all foreign metaphysics. To scholars trembling to see theology fall before the attacks of the positive sciences, it shows a way by which all collision with the natural sciences becomes impossible. To students devoted to history, it unfolds the development of the primitive Church. To timid Christians it says, God has never been angry against you ; He declares to you that you may return to Him. To worn-out Pessimists it cries, Work for the advancement of the kingdom of God ; unite yourselves for the common work   doctrine without Christian life is nothing. To an enthusiastic youth it shows the means of acting on the men of our time. In an age greedy for liberty and equality, it establishes a 'social theology' which makes the individual disappear in the mass."

[2] Stählin's *Kant, Lotze, and Ritschl*, Preface, v : "During the last fifteen or twenty years a controversy has been going on in Germany, which, like some Indian cyclone, has had for its pivot the theological system of Albrecht Ritschl. From year to year, as the number of his pupils and disciples increased, and as others became aware of the true tendency of his teaching, it has grown alike in compass and intensity. Things have looked, in fact, as though the German theological world were destined to split into two great camps, whose respective cries would be—'Here, Ritschl!' 'Here, Anti-Ritschl!'"

VIII

(1) Although Britain is now very ready to borrow theology from Germany,[1] and many British students have, while in Germany, come more or less under the influence of teachers belonging to the Ritschlian school,[2] yet it is only within the last five or six years that the Ritschlian Theology has attracted general attention in this country. Nearly thirty years ago the first volume of Ritschl's great work on *Justification and Reconciliation*,[3] which gives the history of the doctrine, was translated into English, but seems to have had little, if any, influence on English theological thought. In 1889 Principal Simon introduced in an English translation a criticism by Stählin (*Kant, Lotze, and Ritschl*)[4] of Ritschl's theology, with special reference to its philosophical principles; but this work, however acute it may sometimes be, is so disfigured by its violent polemical tone that it is an altogether untrustworthy guide to the study of this movement, and one cannot but regret that Ritschlianism should have had so unfriendly a herald in English theological literature. The translation in 1894 of Kaftan's *The Truth of the Christian Religion*,[5] with a friendly prefatory note by Professor Flint, enabled English readers to gain some understanding of the apologetic attitude of the Ritschlian school; and a like service as regards its distinctive type of piety was rendered by the publication in 1895 of Herrmann's *The Communion of the Christian*

[1] Stählin, *op. cit.* vii : " What Germany thinks to-day, Britain will begin to think to-morrow."

[2] Flint's Prefatory Note in Kaftan's *The Truth of the Christian Religion*, p. v : " Young men from this country who study theology in Germany almost inevitably come more or less under its influence."

[3] Williams & Norgate, 1870.

[4] T. & T. Clark, 1889.

[5] T. & T. Clark, 1894. Translated from the German, under the author's supervision, by George Ferries, B.D.

with God.[1] Harnack's *History of Dogma*, which faithfully represents the Ritschlian attitude towards the development of Christian theology, is still in course of translation, although the first volume was issued in 1894, and the sixth has just appeared.[2] The publication in English of Wendt's *The Teaching of Jesus*, 1893, and of Schultz's *Old Testament Theology*, 1892,[3] enable the English reader to estimate the services being rendered to the study of the Scriptures by scholars in general sympathy with Ritschlianism. A lecture by Harnack on *Christianity and History*,[4] translated in 1896, is very valuable as a distinct statement of the Ritschlian attitude in regard to historical criticism. More important for the English student of Ritschlianism than any of the publications already mentioned, is the promise that has recently been made of a translation of the third volume of Ritschl's *Justification and Reconciliation*,[5] in which Ritschl develops his own theological system.

(2) Professor Orr, of Edinburgh, has probably done more than any other scholar in this country to acquaint those who cannot read German with Ritschlianism. First in articles in the *Thinker* and *Expository Times*,[6] then in numerous allusions in his work, *The Christian View of God and the World*,[7] and, lastly, in his handbook, *The Ritschlian*

[1] Williams & Norgate, 1895. Translated from the second thoroughly revised edition, with special annotations by the author, by J. Sandys Stanyon, M.A.

[2] Williams & Norgate, 1894–1899. Different translators are engaged on the work, which will be completed in seven volumes.

[3] T. & T. Clark, 1892, 1893. The former work is translated by the Rev. John Wilson, M.A.; and the latter by Rev. Professor J. A. Paterson, D.D.

[4] Adam & Charles Black, 1896. Translated by Thomas Bailey Saunders.

[5] T. & T. Clark. The translation is under the joint editorship of the Rev. H. R. Mackintosh, D.Phil., and the Rev. A. B. Macaulay, M.A. It is hoped that the volume will be ready in a few months.

[6] *Thinker*, August 1892; *Expository Times*, v. p. 534, vi. p. 252.

[7] *The Christian View of God and the World*, pp. 29–36, 45, 59–60, 273, 275, 276, 199, 206, 208, 209, 225, 268, 352–5, 387, 434, 440, 441, 445, 448, 462, 513–4, 519, 498–9, 506, etc.

Theology and the Evangelical Faith, he has presented a mass of information on this movement which is simply invaluable to the English student. The present writer makes this acknowledgment of the worth of this work most heartily now, although he feels himself compelled, by an independent study of the original literature, to differ sometimes in what follows from Professor Orr's judgments. A still less sympathetic tone towards Ritschlianism than Professor Orr's is adopted by Professor Denney in his *Studies in Theology*,[1] in which the criticisms are unduly severe. More kindly in spirit than either of these writers is Professor Bruce in several allusions he makes in his *Apologetics*.[2] While he does not accept the philosophical principles of the school, he is attracted by the stress laid on the person of Christ. His criticism of these principles may be found in an article on " Theological Agnosticism " in the *American Journal of Theology*.[3] Dr. Forsyth, of Cambridge, acknowledges indebtedness to Herrmann in his essay on "Revelation and the Person of Christ," [4] but also disassociates himself from " the philosophical position which is the negative side of that school." Professor Mackintosh, in his *Essays towards a New Theology*, accepts some suggestions from, but also expresses censure of, the teaching of Ritschl.[5] Mr. Forrest, in his book, *The Christ of History and of Experience*, gives a brief exposition and a condemnatory criticism of Herrmann's *Communion of the Christian with God* (pp. 158–166); and yet some of the positions stated in dealing with the relation of faith to historical fact show marked affinities to Ritschlian views. Mr. Somerville, in his work on *St. Paul's Conception of Christ*, acknowledges

---

[1] *Studies in Theology*, pp. 10-12, 14, 18, 49, 63, 80, 93-4, 137-9, 141, 143, 145, 156, 181, 220.

[2] *Apologetics*, pp. 155, 399, 355, 405, 502.

[3] *American Journal of Theology*, i. pp. 1-15.

[4] *Faith and Criticism*, pp. 97–144.

[5] *Essays towards a New Theology*, pp. vi, viii, 88, 139.

" special obligations to Albrecht Ritschl, by whose theological method *he is* conscious of having been largely
influenced in *his* treatment of the subject " (Preface, viii–ix).
A severe criticism, both of the presuppositions and also the
conclusions of the Ritschlian school, is offered by Professor
Wenley in his *Contemporary Theology and Theism*,[1] but the
force of the reasoning is lessened by the smartness of the
language used.   Professor Pfleiderer, in his English work,
The Development of Theology,[2] gives a very unfavourable
account of Ritschl's theology, rejects his theory of the origin
of the Old Catholic Church, and condemns severely the treatment of Church history in Harnack's *History of Dogma*.   In
the English translation of his German work on *The Philosophy
of Religion*,[3] there is found a searching examination of
Herrmann's pamphlet, *Metaphysics in Theology*, and his book,
*The Relation of Religion to our Knowledge of the World and
to Morality*, and also of Kaftan's *Essence of the Christian
Religion*.   Mr. Morgan, in the *Expository Times* (ix. 485),
gives a very appreciative account of the Ritschlian teaching
regarding the relation of *Faith and Revelation*.   Dr. Stucken-
berg, in the *American Journal of Theology*,[4] gives a sympathetic presentation of the *Theology of Albrecht Ritschl*.   In
the *Critical Review*[5] there are a number of reviews of books
of the Ritschlian school by some of our leading theologians,
any of which it will repay the student to consult.   The
only work in English hitherto published by one who is said

---

[1] *Contemporary Theology and Theism*, pp. 82–125.
[2] *The Development of Theology*, pp. 183–195, 235–237, 298–299.
[3] *The Philosophy of Religion*, ii. pp. 188–209.
[4] *American Journal of Theology*, ii. pp. 268–292.
[5] *Critical Review*: v. 270, vii. 210, Orr's review of Ritschl's *Collected
Essays* (German): iv. 175, Iverach, *Kaftan's The Truth of the Christian
Religion*: iii. 401, Orr, *Herrmann's The Communion of the Christian
with God* (German): vi. 121, Candlish, *Ibid.* (English): v. 115, Rainy,
Harnack's History of Dogma, i. (English): i. 273, Candlish, *Harnack's
History of Dogma*, iii. (German): ii. 179, Laidlaw, *Herrmann's Certainty
of Faith* (German): viii. 407, Paterson, *Kaftan's Dogmatik*.

to be an avowed adherent of the Ritschlian school is M'Giffert's *History of Christianity in the Apostolic Age*, the subject of which, however, does not allow of any prominence being given to a distinctive theological position. One work has, however, appeared in English, Balfour's *The Foundations of Belief*, which has been warmly welcomed by Kaftan as displaying an affinity to the Ritschlian position in its restriction of the sphere of science, its distrust of speculative philosophy, and in its constructive basis in man's practical needs.[1]   At an earlier date there appeared in England a work, which, independent of Ritschlian influences, approached the history of the origin of dogma with similar intentions and in a kindred spirit.   Hatch's *Hibbert Lectures* on *The Influence of Greek Ideas and Usages upon the Christian Church* set the problem of the contrast between the Sermon on the Mount and the Nicene Creed, and presented a solution, vividly expressed in the sentence, " The one belongs to a world of Syrian peasants, the other to a world of Greek philosophers." [2]   May we not even in this connection recall Hampden's *Bampton Lectures* on *The Scholastic Philosophy considered in its relation to Christian Theology* ?   Has not this sentence a Ritschlian ring, " The Church became unawares Aristotelic " ? [3]   Dr. Dale's argument in his book, *The Living Christ and the Four Gospels*, has a distinct affinity with the Ritschlian position on the relation of the certainty of faith to the results of historical criticism. These brief notes by way of historical introduction are offered in the hope that they will afford needed guidance to the English student of the Ritschlian theology in his reading.   For those who are familiar with German a discussion of the more important literature is added in an Appendix.

[1] See George Ferries' review of Kaftan's article on the German translation of Balfour's book, *Critical Review*, vi. p. 289.

[2] Hatch's *Hibbert Lectures*, p. 1.

[3] Hampden's *Bampton Lectures*, p. 12.

IX

As the writer wishes to avoid repeating what has been adequately stated by others before him, so far as that is possible without giving to this discussion too fragmentary a character, he will not attempt to give a systematic exposition of the teaching of Ritschl and his school. That has been already excellently done by Professor Orr in the book formerly mentioned. What seems most necessary, and therefore will be most profitable, is to concentrate attention on the distinctive principles of the Ritschlian theology, so that as definite a conception and as accurate an estimate of these as is possible may be gained. The Ritschlian theology has a critical as well as a constructive aspect. It clears the ground of a theological structure that seems to it built on a wrong plan, in order that it may build up a theological edifice of the right pattern. Its *critical aspect* may be described by the phrase *theology without metaphysics*. The examination of this principle will occupy the second chapter. Three special applications of this principle demand separate treatment—(1) *the rejection of speculative theism*, (2) *the condemnation of ecclesiastical dogma*, (3) *the antagonism to mysticism*, to each of which a chapter (third, fourth, and fifth) will be devoted. After this examination of the critical aspect of the Ritschlian theology, the constructive will invite scrutiny. What the older theologians called the formal principle of theology, the source of its data, is presented to us in its subjective reference in *the Value Judgments of Religion*, and in its objective reference in *the Historical Character of Revelation*, to each of which a chapter (sixth and seventh) must be assigned. The data having been obtained, there arises the question of the regulative principle to be adopted in arranging these into a system. This for the Ritschlian theology is the idea of the kingdom of God; and accordingly the eighth chapter will discuss *the Regulative Use of the Idea of the Kingdom of God*. In regard to the dogmatic system, there is not general agreement among the members of the Ritschlian school; but as until quite recently, when Kaftan published his volume on *Dogmatics*, Ritschl alone had dealt in a full and orderly way with Christian doctrine, his treatment of the contents of Christian dogmatics will receive almost exclusive attention, although no attempt will be made to offer an exhaustive discussion, but only to present the features of his system that are most distinctive. The test of the genuinely and adequately Christian character of any system of theology is *the Doctrine of the Person and the Work of Christ*, and this, therefore, must first claim our attention in the ninth chapter. But as the work of Christ cannot be discussed without at once raising the question of what is the Christian salvation, and that in turn cannot be understood without a knowledge of the Christian view of sin, the next chapter (tenth) must deal with *the Doctrine of Sin and Salvation*. The sinner as saved is introduced into a community in which he secures privileges, but also incurs obligations. How the relation of the individual believer to the Christian community is conceived, will be shown in the eleventh chapter under the heading *the Doctrine of the Church and of the Kingdom*. In the last chapter the writer will venture to give tentatively *a critical estimate* of the Ritschlian theology as *a solution of the problem* stated in the earlier parts of this first chapter.

APPENDIX TO CHAPTER I

It seems desirable, for the sake of those who may wish to give the subject further study in the original German literature, to give some account of the writings, books, and pamphlets of which use has been made in preparing this volume. (1) Ritschl's great work, *Die christliche Lehre von der Rechtfertigung und Versöhnung* ("The Christian Doctrine of Justification and Reconciliation"), consists of three volumes. The first volume deals with the history of the doctrine, beginning with Anselm ; the second discusses the biblical data for the doctrine ; but it is the third alone which gives Ritschl's own exposition that is of primary importance for the subject here dealt with. As he discusses not only the idea of justification and its relations, but also the presuppositions, including the doctrine of God, of sin, and of the Person and Vocation of Jesus, as well as the proof of the necessity of justification, and of its being grounded in the working and suffering of Christ, and the consequences of justification in the religious life, the volume offers us an almost complete dogmatic system, although there are doctrines that do not receive adequate treatment. This volume may be supplemented by two smaller works, one of which, *Unterricht in der christlichen Religion* ("Instruction in the Christian Religion"), is didactic, being intended for use in higher classes of schools, and gives a brief outline of Christian truth and duty under four headings—the Kingdom of God, Reconciliation through Christ, Christian life, and the common worship of God ; and the other of which, *Theologie und Metaphysik* ("Theology and Metaphysics"), is controversial, and discusses criticisms of Ritschl's position by several of his theological opponents. Although the latter may be described as an occasional writing, it is of very great importance for an understanding of Ritschl's philosophical principles. Several pamphlets also claim notice. Under the title of *Fides Implicita*, Ritschl in one discusses the common faith of Christian believers, the relation of knowledge and faith, and of faith and the Church. In another, *Die Christliche Vollkommenheit* ("The Christian Perfection"), he shows in what sense the Christian believer may claim perfection, qualitatively as regards his religious standing, but not quantitatively as regards his moral character. In a third, *Ueber das Gewissen* ("Concerning Conscience"), he analyses the conceptions of the condemning and of the legislating conscience,

3

and asserts that the former is only a lower stage of the latter.

(2) Herrmann, one of Ritschl's earliest disciples, and now one of the foremost leaders of the school, in his work, *Die Religion im Verhältniss zum Welterkennen und zur Sittlichkeit* ("The Relation of Religion to our Knowledge of the World and to Morality"), examines the philosophical basis of the dogmatic system which he advocates. After discussing the scientific knowledge of nature to prove its necessary limitation by man's practical impulse, he distinguishes two kinds of practical explanations of the world, —the dogmatically metaphysical and the religious,—and admits the possibility of a conflict between them. After condemning the mixture of metaphysics and religion in the traditional theology, he analyses the relation of morality to religion and metaphysics in order to insist on the intimate relation of morality and religion, and to advocate this as the basis of the dogmatic proof of the Christian view of the world, the moral law being the condition of the universality which the dogmatic proof is intended to claim for Christianity. In an earlier writing, a pamphlet entitled *Die Metaphysik in der Theologie* ("Metaphysics in Theology"), he had discussed the general relation of metaphysics and theology, and had indicated the evil consequences that had in his view resulted from their traditional alliance. Of another and more attractive type is his book, *Der Verkehr des Christen mit Gott* ("The Communion of the Christian with God"), in which, after stating the contrast between the Christian religion and mysticism, he discusses God's communion with us, or the revelation of God given in Jesus Christ, as the condition of our communion with God, with which he deals in the second part of the volume. This work, which is marked by intense religious fervour, suffers greatly from lack of proper arrangement, a defect which the English translator by abundant subdivision of the three chapters into sections, and by a continuous marginal analysis, attempts to correct. A pamphlet, *Der Begriff der Offenbarung* ("The Conception of Revelation"), deals with the true character of revelation ; a second, *Warum bedarf*

unser Glaube geschichtlicher Thatsachen ? ("Why does our Faith need historical Facts?"), shows that we who live in history must by facts of history be convinced of God's care for us; but a third, *Warum handelt es sich in dem Streit um das Apostolicum ?* ("What is involved in the Controversy about the Apostles' Creed?"), maintains that acceptance of any of these facts must not be enforced as a condition of either membership or ministry in an evangelical Church. A fourth pamphlet, *Die Bedeutung der Inspirationslehre für die evangelische Kirche* (" The Significance of the Doctrine of Inspiration for the Evangelical Church"), argues that the traditional doctrine of inspiration is not a help but a hindrance to a true understanding of the Christian revelation. A fifth pamphlet, *Die Gewissheit des Glaubens und die Freiheit der Theologie* (" The Certainty of Faith and the Freedom of Theology"), shows how deliverance from the distress in which theology now finds itself can be attained by securing certainty of faith without sacrificing the freedom of theology. The worth of these pamphlets is not to be judged by their size.

(3) Kaftan, as noted a follower of Ritschl and a leader of the school as Herrmann, has written two companion volumes, *Die Wahrheit der christlichen Religion* (" The Truth of the Christian Religion") and *Das Wesen der christlichen Religion* (" The Essence of the Christian Religion"). In the first, which, as already noted, has been translated into English, ecclesiastical dogma as an erroneous method of Christian apologetics is condemned, and a proof of Christianity grounded on the primacy of the practical reason as opposed to the traditional speculative method is offered. In the second, a definition of religion in its varied aspects and relations, and of revelation, is given; and is followed by a discussion of Christianity as the true religion and revelation. One pamphlet, *Glaube und Dogma* (" Faith and Dogma"), argues, against an advocate of an undogmatic Christianity, for the need of dogma, but asserts, as against traditional theology, that this must be a new dogma. Another, *Brauchen wir ein neues Dogma ?* (" Do we need a new Dogma?"), indicates some of the changes

in theology that are now imperative. Recently Kaftan has essayed to supply his own demand by issuing his *Dogmatik* ("Dogmatics"), which has, however, not been made use of in the preparation of this volume.

(4) Harnack's writings are of great importance for the student of Church History ; but in order to understand why he is to be reckoned as an adherent of the Ritschlian school, it is quite sufficient to study his *Grundriss der Dogmengeschichte* ("Outlines of the History of Dogma"), in two small volumes, in which he gives a summary of his great work, *The History of Dogma*, which is being translated into English. From this work, or from the first two volumes of the translation of the larger work, one can learn his distinctively Ritschlian ideas of religion and revelation ; his attitude, which is more advanced than that of many Ritschlians, on questions of the historical criticism of the New Testament ; and his estimate of the theological development of the Church, in which he is in agreement with the Ritschlian school generally. His views of the relation of historical criticism to religious faith are briefly and clearly set forth in a lecture which has been translated under the title of *Christianity and History*. The same problem is discussed by another member of the school, Reischle, in a pamphlet, *Des Glaube an Jesus Christus und die geschichtliche Erforschung seines Lebens* ("Faith in Jesus Christ and Historical Inquiry regarding His Life"), in which the difficulties for faith due to historical inquiry are frankly recognised, the claim and assurance of faith in opposition to historical inquiry are firmly asserted, and even the advantages of historical inquiry to faith are freely admitted.

(5) The value-judgments of religion form one of the most distinctive and yet most difficult features of the Ritschlian theology ; and therefore great importance attaches to the pamphlet, *Ueber Werthurtheile* ("Concerning Value-Judgments"), which Otto Ritschl, the son and biographer of the founder of the school, has published. This writing should serve to obviate some of the objections that are brought against this Ritschlian position, and to explain some of the difficulties that are felt regarding it. The use of

the idea of the kingdom of God in the Ritschlian theology
will be better understood after reading Wegener's *A. Ritschls
Idee des Reiches Gottes im Licht der Geschichte kritisch unter-
sucht* (" A. Ritschl's Idea of the Kingdom of God critically
examined in the Light of History "). Wegener is a severe
critic of Ritschl ; but the historical information which he
brings together is of use even to those who do not altogether share his judgment. In this connection mention
may be made of a French work, Schoen's *Les Origines
Historiques de la Theologie de Ritschl* (" The Historical
Origins of the Theology of Ritschl "), in which all the distinctive features of Ritschl's theology are shown to have
been anticipated in previous theologians, Ritschl's claim to
originality being made to rest on his synthesis of these
elements. His dependence on Kant and Lotze has been
separately dealt with in the German work by Stählin,
Kant, Lotze, und Ritschl, the English translation of which
has already been noticed. A French work covering the
very same ground is Favre's *Les Principes Philosophiques
de la Theologie de Ritschl* (" The Philosophical Principles
of the Theology of Ritschl "). Esslinger in dependence
on Pfleiderer offers, in a short pamphlet, *Eine Studie zur
Erkenntnistheorie Ritschls* (" A Study concerning Ritschl's
Theory of Knowledge "). A more exhaustive treatment
of the same subject is Steinbeck's *Das Verhältnis von
Theologie und Erkenntnis - Theorie* (" The Relation of
Theology and Theory of Knowledge "), in which Sabatier's
as well as Ritschl's theory of knowledge is subjected to a
close scrutiny. The epistemological foundation of the
Ritschlian theology is critically expounded by Pfleiderer in
the first of three essays which he has published in one volume
under the title, *Die Ritschl'sche Theologie*. The second
essay is a very searching examination of Ritschl's use of
the Holy Scriptures, in which it is shown that Ritschl's
claim of a biblical foundation for his theology is deprived
of its worth by his arbitrary methods of exegesis. The
third essay deals with the Ritschlian school in its opposition to the ideas of religion and morality and their mutual
relation, which are characteristic of idealistic philosophies

of religion. From a much more conservative standpoint than Pfleiderer, Frank (*Zur Theologie A. Ritschls*, "To A. Ritschl's Theology") discusses the significance of the theology of Ritschl for the Church as a divine visitation for its discipline, condemns his dogmatic methods, gives special attention to his doctrine of God, and finds no improvement in the successive phases of his thought. A sympathetic and judicious, full and thorough study of the Ritschlian movement is Ecke's *Die Theologische Schule Albrecht Ritschls* ("The Theological School of Albrecht Ritschl"). It deals with the individual peculiarity of Ritschl as a dogmatic theologian, the foreign elements in Ritschl's theology, the origin and development of the Ritschlian school, the true content of the Ritschlian theology in its new dogmatic method, its opposition to rationalism, and its criticism of unsound piety, the noteworthy attempts of the disciples to transform the theology of Ritschl in approach to the unmutilated biblical and Reformed confession as regards the doctrine of sin, of the work of Christ, of the divinity of Christ, of the Holy Spirit, and of prayer. To this work the writer very cordially acknowledges his great indebtedness, although he had studied the Ritschlian literature independently, and had in many cases for himself reached similar conclusions before this book came into his hands. This list of literature makes no profession to be exhaustive, as only those books have been mentioned which have been thoroughly studied in the preparation of this volume; but it is believed it will be quite sufficient to enable any student of this movement to gain such an understanding of it as will enable him fairly to judge its merits or its defects.

A.—CRITICAL

———◆———

CHAPTER II

I

(1) RITSCHL'S position on the relation of metaphysics to theology is by no means consistent. Some of his utterances justify the charge that he desires to exclude metaphysics altogether from theology, while in others he defends himself against the charge, and maintains that it is only the wrong metaphysics he wants to expel. A careful examination of his statements on the subject will probably lead to the conclusion that he was not quite clear in his own mind upon the question, and that therefore, without any deliberation or intention on his part, his statements represent the attitude of the moment rather than any consistent position. One cannot but feel that he was on unfamiliar and uncongenial ground whenever he attempted to deal with philosophical principles, as alike his interests and his capacities were predominantly, nay, almost exclusively, those of a systematic theologian.

(2) "Every theologian," says Ritschl, "as a scientific man, is under necessity or obligation to act according to a definite theory of knowledge, of which he must himself be conscious, and the right of which he must prove. Ac-

cordingly, it is an inconsiderate and incredible assertion, that I exclude all metaphysics out of theology. For if I am scientifically qualified in theology,—and that has not as yet been generally denied me,—then I shall follow a theory of knowledge, which in the determination of the objects of knowledge will be regulated by a conception of 'thing,' accordingly will be metaphysical. Therefore the dispute between Luthardt (one of his opponents) and myself is rightly expressed only in this way, which metaphysics is justified in theology. The right of possession in the theological tradition, which I have abandoned, and which my opponents advocate, belongs to the Platonic theory of knowledge." [1] This emphatic statement of the necessity of a definite theory of knowledge for every theologian as a scientific man, must, however, be accepted with the qualification supplied by another passage which is separated from this by only five pages. " As Christianity," he says, "is neutral in regard to the differences of Jewish and Hellenic morals, so also as a religion it is indifferent in regard to the different theories of knowledge by means of which its intellectual contents may be scientifically arranged." [2] In comparing these two utterances, one cannot but raise the question whether, if the right theory of knowledge is so important to theology as a science, Christianity as a religion can be altogether neutral as regards the theory of knowledge, by means of which theology, as its interpreter, seeks to set forth in order its intellectual contents; or, if Christianity as a religion is neutral as regards all theories of knowledge, any one theory of knowledge can be of so very great value to theology. Surely the relation between religion and theology is too intimate to allow that what is indifferent to the

---

[1] Ritschl's *Theologie und Metaphysik*, Zweite Auflage, pp. 40, 41 ("Theology and Metaphysics," 2nd ed.).

[2] *Op. cit.* p. 46.

former can be important to the latter. Ritschl here shows the uncertainty of his own judgment. While the question which the contrast between these two passages raises is too large for treatment here and now, the qualification of the former passage by the latter must be kept in mind in the discussion to which we now turn. The former passage raises the four questions to which an answer must now be sought. (1) What is Ritschl's own theory of knowledge, or to use the technical term, epistemology? (2) What is the relation of epistemology to metaphysics; can they be identified as by Ritschl? (3) What is the metaphysics Ritschl rejects? (4) What is the effect of this rejection on his theology?

II

(1) The first of these questions must be answered by a quotation, in which Ritschl not only states his own theory of knowledge, but also indicates the theories of knowledge which he rejects. " In European culture we have to deal with three forms of the knowledge of a thing. (1) The *first* has arisen from Plato's impulse, and is at home in the circle of scholasticism. So far as its influence extends, one meets the representation, that the thing indeed *acts* upon us through its changeable signs, and excites our sensation and representation, but that the thing *rests* behind its signs as a unity of attributes which remains unchanged." (2) " The *second* form of epistemology has been produced by Kant, in that he confines the knowledge of our understanding to the world of appearances, but declares unknowable the thing-in-itself, or the things-in-themselves, in the reciprocal changes of which also the changes in the world of appearances will have their origin." (3) " The *third* form of epistemology has been set up by Lotze. We recognise in the appearances, which change

in a limited space in a limited range and a definite order the thing as the cause of its signs which act upon us, as the end to which these serve as means, as the law of their regular changes." [1] It is the third theory which Ritschl accepts.

(2) Against the first theory he brings three objections : (1) the pretence of knowing the thing-in-itself before its activities; (2) the confusion of the thing-in-itself with the image of a thing formed by the memory ; (3) the contradiction involved in thinking of the thing-in-itself as resting, and yet as acting in its apparent signs, and as placed in a space behind that in which its attributes are. All these objections may, however, be included in one charge against the Platonic theory : it separates the thing from its attributes and activities, in which alone it is known by us. Against the second theory he objects, that the objects of our knowledge can be described as appearances only "on the assumption that in them something real, namely, the thing, appears to us, or becomes the cause of our sensation and perception." Kant rejects the scholastic error of claiming a knowledge of the thing-in-itself; but he is at fault, even as scholasticism is, in separating the thing in itself from its appearances. The merit of the third theory, according to Ritschl, is that it attempts no such separation, but claims to know the thing in its appearances and activities.

(3) In criticism of Ritschl's statements it may be pointed out that Plato's and Kant's theories can hardly be placed side by side as they are, since their intentions and methods are different. Plato's theory is, strictly speaking, a *metaphysics*. It is an attempt to discover what are the ultimate principles of existence. These it finds in the universal ideas, of which individual things are the partial

[1] Ritschl's *Rechtfertigung und Versöhnung*, Dritter Band, Vierte Auflage, pp. 19, 20. ("Justification and Reconciliation," iii., 4th ed.).

and imperfect images. These universal ideas it reaches by a logical method of induction and definition. Kant's theory is, strictly speaking, an epistemology. It endeavours to find out the necessary factors of human knowledge. These it discovers to be the data of sensation, the forms of time and space, the categories of quantity, quality, relation. Its method is a criticism of the act of knowing to distinguish its variable content from its necessary form. Even Lotze's view, with which Ritschl claims to be in agreement, is not correctly stated; for Lotze agrees thoroughly with Kant, that the objects of our knowledge are appearances; but he differs from Kant in not regarding the things in themselves as altogether unknowable, as he considers himself warranted in making the metaphysical inference from our own self-consciousness, that things must be soul-like beings. On the one point Lotze clearly declares that " sensible properties are neither directly the content of ' the Existent,' nor are they phenomena which, although in an indirect manner, do nevertheless express the true nature of this Existent; they are rather events which indicate, indeed, the fact and the manner of the *affection* or *action* of things, but never specify what the things *are*." [1] On the other point he asserts that " either we ascribe to all ' things ' as soon as they are assumed to ' be ' *realiter* outside ourselves the most common characteristics of spiritual life—to wit, some form or other of ' Being for self '; or else if we do not want to concede such an ' animating of all things,' we must deny that they can be *realiter* outside ourselves." [2] In other

[1] Lotze's *Outlines of Metaphysics*, translated and edited by George T. Ladd, p. 26. Professor Henry Jones has published the first volume of a work, *A Critical Account of the Philosophy of Lotze*, in which he deals with *The Doctrine of Thought*; and promises a second volume, in which he will deal with Lotze's metaphysical doctrines. The volume already published may, with advantage, be consulted by any who wish to understand Lotze.

[2] *Op. cit.* p. 141. The writer may be excused for here quoting, in illustration, a summary statement of Lotze's epistemology in an article

words, the phenomenalism of our knowledge, which Lotze admits, must lead us to subjective idealism, or the denial of any reality save our subjective states of consciousness, unless we supplement the results of our epistemology by a metaphysical assumption that reality is 'soul-like' 'being for self.' These two features of Lotze's theory Ritschl here ignores, although elsewhere, as we shall see (p. 48), he accepts Lotze's theory, that the conception of a thing is formed on the analogy of our own self-consciousness. He can, however, for his protest against the separation of "a thing" from its attributes and activities claim the support of Lotze, who says: "While we require that the 'Thing' shall be thinkable *before* its properties, we, for all that, never achieve the actual thought of it otherwise than by means of its properties. While we further require that it must first 'be' in order afterwards to experience somewhat or to enter into relations with other things, we, for all that, never in experience find a 'Being' whose apparent rest does not itself rest upon uninterrupted motions and actions; nor are we able even in our thoughts to discover a perspicuous conception of what we mean by such 'Being' as this."[1] But while Lotze follows this statement of the contradictions of the common view by a thorough analysis

on Lotze, contributed by him, to the *Expository Times* (iv. pp. 540–543): "That materiality is a sensible manifestation of supersensible elements of reality; that only *soul-like beings* can claim *thinghood*, which reflection shows cannot be conceived otherwise than as *selfhood*; that all else is but the immediate action of the absolute substance; that all things have their unity only in that substance, and their apparent interaction is the self-modification of that substance; that individuality is not existence distinct from that substance, but a mode of that substance which enjoys its own states; that time, space, and motion are but symbolical representations of the intellectual relations of things; that the world is completed by the spirits, by whom it is subjectively apprehended, and for whose self-realisation—beatitude—it exists as a means,—all these conclusions are very far removed from materialism or monism, and belong to a thoroughly spiritual view of the world."

[1] *Op. cit.* p. 17.

of our knowledge of a thing, Ritschl is content by a *tour de force* to unite what human thought hitherto has been compelled to distinguish.

(4) Ritschl's distinct intention, however much his argumentation (in his work, *Theologie und Metaphysik*, to which he after this statement refers his reader for a further exposition of his theory of knowledge), which moves backwards and forwards, hither and thither, obscures it, is to affirm the proposition, " we know the thing in its appearances," or things-in-themselves are as they are for us. This is the position of *vulgar* as distinguished from *philosophical realism*, which is either ignorant of, or indifferent to, the problem of knowledge and existence.   As Pfleiderer justly remarks regarding the position which Ritschl affirms, " That seems very simple and evident, so simple, that one might only wonder that so sensible people (*gescheidte Leute*) as Plato and Kant could not even already reach it." [1] Ritschl assumes the unity of knowing and being; but the manifest contrast between knowing and being which presents itself even on very slight reflection shows that this unity cannot be an assumption, but must rather be the conclusion reached by a thorough analysis of knowing and being, if such an analysis justifies it.   In Plato this contrast presented itself as a contrast of individual objects and general ideas; in Kant, as a contrast of the subjective and objective elements of knowledge.   To suppose that their efforts have no meaning and no value, is to show oneself incapable of philosophical thinking; and in this respect Ritschl does certainly justify the charge brought against him that he was no philosopher.   A theoretical justification of his own position he has not attempted, but has been content with exposing the contradictions involved in the view which he so strenuously opposes.   As against an abstract

---

[1] Pfleiderer's *Die Ritschl'sche Theologie*, p. 2 (" The Ritschlian Theology ").

dualism between subject and attribute, to which it must be acknowledged scholastic theology has been prone, his polemic is not without justification ; but, on the other hand, the absolute monism of subject and attribute which he would set up involves an assumption, which is disproved by the whole course of philosophical thought.

(5) But it seems to the writer that we must not take too seriously Ritschl's claim to be guided by an epistemology of which he is fully conscious, and which he has fully justified to himself. What he does rather present to us is an empirical method in theology, for which he seeks justification in an epistemology with which it is brought into external connection, but with which it has no necessary relation. There is justification for Pfleiderer's remark : " We may conjecture that Ritschl did not make this theory of cognition the basis of his theology from the first, but rather propounded it subsequently, in its defence."[1] The aim is sincerely and intensely practical. He seeks to lay stress on those relations of the objects of theological knowledge which seem to him of immediate significance and value for Christian experience, and to divert attention from those aspects of these objects, with which theology has busied itself not a little, but which seem to him to be remote from Christian experience. Our immediate empirical perceptions of spiritual realities, such as God and the soul, are the data with which theology is to occupy itself ; and it is to leave alone these secondary rational inferences from the data, which seek to determine what God is for Himself, and what the soul is in itself. It may be frankly conceded that theology has often yielded to the fascination of speculation, and has separated itself from the contents of the religious consciousness ; and in so far as Ritschl seeks to keep theology in close touch with Christian experience we cannot but thoroughly sympathise with him. In this

[1] Pfleiderer's *Development of Theology*, p. 183.

respect, however, he has himself been unfaithful to his own intentions. In his construction of the personality of God, his deduction of the kingdom of God from the love of God, his conception of the divine attribute of eternity, which accounts for his contradiction of Christian conscience in his doctrine of God's wrath, he has himself forsaken the safe ground of Christian experience, and wandered on to the shifting sand of theological speculation. These inconsistencies, however, themselves show that his method is inadequate; for what he ignores is this, that completeness of determination of its objects is a necessity of thought; that theology cannot be content with presenting its objects only in the relations immediately experienced in the Christian consciousness, but is compelled to satisfy an inextinguishable desire for certainty by interpreting these objects as a unity in which these relations find their explanation. Although Ritschl professes " to know the thing in its appearances," yet what his practical method amounts to is rather exclusive attention to the appearances, without any attempt to rationally interpret the thing through its appearances. While he thinks he is maintaining the unity of the thing as " the cause of its signs," to use his own words, " which act upon us, as the purpose which these serve as means, as the law of their regular changes," he is really ignoring the thing, and is fixing his exclusive attention on the signs. This is an inadequate theological method which seeks to justify itself by an epistemology which simply ignores the problem which it professes to solve, the relation between knowledge and existence.

(6) Before leaving this subject it will be necessary to call attention to a serious misconception into which many of the critics of Ritschl have fallen, it cannot be added, without any justification, for he is very far from making his meaning plain. The passage on which this misconception rests must, in justice to Ritschl and his critics

alike, be fully quoted.[1] " The word (absolute) in the sense assigned to it by Frank (one of his most decided opponents), signifies the thing which is represented only as the unity of its internal relations, accordingly incompletely. For one knows completely a self-sufficient thing first in its qualities, namely, its activities on our perceptions and on other things. The appearances which are perceived in a limited space in the same position or succession, and their changes in a definite limit and order, are combined by our faculty of representation in the unity of the thing after the analogy of the cognising soul, which in the change of its corresponding sensations feels and remembers itself as a permanent unity. Accordingly, the thing which we represent for ourselves is an existence in itself (inseity). And as the soul affirms itself as the cause of its changing sensations under the stimulus of the appearances of the thing, and in these perceptions becomes aware of itself as end of itself,

---

[1] Ritschl's *Theologie und Metaphysik*, pp. 19, 20 (" Theology and Metaphysics "), This passage is so important that the German is here given. " Das Wort in der von Frank beigefuegten Deutung bezeichnet das Ding, welches nur als Einheit seiner Beziehungen in sich, also unvollständing vorgestellt wird. Denn vollständing erkennt man ein in sich selbstaendiges Ding erst in seinen Qualitaeten naemlich seinen Wirkungen auf unsere Wahrnehmungen und auf andere Dinge. Die Erscheinungen, welche in einem begrenzten Raumbilde in der immer gleichen Lagerung oder Reihenfolge, und deren Veraenderung in einer bestimmten Grenze und Ordnung wahrgenommen werden, fasst unsere Vorstellung zu der Einheit des Dinges zusammen nach der Analogie mit der erkennenden Seele, welche in dem Wechsel ihrer entsprechenden Empfindungen sich als dauernde Einheit fuehlt und erinnert. Demgemaess ist das von uns vorgestellte Ding Insichselbstsein. Und wie die Seele sich als Ursache ihrer wechselnden Empfindungen unter dem Reize der Erscheinungen des Dinges behauptet, und sich in diesen Wahrnehmungen als Zweck ihrer selbst inne wird, so stellt sich auch das isolirte Ding in seinen Merkmalen als causa sui und als finis sui vor. Demgemaess wird das isolirte Ding auch als Durchsichsein und Fuersichselbstsein gedacht. So gedacht aber entbehrt das Ding aller besondern Qualitaeten. Es ist ein rein formeller Begriff ohne Inhalt. So geringfuegig ist der Begriff des von Frank mit so grossem Gewichte als Gott proclamirten Absoluten ! "

so the isolated thing appears in its attributes as *causa sui* and *finis sui*. Accordingly the isolated thing will be thought as its own cause (aseity) and its own purpose (proseity). But so thought the thing is lacking in all special qualities. It is a purely formal conception without content. So insignificant is the conception of the absolute proclaimed by Frank with so much stress as God."

Looking at the passage as a whole, it becomes clear at first sight that Ritschl is here engaged in controversy, and that he is here giving an account of the way in which he conceives that the idea of the absolute, as his opponent understands it, is formed. But when we look more closely it must be admitted it is not quite clear whether he intends us to regard the analysis he gives of the formation of the conception of a thing as a critical statement of Frank's position, or as a positive exposition of his own views. In favour of the latter position another passage in which he refers back to this passage may be quoted: " The impression," he says, " that the perceived thing in the changes of its marks is one, arises, as has been remarked above (p. 19), from the continuity of the feeling of self in the succession of our sensations excited by the thing. Further, the conception of the thing as cause and as purpose of itself arises from the certainty that I am cause and I am purpose in the activities due to me."[1]   The reference given to Lotze's writings also lends support to this interpretation; for, as Ritschl claims to follow Lotze's epistemology, it is not likely he would appeal to him in support of views which he was ascribing to an opponent. But even if this is Ritschl's own view of how the conception of the thing as a unity, its own cause and end, arises in us, it does not in anyway prove that Ritschl regarded this conception as a pure fiction which the mind imposes upon itself. In the sentence preceding that last quoted he definitely accepts

[1] *Op. cit.* p. 38.

4

this representation as true to reality, and makes the positive statement that "the thing is cause in its operations, and purpose in the orderly succession of its manifest changes." Granting, then, that it is Ritschl's own view that is given in the first part of the passage, there can be no doubt whatever that the last sentence but one, " It is a purely formal conception without content," does not refer to the view of *the thing* Ritschl holds as his own, but to the perversion of that view of which Frank is guilty, in Ritschl's judgment, when he thinks of " the isolated thing," that is, as defined in the next sentence, " lacking in all special qualities," " as its own cause and its own purpose." Whether Ritschl's analysis of the representation of the unity of a thing is psychologically correct or not is not here the question ; nor yet whether he gives a just account of Frank's position or not. The simple issue is, Does Ritschl regard this representation of the unity of a thing as a mental fiction ; and does he apply to it the description of a " purely formal conception without content"? If the careful examination of the passage has proved anything, it has surely shown that a decided denial can be given to both suggestions. Yet Stählin represents Ritschl as describing the unity of the thing conceived on the analogy of the soul " as a represented, not an actual unity,"[1] although, as we have seen, Ritschl assumes a correspondence and not a contrast of representation and reality ; and he actually claims without a trace of hesitation that the phrase, " a purely formal conception without content," is Ritschl's own account of the conception of a thing. " How," he goes on to say, " a purely formal conception without content can be an analogy of the soul, which is regarded as the real unity of its perceptions, is quite unintelligible."[2] In this case, however, the lack of intelligibility is not in Ritschl, but in

---

[1] Stählin's *Kant, Lotze, and Ritschl*, p. 173.
[2] *Op. cit.* p. 175.

his critic. These two misunderstandings of Ritschl are, however, used by Stählin to convict him of reducing all reality to illusion. Having got to this conclusion, again and again in the course of the subsequent discussion it is used to justify such charges as that "it follows from Ritschl's principles, that God Himself has no reality";[1] that "the object of Christology is resolved into a representation generated in the believing mind by its own religious life";[2] and that "even the religious subject itself is mere representation, and wholly lacks reality."[3] Accordingly in his work, which the translator commends on the author's own testimony "as in the strictest sense critical," many of the condemnations of Ritschl's theology draw their apparent justification from "the logical application of principles,"[4] which happen not to be Ritschl's at all, but are statements by Ritschl of an opponent's supposed position. Robert Favre also, who acknowledges his indebtedness to Stählin, asserts on the strength of this same passage that Ritschl must be reckoned with those who ascribe to "our notions of things only a subjective import" (portée subjective).[5] The temper of Stählin's book is such that one understands his misunderstanding of Ritschl; but it is to be regretted that Professor Orr, who is deservedly an authority on the Ritschlian theology, should lend countenance to this misunderstanding, when he says in a note, "In the other passages 'the thing' is described as only a mental fiction."[6] A sympathetic scrutiny of the passage referred to will, the writer is persuaded, bear out his contention that in this respect Ritschl has been grievously misjudged; for, as if to guard against such a misconception he expressly says, "For the doctrine of 'the thing,' it is

[1] *Op. cit.* p. 198.　　　[2] *Op. cit.* p. 226.
[3] *Op. cit.* p. 238.　　　[4] *Op. cit.* Preface, vi.
[5] Favre's *Les Principes Philosophiques de la Theologie de Ritschl*, p. 100 ("The Philosophical Principles of the Theology of Ritschl").
[6] Orr's *The Ritschlian Theology*, p. 63.

assumed that our I is not of itself the cause of sensations, preceptions, etc., but that these distinctive activities of the soul are excited in coexistence with things, to which even the human body also belongs."[1] Ritschl, then, is not a subjective idealist in the sense of reducing all reality to representation. This question has been so fully and thoroughly dealt with because the first introduction of Ritschl to English readers was in this work of Stählin's, in which this misconception plays so prominent and important a part, and which has therefore given to it an extensive currency in English theological thought.

(7) While this passage has been misunderstood, yet on the other hand it must be admitted that Ritschl in discussing the objects of the religious consciousness does not consistently maintain his own theory, that the thing is known in its attributes, but lapses from time to time, probably under the influence of Kant, from which he never entirely delivered himself, into what may be called, in distinction from subjective, *critical idealism*, a recognition of the unknowableness of things-in-themselves (but not denial of their existence, which is *subjective idealism*), and a limitation of our knowledge to appearances. In dealing with the doctrines of God, of Christ, of the soul, and of sin, this tendency to limit attention exclusively to what may be called the phenomenal aspect of reality must be recognised. With some justice, if undue severity, Pfleiderer declares that "the whole Ritschlian theology moves in this Hither and Thither, this swing-play, this absolute confusion of idealistic and realistic judgments of objects."[2] While this tendency to critical idealism in Ritschl must be con-

[1] Ritschl's *Rechtfertigung und Versöhnung*, iii. p. 18 ("Justification and Reconciliation").

[2] Pfleiderer, *Die Ritschl'sche Theologie*, p. 6 ("The Ritschlian Theology").

ceded, yet the epistemology he deliberately adopted was what has been called *vulgar realism*.

(8) Was Ritschl right, however, in insisting on the necessity of a theory of knowledge to the theologian? The question "whether a preliminary (*vorausgeschickte*) philosophical epistemology is necessary for theology or not" is dealt with by Steinbeck as the first part of his work on *The Relation of Theology and Epistemology*; and he comes to the following conclusion: "This demand cannot be fulfilled for this reason, because thereby, in the first place, theology is brought into dependence on philosophy; secondly, it cannot reach any universal validity in this respect; and, thirdly, the difficult and always uncertain solution of the problem of epistemology forbids its being placed at the beginning in a position which controls all subsequent discussions." [1] With this conclusion the writer most cordially concurs. Just as a well-trained mind will reason logically without adopting any theory of the logicians, and an educated man will write grammatically without being conscious of all the rules of grammar; even so the objects of knowledge can be distinctly and correctly known by an intelligence that has been disciplined by gaining knowledge, without any acquaintance with any philosophical theory of knowledge. Attention to, interest in, occupation with, the objects of knowledge will do far more in leading a man to correct methods than any epistemology can. A vivid Christian consciousness and a real Christian experience will make the better and truer Christian theologian. With reason even it may be said that it would have been better for Ritschl himself if he had not formally adopted an epistemology, as his theology does suffer from the tendency to determine the form and limit the range of Christian experience and consciousness, not by

[1] Steinbeck, *Das Verhältnis von Theologie und Erkenntnis-Theorie*,

actual facts, but by formal theory. Another circumstanc
that confirms this conclusion is that while Ritschl and hi
followers are agreed in many of their theological position.
not one of them has followed him exactly in his theor
of knowledge. Herrmann accepts the Kantian theory (
knowledge.[1] Kaftan expounds empiricism in his chapte
on *Knowledge* in the *Proof of Christianity* he offers.[2] Y
both of them from standpoints so dissimilar confess then
selves to be followers of Ritschl in his theological methc
generally, if not in his dogmatic conclusions particularly.

III

(1) So much space has necessarily been given
answering our first question regarding Ritschl's episte:
ology, that the other questions must be dealt with in t
briefest possible compass. The second question, "WI
is the relation of epistemology to metaphysics; can tl
be identified as by Ritschl?" can be dealt with v
shortly. Ritschl assumes that a discussion of the regu
tive conceptions of human knowledge is metaphysics;
having made this assumption he himself only discusses
question what is a thing, or the category of substa:
There are many other categories, such as causa
organism, development, personality, which, even if m
physics were only a discussion of the ultimate princi
of knowledge, would claim scrutiny; but we do not
a recognition of this fact in what Ritschl says about m
physics. Like every other thinker, he must assume t
categories, as they are necessities for our thinking, bt
cannot be maintained that in his use of them he sati

[1] See Herrmann, *Die Religion im Verhältniss zum Welterkenne.*
zur Sittlichkeit, pp. 16–22 ("Religion in Relation to our Knowled
the World and to Morality").

[2] Kaftan, *The Truth of the Christian Religion*, vol. ii. chap. i.

his own tests of the theologian as a scientific man; he is not himself conscious of all that they involve, and he does not attempt to prove their right.   He has not a complete and consistent theory of knowledge.

(2) But, further, Ritschl has no right to claim that his epistemology is a metaphysics.   In a system of absolute idealism, such as that of Hegel is generally understood to be, in which the dialectical movement of thought is claimed to be an exact reproduction of the actual evolution of being, in which the unity of knowledge and existence is asserted, and in which, according to one interpretation at least, the ultimate existence finally realises itself only in human consciousness, an epistemology is also a metaphysics.   But in any other system, in which a relative dualism of knowing and being is recognised, in which the range of possible existence is not measured by the reach of human knowledge, and in which the mind of man claims only to possess partial indications of what the ultimate secret of existence is, imperfect anticipations of the final solution of its problems, epistemology cannot be identified with metaphysics.   It is undoubtedly an introduction to metaphysics, for human intelligence is most certainly one of the approaches to the ultimate reality and final purpose of the universe ; but so is conscience, affection, volition.

(3) A metaphysics is not, then, simply a discussion of the regulative conceptions of knowledge, unless these be claimed as affording an exhaustive report of the ultimate principles of existence.   A metaphysics is an attempt, with all the evidence that is afforded by nature, history, intelligence, conscience, personality, to frame an interpretation of the meaning of the world, to form an estimate of the worth of life, to forecast a goal for the course of history.   A metaphysics is what the Germans call *Weltanschauung*, a world-view.   Such a world-view Ritschl does not offer us.   (He does maintain that there is a Christian

world-view, but it is received by faith from the Christian revelation, and is not established, as a metaphysics must be, on a rational investigation of all intelligible reality.) On the one hand, the *vulgar realism* of his epistemology bars at the very outset the path of inquiry into the relation of knowledge and existence, along which such a world - view must be sought. On the other hand, to anticipate the results of a subsequent discussion, Ritschl's separation of knowledge into two parts, the theoretical judgments of science or philosophy, and the value-judgments of religion, is an express refusal to entertain such a view. If the unity of existence is not reproduced, however partially and imperfectly, in the unity of knowledge, no metaphysics is possible. The charge against Ritschl of attempting a theology without a metaphysics must be held proved, as his identification of metaphysics with epistemology is invalid.

IV

(1) Although Ritschl has not been by any means successful in presenting us with what we can legitimately recognise as a metaphysics, we may now inquire whether he has been more successful in his exposure of the metaphysics which he claims to be the basis of the traditional theology. What then is the metaphysics Ritschl rejects? This is our third question. Although we have seen that Ritschl in one passage declares that it is only against a false metaphysics in theology that he contends, yet he seems at other times to forget this limitation of his purpose, and to write as though no metaphysics were legitimate in theology. This is his description of metaphysics. " Metaphysics is, as is well known, the very accidental title of the ' First Philosophy ' set up by Aristotle. This *discipline* is devoted to the investigation

of the universal principles of all existence. Now the things which occupy our knowledge are distinguished as nature and as spiritual life. In the investigation of the common principles of all existence the distinctive features are ignored, by means of which one represents the distinction between nature and spirit, and recognises these groups as different magnitudes. Natural and spiritual appearances or magnitudes occupy metaphysical knowledge only in so far as they are generally to be regarded as things. For in the conception of the thing there are established the common conditions of knowledge of the appearances of nature and spirit." [1] He then goes on to contrast metaphysics with the philosophy of nature and of the spirit, and expresses a preference for the latter as of greater value, because dealing with reality more exhaustively. Again he continues, ' the metaphysical knowledge of nature and of spiritual life as things is *à priori*; it fixes firmly the forms arising in the knowing spirit of man, in which it proceeds generally to fix the objects of its representation above the current of sensations and perceptions." [2] Here again there is the identification, already fully discussed, of epistemology and metaphysics. In the first passage metaphysics deals with the universal principles of all existence"; in the second, with "the forms arising in the knowing spirit of man." Adopting now the second definition of metaphysics, he admits the necessary priority of metaphysics to all experimental knowledge, as investigating the very conditions of knowledge; yet he maintains that a more adequate knowledge of spiritual " magnitudes " is gained by psychological and ethical in-

---

[1] Ritschl's *Theologie und Metaphysik*, p. 8 ("Theology and Metaphysics"). The terms "discipline," "groups," "magnitudes," are the literal translation of the German terms "*Disciplin*," "*Gruppen*," and "*Grössen*," and have been used as conveying the meaning more exactly than any other English terms could.

[2] *Op. cit.* p. 8.

vestigation than by metaphysical. " For," he says, " only this kind of knowledge (psychology and ethics) is adequate to the reality of spiritual life ; the purely metaphysical determination of a spiritual magnitude cannot distinguish the same from natural magnitudes ; in reference to the nature and the peculiarity of the spirit it is insufficient, and in that measure worthless." [1] With this neglect of the distinction between nature and spirit, Ritschl goes on to contrast the emphasis which religion lays upon this distinction. " The religious world-view (*Weltanschauung*) is," he says, " in all its kinds grounded on this, that the human spirit in some degree or other distinguishes itself in value from the appearances of nature surrounding it, and the activities of nature forcing themselves in upon it." For this reason he sets himself to oppose " the assumption that religion and metaphysics belong closely together, or are very nearly related to one another." [2]

(2) In regard to the account given, and the estimate of metaphysics offered, the following may very briefly be said. In the first place, he here confuses, as has been already indicated, epistemology and metaphysics, and so does injustice to Aristotle, who did not intend his " first philosophy " to be regarded as a mere catalogue of categories. In the second place, he assumes that the sole task of metaphysics is to fix the conception of a thing as if the reality of existence could be summed up under one category. In the third place, he confines metaphysics, which surely, like all branches of human knowledge, is capable of development, to only one of its stages. If the distinction of nature and personality was not adequately recognised in ancient thought, and is being more adequately recognised in modern, metaphysics cannot be bound to the old standpoint, and forbidden to advance to the new. An interesting illustration of this point suggests itself. Canon Gore,

[1] Ritschl's *Theologie und Metaphysik*, p. 9.　　[2] *Op. cit.* p. 9.

in dealing with the terminology which the Christian Church
borrowed from Greek thought, points out that " Christianity
laid all stress on the personality of God and of man, of
which Hellenism had thought but little"; and that, therefore
" even in regard to phraseology, Christianity, in its intense
consciousness of personality, had to infuse its own meaning
into the terms it borrowed." [1]   But if the terms so enlarged
in meaning should prove inadequate for the new truth man
is always learning, nothing forbids that terms more adequate
should be found.   Lastly, here Ritschl's absolute dualism
of nature and spirit would itself require a metaphysics to
justify it; and it may be confidently said that no metaphysics that reckoned with all the facts would be rash
enough to justify it; for to mention only two facts that
contradict such an absolute dualism : first, man discovers
his own intelligence in making nature intelligible; and,
secondly, man develops and disciplines his own personality
in the struggle with what appears a hostile nature, and so
nature even in its opposition becomes a minister of spirit.
To give Ritschl such credit, however, as is his due, it must
be added that his energetic if exaggerated affirmation of
personality in distinction from and superiority over nature
is a distinct service to Christian theology, which under the
influence of the traditional terminology is only too prone
to explain as physical operations what can be fully and
rightly interpreted only as ethical and spiritual processes.
Thus the doctrine of the union of natures in Christ, or of
the operation of the spirit on the soul, needs to be restated
with fuller recognition of all that is implied in personality.

(3) Ritschl directs his polemic particularly against the
place allowed to Plato's doctrine of general ideas in theology.
Of this doctrine he gives the following account : " The
idea in his sense is the image left in the memory (*Erin-
nerungsbild*) of many things which are similar in the

[1] Gore's *Bampton Lectures*, p. 101.

majority of their attributes, and are accordingly of the same kind, the generic concept; but these generic concepts formed by us are said to be the things in the proper sense, in relation to which the things of sensible perception only exist in so far as they participate in the ideas. These eternal archetypes of all individual existence are purely for themselves, untouched by the changes of that which only participates in them in an intelligible place, accessible only to thinking. Things as single are only the shadowy images (*Schattenbilder*) of the ideas." [1] What Ritschl calls the vulgar view of things, of which Plato's theory is only a generalisation, labours in his judgment under two defects: (1) it distinguishes the thing as it exists *for us* from the thing as it exists *for itself*; and (2) the image formed of the thing in the memory by distinguishing its variable accidents from its permanent attributes is practically identified with the thing-in-itself, or the general idea is regarded as equivalent to the reality of the individual thing, which is distinguished from its changeable appearances to us and actions upon us. The objections to this theory are two: (1) these ideas are only generalised images of the memory; that is, they are due to an artificial and often arbitrary mental process; (2) the general idea does not give us a fixed and distinct knowledge.

(4) In answer to these objections it must be said, however, that the mind in forming these general ideas is not acting arbitrarily, but is obeying a necessary condition of all thought, to discover unity in variety, simplicity in complexity; that while many general ideas do not faithfully represent reality, yet the object of science is so to correct ordinary thinking as to make the correspondence as close as possible between the general ideas of our knowledge and the actual types to which individual objects conform;

---

[1] Ritschl's *Theologie und Metaphysik*, p. 36 ("Theology and Metaphysics").

and, lastly, that if spirit be the ultimate reality and the final purpose of the universe, these types may be assumed to be the distinctive ideas of the infinite and eternal mind. While individual objects must be studied carefully in their variable accidents as well as permanent attributes, human knowledge, if mind is to get an understanding of, and command over, nature, must advance to the recognition of common classes and general laws.   While, therefore, one cannot sympathise with Ritschl's polemic against general ideas, yet, on the other hand, if Plato's hypostasis of the ideas is to be taken literally and not figuratively; and if, as Ritschl maintains, popular thought really intends to separate the general idea of a thing (calling it " nature, " substance," or " subject") as an existing entity from the individual thing as it is known to us and acts upon us, then Ritschl's rejection of such a metaphysics from theology is justified.   It must be admitted that scholastic theology did separate a nature or substance or subject from its attributes and activities, and did fix its attention on the former rather than on the latter, nay, even from verbal definition of the former drew logical consequences quite regardless of their correspondence with the reality as known to us in the latter.   A similar tendency has maintained itself to the present day.   To give only one illustration, the two natures of Christ have been elaborately discussed and rigorously defined without regard to, and one might say even in defiance of, the intellectual, ethical, and spiritual characteristics which the actual life displayed.   A habit of premature generalisation from inadequate data has undoubtedly been a hindrance to genuine theological progress.   The facts of Christian consciousness and experience in their variety and complexity need to be carefully studied before the laws can be safely laid down. Much that Ritschl says about the representation of God, the soul, sin and grace, in scholastic theology, or even the modern theology that follows traditional methods, is justified, as will subsequently be shown. What is to be carefully noted now is that Ritschl rejects absolutely the metaphysics which distinguishes the nature, substance, or subject from its attributes or operations.

V

(1) The violent recoil from the Platonic-Aristotelian metaphysics has had, however, an effect on his own theology which is of very serious importance. We have now to seek an answer to the fourth question we set ourselves : What is the effect of this rejection on his theology ? Although we shall be obliged again and again to notice its effect on his theology in particular cases, yet here the matter must be stated in general terms. An indication has already been given in discussing his epistemology. He fixes his regard on what may be called the phenomenal aspects of reality, and averts his gaze from what we may in contrast call its ontological bases. The varied attributes and the variable operations claim his exclusive attention to the neglect of the permanent unity of the subject which shows itself, and acts. While it is quite true that we have no knowledge of the subject apart from its attributes and operations, and here Ritschl's position is justified against a theosophical speculation and a mystical piety, yet, on the other hand, we keep hold for our own knowledge of the attributes and operations only as by a rational synthesis we bind them together in the unity of a subject ; and this Ritschl, in his exaggerated suspicion of metaphysics, often fails to do. God is, so to speak, lost in His kingdom, Christ in His vocation, the soul in its activities.

(2) In this connection there may be mentioned an ambiguous use of the term "metaphysical," which finds illustration in the theology of Ritschl and his school.

Inasmuch as metaphysics seeks besides the empirical perception of reality, a rational explanation of it, it is compelled to go by a speculative inference beyond the data, the sole justification of this speculative inference being the intelligible unity which it gives to the data.   Hence the term "metaphysical" has come to be used in a very loose sense for any idea that is not immediately given in ordinary experience.   Thus the pre-existence of Christ, and His exaltation in glory, may be called "metaphysical ideas." They would be such, if they were speculative inferences from the data of His earthly life, drawn to account for His personality and His influence; but if the former is an assurance given in His own self-testimony, and the latter a promise made for the encouragement of His disciples, they cannot be rightly so described, as, if the gospel records are accepted as correct, both come within the range of historical reality.   Probably doubtful of the gospel testimony to these truths, some of Ritschl's followers show them the aversion that they have for all that is "metaphysical." Even those who do not deny, but accept the facts, make as little of them in explanation of Christ's person as they can. But, as has been pointed out by his critics, Ritschl has sometimes to admit ideas that in this vague sense are metaphysical.   Thus when he assumes the Church, and not its individual members, to be the subject of justification, he assigns to the Church a permanent unity which is certainly not given in experience, but which is a speculative inference, and so in the wide sense "metaphysical."   It may even be maintained that this "metaphysical idea" of "the permanent unity" of the Church has less warrant in experience than some of the "metaphysical ideas," such as the unity and identity of the soul, which he neglects, if he does not deny. His practice is sometimes better than his theory.

VI

(1) As we are concerned not only with Ritschl, but also with his school, it seems desirable to add here as brief an account as possible of the views held on the relation of metaphysics to theology by Herrmann, who has devoted special attention to the subject. An account of his pamphlet, *Metaphysics in Theology* (1876), and of his book, *The Relation of Religion to our Knowledge of the World and to Morality* (1879), is given by Pfleiderer [1] from a very unfavourable standpoint. Herrmann's description of metaphysics in his earlier work is this: "In it we inquire, in what universal forms all being and happening can be represented without contradiction. For the correctness of these representations it does not in any way matter in what relation to the aims of our wills, to our weal or woe, things stand. On the contrary, for the religious view of the world on this all depends, while those metaphysical questions are indifferent," for " the religious view is an answer to the question, How must the world be judged, if the highest good is to be real ? " [2]   Metaphysics deals with facts, religion with aims ; the last question for the former is what is the ultimate cause of the world, for the latter what is the final purpose ; while the former seeks to complete science by discovering the unity of all reality in God, the latter endeavours to meet the needs of man's spirit by assuring man that his ideals are of God, and so not vain imaginations but assured promises. The religious man believes that reality subserves the ideal, in other words, that the world of fact is a means to the world of aims as an end ; but this assurance he draws " not from an insight into the actual

---

[1] *The Philosophy of Religion*, vol. ii. pp. 188-203.

[2] Herrmann, *Die Metaphysik in der Theologie*, p. 8 (" Metaphysics in Theology ").

construction of the world, but from the power of the highest good over his inner life." [1]   Metaphysics with any conclusions about the ultimate reality of the world it may reach, cannot reach up to the final purpose which religion recognises in the world; but Christianity does not need any speculative assistance, for it has the sufficient assurance of faith.   For Christian theology to seek a basis in metaphysics, and not in the certainties of the religious experience, would be to lean on " an arm of flesh " and to distrust " the spirit of the living God," for " the refusal to recognise the irreducible difference that exists between the feeling of the value of goodness and the knowledge of facts, may come perhaps from the relinquishment of the supramundane character of the Christian idea of God." [2]   The moral and religious life is so distinctive and unique, that it and all that immediately belongs to it cannot possibly be viewed from the same standpoint as existence generally.   " The consideration of this peculiarity forces us to acknowledge that what we speak of as real in Christianity, is quite different from what is spoken of as real in metaphysics. Here it means the producing real, by which we explain to ourselves the possibility of all being and becoming; in the former case its certainty is connected with the incommunicable experience of the value of Christian goodness. To attempt therefore to mix up the two kinds of reality, is to deny that the ethical fact in which the religious view of the world has its root is a separate thing, not to be grasped in the general forms of being and becoming, not within the view of metaphysics at

[1] *Op. cit.* p. 9 ; " Inner life " seems the best rendering which can be given of the word *Gemüthsleben.*

[2] Quoted by Pfleiderer, *The Philosophy of Religion*, vol. ii. p. 189. Herrmann's *Die Metaphysik in der Theologie*, p. 12.   The sentence that follows in Pfleiderer's book must be his paraphrase of Herrmann's words, although it is marked as a quotation from Herrmann, as the writer has failed to find in the immediate context in Herrmann's pamphlet any sentence corresponding to it.

5

all." [1]   This independence of religion from metaphysics involves, that theology must not occupy itself with the same problems as metaphysics, for "the task of theology is the proof that the problems of the moral spirit are solved, when, by appropriation of what Christianity regards as good (*des Christlich-Guten*), it participates in the religious view of the world which belongs to Christianity." [2]   There are two demands that theology must make on metaphysics.   "It should allow us to recognise, in the first place, the modification of our conceptions involved in the change of their reference to things and spirits, and it should respect the frontier, which separates the sphere of independent knowledge from the dominion of the concrete moral ideal." [3]   In all other respects theology can be quite indifferent to metaphysics.   "Whether in other respects philosophy is deistic, pantheistic, theistic, or anything else, is a matter of indifference to us as theologians." [4] Herrmann in the rest of his pamphlet discusses some theological problems in which the introduction of metaphysics has had an injurious effect, the freedom of the will and the person of Christ.

(2) In his larger work there is a more thorough treatment of the question, and accordingly what has now been stated may in several respects be supplemented.   He very emphatically asserts that metaphysics is, even as religion itself, due to a practical motive, the desire of man to view the world as a whole, which he can understand and use as a means to his ends.   The results that any metaphysics may reach can never compare in certainty with the conclusions regarding individual objects and events which

---

[1] Quoted by Pfleiderer, *op. cit.* p. 189.   Herrmann, *op. cit.* p. 17. It may be remarked that the word "real" in the first sentence renders *Wahrhaftwirklichen*, in the second the simple *Reale*.

[2] Herrmann, *op. cit.* p. 22.

[3] *Op. cit.* p. 21 ; see Pfleiderer, *op. cit.* p. 190.

[4] Herrmann, *op. cit.* p. 21.

science can reach.   It is an illusion that any metaphysics which strives to represent the world as a whole, can claim to be objective truth in the same sense as the sciences, which investigate the relations of the parts to one another. It has not, and cannot have, adequate data; it does not, and cannot, use any certain methods.   It is "rooted in convictions, which neither are gained by a knowledge of the actually given world, nor can be contradicted by this." Yet as it tries to bring to some intelligible unity the data of all the sciences, "the fate of individual metaphysical attempts is influenced by the progress of the scientific knowledge of the world."[1]   As there is no finality in science, so metaphysics must always anew be attempting the task of representing man's interpretation of the universe as an intelligible unity.   Religion also aims at viewing the world as a whole, a means to man's ends; but inasmuch as it does not adopt the same method, it is not subject to the same fate.   "Religion is in a position to satisfy permanently in a higher way the need which metaphysics seeks in this way to meet for a short time, and accordingly can make metaphysics as a system superfluous."[2] In allying itself with metaphysics, theology is attempting to do with inferior tools what it can do much more efficiently and satisfactorily with the superior tools which religion puts into its hands.   Nay more, in seeking the assistance of metaphysics in its tasks, it is subjecting itself to a foreign authority, with laws and tests other than those that properly belong to religion.   To give one illustration, the idea of God which the early Christian Church adopted from Aristotle became the dominant conception of Christian theology to the practical exclusion of the Christian idea

---

[1] Herrmann, *Die Religion im Verhältniss zum Welterkennen und zur Sittlichkeit*, p. 78 ("Religion in Relation to our Knowledge of the World and to Morality").

[2] *Op. cit.* p. 75.

of God, the content of which is intelligible to faith alone.[1]

(3) Herrmann's position challenges dissent as well as invites assent. He is altogether right in maintaining that Christian theology has suffered by the alliances it has formed with philosophical systems, the intention and motive and spirit of which was different from Christian faith in its full vitality and free vigour. The contents of the Christian consciousness have not come to an adequate and distinctive expression. Further, he is right, too, in maintaining that theology must be a faithful interpretation of Christian faith, recognising no other authority than the revelation appropriated by that faith, and disowning subjection to any metaphysics which claims to test and judge the truth of Christian ideas by their conformity with speculative principles, based on what claims to be a rational interpretation of the world. Lastly, he is right also in making plain that no system of metaphysics can claim to be objective truth, independent of the subjective convictions of the individual thinker, in the same sense as the facts and laws of science ; and that therefore metaphysics has no right to claim greater certainty for its speculations than Christian theology may claim for the assurances and promises of faith. But to turn now from assent to dissent, he concedes too much to metaphysics, when he allows it to supply theology with "the instruments of its work,"[2] the conceptions of things and of spirit, for these conceptions must have a definite content, depending on the distinctive standpoint of the metaphysics from which they are borrowed, and so affecting the expression of the Christian faith in the theology that borrows them. Theology cannot borrow its materials in this way. The theologian

[1] See *op. cit.* p. 131.

[2] Herrmann, *Die Metaphysik in der Theologie*, p. 20 (" Metaphysics in Theology ") ; see Pfleiderer, *op. cit.* p. 190.

must be a metaphysician as well, in as far as he from the Christian standpoint independently examines the significance and estimates the value of all the conceptions he may employ. The great contrast between nature and spirit, things and persons, which is implied in the Christian consciousness and experience, but which has not been adequately recognised in the metaphysics of past times and in the traditional theology depending thereon, must be rendered explicit in a Christian metaphysics which must essay a problem Herrmann rejects, to show the latent unity in the patent difference. Such a metaphysic from a distinctively Christian standpoint is not to be assumed as impossible, for Herrmann and Ritschl as well are unjustified in identifying as they do metaphysics with only one stage in its development. Theology need not adopt any metaphysics, for it can beget its own.

CHAPTER III

THE REJECTION OF SPECULATIVE THEISM

I

(1) RITSCHL is, as we have seen, inconsistent in his statements about the relation of metaphysics to theology. He, on the one hand, by his words generally gives the impression that there is no place for metaphysics in theology. The definition, in giving which he considers himself justified by Aristotle's writings as an example, is intended to prove that metaphysical knowledge as regardless of the distinction of nature and spirit is opposed to religious knowledge, which lays stress on the superiority of spirit to nature. Again, he considers the Platonic doctrine of general ideas as responsible for a very injurious method of theological investigation. He, on the other hand, however, in one passage denies that he excludes metaphysics from theology, and affirms that his sole aim is to reject a false metaphysics that has done harm in theology. But when we examine more closely what he means by metaphysics, we discover that it is theory of knowledge, and theory of knowledge that limits itself to a definition of a "thing." This definition so completely ignores the problems involved in any theory of knowledge, that its claim to be even the first step towards a metaphysics must be pronounced a vain pretension. To sum up the results of the previous discussion, we may assert that Ritschl's attitude to philosophy was one of estrangement and aloofness; but we cannot estimate the excellence or the

defect of that attitude aright until we ascertain its motive.

(2) He himself very clearly expresses that motive in the following sentences : " The application of metaphysical categories as the highest rules of guidance in systematic theology is explicable, if one conceives its task to be this, to prove the harmony of the Christian revelation, especially the Christian view of the world with a superior general view of the world, which is claimed to be the universal and the rational one." This, however, he declares to be a mode of proceeding which is " rationalistic, and an abuse of reason in theology, which lessens the worth of the knowledge of God got from revelation."[1] It is not on behalf of unbelief, but in the interests of faith, that Ritschl thus earnestly, sometimes even violently, contends for the exclusion of metaphysics from theology. When he rejects speculative theism, it is not from any sympathy with atheism or agnosticism, materialism or pantheism, but from a passionate devotion to the Christian revelation, the distinctive significance, the unique value, and the absolute independence of which, he thinks, are endangered by any alliance with philosophy. In support of his position he appeals to Luther's sayings, " that a knowledge of the being of God as such, as undertaken by the scholastics, is without power to save, and destructive ; that the knowledge of the gracious will of God can be understood only as the correlate of the knowledge of Christ, and that Christ's divinity can be understood only in His activity, in His vocation."[2] When we remember, as has been already stated, that the application of Hegelian principles and methods to Christian theology had resulted, on the one hand, in Strauss' " mythical " theory of the life of Christ, and, on the other, in Baur's " tendency "

[1] Ritschl's *Theologie und Metaphysik*, p. 24 ("Theology and Metaphysics").

[2] *Op. cit.* p. 59.

theory of the history of the Apostolic Age, we cannot be altogether surprised at Ritschl's suspicion of philosophy. It is even not at all improbable that the separation of theology from philosophy as attempted by Ritschl will in the end prove profitable to both, as compelling each to define its own functions more accurately, and to determine its own method more exactly, and consequently enabling both to agree on their mutual boundaries, and to settle the terms of their possible co-operation. Whether this be so or not, we must do Ritschl the justice of recognising his genuinely and intensely religious motive ; and this recognition will enable us to understand better the grounds on which he rejects speculative theism.

(3) Ritschl's own words justify the prominent place here assigned to his rejection of speculative theism in our treatment of his attitude to metaphysics. " Apart from the doctrine of God," he says, " Christian dogmatics offers no opportunity to set up a metaphysical idea directly as a theological." [1] He admits here that there is a borderland common to theology and philosophy, or at least he allows that it may be claimed that there is such a borderland. This question demands closer scrutiny.

II

(1) Ritschl's mind seems to have wavered upon this question, whether there was any ground common to theology and philosophy. Of the views expressed in the first edition of his great work on *Justification and Reconciliation*, Pfleiderer gives the following account : " The peculiarity of the religious view of the world is, that it aims at the representation of a whole. Everywhere the representation, however indistinct, of the divine unity involves a representation of the *wholeness* of the world, of the *enclosedness* of the appearances of nature, in which the divine being lives, or

[1] *Op. cit.* p. 40.

over which it rules.   The representation of the world as a unity and as a whole expresses everywhere, where it is reached, a product of religious knowledge, as it is not at all attainable by actual experience and observation.   On the contrary, theoretical knowledge in philosophy and in the single sciences aims at the universal laws of knowledge, and of the existence of nature and spirit.   With the intention of scientific knowledge there is not combined the security that it will find with its means of experience and observation, and the arrangement of its observations according to law, the highest universal law of existence, from which the differing arrangements of things could be understood. Were this result possible, and in every case necessary, as often as one has advanced to this in philosophy, then the collision of science with religion would be inevitable. . . . The collision is not in itself therefore necessary , it is avoided, where philosophers abstain from the claim, which is unjustified in their case, to possess a view of the world as a whole.   But it enters, where they aim at this, and so trespass on the province of religion." [1]

(2) In the third edition of the same work, Ritschl, while retaining much of his previous argument, makes this statement: " The possibility of the mixture and again of the collision of the two kinds of knowledge lies herein, that they are directed to the same object, namely, the world.   One cannot soothe oneself with the peaceful decision that the Christian knowledge understands the world as a whole, the philosophical establishes the special and the general laws of nature.   For every philosophy combines with this task also the intention, to understand the world-whole in a highest

[1] Pfleiderer, *Die Ritschl'sche Theologie*, pp. 13, 14 (" The Ritschlian Theology "). In the translation of this passage, the words wholeness and enclosedness render the German words *Ganzheit* and *Geschlossenheit*. As the writer has not been able to get access to the first edition of Ritschl's work, he has been compelled to rely entirely on Pfleiderer's representation of the differences between the first and the third edition.

law. And a highest law is also for Christian knowledge the form in which the world is understood as a whole under God. Also, the thought of God, which belongs to religion, is made use of in every philosophy that is not materialistic in some form or another. Accordingly, in the object no distinction between the two kinds of knowing is provisionally, at least, to be reached." [1] As we shall afterwards see, Ritschl explains the difference between philosophy and religion by a difference of mental functions in the subject of knowledge, philosophy consisting of *theoretical*, but theology of *value* - judgments. It may be questioned, however, whether he has consistently applied his own theory. Having accepted a fundamental distinction between the two kinds of knowledge, that of religion and that of philosophy, he should have left the latter severely alone as altogether insignificant and valueless for him as a theologian; but his actual procedure seems to be controlled by the theory that philosophy cannot of itself reach the idea of God, as his endeavour is to show that all the attempts which philosophy has made to prove God's existence have invariably resulted in failure.

(3) That he has still an interest in theoretical knowledge, and desires to avoid a collision between it and religious knowledge without availing himself of his own theory of two kinds of knowledge, is made evident by the following facts, each of which will claim our separate notice. He examines the speculative proofs for the existence of God, the cosmological, the teleological, and the ontological, and concludes that these do not yield the idea of God (III). He discusses the moral argument as given by Kant; and in the first edition of his great work he dissents from Kant, and maintains that the idea of God thus reached is not a practical belief, but an act of

[1] Ritschl's *Rechtfertigung und Versöhnung*, iii. pp. 193, 194 ("Justification and Reconciliation").

theoretical knowledge, thus allowing a common ground for theology and philosophy ; but in the third edition he, at the close of the same argument, states the contradictory conclusion that " this assumption of the idea of God is, as Kant remarks, practical belief, and not an act of theoretical knowledge "[1] (IV). He rejects alike the Socinian and the orthodox conception of the moral order of the world, regards conscience as not an original testimony to the existence of God, but as a secondary product of social evolution ; and thus condemns any attempt philosophy may make to discover an ethical purpose in man's history (V). He admits that the religions of the world may be arranged in an ascending scale of value, with Christianity at the top, but he denies at once that this judgment can be made universally valid (VI). He rejects as intellectually unverified the two theories of the world-whole which compete with the Christian view, materialism and pantheism, and thus, contrary to his own theory, allows Christianity to meet its rivals on the same open field, instead of confining it, as according to his theory he properly should, to its own narrow enclosure (VII). He expels from theology the idea of God as the *absolute*, which he regards as a product of philosophy, although in his own idea of personality he seeks to recover for theology whatever of value there was in the idea of the absolute (VIII). In all these ways Ritschl seeks to prove the incapacity of philosophy to reach any idea of God that can be regarded as sufficient by Christian faith. The admission, then, that philosophy may reach the idea of the world as a whole, and even the idea of God in some form or another, is an empty compliment that he offers to it. His true attitude is one of absolute scepticism as regards the ability of human thought apart from Christian faith to reach any view of the world which offers any completeness or certainty. But over against this philo-

[1] *Op. cit.* p. 214.

sophical scepticism must be placed a religious positivism. Whatever he takes away from us as illegitimate profession of philosophy, he gives back to us as a warranted assurance of religion. While we are observing the work of destruction, we must always remember that Ritschl is only preparing himself for a work of construction.[1]

(4) The exposition and criticism of Ritschl's positions which follows will be made more intelligible, it is hoped, if a brief statement be now added regarding the general bearings of the question of the relation of philosophy and theology. If philosophy be an attempt to give a rational interpretation of the Universe, it must neglect no facts, ignore no truths. Morality and religion are the most distinctive features of human history, and for the moral and religious consciousness have supreme significance and absolute value. Christianity for Christian faith offers not only a practical solution of the problem of life, but also a theoretical explanation of the mystery of the world. What attitude is philosophy going to assume to this claim of the moral and religious consciousness, this certainty of Christian faith? Shall it occupy the same standpoint, and recognise that the moral and religious consciousness is the key to the Universe, and that the Christian faith, as the truest expression and the fullest satisfaction of the moral and religious consciousness, is the best means of interpreting the world and life. If it did so, it would become a Christian apologetic, an attempt to show that

[1] While it is convenient thus to distinguish and contrast Ritschl's *philosophical scepticism* and his *religious positivism*, it is to be always remembered that religion and philosophy are different functions of the same spiritual personality, and accordingly what he denies to the one function that he may attribute it exclusively to the other, is not denied to the subject to which both belong. If the reason of man be conceived abstractly as distinct and separate from religion, then Ritschl may be held to teach that reason cannot discover God ; but if, as is probably his meaning, he regards reason as exercised in religion, then no such opinion can be ascribed to him.

Christian ideas do really offer the best explanation possible
of the problems of existence. But is such an attitude conceived as inconsistent with the impartiality towards all
distinctive moral codes or religious beliefs which philosophy
should display? Must the philosopher divest himself of
his moral obligations and his religious aspirations, and if
he is confessedly a Christian of his Christian faith, in order
that he may assign to these as facts of human history
merely the same value as he assigns to the intellectual conceptions, to which science by observation, experiment, and
induction leads him? Is philosophy to be a general view
of the Universe, resulting from a comparison of all the facts
without any personal estimate of their relative value? Is
Christianity to be treated by such an impartial philosophy
as one of the religions, the truth of which is to be tested by
its conformity with this general view of the Universe?
Can this philosophy yield such an idea of God as Christian
faith can recognise as adequate? Can Christian faith
consent that the truth of its contents should be made to
depend on conformity with such a philosophy? It is
against a philosophy which does not give its due authority
to the moral and religious consciousness, which does not
adequately recognise the full value of Christian faith, that
Ritschl contends. Rightly he maintains that such a
philosophy cannot yield an adequate conception of God,
and that the contents of Christian faith cannot be subordinated to the conclusions of such a philosophy. Of
course it may be said that such a philosophy as a philosophy
is inadequate, and that an adequate philosophy would be a
helpful ally of theology; but Ritschl is concerned, not
with philosophy as it might be, but philosophy as it has
been. But an appeal may be made to reason, and it may
be said that religion and morality, Christianity itself, must
be tested by reason. But what is this reason? Did it
appear all at once full grown, as Athena from the head

of Zeus? Is it not rather a complex and continuous development in human history? And have not morality and religion as well as science been factors in this development? When we assert that reason gives us an adequate conception of God, do we mean reason, in the development of which the Christian religion with the divine revelation it implies has been determinative, or do we mean a reason that recognises no dependence on, and asserts a superiority to, the Christian religion? If we mean the former, Ritschl would not deny this, because he does maintain that the Christian religion can give for man's practical purposes an adequate idea of God. If we mean the latter, then Ritschl would deny, and rightly, that reason in such isolation and independence can yield an idea of God which can in value be compared with the Christian idea, or can be used as a standard to which the Christian idea must conform. This, be it remembered, is the question, stated in its simplest terms, which is now under discussion.

III

(1) Of the speculative proofs for the existence of God, Ritschl says that, " since the Middle Ages these have the intention, to prove the representation of God which is taken for granted as given in the Christian religion, to be scientifically justified," and that " they are not capable of proving the being of God, but only His being for thought," [1] and even then only on the assumption of Christian ideas. His aim is to show that these proofs do not afford an adequate idea of God, and that when an attempt is made to reach by these proofs an adequate idea, the independence of these proofs is surrendered as

---

[1] Ritschl's *Rechtfertigung und Versöhnung*, iii. pp. 203, 204 (" Justification and Reconciliation "). In this passage the contrast is between real existence (*Dasein*) and ideal existence (*Gedachtsein*).

Christian ideas are assumed. " Now usually," he says, " the cosmological proof is so stated, that when one is seeking a conclusion for the succession of operations and causes, in which things are arranged, one must think of the first cause as *causa sui*, which is not *res causata*, which accordingly is God. And the meaning of the teleological proof is, that when one seeks a conclusion for the succession of the means and ends in which things are arranged, one must think the final end, which is no longer means, as God. Now, certainly the Christian representation of God our Father in Christ includes the representation of the first cause and the last end as subordinate attributes ; but placed, as self-sufficient things, the conceptions of first cause and final end do not reach beyond the conception of the world, therefore, not to the Christian conception of God." [1]   Elsewhere he asserts that " the cosmological argument has its peculiarity in this, that it considers things as causes and operations, regardless of their distinction as nature and spirit. As a metaphysical argument it, in fact, leads only to the idea that the world is the substance of all things, the one thing in all appearances." [2]   Here he also gives the following account of the teleological argument : " If we in the observation of purposeful relations of things consider ourselves justified in forming the idea of a world-whole on the assumption of a final purpose, then Aristotle has already clothed this idea with highest intelligence. When one puts forward this side of the matter, then the final purpose of the world is to be represented as world-soul. But if one is statistically accurate with the teleological induction, then others have already proved that in an immeasurable compass one finds relations of things contrary to purpose besides those according to purpose,

[1] *Op. cit.* p. 205.
[2] Ritschl's *Theologie und Metaphysik*, pp. 13, 14 (" Theology and Metaphysics ").

so that one does not reach to any goal in this metaphysical view of the world, to say nothing of an assured
inference to a transcendent God."[1] But he goes on
to argue, even if these two proofs could accomplish what
they profess, yet the certainty of God's existence would not
be established, "for they only express the thought that *if*
one wants to recognise the world as a whole, one must
necessarily add to it *in thought* God as first cause and final
purpose. But with this no security is given that anything
real corresponds to our thought, though necessary under
the conditions indicated."[2] The ontological proof, alike in
the form given to it by Anselm, that the idea of the
perfect being necessarily involves the predicate of existence, and in the modification by Descartes that an infinite
reality alone can be the cause of the idea of the infinite in
our minds, is rejected as not carrying us beyond thought
to reality. "This argument is valid for our thoughts, not
for the reality opposed to our thoughts." The ontological
argument thus is regarded as failing to compensate for the
manifest imperfections of the cosmological and teleological
proofs.

(2) This is not the occasion for a full statement and
a thorough vindication of these proofs in the form in which
they are still valid for human thought; but in criticism of
Ritschl it may be pointed out : (1) that the ultimate cause
which explains the coexistence and co-operation of all
secondary causes cannot be conceived as either the sum of
all these causes, or as of the same kind as these are; (2)
that the relation of the human will to the coexistent and
co-operant activities of the human body suggests, at least,
a transcendence, as well as an immanence, of this ultimate
cause; (3) that similarly the final purpose of the universe

[1] *Op. cit.* p. 14.
[2] *Rechtfertigung und Versöhnung*, iii. p. 206 ("Justification and
Reconciliation ").

cannot be identified with any of the secondary ends, or with the totality of secondary ends ; (4) that the self-end of human personality which seeks realisation through all lesser ends as means, suggests at least that the final purpose of the Universe reaches out beyond, and rises above, all the secondary ends which serve as the means of its realisation ; (5) that any conclusion which human thought is compelled to reach in order that it may give to its contents an intelligible unity, cannot be dismissed as an idea which need not have any corresponding reality, without abandoning the assumption that there is a correspondence between intelligence and existence,—an assumption without which all our knowledge would be reduced to an illusion. The polemic which Ritschl directs against these proofs is for his own purpose exaggerated. All that he need have shown is the inadequacy of these proofs to yield us the full Christian idea of God on the one hand, and the injury done to Christian faith on the other hand, when the Christian idea is subordinated to any idea of God, formed by means of these proofs. As regards the one point, it needs no argument to show that the ultimate cause, the final purpose, and the pervading intelligence of the Universe are lower and poorer epithets for God than the Father of our Lord and Saviour Jesus Christ. As regards the other point, the cosmological proof suggests a conception of the unity of the Universe in its immanent ultimate cause, which may be used in the interests of pantheism, and may lead to a denial of human freedom. Again, the teleological proof suggests an idea of the invariable rationality of history as controlled by its final purpose, which may be held to involve the admission of the necessity of sin as a means of moral development, and to exclude the recognition of miracles as possible or necessary factors in the realisation of the divine purpose. Lastly, the assumption of a correspondence between intelligence and existence, which is implied in the

6

ontological argument, may be pushed so far as to make the
human mind the measure of all possible reality, and so to
encourage an impatient disbelief in any mystery in God's
dealings with men.   Attempts may be made, and have
been made, to discredit the Christian revelation in the
interests of such speculative constructions of the Universe,
which deny freedom, exclude miracle, and ignore mystery.
As a protest against any subordination of Christian truth
to any speculative thought of this kind, Ritschl's argument
deserves cordial sympathy.   Yet it is not necessary in
making such a protest to deny absolutely all virtue and
validity to these proofs.   If the speculative interpretation
of nature and history yields the idea of an infinite spiritual
unity, the ultimate cause, the final purpose, and the pervading intelligence of the Universe, and so advances towards
the Christian belief in God, Christian thought need not
regret that result, or refuse that approach.   As the law
was for the Jews a tutor to bring unto Christ, so for some
minds may these theistic proofs prove; and therefore
they should not be despised by Christian faith.

(3) That it is the danger of narrowing and lowering
Christian ideas which Ritschl seeks to guard against, is
shown by one of the inconsistencies on which Pfleiderer,
with a quick eye for any defect in a theological tendency
so opposed to his own, eagerly seizes.   In arguing against
Strauss for a personal God, and not an impersonal Universe,
as the ultimate cause and final purpose, Ritschl declares
that "a universe which is at the same time cause and
operation, inner and outer, is by these statements withdrawn from the conditions of scientific knowledge"; that
"into this conception there does not enter the consideration
that a law, a thing posited, points back the understanding to
the positing spirit and will, the moral order of the world to
a law-giving and purposefully guiding first cause"; and
that "it is only a leap of the imagination, when the

æsthetic action on our feelings of a law perceived in nature and history is objectified into the proposition, that every recognised law of reality, *eo ipso*, is the power and sufficient reason thereof; and one must not allow oneself to be imposed on by the accompanying assurance, that it is a sign of a limited understanding to put before the law the ordering will, and to derive from it also the energy in the appearances conformable to law." [1]   Here Ritschl himself defends an inference from the world to a cause and a purpose beyond the world, which he had himself declared illegitimate in the speculative theistic arguments.   The explanation, if not justification, of the inconsistency is this, that while Ritschl denies that the world itself, viewed from the standpoint of philosophy, can yield the idea of God, yet he maintains that from the standpoint of religious faith in God an inference may be drawn from the order and law of the world to an active and rational will.   What he forbids philosophy to do, that he will allow to theology.

IV

(1) As might be expected from the emphasis with which Ritschl is never weary of asserting the distinction between nature and spirit, the moral argument of Kant strongly appeals to him; but even here there is a change of view to be noted.   According to Pfleiderer, Ritschl's argument in the first edition of his great work is as follows : " He accepted the proof for the existence of God given by Kant in the *Critique of Judgment*, because it fulfils the conditions under which the idea of God can be proved as a scientifically necessary idea "; for, on the one hand, " the idea of God herein suffers no mutilation, as God is expressly recognised as rational and moral author and guide of the world "; and, on the other hand, " the knowledge of the laws

[1] *Op. cit.* pp. 219, 220.

of our conduct is at the same time theoretical knowledge, that is, knowledge of the laws of our spiritual life; and theoretical knowledge has also the task to seek a law of the coexistence of the two systems of reality, the sensuous and the moral." To put the argument in other words, even science has to recognise as a reality the moral life on the one hand, and the sensuous experience on the other; it must, unless it abandons its endeavour to find a unity in all objects of knowledge, seek some explanation of the relation between them; the Christian idea of God offers such an explanation, assuring, as it does, an ultimate correspondence between holiness and happiness, character and circumstance. To bring its view of the world to completeness and unity, science in its own interests is under obligation to accept this idea of God. "*The acceptance of the idea of God is not a practical belief, but an act of theoretical knowledge.*"[1]

(2) In the third edition, however, Ritschl states the same argument in almost similar terms until he reaches the conclusion; and now he rejects what he had before accepted, he agrees with, instead of dissenting from, Kant. "This acceptance," he say, "of the idea of God is, as Kant observes, practical faith, and not an act of theoretical knowledge"; and then adds, "if, accordingly, the correspondence of Christianity with reason is hereby proved, it is still taken for granted that the knowledge of God finds expression in another kind of judgment than that of the theoretical knowledge of the world."[2] What this means is, that he now holds, that in the interests of knowledge as such, for the explanation of facts, the idea of God is not sought, and cannot be found; but that, in the interests of the moral life,

---

[1] Pfleiderer, *Die Ritschl'sche Theologie*, pp. 23, 24 ("The Ritschlian Theology").

[2] Ritschl's *Rechtfertigung und Versöhnung*, iii. p. 214 ("Justification and Reconciliation").

that it may be lived in the confident expectation of an ultimate reward of virtue, the idea of God must be assumed. To anticipate a later discussion God is known by a *value-judgment*, not a theoretical judgment, that is, a judgment formed by a practical impulse, and not in a speculative interest.

(3) This change of opinion is due to Ritschl's growing distrust of the capacity of the speculative reason apart from Christian faith to solve the problems of existence, and to his growing conviction that Christian faith alone could lay hold on and keep hold of the idea of God.   In the first edition he thought that science, recognising its need of a unifying principle for the natural and the ethical life, might so far stretch itself beyond its usual reach as to grasp the Christian idea of God; in the third edition, while he still maintains that science must recognise the same need, yet he now denies that science can meet its own wants, unless to its weakness religion affords some of its strength.   As has already been noticed, a growing philosophical scepticism is accompanied by a growing religious positivism.   On the one hand, he is anxious that theology should maintain and defend "the uniqueness of the idea of God, that it can be represented only in value-judgments"—that is, as we shall afterwards see, personal convictions, affirmations of faith; yet, on the other hand, he wants theology to be recognised as a science by the other sciences.   The former motive would lead him to affirm that along the path of common knowledge and thought no idea of God can be reached; the latter motive would compel him to discover some common grounds on which theology can meet the other sciences. In order to secure from the other sciences a recognition of the claim of theology to be a science, he tries to show that even science generally in carrying out its task must recognise the object of theology, God, as a reality; but in order to maintain the necessity of faith to the knowledge

of God, he is driven to deny that science by itself can
reach such a recognition. The inconsistency is evident.
Inexcusable it will appear only to those who have never
passed through an intellectual crisis, when an old standpoint
was abandoned and a new was chosen, and yet the mind
could not be kept from passing from the one to the other.
As regards the question itself, regarding which Ritschl
shows so wavering a mind, surely these mutually exclusive
alternatives are not justified. Scientific thought on the
moral life in its relation to the natural may suggest the
necessity of an ultimate harmony, the certainty of which
Christian faith may affirm. Because, as regards the idea
of God, science cannot give us all we want, need we forbid
its offering us anything at all?

V

(1) Although Ritschl does not recognise the moral
argument, as stated by Kant, as valid for science, seeking
to find a unity for its data which is not directly given in
the data, yet may not the moral argument be accepted by
him in another form? Conscience has been regarded by
many as one of the most certain evidences of the existence
of God. Ritschl has published a lecture on Conscience of
which the following account has been given: "The lecture
on 'Conscience,'" says Professor Orr, "is chiefly remarkable
for its discussion of the right of conscience to be regarded
as 'the voice of God,' and for the remarks which grow out
of this on the idea of Revelation. It is characteristic of
Ritschl, with his dread of anything that bears the semblance
of a natural theology, that he refuses to see in conscience
an immediate witness for God, and views it as a product of
education and social environment. How this is to be reconciled with the unconditioned worth which he, in common
with Kant, ascribed somewhat earlier to moral law, does

subject to the ethical education and social evolution of the race, it must be admitted that in his view conscience is not as distinct or certain a witness for God as has often been held.

(2) But does not this ethical education and social evolution of the race display a divine purpose? Is there not a moral order in the world which bears testimony to a moral Governor? This argument Ritschl recognises only to reject it. " The completion of the idea of God," he says, " by a moral order of the world has been attempted in theology in two ways. The one theory attaches itself to the affirmation that God as the possessor of unlimited power over all His creatures, from an arbitrary motive, treats with equity (*Billigkeit*) mankind, which in itself has no rights as against Him. The other determines the relation of God to man in this way, that God orders the reciprocal relations of the mutual rights between Him and mankind by a law and a practice of righteousness which are a necessity for Himself"[1] The first Ritschl calls the Socinian and Arminian, the second the orthodox theory; but of both he declares that " although they attach themselves to different elements of the biblical mode of representation, yet they bear the stamp of natural theology; each of them is accompanied by the claim that it exhibits what is self-evident in the rational observation of the moral order of the world."[2] After a close scrutiny of the first theory, he declares that " in so far as it expresses a moral order of the world, it is self-contradictory, as a universal and public order of the moral law cannot find its sufficient reason in the indefinite moral relation of equity in private dealings."[3] A severe criticism of the second theory is also given; but what alone concerns our immediate purpose is his assertion that, on the one hand, " the idea of a double

---

[1] Ritschl's *Rechtfertigung und Versöhnung*, iii. p. 227 (" Justification and Reconciliation ").
[2] *Op. cit.* p. 228.   [3] *Op. cit.* p. 233.

recompense (which is a necessity for God) of man's varying actions that rules this theory is not the fundamental conception in Christianity ";[1] and that, on the other hand, " the filling out of the idea of God by the double co-ordinated recompense is not an innate or universal knowledge, but has its historical place in the religion of the Greeks."[2]   As this view is not Christian in character, but is Greek in its origin, it has no rightful place in theology.   " The assumption," he declares, " that the double recompense of God as an innate idea, as an element of natural religion, is also the fundamental representation of the moral order of the world, which is to be taken for granted by Christianity, is in reality the recognition of the Greek religious view of the relation between gods and men as the highest standard for all else which belongs to the Christian order of the world."[3] On these conclusions of Ritschl's it is to be remarked, that because an idea is Greek in origin it is not necessarily false.   The Greeks in their philosophy brought to conscious expression intellectual and moral laws of universal validity, which were not previously made the subject of deliberate reflection.   That the forms of expression in which these mental and ethical discoveries were presented were always adequate, need not for a moment be maintained.   That the moral ideas of the Greeks especially needed the correction and improvement which Christianity could afford them, must be at once conceded.   Yet surely these conceptions of a moral order, of reward of virtue and of punishment of vice, were not pure invention, but were derived from experience and observation.   That either the one theory or the other which Ritschl criticises is correct need not be affirmed ; but we must regret that he did not seek to discover and to display whatever truth might be latent in them, for surely there are some facts of life which certainly justify the assumption of some moral order in the world.

[1] *Op. cit.* p. 247.   [2] *Op. cit.* p. 248.   [3] *Op. cit.* p. 249.

(3) In rejecting these two theories does Ritschl offer us a satisfactory substitute for them, for he cannot deny that God has had some dealings with the human race? He attempts to do this in the first edition of his great work, but refuses to do so in the third edition. In the first edition, according to Pfleiderer, " It is still the human race generally which God loves under the aspect of its destination for the kingdom of God, and the training of which for this forms the content of all history. The Christian idea of the kingdom of God is regarded in the representation of the first edition as the *highest stage* of the moral community of men, which is not more distant from the earlier stages than these are from one another ; it is only more complete in degree of extension, but not essentially different in its kind, as the earlier communities also owed their existence to love." [1] In the third edition, however, it is stated that " God is love in that He reveals Himself through His Son to the community founded by Him, to form it into the kingdom of God, so that He realises in this purpose for mankind above the world, His honour, the fulfilment of His end for Himself " ; [2] that in the kingdom of God which is above the world mankind " reaches a supernatural unity in the mutual and common dealings from love, which no more finds a limit in family, rank, or nationality " ; [3] and that " all love of men springs, according to the Christian representation, out of the revelation of God in Christ." [4] While in the first edition it is recognised that the social communities, which are based on natural relationships, have an ethical value, as expressing and exercising love, and so show an affinity with, and offer an anticipation of, the perfect community of the kingdom of God ; in the

[1] Pfleiderer, *Die Ritschl'sche Theologie*, p. 31 ("The Ritschlian Theology").

[2] Ritschl's *Rechtfertigung und Versöhnung*, iii. p. 268 (" Justification and Reconciliation ").

[3] *Op. cit.* p. 267.   [4] *Op. cit.* p. 226.

third edition the kingdom of God as supernatural is distinguished from and opposed to all other social communities as natural, and accordingly love of home and kindred, country and people, is not regarded as a preparation for and a prophecy of love for mankind. God is represented as introducing His purpose for mankind in the kingdom of God without any previous discernible indication of His intentions. Such a view does injustice, on the one hand, to human history which does afford evidence of a moral progress towards wider sympathies and more extended obligations; and it shows dishonour to God, who cannot be conceived as having rested from His labour after the Creation throughout the ages of pre-Christian history, as having left Himself without witness in the consciousness and the experience of man. This tendency to reject as meaningless and worthless for Christian thought all that falls short of the full measure of Christian faith, is one of the conspicuous defects of Ritschl's theology.

VI

(1) But if human morality does not lead us to God, surely religion must? In his controversy with Luthardt Ritschl rejects Luthardt's assumption that a universal consciousness of God finds its completion in the Christian idea in words of harsh contempt. " If this alleged natural consciousness of God is to find its truth first by means of something else, then it has no truth in itself. It is in itself a false doctrine of God. Or is this natural theology to be reckoned as a half-truth, until by the revelation of salvation it is completed to be the full truth. Alas! falsehood on that account still cleaves to it; for what is truth cannot be added together out of two different halves." [1]

[1] Ritschl's *Theologie und Metaphysik*, p. 7 (" Theology and Metaphysics ").

It is true, however, that he discusses Christianity as one among other religions, having common features with them, and one of these revelation. " No religion," he says, " can be fully understood in its kind, when the attribute of revelation belonging to it is either denied or set aside as indifferent." [1]   But if there be no universal consciousness of God, then it would seem that the revelation which all religions claim must be declared an illusion, however necessary to the very existence of religion.   If we are to escape this conclusion, then we must assume that in the heat of controversy Ritschl went further than he would have ventured in calmer moments.   All he needed to say was that this universal consciousness of God is from the Christian standpoint inadequate and imperfect; but he went further, and said that it was altogether false.   The image he uses of a half-truth to which another half-truth is added cannot be otherwise regarded than as a controversial lapse from fairness.   The opponent's meaning would be more fully represented by the figure of an organism which develops from immaturity to maturity, and then there would be no occasion for ridicule, for surely Ritschl would admit that truth may grow from lower to higher stages of thought.   The judgment of Ritschl's calmer moments, when he is not engaged in controversy, is undoubtedly that there is a kinship and a likeness between Christianity and other religions.   " The observation and the comparison of the several historical religions," he says, " from which the common conception is abstracted, teach that these are related to one another, not as kinds, but at the same time as steps.   The expression of the leading features in the religions is always richer and more distinct, their texture closer, their aims more worthy of man. . . . In this care they rank as members in the spiritual history of man

[1] Ritschl's *Rechtfertigung und Versöhnung*, iii. p. 192 (" Justification and Reconciliation ").

kind." [1]   Yet he will not acknowledge that from any stand-point except that of Christian faith the significance and the value of the religious history of mankind as a testimony to God can be recognised or appreciated, for he goes on at once to qualify his statements. " When, accordingly, we, as Christians, determine the successive stages of the religions in this way, that all are transcended in Christianity, that in it the tendency of all others has come to its perfect result, then the claim to the universal validity of this knowledge seems to be offered up to the prejudice of one's own individual conviction. But that intention to claim universal validity for this succession of the stages of the religions, which can be indicated, is aimless and unattain-able. Can one find a way to prove scientifically to Mohammedans or Buddhists that not their religion, but the Christian, holds the highest place ? " [2]   It is our personal convictions as Christians which we express in this judgment on the relations of the religions to one another, for " we understand in the other religions the attributes by which they are stages, principally by the standard of the completeness which these appear with in Christianity, and of the distinctness which distinguishes the perfect religion from the imperfect religions." [3]   A philosophy of religion which claimed to prove that Christianity is the absolute religion, as fulfilling the promise of all other religions, would in Ritschl's opinion be a vain assumption. While, looking from Christianity downward, a continuity of stages can be discovered, there is for human thought, apart from Christian faith, no outlook from religion generally upward to Christianity.

(2) Surely the experience of missionaries of the gospel in dealing with educated inquirers belonging to other religions contradicts this dictum of Ritschl's. That the superiority of Christianity to Mohammedanism or Buddhism

[1] *Op. cit.* p. 187.   [2] *Op. cit.* pp. 187, 188.   [3] *Op. cit.* p. 188.

can be proved " scientifically," to use Ritschl's own word, need
not be maintained, for religion never appeals exclusively to
the understanding, never is based completely on logic.   The
whole man as moral and religious as well as rational must be
dealt with.   Then it is often found that, once the natural
prejudice against the religion of a foreign race has been
overcome, spiritual necessities become clamant, which find
their satisfaction only in " the truth as it is in Jesus."   There
is a way, not of logical demonstration solely, but of personal development generally, which leads from Mohammed
or Buddha to Christ.   Ritschl's son and biographer, in
dealing with the subject of the value-judgments, refers
to the rivalry of the religions of the world, and declares
that that one of them all will gain the victory " the objects
of faith of which will prove themselves also necessary as
the only true and real ones."   " We Christians," he adds,
" anticipate, if only provisionally from reasons of subjective
validity this highest standard of objectivity in our faith, not
only in so far as this proves itself power and truth to every
pious man in the practice of life, but in so far also as it
teaches us to hope for the final victory of our religion." [1]
This strikes a truer note than Ritschl's own statement.

VII

(1) While Ritschl thus rejects the assistance offered to
Christian faith by speculative theism, he opposes himself
to the two theories of the world, pantheism and materialism, which are its rivals.   In the third edition of his great
work, Ritschl admits, as has already been indicated, that
philosophy may aim at the representation of the world as a
whole under a highest law; but nevertheless he retains
from the first edition the assertion that whenever it does so

[1] Otto Ritschl's *Ueber Werthurtheile*, p. 32 (" Concerning Value-
Judgments ").

" there betrays itself herein an impulse of a religious kind, which the philosophers should distinguish from their method of knowledge." [1]   The method of scientific knowledge does not yield the idea of a highest law, and it is an illusion when it is claimed that it does.   Accordingly, he meets the two rival theories of the world, materialism and pantheism, not as legitimate results of science, but as due to an obscure religious impulse to discover unity in the world, combined with an abuse of the imagination in assuming a highest principle without sufficient evidence.   Of materialism, he declares that " its claim to disprove the world-view of Christianity rests on the expectation that it must succeed in tracing organism out of mechanism, and in the same way the other complex stages of existence out of the always subordinate.   In the chase for these empty possibilities the materialistic view of the world moves about." [2]   Of pantheism in its varied forms he asserts that " none of these laws is the key to an exhaustive view of the world as a whole " ; and of Hegelian idealism especially does he hold that it makes an unwarranted assumption when it declares that " the law of theoretical knowledge is the law of the human spirit in all its functions," for " as certainly as feeling and willing cannot be reduced to knowledge in representations, the latter is not justified to impose its law upon them." His great objection to pantheism is that here " one reaches anything but the appreciation of the destiny and the value of the human person, which is regulative in Christianity." [3] Both of these theories are invalid, because essaying a task for which knowledge in itself is not fit; and both are inadequate, because neglecting essential elements in reality, especially personality in its three functions of feeling, willing, knowing.

[1] Ritschl's *Rechtfertigung und Versöhnung*, iii. p. 197 (" Justification and Reconciliation ").

[2] *Op. cit.* p. 199.   [3] *Op. cit.* pp. 200, 201.

(2) It is doubtful whether Ritschl is justified in ruling these theories out of court as invalid. Surely knowledge from its own impulse and in its own interest must seek unity in the world. Even Kant admitted that the three ideas of reason—the soul, the world, and God—had a regulative value, although he denied to them a constitutive validity. Knowledge must proceed on the assumption of an ultimate unity in its objects. Herrmann, however, although he usually follows Kant, maintains that we set a limit to our knowledge of nature by the representation of a world-whole by an " immanent practical impulse." " The reality of a world-whole arranged in accordance with our purposes is assured for us, because by a value-judgment an organic (*solidarische*) connection between it and our individual existence is established." [1] Without entering into the discussion of this interesting problem, the writer must briefly express his own conviction that Kant was right in including the three ideas of Reason in his *Critique of Pure Reason*, and not in his *Critique of Practical Reason*, as he should have done were Herrmann right in his position. There is a theoretical necessity, as well as a practical impulse, to regard the world as a unity. Ritschl's criticism of the two theories regarding the nature of this unity commends itself as reasonable, but its interest lies chiefly in this, that it shows that Ritschl does not intend his theory of value-judgments to be a refuge for intellectual cowardice ; but is prepared to meet any theory of the world which sets itself up as a rival to the Christian view in the open field of theoretical judgments. As a misrepresentation of Ritschl's theory of value-judgments is in this respect common, his frank and bold criticism of materialism and pantheism is a fact to be noted and remembered.

[1] Herrmann, *Die Religion im Verhältniss zum Welterkennen und zur Sittlichkeit*, p. 40 (" Religion in Relation to our Knowledge of the World and Morality ").

7

VIII

(1) One last refuge seems to be left to metaphysics.
It cannot offer any proof of the existence of God ; but that
existence having been given on the testimony of Christian
faith, may not metaphysics determine the intellectual form
in which the idea of God must be presented ?   If it has no
constitutive value, may it not have a *regulative* for Christian
theology ?   This, too, Ritschl denies.   The idea of God as
the Absolute he declares to be " an illegitimate mixture
of metaphysics in the religion of revelation."   " Literally,"
he continues, " it means what is set loose, what stands in no
relations to others ; and Frank (the theologian against whom
Ritschl is here writing) understands it even thus, because
he puts instead of it the expressions being through, in, for
self (aseity, inseity, proseity)." [1]   Consequently, " the
absolute is no product of religious reflection, but a metaphysical conception, which is quite foreign to Christians,
and is familiar only to the mystics." [2]   This absolute
cannot be defined by any predicates, as personality or as
love, for " if the absolute, that is, the isolated, qualityless
thing, is to be thought with such predicates, then either the
subject is denied by them, or it is impossible to keep hold
of these predicates for the assumed subject." [3]   In other
words, if God be defined as personality or as love, He
cannot be thought of as the Absolute, or the Being out of
all relations ; or if He be thought of as the Absolute, personality or love cannot be ascribed to Him.   Although
Plato, Plutarch, and the Neo-Platonists (to continue Ritschl's
argument) identify this Absolute with God, it is " the
universal, indistinguishable, indeterminate, unlimited existence," which is " nothing but the shadow of the world." [4]

[1] Ritschl's *Theologie und Metaphysik*, p. 18.   [2] *Op. cit.* p. 19.
[3] *Op. cit.* p. 20.   [4] *Op. cit.* p. 37.

A few words will explain this statement.   Our general ideas may be arranged in a scale of increasing extension and decreasing intention, as, for example, human, animal, animate, existent.   The idea of greatest extension and least intention is the idea of existence, or the world thought of without any definite content.   With this Ritschl holds that ancient thought identified God as the Absolute. The introduction into Christian theology of this metaphysical abstraction is this, that instead of God being known as the Father of our Lord Jesus Christ, He is "subordinated to a general idea which is called the absolute, the substance." [1]

(2) This polemic is justified against the use of the idea of the Absolute, which under the influence of Greek philosophy has unfortunately been not uncommon in Christian theology.   God has been conceived as the Infinite Being which excludes determinations and relations.   The distinction and separation of the Creator from His Creation has been so insisted on as to banish God to a transcendence which makes Him inaccessible to human thought.   Every determination of His character has been regarded as a negation of His absoluteness.   The *via negationis* has been considered the appropriate method of intellectual approach to Him.   From this standpoint it is possible to ask the question, Can God be conceived as personal? and to incline to a negative answer.   Some Christian thinkers have found it difficult to combine the idea of the Absolute and the idea of personality.   But Ritschl in his polemic has been unjust to his opponents.   They meant, it is probable, a Being abounding in determinations and relations, but self-determined and self-related, a Being self-sufficient, and not dependent on others.   In this sense God must be regarded by every theologian as Absolute.   It is a defect of Ritschl's theology that he does not clearly and fully recognise the

[1] *Op. cit.* p. 41.

need of this conception ; although it must be admitted that in his definition of the divine personality, and the distinction he recognises between human and divine personality, he grants much that may be in this respect required. Another proof this that he will allow Christian theology to bestow what he forbids metaphysics to offer, that his philosophical scepticism has its counterpart in a religious positivism.

CHAPTER IV

The Condemnation of Ecclesiastical Dogma

I

THE antagonism of the Ritschlian theology to any alliance between metaphysics and theology is maintained on the ground that the past history of Christian theology shows how injurious to the vitality of Christian faith, the vigour of Christian life, any combination of Christian doctrine with philosophical speculation is. The Ritschlians do not shrink from appealing to facts in defence of their position; for they are sure that the development of dogma in the Church is itself the most convincing testimony to the value of their theological method as opposed to that which has hitherto been regarded as valid. They present the history of ecclesiastical dogma as its own judgment; for the unprejudiced Christian mind it pronounces its own condemnation. The first volume of Ritschl's work on *Justification and Reconciliation* is a history of the doctrine which he is discussing; and even in the third volume, in which he offers his own exposition of the doctrine, he criticises as he constructs; his own views are always stated in opposition to the views of those who have gone before him; and he exhibits not only a difference in his results, but also an antagonism in his method. Herrmann, in his *Religion in Relation to our Knowledge of the World and Morality*, devotes one chapter to a condemnation of " the mixture of religion and metaphysics "; and there accounts for this combination in Aristotle as due " to the abnormal character of a nature-religion." In his last chapter he seeks to show that Christianity has finally separated religion from metaphysics. Kaftan, in his work on Christian apologetics, *The Truth of the Christian Religion*, before stating in his second volume the argument for Christianity which he adopts, seeks to justify his departure from the traditional method of theology by offering in his first volume "the judgment of history" on ecclesiastical dogma. It is Harnack, however, who has given to the Ritschlian attitude to ecclesiastical dogma its clearest and fullest expression. In his *History of Dogma* the theologian's personal convictions have controlled the historian's conscientious labours. While the facts are stated, yet they are so stated as to pronounce their own condemnation. This work of Harnack's may therefore now claim our exclusive attention.

II

(1) Harnack's definition of religion generally, and of Christianity especially, first claims notice. "Religion," he says, "is a *practical* affair of humanity, for it is concerned with blessedness and the *powers* for a holy life. But in all religion these powers are attached to either a definite *faith* or a definite *worship*, which is traced back to a divine *revelation*. Christianity is the religion in which the power for a blessed and holy life is attached to faith in God as the Father of Jesus Christ. In so far as this God is believed in as the Almighty Lord of heaven and earth, the Christian religion includes a definite *conception* of God, the world, and the world-aim ; in so far, however, as it teaches that God can be fully known only in Jesus Christ, it cannot be separated from historical knowledge."[1] In this definition

---

[1] *Grundriss der Dogmengeschichte*, i. p. 1 ("Outlines of the History of Dogma"). This smaller work has been used rather than the larger, as it usually expresses more briefly and yet more clearly the distinctive features of Harnack's treatment of the subject.

the following features are to be carefully noted : (1) the practical purpose of all religion ; (2) the exclusive signifi-cance of faith, not worship, in Christianity ; (3) the double reference of faith to permanent elements of human thought on the one hand, to temporary events in human history on the other. This last feature is one that specially demands attention ; for, as we shall afterwards see, one of the serious problems of theology is just to determine the relation of the permanent elements to the temporary events, or, to put it in other words, how can facts express and guarantee truths ?

(2) Faith cannot remain long in an irreflective stage ; it must make its own contents clear to itself, and so sure for itself. But the impulse to this development generally comes from without. Error or doubt compel faith to define correctly or to demonstrate convincingly. The Ritschlian school, however severe may be its condemnation of the methods of ecclesiastical dogma, does not cherish the delusion of an undogmatic Christianity in the sense of a faith which has not examined the significance and estimated the value of its objects. Accordingly Harnack at once goes on to affirm that " the impulse to combine the contents of religion in *propositions of faith* is therefore just as essential to Christianity as the effort to prove these proposi-tions to be the *truth* in reference to knowledge of the world and history." [1] Faith seeks to define as well as to defend its objects ; it is constructive as well as apologetic. Inasmuch as, on the one hand, faith becomes more and more self-conscious, and, on the other hand, as knowledge of the world and of history is always advancing, this task which faith sets itself is a never-ending one, is never fully dis-charged.

(3) One of the attempts to fulfil this purpose of faith claims the pre-eminence, according to Harnack. " The hitherto most impressive attempt at a solution is that which

[1] *Op. cit.* p. 1.

Catholicism has made, and which the Churches of the Reformation took over, even though with very great qualifications. It is this : (1) the assumption of the divine origin of a succession of Christian and pre-Christian writings, and of an oral tradition ; (2) the abstraction from these of propositions of faith logically formulated, expressed for scientific and apologetic purposes, and mutually connected, the contents of which are the knowledge of God the world, and the divine provisions for salvation ; (3) the proclamation straightway of this structure (*dogmas*) as the *content* of Christianity, the believing acknowledgment of which must be required of every mature member of the Church, and should be at the same time the condition of the blessedness held in prospect by religion." [1]   In this description three features of ecclesiastical dogma are brought to our view, their authoritative source, their logical method, their religious value. As regards the first feature, Catholicism differed from Protestantism in recognising oral tradition as well as the written Scriptures, thus allowing the Church in its alleged apostolic confessions and its assumed apostolic offices a determinative influence in the formation of dogma.   The stream thus begins to be polluted at its very springs.   As regards the second feature, the forms in which and the purposes for which ecclesiastical dogma came into being were in harmony with and subordination to Greek intelligence in its decadence rather than Christian faith in its vigour. Thus the current is diverted into a strange channel.   As regards the third feature, the privileges of the Church on earth and the promises of the life in heaven were made dependent, not, as in the Gospels, on faith in Christ, but on

[1] *Op. cit.* p. 2 ; cf. *History of Dogma*, Eng. trans. i. p. 1.   As the language of the larger and the smaller German works is not identical, the passages in the English translation of the former, to which references are given, will be found to correspond with the translated quotations from the latter work given here, generally only in substance, but not in language.

an intellectual assent to a creed, many of the articles of which were either unintelligible to the mind or uninfluential for the life of the believer. The water thus polluted in its source and thus diverted in its course is forced on those who have no living thirst for it, and find no refreshing taste in it.

(4) Incapable of serving the interests of faith in its original purity, this movement served for the establishment and the maintenance of the Church. "With this content," says Harnack, "the Christian community, whose character as 'Catholic Church ' is quite essentially defined by this way of looking at Christianity, assumed a definite, a pretendedly immovable position to knowledge of the world and history, brought its religious faith in God and Christ to expression, and gave, while binding all its members to these propositions of faith, nevertheless to those who were thoughtful material capable of further extension in an unlimited measure."[1] The essential circumstance to be remembered in this connection is that through its dogmas the Church claimed an absolute authority over the thought of its members in opposition to any other intellectual influence.

III

(1) The history of dogma, according to Harnack, falls into two periods — (1) its origin, (2) its development. "The history of the origin of dogmatic Christianity," he says, "seems completed when first of all a proposition of faith, logically formulated, and expressed with the means of science, has been raised to be *articulus constitutivus ecclesiæ*, and as such has been universally enforced in the Church. But that happened at the end of the third and the beginning of the fourth century, when the Logos-Christology asserted itself."[2] At this time, then, the period

[1] *Op. cit.* p. 2.
[2] *Op. cit.* p. 2 ; cf. *History of Dogma*, Eng. trans. i. pp. 1, 2.

of origin closes, and the period of development begins. But a more difficult question is to determine whether the period of development has closed, and, if so, at what time. The decision of this question by Harnack reveals his distinctive conception of dogma. " The *development* of dogma," he says, " is in the abstract unlimited, but in the concrete it is closed; for (*a*) the *Greek Church* declares that her system of dogma has been completed since the end of the controversy about images ; (*b*) the *Roman Catholic* Church, it is true, leaves open the possibility of the formulation of new dogmas, but she has completed her dogma in the Tridentine and still more in the Vatican decrees essentially on political grounds and as a legal code, which before all else demands obedience, and only secondarily conscious faith ; therewith she has abandoned the original motive of dogmatic Christianity, and put quite a new one in its place, maintaining little more than the appearance of the old ; (*c*) the *evangelical* Churches have on one hand taken over a great part of the formulations of dogmatic Christianity, and seek to establish the same, as the Catholic Churches, from the Holy Scriptures ; but, on the other hand, they have otherwise conceived the authority of the Holy Scriptures, have rejected tradition as a source of doctrines of faith, have placed in dispute the significance of the empirical Church for dogma, and, above all, have attempted a conception of the Christian religion which goes back directly to ' *the pure understanding of the word of God.*' " [1]   Accordingly Harnack holds that the history of Protestant theology can be excluded from the history of dogma, the results of the latter only in so far as they are factors in the development of the former having been indicated.   Thus the history of dogma can be treated as a completed unity.

(2) In this history there are four divisions : " I. the origin of dogma ; II *a*. the development of dogma in accord-

[1] *Op. cit.* pp. 2, 3 ; cf. *History of Dogma*, Eng. trans. i. pp. 2-4.

ance with its original idea (the Oriental development from
the Arian controversy to the controversy about images);
II *b*. the Western development of dogma under the influence of the Christianity of Augustine and the policy of
the Roman chair; II *c*. the threefold issue of dogma (in
the Churches of the Reformation, in Tridentine Catholicism, in the criticism of the Enlightenment, especially of
Socinianism)." [1]   In the first period of the development,
Theology and Christology were the dominant interest; in
the second, owing to the influence of Augustine, the
doctrines of freedom, sin, grace, and the means of grace
came to the front; in the third, Roman Catholic dogma
was formulated in antagonism to the positions of the
Reformers, which implied a revision of all dogmas from the
new standpoint of faith then reached, a revision which
unfortunately was not thoroughly carried out.

(3) There are four lessons which the history of dogma
teaches; and, as these are of importance for an understanding of Harnack's position, they may be given in his
own words.   (1) " The assertion of the Churches, that the
dogmas are exclusively the exposition of the Christian
revelation alone, because drawn by inference from the Holy
Scriptures, is not confirmed by historical research.   On
the contrary, this shows that dogmatic Christianity (the
dogmas) in its conception and execution *is a work of the
Greek spirit on the soil of the gospel.*   The logical means,
by which the attempt was made in the ancient times to
make the gospel intelligible and to confirm it, have been
fused together with its contents." [2]   (2) " As the view of
dogma as a *pure* representation of the gospel shows itself
an illusion, even so historical research disturbs also the
other illusion of the Churches, that dogma has always been
the same in them, therefore has only been unfolded, and

---

[1] *Op. cit.* pp. 4, 5 ; cf. *History of Dogma*, Eng. trans. i. pp. 5–8
[2] *Op. cit.* p. 3 ; cf. *History of Dogma*, Eng. trans. i. p. 11.

that Christian theology has never had another task than to expound the always similar dogma, and to refute the false doctrines coming in from without. It shows rather that theology has formed dogma, but that the Church was compelled always to conceal with a grudge the work of the theologians, and these were therewith put in a bad position."[1] (3) "Although Dogmatic Christianity in the course of development never lost its original form and character as the work of the spirit of decadent antiquity on the soil of the gospel, yet it has experienced a deep-reaching transformation, first by *Augustine* then by *Luther*."[2] (4) "The history of dogma, while exhibiting the process of the origin and development of dogma, yields the most appropriate means to free the Church from dogmatic Christianity, and to hasten the unceasing process of emancipation, which began with Augustine. But it also bears witness to the *unity* of the Christian faith in the course of its history, in so far as it proves that certain fundamental ideas of the Gospel have never been lost, and have bidden defiance to all assaults."[3] Such, then, is Harnack's definition of the nature, limitation of the scope, and estimate of the worth of dogma. Each of these subjects claims a few remarks.

IV

(1) The definition of dogma seems to many too narrow, as dogma has often been used in a wider sense as synonymous with doctrine. "Harnack," says Principal Rainy, "takes dogma in a special sense. He distinguishes dogma from doctrine, in so far as doctrine may be propounded by any Christian; but dogma is doctrine which

---

[1] *Op. cit.* pp. 3, 4 ; cf. *History of Dogma*, Eng. trans. i. p. 9.
[2] *Op. cit.* p. 4 ; cf *History of Dogma*, Eng. trans. i. p. 8.
[3] *Op. cit.* p. 5 ; cf. *History of Dogma*, Eng. trans. i. p. 11.

the Church lays down, and which she lays down as essential,
pertaining to the basis of faith, life, and fellowship. Harnack
lays stress on the point for this reason partly: he wishes
to show that, when doctrine assumes the character of
dogma, it begins to occupy a new place, and to operate
in quite a new way on the very process to which it owes
its own formation." [1]   Whether the history of the word
justifies this narrower use is a question that need not now
detain us, as a mere definite sense may be assigned to a
word, if practical convenience or scientific accuracy is
thereby served.   Now it does seem at first sight an
advantage to distinguish doctrine in general from doctrine
which has been invested with ecclesiastical authority, and
has been enforced as a religious obligation ; especially if,
while the necessity of doctrine to faith is admitted, the
legitimacy of thus imposing doctrine on faith is denied.
But, on the other hand the relation between doctrine and
dogma is so organic, doctrine the source of dogma, and
dogma in turn the basis of doctrine, that it is hardly
possible to separate the one from the other.   In fact,
Harnack does not succeed in doing this, as necessarily he
is oftener dealing with doctrine generally than with dogma
particularly.   But while one may question the utility of his
distinction, there is one feature in the history of theology,
to which his definition does call attention, of which one
must not lose sight.   Doctrine ceases to serve its legitimate
purpose as the intellectual expression of faith whenever
the Church makes it a restraint on, or a compulsion of,
theological thought.   This seems to the writer a more
serious defect in ecclesiastical dogma, as Harnack defines
it, than the imperfect philosophical principles or the inadequate logical methods, by which reasonable form was
given to the contents of Christian faith.   It is to be noted,
however, that this restriction of the term dogma is not a

[1] *Critical Review*, v. p. 116.

common feature in the Ritschlian school. Kaftan does
not adopt it, but defines dogma as " a doctrine which is to
be valid in the Christian Church"; and explains "that
the Christian faith of itself and necessarily leads to a
doctrine; that the Christian community cannot dispense
with a doctrine, which is to be valid, accordingly a dogma
in the original sense ; that also the evangelical Church, and
she especially, in her condition must have recourse to such
a dogma."[1] He distinguishes dogma from doctrine only
in so far as the former claims a more or less general
recognition in a Christian community which the latter
may lack; but he does not consider enforcement by
ecclesiastical authority as an essential feature of dogma,
as Harnack does.

(2) The limitation of the scope follows from the
definition of the nature of dogma. If dogma be what
Harnack defines it, then he is altogether justified in making
the close of the period of origin and the beginning of the
period of development coincide with the first Christological
decision of the Catholic Church, whose ecclesiastical
authority was enforced by the legal sanction of the imperial
power. The development of dogma, too, may be fitly
regarded as closing at the Reformation, when a large
section of the Christian Church assumed a new attitude
towards the theological tradition, the logical method, and
the ecclesiastical authority which had been combined in
dogma. The Churches of the Reformation lacked the
authority to enforce dogma as the Catholic Church had
done ; and the two principles of the sole authority of the
Scriptures, and the individual right of private judgment
affirmed by Protestantism, made it impossible for believers
in the same way as hitherto to recognise the obligation
of dogma. Harnack's recognition of the fact that in
Augustine there appeared a religious vitality combined

[1] Kaftan's *Glaube und Dogma*, p. 21 ("Faith and Dogma").

with an intellectual vigour, which, if it could not transform the character, yet modified the tendency of ecclesiastical dogma, must command ready assent, and so secure a willing acquiescence in his separation of the Oriental or Greek Christological development from the Occidental or Latin Soteriological. Even if his distinction between doctrine and dogma is not accepted, yet his distribution of the contents of the history brings into due prominence important features of the course of Christian theology.

(3) Harnack's estimate of the value of ecclesiastical dogma provokes strong dissent. Pfleiderer thus expresses his judgment of Harnack's book : " Perhaps we can most simply describe its character by saying that to Baur's optimistic evolutionary theory of history it opposes a pessimistic view of Church history, which makes this history to consist, not in a progressive teleological and rational development, and ever richer unfolding of the Christian spirit, but in a progressive obscuration of the truth, in the progress of disease in the Church, produced by the sudden irruption of Hellenic philosophy and other secularising influences. We can understand that such a view is acceptable to a realistic and practical age which has long lost all touch with the ancient dogmas; we cannot deny that it contains relative truth, and might, in fact, serve as a salutary complement to Baur's optimism ; but is it adapted to form the supreme guiding principle of ecclesiastical history, or can it justly claim to be the only scientific view, or the right to condemn as unscientific scholasticism the teleological theory of evolution which in the manifold play of individual causes, recognises the governance of a higher Reason ? These are questions to be seriously asked." [1]   This must be admitted a just judgment. There were human error and sin in this development of dogma ; and therefore one cannot apply

[1] Pfleiderer's *Development of Theology*, pp. 298, 299.

to it without numerous and serious qualifications the optimistic, idealistic formula, "the real is the rational." But if one has any belief in God's guidance and guardianship of the Church, one cannot hold with Harnack that the movement was thoroughly a mistake and wholly a wrong; for, as Principal Rainy asks, "Is it not likely also that the Church, providentially placed in these circumstances, did think to *some* good purpose?" In accepting the philosophical principles and the logical methods of ancient thought, the Church was following the only course possible to it. "It is inconceivable and untrue that she could have any right to decline to use human thought in the best methods of it which the world had seen."[1] Greek thought, even as Roman law, was included in the preparation for Christianity as well as Hebrew religion.[2] There was surely not an accidental but a providental relation between the Christian organism and the historical environment, amid which it was born and grew.

(4) Yet Harnack's estimate, although it is unduly pessimistic, has undoubted value as a corrective of a tendency, only too prominent in English theology, to regard this ecclesiastical dogma as universally valid and permanently authoritative. The progress of theology depends on our always maintaining the distinction between "the heavenly treasure" of Christian faith and "the earthen vessels" of ecclesiastical doctrine in which it has been handed down to us. The Creeds of the Councils are not altogether and only "the faith once delivered to the saints." One illustration of this tendency may be given. "What the Church," says Canon Gore, "then

---

[1] *Critical Review*, v. p. 118.

[2] See on this subject Wenley's *The Preparation for Christianity in the Ancient World.* The passage quoted in chapter vii. from Herrmann's *The Certainty of Faith and the Freedom of Theology*, makes due acknowledgment of this fact.

borrowed from Greek thought was her terminology, not the substance of her creed."[1]   But terminology and substance are not so easily held apart; the terminology chosen to express the substance modifies it.   "The phrases 'hypostasis' and 'persona,'" he goes on to say, "used to express personality, have an altogether new shade of meaning given to them to meet new needs of thought." But are not the old shades of meaning likely to show themselves so as to hide the new thought?   But Canon Gore makes even a bolder claim for "the earthen vessel." "Its language is permanent language, none the less permanent because Greek.   The Greek language was, in fact, fitted, as none other ever has been, to furnish an exact and permanent terminology for doctrinal purposes.   The ideas of substance or thing, of personality, of nature, are permanent ideas; we cannot get rid of them; no better words could be suggested to express the same facts."   He does admit that "we need always to distinguish the permanence from the adequacy of our dogmatic language. It is as good as human language can be, but it is not adequate"; but then he neutralises the admission by saying that "human language can never express adequately divine realities."[2]   Of course, if modern philosophy can do no more than add critical and exegetical notes to Plato's *Republic* or Aristotle's *Ethics*, this judgment must be accepted as final.   But if experimental psychology, and critical epistemology, and idealist metaphysics have taught us something; if Bacon, and Kant, and Hegel have not lived altogether in vain, we may venture to believe that we can now give a fuller content to, and a clearer expression of, the categories that control our thought than even the Greeks could.   We must dissent from Harnack, and hold that the alliance of Christian faith with Greek thought in the centuries when ecclesiastical dogma was being formed,

[1] *Bampton Lectures*, p. 101.   [2] *Op. cit.* p. 105.

8

was not only inevitable but even desirable and profitable; but we should learn from his treatment of the origin and development of ecclesiastical dogma that there is not an essential and so permanent and universal unity presented to us in dogma, but only an historical, and so temporary and local union between two elements, one of which, Christian faith, needs that it may win mankind, to enter into new alliances, to meet new dangers and new duties.

V

(1) Having thus considered and estimated Harnack's position in dogma generally, we may now confine our attention to that feature in the history of dogma in estimating which Harnack shows himself most distinctly a Ritschlian, namely, his attitude towards metaphysics. In doing this we need no longer take into account the two latter parts of the history; as, although scholasticism flourished during the Middle Ages in the Latin Church, yet the problem which claimed special attention was a genuinely religious, practical one, the plan of salvation and the means of grace, and the spirit of the solution, too, was in some measure controlled by the vital spiritual experience of Augustine; and, further, even although at the Reformation scholasticism survived in the Protestant Churches (to some instances of which we shall return at a subsequent stage of the discussion), yet the force and the fulness of the religious revival did bring back theology to the control of a living faith, as the Ritschlians frankly acknowledge in claiming to be in their theology more faithful in their application of essential Protestant principles than the Reformers, owing to their position in a transition age, could possibly be. The metaphysical interest is most prominent in Christian theology in the second period of the history of dogma, the Christological

development of the East; but already begins to assert itself in the first period, the preparation for dogma. While the second period will claim a passing glance, yet it is the first period on which attention must be specially fixed, for, on the one hand, as being the nearest to the origins of Christianity, it possesses greatest interest for us; and, on the other hand, the Ritschlian estimate of the earliest development of Christian doctrine has for us most importance, as affording the surest test of the soundness of the position generally.

(2) As presuppositions of the history of dogma, Harnack deals with the following: (1) "the gospel of Jesus Christ according to His own self-witness"; (2) "the common preaching of Jesus Christ in the first generation of believers in Him"; (3) "the current exegesis of the Old Testament and the Jewish hopes for the future in their significance for the oldest expression of the Christian preaching"; (4) "the religious conceptions and the religious philosophy of the Hellenistic Jews in their significance for the transformation of the gospel"; (5) "the religious disposition of the Greeks and Romans in the first two centuries, and the current Greco - Roman religious philosophy."[1] In a note he adds, "The right of distinguishing 2 and 3 may be contested. But if we surrender this we therewith surrender the right to distinguish kernel and husk in the original proclamation of the gospel. The dangers to which the attempt is exposed should not frighten us from it, for it has its justification in the fact that the gospel is neither doctrine nor law."[2] Thus is indicated the attitude of the writer even to the apostolic preaching and teaching; he claims the right to distinguish kernel and husk.

[1] *Grundriss der Dogmengeschichte*, i. p. x ("Outlines of the History of Dogma"). See *History of Dogma*, Eng. trans. i. p. 57.
[2] *History of Dogma*, Eng. trans. i. p. 57, note.

(i.) The content of the gospel is described as embracing three moments, the dominion of God as Father and Judge, the better righteousness or the command of love, and the forgiveness of sins; and this content is said to be inseparably attached to Jesus Christ as Son of God who knows the Father; it is recognised that Jesus at the end of His life assigned a special significance to His death in relation to the forgiveness of sins, claimed a unique dignity as Saviour and Judge, regarded His death as His passage to glory, and was able to persuade His followers that "He was still living, and was Lord over the living and the dead."[1]   (ii.) The common preaching about Jesus included His Messiahship, His second coming, the possession of the grace of God, and the participation in the coming glory by all who believed in Him, and surrendered themselves to Him. The ground on which the certainty of Christian faith rested was the resurrection of Jesus; and the guarantee of the fulfilment of all God's promises to the Christian community was, on the one hand, Christ's sacrificial death, on the other, the gifts of the Spirit. But already in the Apostolic Age the study of the Old Testament in order to find proofs for Jesus' Messiahship, the self-testimony of Jesus regarding His relation to the Father, the belief of the disciples in His exaltation, and the extension of the gospel to the Gentiles, introduced speculation, which found expression in new statements about the Person and the Dignity of Christ. This speculation included an expansion of the Jewish idea of the theocracy, an interest in the beginnings of His existence, an estimate of His significance for all mankind, an examination of His unique relation to God. At this stage already Harnack detects a false and a foreign element introducing itself into the gospel. "It is evident," he says, "that hereby a

[1] *Grundriss der Dogmengeschichte*, p. 10 ("Outlines of the History of Dogma"). See *History of Dogma*, Eng. trans. i. p. 66.

serious displacement for the future was brought about; for, although the important matter is the appropriation of the person of Christ, yet personal life cannot be appropriated by *judgments* about the person, but only by the tradition of the *concrete* picture." [1] In other words, the apostles should have been content to be reporters of Jesus' words, recorders of His deeds, instead of becoming, as they did, interpreters of the significance and the value of His person : an error was committed when explanation took the place of testimony. But the original apostles did not go very far in theological interpretation. " Paul," he says, " was the first on the basis of the death and resurrection of Jesus to develop a theology as a means of separation from the religion of the Old Testament." [2] (iii.) The apostles accepted the Jewish exegetical method, and the result of their application of it to the Old Testament was that " a foreign meaning was given to many Old Testament passages," and that " the life of Jesus was enriched with new facts, while attention was directed to single events which often were unreal, and seldom pre-eminently important." [3] They were influenced, too, by Jewish apocalyptic literature, and " consequently the reproduction of the eschatological sayings of Jesus must needs become uncertain ; yes, even what was quite foreign was mixed up with them, and the true aims of Christian activity and hope in life became vacillating." [4] But the most important foreign element introduced even into apostolic Christianity was the doctrine of pre-existence. " Already long before," he says, " one had in the Jewish religion assigned an existence in the divine knowledge to all being and happening, but one had applied this representation, as was

---

[1] *Op. cit.* p. 12.   See *History of Dogma*, Eng. trans. i. p. 82.
[2] *Op. cit.* p. 12.   See *History of Dogma*, Eng. trans. i. pp. 86–96.
[3] *Op. cit.* p. 14.   See *History of Dogma*, Eng. trans. i. p. 100.
[4] *Op. cit.* p. 14.   See *History of Dogma*, Eng. trans. i. pp. 100, 101.

natural, in fact only to what has great worth.   Advancing
religious thought had before all drawn into this speculation,
the sole aim of which was to glorify God, individuals also,
that is to say, the pre-eminent ones, and accordingly pre-
existence was assigned to the Messiah, but such an one that
in His earthly appearance He abides with God.   On the
contrary, the Hellenic representations of pre-existence were
rooted in the distinction of God and matter, spirit and
flesh.   According to these the spirit pre-exists, and the
sensuous nature is only a veil which it assumes.   Here was
given the soil for ideas about the incarnation, the assumption of a second nature, etc.   In the time of Christ these
Hellenic representations influenced the Jewish, and so
widely extended were both, that the pre-eminent Christian
teachers even accepted them."   Accordingly the conclusion
was reached that "Jesus had pre-existed, especially that
in Him a heavenly being, equal in position to God, who
is older than the world, yea, its creative principle, had
appeared and assumed flesh." [1]   This idea was accepted
by the fourth evangelist; but other conceptions were also
current, such as "a communication of the Spirit at Baptism
for the qualification of the man Jesus for His vocation," or
"a miraculous birth in which was posited the germ of His
unique existence." [2]   (iv.) Still another modifying influence
was the Jewish-Alexandrian philosophy of religion, which
had "its most important representative in *Philo*, the complete Greek and the convinced Jew, who developed the
religious philosophy of the age in the direction of Neo-
Platonism, and prepared for a Christian theology which
could enter into rivalry with philosophy." [3]   The most
prominent feature of his philosophy was his doctrine of the
Logos, a personal-impersonal existence, bridging the gulf

[1] *Op. cit.* p. 15.   See *History of Dogma*, Eng. trans. i. pp. 102–104.
[2] *Op. cit.* p. 16.   See *History of Dogma*, Eng. trans. i. p. 105.
[3] *Op. cit.* p. 17.   See *History of Dogma*, Eng. trans. i. p. 108.

between Creator and creature, nature and history, the
explanation of the world as well as religion. "At the
beginning of the second century," says Harnack, "the
philosophy of Philo, especially his *doctrine of the Logos* as an
expression for the unity of religion, nature, and history, and
above all his hermeneutical principles, gained influence among
Christian teachers."[1]   (v.) The last factor in this process
of development, or degeneration, as it should be called
from Harnack's point of view, was the religious disposition
and philosophy of the Greco-Roman culture. "Out of the
decay of political cults and out of Syncretism there was
developed under the influence of philosophy the disposition
for *Monotheism*"; for "philosophy in nearly all its schools
had more and more pushed ethics to the front, and had
deepened it," and "common to all" the schools, "was the
high value set on the *Soul*."[2]   But these schools could
offer only an aspiration, and no assurance. "One possessed no certain *revelation*, no embracing and satisfying
religious communion, no potent religious *genius*, and no
view of *history* which could take the place of the political
history which had lost its value; one possessed no *certainty*,
and one did not escape from the vacillation between fear of
God and deifying of nature."[3]   Nevertheless an alliance
was made by the gospel with this inadequate and defective
philosophy, and hence there is an exact correspondence
between the development of dogma and the course of the
Hellenic philosophy of religion. Thus did the gospel pass,
to use Hatch's words, from "a world of Syrian peasants"
to "a world of Greek philosophers."[4]

[1] *Op. cit.* p. 18.   See *History of Dogma*, Eng. trans. i. pp. 113, 114.

[2] *Op. cit.* pp. 19, 20.   See *History of Dogma*, Eng. trans. i. p. 116–
118.

[3] *Op. cit.* pp. 20, 21.   See *History of Dogma*, Eng. trans. i. pp. 124,
125.

[4] Hatch's *Hibbert Lectures*, p. 1.

VI

(1) The origin of ecclesiastical dogma, according to Harnack, was marked by two stages, the preparation and the foundation. (i.) In the course of the second century the idea of salvation was deprived more and more of its apocalyptic character, and assumed an intellectual and ethical form. Salvation was thought to consist of a certain and complete knowledge of God in contrast to the errors of heathenism, combined with the hope of life and every good; but the fulfilment of this hope was made to depend on good works, and so the gospel itself came to be regarded as a new law. Christianity finally separated itself from Judaism, and found a home in the Gentile world. Gnosticism, on the one hand, attempted to create an apostolic doctrine and a Christian theology, an attempt described as " the acute secularisation of Christianity." Marcion, on the other hand, tried to separate the gospel from the Old Testament, to purify tradition, and to reform Christianity on the basis of the Pauline gospel. While Jewish Christian sects continued in existence, Jewish Christianity, as distinguished from, or opposed to, Gentile Christianity, ceased altogether to be a factor in the history of the Church. (ii.) " The secularisation of Christianity " (for in this phrase Harnack describes the establishment and defence of the Christian faith and life which took place in the second and third centuries) assumed two forms, one ecclesiastical, the other doctrinal. Christianity was steadily and surely secularised, conformed to the world, as Church and as creed. It was assumed that the Christian character of both was being preserved by an apostolical rule of faith, an apostolical collection of writings, and an apostolical office. Protests in favour of the older order of faith and life were mainly made by Montanism and Novatianism,

and served only to strengthen the tendency to ecclesiastical organisation. Christian ministers came to be regarded as priests, and the Christian ordinances as sacrifices. This ecclesiastical development was accompanied by a doctrinal of the same tendency and intention. The efforts of the apologists to commend Christianity to ancient thought resulted in a transformation of Christian truth. " The whole positive material of Christianity," says Harnack, " is changed into a great *instrument of proof*; religion does not receive its contents from historical events,—it receives this from the divine revelation, which evidences itself in the innate reason and freedom of man,—but the historical events serve for a *confirmation* of religion, for its greater *distinctness* over against partial obscurations, and for its universal *extension*." " While the Gnostics," he continues, " sought in the gospel a *new religion*, the apologists used it as a confirmation of their *religious ethics*."[1] " The apologists," he again states by the way of summing up their position, " held these doctrines of God, the Logos, the world and man as the essential content of Christianity."[2] The attempt of Irenæus and his followers to arrest this Hellenisation, by the prominence which they gave to the Scriptures, faith in Christ as Saviour, the reality of Christ's human life, was made ineffective by " the superstitious view of salvation," which gave it a physical character, and by the stress laid " on the natures instead of the living person of Christ."[3] These theologians themselves were " double-minded," and so " unstable in their ways." Themselves attached to the older and simpler views, they were compelled to adopt the Logos doctrine in controversy with Gnosticism. In Clement's theology "the religious philoso-

---

[1] *Grundriss der Dogmengeschichte*, i. p. 66 ("Outlines of the History of Dogma"). See *History of Dogma*, Eng. trans. ii. p. 172.

[2] *Op. cit.* p. 71. See *History of Dogma*, Eng. trans. ii. p. 203.

[3] *Op. cit.* pp. 74, 75. See *History of Dogma*, Eng. trans. ii. p. 247.

phy of the Greeks serves not only apologetic and polemical purposes, but is *the means of first opening up Christianity for thinking men*"; for while "faith (πίστις) is given, it is to be transformed into knowledge (γνῶσις), that is, a doctrine has to be developed which will meet the scientific demands for a philosophical view of the world and ethics."[1]   In Origen's theology "*the Christian religion is the only religion, which also in the mythical form is truth,*" that is, it is true as *pistis* for the multitude, even although for the thoughtful man it must be translated into *gnosis*, which "neutralises all that is empirically historical, if not always in its historicity, yet throughout in its value" (that is, without denying the facts is indifferent to them as facts), for "behind the historical Christ rests the eternal Logos; he who appears at first as physician and saviour appears on deeper consideration as teacher; but also the teacher is at last no longer necessary to the perfect man; he rests in God. Thus here the Christianity of the Church is slipped off as a veil and cast away as a crutch."[2]   In spite of the opposition of the *monarchian* schools, whether adoptionist or modalist, the Logos Christology was enrolled " in the faith of the Church— and that as a fundamental article " about the end of the third century, because it "allowed an alliance of faith and science, corresponded with the formula, that God became man that we might become gods, and so supported Christianity both outwards and inwards." Yet the result was very serious to Christian faith and life. " It meant the change of faith into a *doctrine* of faith with a Greek philosophical character; it pushed back the old eschatological represen- tations, yes, pushed them out; it placed behind the Christ of history a logical (*begrifflichen*) Christ, a principle, and changed the historical into an appearance; it referred the Christian to 'natures' and natural magnitudes

---

[1] *Op. cit.* p. 84.   See *History of Dogma*, Eng. trans. ii. p. 324.
[2] *Op. cit.* p. 87.   See *History of Dogma*, Eng. trans. ii. p. 342.

(*Grössen*) instead of to the Person and the Moral; it gave the faith of Christians decisively the bent towards the contemplation of ideas and doctrines, and therewith prepared, on the one hand, the monkish life, and, on the other, the Christianity under guardianship of the incomplete active laity; it made legitimate in the Church a hundred questions of metaphysics, of cosmology, of secular science, and demanded a definite answer on pain of loss of blessedness; it led to this, that one preached instead of faith rather faith in the faith, and it burdened religion, while it seemed to widen it." [1]

(2) That the pursuit of *metaphysical ideas* drew away interest from *historical facts*, that the *cosmical relations* of the Logos obscured the *soteriological activities* of the Christ, that *doctrine* claimed an exaggerated importance in comparison with *practice*, that *orthodoxy* came to be more highly prized than *piety* or *morality*, that, in short, the expression of Christian faith in Greek modes of thought meant its modification, nay, even in some respects its perversion, we are with Harnack compelled to admit, although with modifications and qualifications. But then, on the other hand, it is to be noted how inadequate is his account of the self-testimony of Christ; how suspicious, and even censorious, is his attitude to the apostolic interpretation of Christ; how many features of the evangelical record, such as the pre-existence, the miraculous birth, the baptismal endowment with the Spirit, the heavenly exaltation, the " Logos " incarnation, he is compelled to exclude from the original testimony, and to attribute to foreign influences; how inappreciative he is of the necessary impulse of faith to define and verify its objects, and so clarify and justify itself; how forgetful he generally is of the fact, which he at times admits, that the doctrinal development

---

[1] *Op. cit.* pp. 93, 94.   See *History of Dogma*, Eng. trans. ii. p. 380, and iii. pp. 2–4.

served to guard religion from dangers at the time threatening it, and to commend it to thoughtful and earnest men in the Gentile world who had been formed by Greco-Roman culture. That the metaphysics the Church used was inadequate, and that an exaggerated importance was assigned to it, that he has proved; but he has not proved what it was his intention to prove, that Christian faith may do without a metaphysics, and that the Christian Church erred in having anything to do with a metaphysics. The necessity he is under of justifying his position by excluding from the objects of faith so many elements hitherto included in them, shows conclusively that the expulsion of metaphysics from theology would involve a narrowing and a lowering of its objects. On the ground, then, that ecclesiastical dogma admits metaphysics into theology we cannot accept the Ritschlian condemnation of it, for the indictment which Harnack with all his learning and his great skill has drawn up is not convincing.

(3) Harnack's account of the presuppositions of the history of dogma, and of the origin of dogma, raises one of the most serious problems which Christian thought is called to face. It is nothing less than the significance and value of apostolic Christianity, and the authority of the New Testament as its record and interpretation. Historical and literary criticism cannot be condemned, or even treated with suspicion by the Christian Church. That there is a temporary, local, and derived element in the New Testament as well as a permanent, universal, and original element, and that the former has only a relative interest while only the latter has an absolute importance, must be admitted. Further, that it is a legitimate endeavour to distinguish these two elements, so that the Church may hold fast only what is essential to Christianity, and may not be burdened with what was only accidental in the period of its origin, must also be conceded. But is the

meaning and worth of Jesus Christ for the world adequately
expressed in Harnack's statement of " the Gospel of Jesus
Christ according to His self-testimony." Can He be
recognised as all that Harnack admits Him to be without
being also confessed a great deal more than Harnack
states ? The explanations of His nature (the miraculous
birth, the anointing with the Spirit at Baptism, the pre-
existence, the " Logos " incarnation), all of which Harnack
excludes from essential Christianity, and derives from
Jewish or Gentile thought of the age, are, to give them
even their lowest possible value, at least witnesses that the
Person of Christ offered a problem which the first century
was conscious needed solution, and which the nineteenth
century cannot afford to ignore or neglect. But if this
be acknowledged, more will be conceded ; instead of
treating these explanations with suspicion, the Christian
thinker may be led to assign to them a very high value
indeed, as affording an interpretation of Christ as necessary
and as authoritative now as it was then. To the apostolic
experience, including even what some are pleased to call
the speculations of a John or a Paul about the person and
work of Christ, the Christian thinker may find himself
constrained to assign a normative authority for Christian
thought and life in every land and age. But if, without
the assumption of any doctrine of inspiration, such a
position is assigned to the New Testament, the Ritschlian
assumption that metaphysics can and should be excluded
from Christian theology is disproved ; for John and Paul
alike, the two greatest thinkers of the apostolic age, recognise that the historical can be clearly seen only in the light
of the eternal, that the phenomenal is unintelligible without
the noumenal, that Jesus the Christ on earth is completely
apprehended only as the Word and the Lord in heaven.
The Ritschlian position as regards metaphysics in theology
is not independent of criticism ; for it is only when criticism

has done even more than what many will regard as its necessary and legitimate work on the New Testament, that the exclusion of the metaphysical elements from primitive Christianity is made possible. May not Harnack's aversion to metaphysics have influenced even his critical conclusions? It must be added by way of caution that Harnack is more advanced in his critical attitude to the New Testament than Ritschl himself was, and other members of the school even now are.

VII

(1) Although the most important question raised by Harnack's *History of Dogma* emerges in the first period, yet his treatment of the subsequent period is not without interest or importance, and may be very briefly indicated. At the end of the third century the Holy Scriptures and Neo-Platonic speculation were united in the Church of the East. Doctrine, Cultus, and Polity were all traced back to "apostolic" origin; but in reality Hellenic speculation, pagan superstition, and Roman imperialism found a home in the Church. Athanasius, although on the basis of Greek speculation, arrested the process of deterioration by his insistence on "the redemption of humanity by God Himself, the God-man, of the *same substance* as God."[1] (i.) The first controversy of this period dealt with the divinity of the Redeemer, and ended in the adoption of the doctrine of the *homoousia* of Father and Son, the value of which Harnack recognises to be this, that the "Logos" doctrine fell into the background, the soteriological rather than cosmical interests were pushed to the front, and expression was given to "the faith that in Christ God Himself has saved man, and brought him into fellowship with Himself."[2]

[1] *Grundriss der Dogmengeschichte*, i. p. 111 ("Outlines of the History of Dogma"). See *History of Dogma*, Eng. trans. iii. pp. 140, 141.
[2] *Op. cit.* p. 141. See *History of Dogma*, Eng. trans. iii. pp. 290–295.

Although this result was in the interests of religion, yet Athanasius, as much as Arius, placed himself on the ground won by previous metaphysical speculation; and therefore the creed adopted by the Church suffered from an alliance of Hellenic metaphysics with Christian faith. As an authoritative confession enforced by ecclesiastical allied with imperial power, it became, not an expression of faith, but a legal obligation as the condition of salvation. (ii.) The second controversy of this period was concerned with the humanity of the Son of God. The so-called heresy of Apollinaris aimed at securing the unity of the person of Christ, and at the same time the full humanity; yet the latter had to be sacrificed in order to make the former intelligible on the presuppositions of the previous dogmatic development. The Church affirmed the complete humanity, but did not show how this was to be united in one person with the complete divinity. (iii.) This was the problem of the next great controversy. The Antiochians surrendered the unity of the person for the distinctness and completeness of the two natures; but their merit was to keep before the Church the picture of the historical Christ, which it was fast losing. The Alexandrians started " from the God who became man," [1] and asserted an assumption of a humanity (not of an individual man) by the unchangeable Logos. The picture of the real Christ disappeared from view, and docetic explanations were accepted. Eutychianism was the logical result of this position; the humanity was affirmed to be absorbed in the divinity. The Council of Chalcedon affirmed the two natures and the one person; and so virtually asserted three distinct magnitudes. It did not do justice to the interests of piety; it excluded any concrete conception of the historical Jesus; as a political compromise it alike sacrificed faith and intelligence. (iv.) A fourth controversy was the result.

[1] *Op. cit.* p. 159. See *History of Dogma*, Eng. trans. iv. p. 175.

The monophysites in the interests of the unity of Christ tried to combat, evade, or explain this dualistic formula; but the fortunes of this unworthy warfare need not be noted. In the *monergist* and *monothelite* controversies theology drifted further and further away from piety, and became a scholasticism, which instead of apprehending realities, manipulated formulæ. The subtle Christology of John of Damascus marks the last stage of this dogmatic development. He not only gave the Greek Church its orthodox system, but afforded also the basis for the Mediæval theology. He was a thorough scholastic. "Every difficulty," says Harnack, "was for him only a demand, skilfully to divide conceptions, and to find a new conception, to which nothing in the world corresponds, except just that difficulty which is to be removed by the new conception."[1] As theology drifted to scholasticism, so piety moved towards ritualism and mysticism. It may be that Harnack, in his aversion to all speculation in theology, has not been altogether fair in the account he gives of this Christological development in the East; but the writer cannot but express his general agreement with Harnack's estimate of the decisions of the Councils in regard to the Person of Christ. Probably in the historical conditions no other decisions were possible, and these given were, in the existing circumstances, the most desirable; but it were a grievous misfortune if Christian theology held itself bound by the letter of any of the creeds, and Harnack has rendered a service in helping us to free ourselves from these dogmas by showing us their origin and development.

(2) With the piety of the Western Church, more practical and less speculative than that of the East, Harnack shows greater sympathy. He does justice to Augustine as the disciple of Paul, who fixed the attention of the Western Church on man's individual relation to God, on the doctrines

[1] *Op. cit.* p. 182. See *History of Dogma*, Eng. trans. iv. p. 264.

of sin, grace, and the means of grace.   Yet his speculative
tendencies, his ecclesiastical sympathies, and his sacrament-
arian beliefs are shown in large measure to have neutralised
his efforts as a reformer of piety.   While in the Middle
Ages the old dogmas became petrified, the teaching of
Augustine was the beginning of a theology still fluid,
neither condemned nor approved by the Church.   The
problems raised by Augustine continued to be discussed;
and while Augustine's authority was still recognised, the
doctrine of the Church gradually moved away from his
positions.   The doctrine of the atonement and of the
sacraments came into prominence.   The Aristotelian
logical method appeared as a rival of the Platonic speculative philosophy.   Scholasticism set itself the task of
(1) "scientifically manipulating the old *articuli fidei*";
(2) "developing the doctrine of the sacrament; and,"
(3) "reconciling the principles of the ecclesiastical practice
with Augustinianism."[1]   While scholasticism recognised
the absolute authority of the Church, it nevertheless
attempted an independent activity.   The result was
nominalism, in which theology came in conflict with piety.
This period also, even as the preceding, showed that the
methods and intentions of the theology approved by the
Church were distinct from, where not opposed to, the
interests and demands of piety.   This, too, is a conclusion
with which general agreement must be confessed.

(3) This history of dogma had a threefold issue,
Roman Catholicism, Anti-trinitarianism and Socinianism,
and Protestantism.   "In these three formations," says
Harnack, "there present themselves *issues of the history of
dogma*; the post-Tridentine Catholicism surely finally completes the neutralising of the old dogma as an arbitrary
papal legal ordinance; Socinianism breaks it up by the
understanding, and takes it away; the Reformation, while

[1] *Op. cit.* ii. p. 79.   See *History of Dogma*, Eng. trans. vi. pp. 23–44.

9

it at the same time has set it aside and kept it up, points beyond it, backwards to the gospel, forwards to a new formulation of the evangelical confession, freed from dogma, and reconciled with reality and truth."[1]   Of these three issues that which concerns us most is the last, and of the characteristics of this Harnack gives the following description : " The Reformation, as it is represented in the Christianity of Luther, is in many respect an old Catholic, especially a mediæval appearance ; but judged, on the contrary, by its religious kernel, it is not this, rather a restoration of Pauline Christianity in the spirit of a new time."[2]   While Luther kept the old dogmas, he put a new meaning into them.   He saw in them only " *a divine deed through Jesus Christ for the forgiveness of sins and for eternal life*," and " all else in them he overlooked."[3]   Luther met the old Church with these four positions : (1) " he set up *the word of God according to its pure sense* as the foundation of the Church " ; (2) " he restored *the gospel in the gospel*" ; (3) " he led back *the Church to faith*" as its sphere and its charge ; (4) " he restored their independent right to the natural ordinances in marriage, family, vocation, and State."[4]   Yet he kept Catholic elements, and so " he did not render anything final, but only made *a scanty beginning of reformation according to his peculiar principles*."[5]   He confused the gospel and the doctrines of the gospel, the evangelical faith and the old dogma, the Word of God and the Holy Scriptures, Grace and the Means of Grace.   His greatest error, however, was his doctrine of the Lord's Supper, involving a Christology which outstripped even Mediæval Scholasticism in its unintelligibility and its incredibility.   Thus the later Lutheran Church " threatened

[1] *Op. cit.* ii. p. 105. The seventh volume of the English translation of the *History of Dogma* has not yet appeared.
[2] *Op. cit.* p. 123.   [3] *Op. cit.* p. 125.
[4] *Op. cit.* p. 127.   [5] *Op. cit.* p. 134.

to become," in many respects, only "a pitiful repetition of the Catholic Church."[1]   The conclusion of the whole matter is that "the form which the Churches of the Reformation received in the sixteenth century was no consistent and no conclusive one; that the history of Protestantism to the present day shows. Luther placed the gospel again on the candlestick, and subordinated dogma to it. Our task is to maintain and continue what he began."[2]   In dealing with individual doctrines, it will be shown in subsequent discussions in what respects the Ritschlian school claims not only to continue, but even to correct the work of the Reformation. That the return to primitive Christianity was not thorough cannot be denied, that Protestant principles demand more faithful application must be admitted; but whether Ritschlianism has made the return, and so has applied these principles, remains yet to be shown.

[1] *Op. cit.* p. 138.   [2] *Op. cit.* p. 138.

CHAPTER V

THE ANTAGONISM TO RELIGIOUS MYSTICISM

I

(1) WHILE many Christians might view with indifference *the exclusion of metaphysics* from theology, if that were possible, and, confident in their own religious experience, might be in no way troubled, even if Christian thinkers agreed to *the rejection of speculative theism*; nay even, holding the Scriptures to be the sole and sufficient source of Christian doctrine, might welcome *the condemnation of ecclesiastical dogma*; while all these concessions to the Ritschlian position might be made by many believers without any sense of spiritual loss, yet it is not at all unlikely that *the antagonism to mysticism* of the Ritschlian theology would excite suspicion, as appearing to threaten what is the most precious possession of the Christian life, personal communion with God in Jesus Christ our Lord. While, on the one hand, it may, at the very beginning of this inquiry, be admitted that the language in which this antagonism to mysticism is expressed often appears to justify a charge of the denial of any "direct spiritual communion of the soul with God," yet, on the other hand, the results of this inquiry may show that such a statement needs to be so largely qualified as to be deprived of much of its force as an objection to Ritschlianism in the interests of piety.

(2) What first of all demands our close attention is the direct connection between this *antagonism to mysticism* and the exclusion of *metaphysics from theology*. Ritschl and

his followers are opposed to mysticism, because they regard it as an intrusion of metaphysics into religious life. While the term " mysticism " is often used in a vague sense for any individual religious experience in which there is an intense consciousness of God's Presence, and a passionate desire for communion with Him, the Ritschlian school uses the term in its strictly historical meaning, as the name of a very distinct type of religious life, which (1) was inherited by Christianity from decadent paganism ; (2) was most evident and potent when the truest and best souls turned away from the superstitions and corruptions of the mediæval Catholic Church ; and (3) has appeared, but in a greatly modified form, in some religious movements in Protestantism. Using this term in this restricted application, the Ritschlians cannot merely on account of their antagonism to mysticism, be condemned as rejecting all direct spiritual communion of the soul with God, although, of course, the grounds on which they base their opposition may justify, or appear to justify, this charge. This type of religious life which they condemn is, they contend, based on a false metaphysic, which has been allowed to invade the religious life to the subordination in all cases, and the exclusion in some cases, of the historical element, which is essential to Christian faith ; for if, on the one hand, this antagonism is but one among other expressions of their unfriendly attitude to metaphysics, it has, on the other hand, had a deeper motive, even a genuinely religious and Christian one—their desire to assert the value for, and maintain the authority of, the Christian revelation over the Christian life. All these elements in the Ritschlian antagonism to mysticism, which have been thus briefly indicated in their mutual relation, demand a more thorough separate treatment.

II

(2) " Mysticism," says Ritschl, " is the practice of the Neo-Platonic metaphysics ; and this is the theoretical rule of the alleged mystical enjoyment of God." " Between mysticism and *this* metaphysics," he says again, " there exists so close a kinship that it is quite the same whether one attributes certain propositions to mysticism or to false metaphysics." " In the mystical method," he continues, " the intention is to transcend the individuality of the spiritual life, which maintains itself in discursive know-ledge, and in moral activity, socially beneficent, and to retire to one's own real actual self. This is said to be reached when, either through theoretical speculation or through extinction of one's own will, one is dissolved in the universal Being, which is reckoned as God. The intellectual framework in which alone this task is intel-ligible is the Neo-Platonic depreciation of all individual definite Being and Life in comparison with universal existence, according to the standard of judgment, that the former is predominantly illusive and unreal, but the latter is the reality in the true sense." " The Neo-Platonic God " (to complete his description with one other quotation) " is Himself the idea of the world, the universal vague form in which all the peculiarities and mutual relations of things are excluced, but which is declared to be, as the Idea in the Platoric sense, the actual, real thing." [1] The character-istic feature of Neo-Platonic mysticism, to put Ritschl's statement in a few words, was the effort to get rid of individual consciousness by absorption into the universal existence, which was conceived, according to the Neo-Platonic metaphysics, to be God. A single sentence may

[1] Ritschl's *Theologie und Metaphysik*, pp. 27, 28 (" Theology and Metaphysics").

be added to confirm Ritschl's description. "This mystical absorption into divinity," says Schwegler, "or the One, this trance or swooning into the Absolute, is what gives so peculiar a character to Neo-Platonism as opposed to the Greek philosophical systems proper." [1]

(2) This mysticism, although necessarily in a form more or less modified, as it was more or less strongly affected by Christian ideas and habits, was inherited by the mediæval Catholic Church. What it then and there became a few sentences of Harnack's will show: "Mysticism is the conscious, reflective, Catholic piety, which just by reflection and contemplation wishes to intensify itself; Catholicism knows only it or *fides implicita*" (the unquestioning, submissive acceptance by the laity of the doctrines and ordinances of the Church) "The type," continues Harnack, "is due to a combination of Augustine and the Areopagite, vivified by the self-committal to Christ, taught by Bernard. Mysticism has many shapes, but it is little distinguished nationally or confessionally. As historically it has a pantheistic starting-point, so also it has a pantheistic (acosmic) end. In the measure in which it more or less attaches itself to the historical Christ and the directions of the Church, this aim becomes less or more strongly evident; but even in the churchly form of mysticism there is never altogether lacking the inclination to go beyond the historical Christ; God and the soul, the soul and its God; Christ the brother; the birth of Christ in every believer (the last thought conceived, sometimes fantastically, sometimes spiritually)." "The instructions of mysticism," he says further, "move in the framework, that the soul distant from God must return to God by *purification, illumination,* and essential *union*; it must be 'unformed,' 'informed,' and 'transformed' (*entbildet, gebildet, überbildet*)." "The sacrament of penance especially plays a great part, as a

[1] Schwegler's *History of Philosophy*, p. 140.

rule, in the 'purification.' In the 'illumination,' the Contemplations of Bernard are much in evidence. Besides very dubious instructions about the imitation of Christ, there are found also evangelical thoughts—believing trust in Christ." "In the 'essential union,' finally, there appear the metaphysical thoughts (God as the All-One, the individual nothing; God the 'abysmal substance,' 'the silent silence,' etc.)." "But dubious as these speculations were, the highest spiritual *freedom* was, in fact, intended, which is to be won in full separation from the world in the feeling of the supramundane." "The mystics taught that the soul already here on earth can so absorb God that in the fullest sense it enjoys the vision of His essence, and already dwells in heaven." "The Thomist Mysticism had the Augustinian confidence that it could free itself by knowledge, and mount up to God; the Scotist had this confidence no longer, and sought by discipline of the will to reach the highest mood: *unity of will with God, submission, resignation.*" [1] In Roman Catholic Mysticism there still remain, according to this account, as a lurking danger, an indifference to the historical revelation, a tendency to an acosmic denial of the reality and the value of our present earthly life, and a pantheistic affirmation of God as the exclusive existence which absorbs all other forms of being.

(3) This mysticism survives in Protestant theology in the form of the doctrine of the *unio mystica*, which may be described in the words of Luthardt, as quoted by Ritschl: "The Father and the Son are to be the element in which believers live and move: *unio mystica.* . . . In God and Christ believers are not only according to their wills and disposition, but according to their *real actual self*, without, nevertheless, ceasing to be creaturely and sinful." Of this

---

[1] Harnack's *Grundriss der Dogmengeschichte*, ii. pp. 64–66 ("Outlines of the History of Dogma"). See *History of Dogma*, Eng. trans. vi. pp. 97–108.

statement Ritschl gives the following historical explanation : " Doubtless, he means the conception which in the
seventeenth century was introduced into Lutheran dogmatics as a predicate of every single believer, in whom,
after justification, the Trinity assumes a place with this
qualification that this *unio cum patre, filio et spiritu sancto*
is not *substantialis*, and not *personalis*, but even *mystica*—
that is, undefinable." " This means," he adds, " that one
must not with Philip Nicolai so think this unity as that the
believer is fused together with God into one cake or lump,
and participates in divine nature ; nor yet with Stephen
Pretorius, so that the believer becomes deified, and can say
with right he is Christ." [1]   Calvin and his followers, according to Ritschl, knew the *unio mystica* as " the union of
Christ with the community, which embraces and conditions the justification of the individual."   But this idea
Calvin borrowed from Luther, " who describes the idea of
justification in the form of a marriage of Christ with the
community, in accordance with which a mutual exchange
of possessions lawfully takes place, which in the present
case comes about in this way, that Jesus takes the sins of
the members of the community on Himself, and transfers
His righteousness to them."   Not until the seventeenth
century did Nicolai and Arndt, regardless of the true
intentions of the Lutheran theology, which places justification by faith in the forefront, and influenced by mediæval
modes of thought, introduce the idea of *unio mystica* as
defined by Luthardt.   " At last," he says, in finishing his
historical sketch, " John Arndt, and after him Christian
Hohburg and others, interpreted this practice of union with
God as the tender, loving intercourse with the bridegroom." [2]
The importance for Ritschl of this historical argument is,

[1] *Theologie und Metaphysik*, pp. 25, 26 (" Theology and Metaphysics ").

[2] *Op. cit.* pp. 52, 53.

that here as elsewhere he claims to reject only later scholastic developments of Lutheran theology, and to apply faithfully the essential principles of Luther as a Reformer.

III

(1) Ritschl's argument against mysticism must now be sketched in outline. He rejects, as might have been expected, the Neo-Platonic idea of God as Being without determinations or relations, and also the personal absorption in God which the mystic sought, as the dissolution of his individual in the universal existence of God. With this rejection of mysticism in its extreme form no Christian man will surely have any desire to find fault. But Ritschl goes much further than this. In his rejection of the *unio mystica* as taught by later Lutheran dogmatics, he appears in the opinion of some critics to be rejecting all personal communion with God; and, therefore, his statements need to be very closely and very carefully examined.

(2) In this controversy he starts with a negative and a positive statement. The negative statement is this : " Of my (according to Luthardt) real and actual, that is, metaphysical, being I know nothing, I experience nothing; according to it I cannot, therefore, be guided. And Luthardt cannot teach me anything about it, for he, too, knows nothing about it."[1] His positive statement is that " in a personal life reality attaches to the spiritual activity and nothing else."[2] His opponents, however, are as opposed to the one statement as to the other. " Weiss and Luthardt," he says, " declare their inclination to metaphysics in their common statement that the reality of the human spirit is not grasped in its willing (which naturally includes knowledge and the guiding feeling of self), but that we must think behind, under, and over these functions the

[1] *Op. cit.* p. 25.   [2] *Op. cit.* p. 30.

actual real being in a form of objectivity, which is also distinctive of nature." [1]   The metaphysics which their position betrays is one which he is never weary of condemning, the Platonic doctrine of ideas in its scholastic form, in which substance is separated from its attributes, and subject from its operations.

(3) Now Ritschl does well in protesting against such separation of the two aspects of reality, each of which is unintelligible without the other.   The permanent unity of self or thing cannot be mentally represented apart from its varied relations and its manifold changes, although it may be formally abstracted ; far less can it be believed to have a separate and independent existence of its own.   But, on the other hand, attributes and operations cannot be rationally construed unless on the assumption of such a permanent unity, which is manifest and active in, but is not exhausted by, these attributes and operations.   Accordingly Ritschl's statement goes beyond the psychological facts. There is a mental latency, an organic basis, which must be taken into account in a rational construction of personality as well as the conscious functions and empirical variations. The unity of the self in all its functions is not simply the totality of these functions ; the identity of the self through all its variations is not simply the succession of these variations.   With some show of reason, then, does Pfleiderer bring the following severe indictment against Ritschl's view : " It explains," he says, " the unity of the ego as appearance, and only the manifoldness of the functions as the reality ; but how this appearance could even be brought about, how the actual consciousness of an identity of the ego, how the continuity of the consciousness, how recollection from one day to another, is to be possible if there were in us only changing functions, and not a permanent unity, from which they proceed, and into which they return, depositing

[1] *Op. cit.* p. 47.

there their results; that is, and remains hereby wholly incomprehensible."[1] Ritschl, as we shall see, attaches great importance to a self-sufficient moral character; and Pfleiderer justifiably asks: "Where, then, does there remain the *possibility* of such a character, if our being were nothing else than the ever-changing current of the conscious activities and appearances, if behind this manifold and changeable there were not to be assumed *an existent unity* as the ground of the unity of consciousness, and as the ordering and ruling power in the surging chaos of the appearances of consciousness?" A still more important question does he press home, "whether a doctrine of the soul which wishes to do without a soul, could keep hold of the immortality of the soul?" While we must admit that Ritschl has expressed himself very incautiously, and has laid himself open to such an attack, yet when we ask ourselves whether he really intended to deny such a permanent unity of the self, we are led to recognise that his language here does injustice to his thought; for, first of all, let us recall his definition of a thing (which with the necessary modifications is applicable to "self") "as the cause of its signs which act upon us, as the end to which these serve as means, as the law of their regular changes";[2] secondly, let it be remembered that Ritschl acknowledges his agreement with Lotze's epistemology, and, so it may be assumed, shares his views of personality; and, thirdly, as will be afterwards shown (chap. viii.), he gives a valuable and significant analysis of the idea of personality in proving the personality of God, which very conclusively shows that he did not favour the phenomenalism which his words in controversy at least suggest. One sentence may here be quoted. "The truth of the idea of the divine personality is proved

---

[1] Pfleiderer, *Die Ritschl'sche Theologie*, pp. 11, 12 ("The Ritschlian Theology").

[2] See the discussion of this question in Chapter II. Section II.

just in this, that by means of it as a standard we recognise, whether and in what degree the same predicate belongs to us."[1] We are only becoming persons, and are destined for personality; God is personality without any contradiction of the idea.

(4) While, then, we must so far modify Ritschl's statement as to recognise that consciousness does not exhaust personality; yet surely we are ready to agree with him rather than with the mystics, that what is of greatest worth, and has most meaning for us, is not the subconscious condition of our personality, but the conscious.   Not through the unconscious self does God approach us; but in the conscious self God reveals Himself to us.   The abstract possibility of such an approach through the unconscious we may admit; but for the simple reason that we have no certain knowledge of it, we must hold the revelation in the conscious self as alone significant and valuable.   " In this circle of the reality of the spiritual life," says Ritschl, " can the operations of God, which establish religion, alone be understood.   But even as we also can recognise God only in His operations on us, which correspond with His open revelation, even so do we in these operations recognise the presence of God for us "; for " the religious evidence of the presence of God depends on a combination of religious community and education with moral self-culture and self-judgment."[2]   The presence of God must be revealed within our consciousness; but this consciousness has a varying and a varied content; how shall we distinguish the operation of God upon us, which are the proofs of His Presence with us, from the movements of our own spirits ?   We must have a standard of objective validity as well as of subjective

[1] Ritschl's *Rechtfertigung und Versöhnung*, iii. p. 225 (" Justification and Reconciliation ").

[2] Ritschl's *Theologie und Metaphysik*, p. 48 (" Theology and Metaphysics ").

value. The mystic, who seeks an individual subjective revelation, dispenses with this test of his experiences; but then he cannot possess the security that it is verily God that is with him, and working in him. But the Christian believer (according to Ritschl, and this is another feature in which he contrasts Christian faith with mysticism) recognises God's Presence with him only in those operations on him which correspond with the objective Christian revelation, which is mediated for each believer by the Christian community, which not only bears testimony to the content of that revelation, but also gives to the moral and spiritual faculties of each man the training which makes him capable of appreciating and appropriating that testimony. The communion between God and the soul is thus mediated alike in its subjective and objective reference. Subjectively it is mediated by the exercise of the spiritual functions of the soul; and objectively it is mediated by the historical revelation of God in Christ, and by the Christian community, by which the revelation is made accessible to, and available for, the individual believer. The mystic on the other hand, claims both an immediate receptivity of the self apart from its conscious functions, and an immediate communication from God apart from His historical revelation. At first sight it might appear as if mysticism offered nearer access to God than Christian faith; but on closer view we discover that, as the alleged religious experience is without any content, so the assumed divine contact is without any evidence.

IV

(1) Yet there is a desire for a close present communion with God in the living Christ; and to this desire mysticism is a witness. It is thought by many critics that Ritschl shows himself ignorant of, or indifferent to, this genuine

spiritual necessity in his antagonism to mysticism. Professor Orr, for instance, says, " Ritschl will hear nothing of direct spiritual communion of the soul with God.   Pietism in all its forms is an abomination to him.   The one way of communion with God is through His historical manifestation in Jesus Christ, and experiences due to a supposed immediate action of the Spirit in the soul can be regarded as only illusion.   This is the side of Ritschl's teaching which has been specially taken up and developed by his disciple Herrmann.   It will be difficult, we fancy, to persuade most people that this is a nearer approach to the primitive type of Christianity than is found in the ordinary theology." [1] With all possible respect to the author of this indictment both as a scholar and a thinker, the present writer feels bound in the interests of truth and justice, however reluctantly, to challenge it both as a misunderstanding of the Ritschlian position, and, what is still more serious, as an ambiguous use of language, where definiteness is necessary.

(2) The second objection may be dealt with first of all. What is meant by " direct " as an adjective qualifying " spiritual communion " ; and what is to be understood by " immediate " as a predicate applied to the " action of the Spirit " ?   Principal Simon appears to attempt an answer. " I believe," he says, " that as we are endowed with a sensitivity through which the material world finds access to the mind, so are we endowed with a sensitivity through which the invisible sphere, especially God, finds access to the mind."   " As we perceive the outward world by eye, ear, and the other senses so have we an eye and ear for the invisible and divine—we perceive them by our ' reason.' In the one case, as truly as in the other, there is perception." [2]

[1] *Expository Times*, v. p. 539.
[2] Stählin's *Kant, Lotze, and Ritschl*, xvi, xvii. This work, from the preface of which this passage is a quotation, has been consulted only in the English translation.

Let us venture to assume that this passage at least approximately describes what the adjectives "direct" and "immediate" are intended to convey; for we ordinarily assume that our perception of the external world is "direct" and "immediate"; at least, it would not be generally claimed that our knowledge of God was more "direct" and "immediate." But this directness and immediacy of sensuous perception are proved on closer examination to be only apparent. Although we are not conscious of the process, yet psychological analysis of the act of perception shows a very complicated process, in which the connection between mind Knowing and thing Known is by no means as direct as it seems, being mediated by the physical properties of the object, the physical medium between it and the body, the organs of sense, and the mental activities responding to the stimulation of these organs. There need be no objection whatever to the admission of a spiritual perception in man, provided it is recognised, as on closer inspection we are bound to recognise in regard to sensuous perception, that here too there is a process of mediation, media of communication on the part of God, the object of knowledge, appropriate to the media of receptivity on the part of man, the subject of knowledge. Just as in sensuous perception there is necessarily no consciousness of the process of mediation, so in spiritual there need be no consciousness. In this sense we may speak of a direct spiritual communion and an immediate action of the Spirit. But if, on the contrary, these adjectives are intended to deny, not the subjective consciousness, but the objective reality of such a process, then it must be said that we can know nothing about any such "direct" communion, nor can we experience any such "immediate" action; for our knowledge and our experience are so complex processes, that such adjectives taken literally are inapplicable to any object or any operation that comes within their range.

These adjectives cannot mean that a "self" without any faculties or activities can "commune" with a "God" without any operations or attributes; or that a "Spirit" that uses no means "acts" on a soul that is subject to no conditions. Admitting that there is a process of some kind, it cannot be an objection to the Ritschlian theology because it seeks to distinguish and define the features and the factors of this process, and to exclude from it whatever seems injurious to it. On the contrary, our religious life would be more healthy as our religious thought would be more clear, if all Christian theologians paid as much attention as Ritschl does to the process of communion with God, or of the Spirit's action.

(3) If, however, the critic means that Ritschl's analysis of this process is such as to exclude a real Presence and an actual operation of God in communion with God, or the Spirit's action, then it can be shown that while isolated statements of Ritschl give an apparent justification for the charge, his general intention, taken along with specific statements, contradicts it. In answer to just such an objection, Ritschl affirms that "when one rightly thinks operations, then one thinks the cause in the operations. It is only the false application of the common understanding, that one represents the causes in the plane behind the plane in which one sees the appearances, which one represents as the operations of these causes, or that one sets the causes in an earlier point of time than the operations.— Accordingly, what we religiously affirm as the operation of God or Christ in us, that assures us not of the distance, but of the presence of these authors of our salvation. And, in fact, in the form of a relation of person to person."[1] These words expressly affirm that God or Christ is really present and actually operative in our religious experience;

[1] Ritschl's *Theologie und Metaphysik*, pp. 49, 50 ("Theology and Metaphysics").

10

and unless it can be proved that Ritschl was so stupid that
he did not know the meaning of the words he used, or that
he was so dishonest that he did not intend the words to
mean what they must be taken to mean, his assurance may
be accepted against the objections critics may bring forward.
Two observations may here be added to obviate further
criticism. In the first place, what is here generally affirmed
of the relation of operations and their causes is surely in a
fuller sense true of God than of any finite agent. Only
deism can so detach second causes from the First Cause, as
to make even conceivable the assumption of an operation
of God in the absence of God Himself. The manifest
imperfection of the analogy does not weaken, but strengthen
Ritschl's position. In the second place, we must not
distort Ritschl's words " think " " assures " to mean merely
a subjective representation. In a theological statement of
the spiritual process we do logically separate the factors
of the process, and then logically combine them ; but in
religious experience they are a vital unity. This here
is a theological statement, and not the report of religious
experience. As if to anticipate further objections, Ritschl
is careful to show that the process of mediation does not
make the Presence of God less real, or the operation of
God less actual. " Accurate and copious memory is for
the human spirit the form of the appropriation of all operative and valuable motives, by following which our life
attains its distinctive content. In this the self-feeling
of our spiritual reality is the sufficient evidence of the
reality of all that which contributes to our reality as a
valuable and operative existence. By accurate remembrance particularly are reciprocal relations in life mediated,
namely, that the one person works on in the other, accordingly is present herein, when this one acts from education
or impulse experienced from that one. And in the most
comprehensive sense this is valid of the religious attach-

ment of our life with God through the accurate remembrance of Christ." But this mediation by the remembrance of Christ does not lessen the reality of the communon with God, "for," Ritschl goes on to say, "without much mediation there is nothing real. The personal relation of God or Christ to us, however, is and remains mediated by our accurate remembrance of the word, that is, the law and the promise of God, and God works on us only through the one or the other of these revelations."[1] The word "remembrance" (*Erinnerung*), unless carefully explained, may mislead. It does suggest distance and absence; but Ritschl does not intend this. What he means may be put thus. The intercourse which others have with us, and the influence they excite upon us, would be transitory and ineffective, unless by the exercise of memory their teaching and example became absorbed into our spiritual substance, and continued to be active in us as purpose or as motive. Whatever is to be potent and effective in us must first of all be appropriated by us. But this is not all. The intercourse which we on any occasion enjoy with another, or the influence we receive from another at any given moment, depends, on the one hand, on our own past, so far as that survives in our memory, but it also depends, on the past of the other, on the relations which he has already had with us. The words of a friend and of a stranger may be the same words; our intelligence may apprehend, and our conscience approve both utterances alike; but the speech of the former has a power, the speech of the latter has not, because the memory recalls the close relationship of many years with the one, but has no testimony to offer regarding the other. Memory gives a larger content, and so a stronger influence to our relations to others than belong to present words or deeds. Christ is not distant or absent from us, but His communion with us and action on us are

[1] *Op. cit.* p. 50.

conditioned by what we have learned regarding Him from
the Gospels, and by what He has already done for and in
us. This, as it seems to the writer, is the meaning to be
given to Ritschl's words; although it must be frankly
conceded that his language does admit of serious misunderstanding. In giving an account of the subjective process
of communion with Christ, he does allow the objective
cause of that process, Christ's communion with us, to fall
out of sight; but he does not intend to ignore or deny it.

(4) What we remember is Jesus as He is presented to
us in the Gospels. The history gives content to our communion. But it may be said that God has a more direct
and immediate mode of presence with us, and operation on
us, in the living Christ than in the historical Jesus. But to
this suggestion Ritschl, too, has a reply: " In this respect
no change is effected by the consideration that Christ is at
present in His exaltation. For the representation which
one has to form of this case can only contain the content,
which is assured by the historical account of Christ." If
the attempt is made apart from this historical account to
represent Christ as risen, ascended, and glorified in the
actual present conditions of His exaltation, fancy can in no
way be distinguished from fact; for we do not here and
now know, we have no means of knowing, a mode of existence so different from our own. The extravagances into
which mystics have run in trying to imagine the unimagin-
able should be a warning. While we know Christ present
and operative, the content we give to His personality and
activity must be derived from the history of His earthly
life. Ritschl therefore is quite justified in concluding that
" without the means of the word of God, and without the
accurate remembrance of the personal revelation of God in
Christ, there is no personal relation between a Christian
and God." [1]   If this conclusion is to be challenged, then, on

[1] *Op. cit.* p. 51.

the one hand, it must be shown that the personal revelation of God in Christ has not exclusively permanent value
and universal validity; and, on the other hand, it must be
shown that valuable and valid revelations of God have been
received in Christendom apart from any illumination or
influence from the personal revelation of God in Christ.
Can any mystic claim that he has gained any knowledge
of the Father apart from the Son? Has any new truth
about God been added to the store of wisdom given by
Christ? Is not all progress in Christian knowledge simply
a clearer understanding and a keener insight of " the truth
as it is in Jesus." If there is an immediate communion
with Christ, or a direct action of the Spirit, unconditioned
by the historical revelation, why contend so earnestly for
the defence of the New Testament, why preach the gospel
in all the world, why maintain the Church and its means of
grace? If Christ needs no mediation, and the Spirit uses
no agency, why all this effort and testimony? The truth
is, that Ritschl and his school are contending for what is
recognised practically in all the Christian Churches, the
dependence of Christianity on the historical revelation of
God in Christ, as recorded in the New Testament. Its
antagonism to mysticism, it cannot be too often insisted on,
is due to its appreciation of the permanent value and
universal significance of the historical revelation. One
might have expected that such an attitude would have
commanded the sympathy and support of all Christian
theologians instead of their criticism and censure. That
this expectation has not been fulfilled is due to the fact,
that Ritschl fails to give due attention to a feature of
Christian experience which is rightly regarded as of very
special importance. The Christian recognises, on the one
hand, that he cannot picture to himself Christ as He is in
His exaltation; and, on the other, that the Gospels give the
content to his conception of Christ; but, at the same time,

he has a vivid and intense consciousness of Christ's presence with and action in himself. His own religious experience, with its growth in grace and truth, is quite inexplicable to him as a psychological process, of which all the factors can be measured and weighed. He can understand it only as the result of Christ's presence and action. There are some Christians in whom this consciousness is less distinct and potent, while there are others in whom it is found in exceptional vividness and intensity. Nevertheless, no account of Christian experience can claim to be accurate and complete that does not recognise this feature of it. Ritschl, owing to the peculiarity of his religious experience and character, failed to do justice to this fact of Christian life. His logically reflective, rather than spiritually intuitive, mind fixed on the psychological process and the historical mediation instead of grasping the Person who lives and works in both.

(3) Another question still remains. It may be urged, why then this desire for direct and immediate communion, to which mysticism witnesses? The history of mysticism affords the answer. The origin of mysticism is due to the insufficiency and imperfection of the current, authoritative means of communion with God. Mediæval Catholicism had separated God in Christ from the faith and life of the individual believer; it had transformed the truth of Christ into unintelligible dogmas, and had changed communion with Christ into burdensome cultus. "The Catholic conception of Christ," says Herrmann, "is so formed, that its content cannot accompany any pious man in his communion with God." "Catholic piety," he says again, "shows itself incapable of holding fast faith in the revelation of God in Christ, so far that it could decisively determine religious practice." When the historical mediation of Christian faith and life is so perverted and corrupted, it is inevitable that genuine and intense piety

should seek to get beyond.   "The desire for God," says
Herrmann, "presses out beyond the historical.   Accordingly in Catholicism all that belongs to positive Christianity is degraded to be a means of preparation for the
highest stage of the religious life." [1]   As a temporary
protest against the superstition and corruption of the
Church, mysticism has its historical justification, but as a
permanent tendency in Christian piety it is without
warrant; for the revelation of God in Christ is itself
sufficient for the whole of man's religious life, and the
aim of Protestantism is to make the historical mediation
of that revelation in the teaching, worship, and life of the
Church so adequate and so complete, that there will be
no sense of God's distance, but ever and only an assurance
of His presence and activity in Christ.   Mysticism is a
demand for the purification and the elevation of the
historical mediation of the Christian revelation, but not a
reason for its rejection.   It must not here be forgotten
that Ritschl and his followers seek so to interpret the
historical revelation, that it will afford to the religious
experience the certainty and satisfaction that mysticism
vainly sought.

(6) An objection to Ritschl's theology, which is based
on his antagonism to mysticism, must be briefly noticed
before we leave this subject.   "An immediate Revelation
of God to the soul of Christ," says Professor Orr, "would
come under the ban of mysticism, and would be exposed
to all the philosophical objections which Ritschl urges
against the view that God and the soul can come directly
together."   Accordingly it is argued that according to
Ritschl, "however great the worth of the Revelation
of Jesus, it does not imply an origin outside of, or
transcending, the inherent laws of the human

[1] Herrmann's *Verkehr des Christen mit Gott*, pp. 16, 22 ("Communion
of the Christian with God," pp. 20, 25).

spirit." [1]　This criticism is an excellent example of a theological method which Ritschl very strenuously opposes. Here a deduction is made from a general idea, without due consideration whether the general idea does correspond to any reality, or whether, granted that the general idea is true, it is applicable to this particular instance.　As regards the first point Ritschl does not, as far as the writer is aware, commit himself to any positive statement as to what is or what is not possible in the relation of the soul to God. Probably he would condemn such a statement as an instance of the Platonic metaphysics which he opposes. The recognition of revelation in all religions, and especially his acceptance of the Old Testament as the necessary preparation for the New Testament, are evidence that he admits modes of relation between God and man other than that which is distinctive of Christianity.　What in his antagonism to the mystics he is exclusively concerned about is to show that the genuinely Christian experience is dependent on the historical revelation in Christ.　He is not defining general laws about the relation of God and the soul; he is describing particular facts of the Christian experience.　It is his intense conviction of the significance and the value of this Christian revelation, which leads him at times to use language that may be construed into a denial of any relation between the soul and God except that which is mediated by the Christian revelation; but we have always to beware of hasty generalisation of his statements, and to supply the necessary qualifications which a sympathetic interpretation in view of his distinct purpose legitimately suggests.　But even granting that Ritschl is intending to deal in his statements with the relation of the soul to God generally, yet the criticism may be shown to be invalid.　As will afterwards be

[1] Cirrs *The Ritschlian Theology and the Evangelical Faith*, pp. 212, 213, note.

proved, Ritschl and his followers do not put Christ into the common category of humanity, but expressly recognise His unique relation alike to God and to man.   Their aim and end in their controversy with mysticism is to magnify and exalt Christ by claiming for Him, and Him alone, the sole and sufficient mediation between God and man, which can be legitimately recognised by the Christian Church.   Surely the statements which are so fervently and frequently made regarding the Christian's constant and complete dependence on Christ, cannot be regarded as equally applicable to Christ in His relation to God. Just because our relation to God is mediated by Christ, Christ's relation to God cannot be regarded as subject to the same conditions and limitations as ours is.   "The ban of mysticism" has no application to Christ at all ; for the Ritschlians affirm so unique a relation of Christ to God, that every Christian is altogether and always dependent on Him.

V

Herrmann is included by Professor Orr in the same condemnation as Ritschl ; he is even described as having "specially taken up and developed this side of Ritschl's teaching."   What justification do Herrmann's statements afford for the charge against the Ritschlian position which we are now examining ?   "We are agreed," he says, "in this, that the inner life of religion in the last resort is something secret and incommunicable.   Every man to whom religion is more than a store of knowledge or a burden of commandments, does, in fact, experience at times an excitement of feeling, in which he can first appropriate for himself the result of all that has meaning for religion.   This possession by God is of such a kind that he must find his God in it, who makes himself felt by him, and translates him into that inward state which makes him blessed." [1]   This is a feature common to all religion ; but this is not mysticism the distinctive feature of which is thus described.   " When the working of God in the soul is sought and found exclusively in an inner experience of the individual ; when an excitement of feeling is taken without further question as a proof of God's possession of the soul ; when nothing external is at the same time grasped and held with clear consciousness ; when no thoughts which elevate the spiritual life are produced by the positive contents of a contemplation which rules the soul,—then that is mystic piety." [2]   An individual internal communion with God without any definite intellectual content, without direct spiritual result, without any external historical mediation — that is mysticism.   One result of this is that " in the Highest, which it seeks to reach, it leaves Christ and His kingdom behind it."   This is inevitable and explicable when, as in Catholicism, " the historical in Christianity has been transformed into an unintelligible mystery."   Even   in Protestantism this tendency must continue so long as " the historical in Christianity is preserved by us as something unintelligible in the form of the slightly modified Catholic dogma." But as the evangelical conception of Christ is made distinct, there will be no desire to press to God beyond Christ, for the Christian will " find nothing else in God Himself than Christ," for he " has in the personal life of Jesus a positive view of God." [3]   Now this personal life of Jesus belongs to the historical reality to which the Christian himself belongs ; and therefore in it alone does God really reveal Himself. Any other revelation, such as the mystic claims in his individual internal experience, can offer no conclusive

---

[1] Herrmann's *Verkehr des Christen mit Gott*, p. 13 (" The Communion of the Christian with God," p. 17).

[2] *Op. cit.* Ger. pp. 15, 16 ; Eng. p. 19.

[3] *Op. cit.* Ger. pp. 16, 17, 18, 23, 24 ; Eng. pp. 19, 21, 22, 26, 28.

evidence of its reality.   The evangelical Protestant position
is this : " Our certainty of God has its roots in the fact that
in the historical sphere, to which we ourselves belong, we
meet the man Jesus as an undoubted reality.   Inasmuch as
Jesus lifts us to communion with God, He becomes the
Christ to us.   The confession that Jesus is the Christ is
the true Christian confession.   But, rightly understood, it
means nothing else than this, that we through the man
Jesus are first lifted up to a real communion with God." [1]
It is Christ Himself, and not the tradition about Him, that
is part of our present reality.   While mediated by that
tradition, Jesus Himself presents Himself to us " as the free
revelation of the Living to the living."   He Himself
" becomes for us, while His inner life is unveiled for us, a
real power, which we experience as the best content of our
own existence." [2]   These words have no meaning at all if
they do not mean that God in Christ Himself is present
and active in our religious experience.   It is said, however,
by critics that all that Herrmann means is that we have a
present remembrance of the historical life of Christ which
belongs to the past, but not a present experience of the
living Christ Himself who is with us now ; that His teaching
dissevered from His person exercises on us a posthumous
influence, but that there is no present continuous activity
of Christ.   Herrmann himself notices such criticism, and
describes it as " the very contrary of what he seeks to
prove," adding, " I myself should feel myself only as an
opponent of a theology which taught what is ascribed to
me." [3]   The late Professor Candlish, who could not possibly
be charged with any bias towards Ritschlianism, well states
what seems to the writer to be the truth of the matter.
" Great stress," he says, ' is laid in this work on the asser-

[1] *Op. cit.* Ger. p. 47 ; Eng. p. 52.
[2] *Op. cit.* Ger. p. 59 ; Eng. p. 62.
[3] *Op. cit.* Ger. p. 82, note (Eng. trans. p. 84, omits this part of the note).

tion that it is through a historical fact that God communes with us ; and at some points the suspicion is apt to arise that he means merely that in an event of the past we get a conviction of God's Presence without recognising Christ as present to us now. But ere long we find that that would be a very unjust suspicion, and misrepresent the author's meaning. He expressly teaches that the inner life of Jesus is now present before our souls, and that God works on us by the spiritual power of Jesus. While, therefore, he contemplates almost exclusively the earthly life of Jesus, he avoids the fatal error of a merely humanitarian view, that of making our Saviour a mere departed man. He believes that He is living now, able to help and bless us. Only, he insists that we should always look at Him through His earthly life because as to His present activity we have only general statements, and those actions of His that reveal His character and will all belong to His life on earth. It is perhaps an excessive dread of an unreal mysticism that prompts to so strong an assertion of our communion with God being through a historical fact ; but the position seems on the whole a sound one, and favourable to a due appreciation of the value of the gospel records. He has some very true and beautiful remarks on the difference of true love to the real Jesus, and an emotional sentiment." [1] It must be reserved for a subsequent discussion to deal with the Ritschlian doctrine of the action of the Holy Spirit, which is condemned in Professor Orr's criticism of the Ritschlian antagonism to mysticism ; but meanwhile it may be hoped that enough has been said to justify Ritschl and Herrmann against the charge that the vital interests of Christian piety are endangered by the condemnation which they pronounce on, and the opposition they offer to, religious mysticism.

[1] *Critical Review*, vi. pp. 123, 124.

VI

Kaftan, with Ritschl and Herrmann, condemns mysticism in the two types which they describe, both as an attempt to secure union with God conceived as the Absolute, and as an endeavour to be joined through the imagination and the affections to Christ in His glorified state. But in his antagonism to mysticism he is not led, as Ritschl is, to deny that there is in Christian experience a mystical element, a real communion of the soul with Christ, which cannot be fully expressed in any psychological analysis of the religious consciousness. As we have already seen, Herrmann too acknowledges that "the inner life of religion is in the last resort something secret and incommunicable." Kaftan, however, goes beyond Herrmann even in not only acknowledging an element of truth in mysticism, but in also using the term mystical to express an essential feature of the Christian experience. He justifies his use of the term, in opposition to Ritschl and Herrmann, in words worth quoting. "The word 'mystical' has for a long time been recognised among us in a less definite signification, and, so far as I know, there has not been hitherto any dispute as to how it was meant. The innovation lies on the side of those who contend against this usage, not of those who accept it, and the confusion would be soon set aside if one simply allowed the recognised usage." [1] What he understands by the term "mystical" will clearly appear, if we consider his conception of the kingdom of God. "The highest good of Christianity," he says, "is the kingdom of God *above the world*. What that means can only be recognised if at the same time the moral ideal of the kingdom of God *in the world* is kept in view." In other words, the

---

[1] Kaftan's *Das Wesen der christlichen Religion*, p. 263, note ("The Essence of the Christian Religion").

kingdom of God is a hope to be fulfilled beyond this world, and a duty to be done in this world, and the fulfilling of the hope is dependent on the doing of the duty. " *To this religion,*" he continues, " *there is accordingly equally essential a mystical side, turned away from the world, and an ethical side turned towards the world. The former* is the life of the soul hidden with Christ in God, a blessedness which lifts above the world ; *the latter* is the moral activity for the realisation of the kingdom of God in ourselves and others, a system of duties which fetter us to the world." [1] While he calls attention to the fact that neither in the Synoptists nor in John does Jesus give His disciples any " *instruction regarding mystical contemplation,*" yet he states regarding the disciples after the Ascension that " *the preaching of the kingdom became in their mouths a proclamation of the risen and transfigured Jesus* " ; and, regarding Paul, " *one can exactly say that the glorified Christ here fills the place which in the teaching of Jesus the kingdom of God above the world holds, which has appeared in His person, and which through faith in Him is accessible to the possession of His disciples.*" [2] This he does not regard, as Harnack does (see page 116), as a wrong direction given to Christian faith even in the apostolic age ; but considers that only by combining the evangelical testimony and the apostolic interpretation can we get a complete view of " the highest good of the Christian religion." Even as " *the exalted Christ is the highest good of the Christian faith,*" so " in participation in His glorified life the blessedness of Christians consists." But Kaftan is just as distinct and emphatic as Ritschl or Herrmann in asserting the value of the historical Jesus. " The predicate of *the revelation* of God in the sense of making known attaches to the *historical* activity of Jesus, as it closes with the appearance of the Risen One among His disciples ; the predicate of *the highest good,* on the contrary, attaches per-

[1] *Op. cit.* pp. 262, 263.   [2] *Op. cit.* pp. 242, 262, 251, 253.

manently for the community to the *glorified* Christ.   And
that claims attention.   No man has a right to make bold
to receive through the exalted Christ new revelations, which
should complete or ever transcend what has been given in
the historical Jesus.   And just as little can or dare the
Christian artfully put himself into the position of the
disciples of Jesus during His earthly course ; but he who
would do this, would with such intimacy sin against the
heavenly Head of the community." [1]   In this statement it
is clearly and firmly asserted that the Christian now enjoys,
as his highest blessing communion with the living Christ ;
that the historical Jesus alone, however, is the revelation of
God to man ; that, consequently, no man has a right to
claim that he has received new revelations from the living
Christ other than those given in the historical Jesus ; and
that as a further consequence the exaltation of the living
Christ forbids such familiarity of intercourse with Him as
the disciples enjoyed in the earthly life, or as many of the
mystics strove to indulge in.   Accordingly Kaftan seems to
the writer to grant all the legitimate demands of Christian
experience, and in so far to correct Ritschl, where correction
is necessary, while at the same time guarding against the
exaggerations and extravagances that Christian pietism has
sometimes fallen into, and in this respect agreeing with
Ritschl where his criticism is just.   If such criticism of
pietism is necessary in Germany, there can be very little
doubt that it is as much, if not more, needed in Britain.
There is a great deal said and written about " fellowship with
the living Christ," which very much needs intelligible
explanation and judicious examination.   Individual vagaries
and eccentricities of creed and conduct take shelter under
cover of communications from the living Christ.   Some of
the methods for the deepening of the spiritual life, which
find a confident and even censorious advocacy among us,

[1] *Op. cit.* pp. 334, 336.

would scarcely stand the test, if tried by the standard given in the historical revelation in Christ. Even in the "Keswick" movement, however valuable has been its persistent testimony to the need of holiness, and of the Spirit's presence and power in the Christian life, there is sometimes seen a mysticism of the illegitimate type, which challenges censure. The Ritschlian antagonism to mysticism for these reasons deserves careful attention from religious thinkers and leaders of our own land, as, although not free altogether from defects, it does bring to view dangers in common tendencies of pietism which are often overlooked, and suggests considerations which very much need to be emphasised.

B.—CONSTRUCTIVE

CHAPTER VI

THE VALUE-JUDGMENTS OF RELIGION

I

THE critical enterprise of Ritschlianism is but a preparation for its constructive endeavour. It takes away much
that has hitherto been thought significant for Christian
thought and life, only that it may offer what it deems to
be very much more valuable. It rejects metaphysics from
theology, speculative theism, ecclesiastical dogma, religious
mysticism, not merely as helps so slight in themselves as
not worth keeping, but altogether as hindrances so great that
they must by all means be set aside. There is a better
method in theology than that in which an alliance with
metaphysics finds recognition ; there is a truer idea of God
than can be reached by any of the proofs which speculative
theism can offer ; there is a more faithful expression of the
contents of the Christian faith than has been given in
ecclesiastical dogma ; there is a worthier type of piety
than that which is presented in religious mysticism. On
the principle that the good is the enemy of the better is
the polemic against the traditional theology, the prominent
features of which we have been considering, carried on with
so much zeal and labour. How far the polemic is justi-

fied, this must depend on how great is the success of
Ritschlianism in offering us a new theology which will
take the place of the old.   But, on the other hand, acceptance of the new theology must involve rejection of the old.
The contrast, and even the contradiction, between the two
types as regards method, purpose, and results have been
stated so plainly and so strongly by the Ritschlian school,
that a policy of compromise, although it dignify itself with
the title of a mediating theology, or a theology of con-
ciliation, is entirely excluded.   The British people is
prone to congratulate itself on the fact that it is so
successful practically, because it is so inconsistent logically ;
the Ritschlian tendency does not claim any such excellence.   Its intention, if not always its execution, is
" thorough.'   The new patch will not be put on an old
garment, nor will the new wine be poured into old bottles.
Let us then be prepared for much that at first sight may
appear not only unfamiliar and new, but uncouth and
strange

II

(1) The starting-point of an inquiry into the character
and value of this " new " theology must be the view taken
of religion.   " In all religion," says Ritschl, " the endeavour
is made, with the help of the exalted spiritual power which
man adores, to solve the contradiction in which man finds
himself as a part of the natural world, and as a spiritual
personality, which makes the claim to rule nature." [1]   In
another place his definition is: " All religion is interpretation of the course of the world, in whatever compass it is
recognised, in the sense that the exalted spiritual powers
(or the spiritual power), which rule in or over it, maintain
or confirm for the personal spirit its claims or its inde-

[1] Ritschl's *Rechtfertigung und Versöhnung*, iii. p. 189 (" Justification
and Reconciliation ").

pendence against limitation by nature or the natural
operations of human society."[1] As these definitions appear
at first sight to bring the intellectual factor in religion into
undue prominence, it is necessary to add two sentences
which indicate its coexistence with and subordination to
other elements. Ritschl says that "it can be easily shown
regarding all other religions, that the knowledge of the
world, which is made use of in them, is constituted not
theoretically without interest, but according to practical
objects"; and that "the historical religions lay claim to
all the spiritual functions, knowledge for the doctrinal
tradition, that is, for the special view of the world, willing
for the common cultus, feeling for the change of satisfaction,
or dissatisfaction, in which moods the religious life is distinguished from ordinary relations." Only one other trait
needs to be added to this description; and it is that "the
historical religions are always a social concern, belonging
to a number of men."[2]

(2) In what way are we to regard this description?
Is it an attempt to describe what is the common element
in all religions, or is it intended to be the universal ideal
to which all religions tend? It is, on the one hand, not
merely the first, for Ritschl himself tells us that "for this
purpose it is not indefinite enough," and "language does
not offer a sufficiently indefinite or neutral expression to
convey the desired general idea of religion." Nor is it, on
the other hand, altogether the second; for while, on one
hand, "the religions are related to one another not only
as kinds, but at the same time as stages," so that "the
expression of the chief features in the religions is always
richer and more definite, their connection closer, their aims
more worthy of man"; and while "we as Christians
determine the successive stages of the religions in this
way, that all are transcended in Christianity, and that in

[1] *Op. cit.* p. 17.   [2] *Op. cit.* pp. 186, 188, 189.

it the tendency of all others comes to a perfect result ";[1] yet, on the other hand, this description is not intended as a standard by which Christianity may be measured, for it falls short of what Christianity actually is, and Christianity gives the ideal as a reality. The common element in religion is in many religions in so indefinite a form that it cannot be even understood there, unless as interpreted by the more definite form assumed in other religions. In any description there must, therefore be intelligible interpretation. But this must not, on the other hand, go as far as an ideal presentation of religion, for that would be to ignore the great difference there is between the one religion in which this ideal is realised, and all the others in which it can be discerned only as an imperfect tendency. To Christianity we must turn to discover what religion in its ideal is. "Christianity," says Ritschl, "is the monotheistic, completely spiritual, and ethical religion, which, on the basis of the life of its author as Redeemer and as Founder of the Kingdom of God, consists in the freedom of the children of God, includes the impulse to conduct from the motive of love, the intention of which is the moral organisation of mankind, and in the filial relation to God as well as the Kingdom of God lays the foundation of blessednesss."[2]

(3) Herrmann is thoroughly in agreement with Ritschl, but he renders an undoubted service in laying greater stress than Ritschl does on the fact that the human personality which finds itself in contradiction with nature, and seeks in religion to escape that contradiction, is determined in its desire and effort by a moral law, recognised as of absolute authority and universal validity. "Every religious view of the world," he says, "is an answer to the question : how must the world be judged if the highest good is to become real? With his hopes and strivings the personal human spirit finds himself in an unceasing conflict with nature.

[1] *Op. cit.* pp. 185–187.   [2] *Op. cit.* pp. 13, 14.

His dependence thereon inevitably forces itself upon him, but just as strongly the conviction that this relation does not in any way mean for him the regular furtherance of his good (*Gueter*). The removal of this contradiction man seeks in his religion, which, while it puts the natural world, either partially or totally, into a position of dependence on a deity favourable to us, in the same measure causes that hostile contradiction against us to disappear. Against the appearance that what his heart clings to will go down in the course of nature, the religious man affirms that the whole of his good is hidden in the hand of his God. Everywhere, where real religion exists, there will be no denial of this its fundamental feature. Clearest of all this comes to the front in Christianity, which completely removes that contradiction of the personal spirit and nature, in that it combines the completely supramundane character of the highest good with the thought of the Almighty God as Father."[1] On this important matter, although not on all others, Herrmann is a true disciple of Ritschl.

III

(1) Kaftan differs both from Ritschl and Herrmann. It is important to notice that, under the heading of "A Critical Statement" (*Kritisches*), he devotes a number of pages of his book on *The Essence of the Christian Religion* to a discussion of their views, in order to express his dissent from them. His criticisms are well worthy of mention. (1) "First and before all," he says, "it is wrong to speak of a contrast or a contradiction in the position of man in the world, which on emerging in experience becomes the motive of religion," for (2) "the consciousness of a specific dignity in man is altogether lacking in some subordinate

[1] Herrmann's *Die Metaphysik in der Theologie*, p. 8 ("Metaphysics in Theology").

stages of religion"; and (*b*) "if they were right, then religion
—so to express it, the actually religious in religion—would
consist in a new relation to the world," and "who will set
that forth as the distinctive content of religion?" and
(*c*) "the core of Christianity is *the life of the soul hidden with
Christ in God*, and the relation to the world an aspect, a
further determination of this life in God." (2) Secondly,
in these formulæ "the reference to theoretical knowledge
plays too great a part." "But this does not correspond
with the real fact of the historical religions," for "they are
concerned about life and not about knowledge—about
knowledge only in so far as it is a means of life, or itself as
a good is reckoned as a part of life." (3) "Thirdly and
lastly, I have to object that the ideas employed in these
formulæ do not correspond to the fact," for "the conception of a spiritual sense of self appears to me too
ambiguous to allow me to think Ritschl's and Herrmann's
use of it correct." This third objection leads Kaftan to
notice a difference in method between him and Ritschl.
While Ritschl has, on the one hand, objected to Kaftan's
description, which aims, as we shall see, at defining the
common element of all religions, "that so conceived it is
too universally and indefinitely described"; and has, on
the other hand, "defined as the right method, to start from
the knowledge of Christianity as the perfect religion, and
to draw the other religions into comparison in such a
way that one perceives in them imperfect attempts to
secure that which Christianity alone really secures," Kaftan
holds that his is the scientific method, as its validity does
not depend on personal conviction, and that it serves "to
bring to expression an essential and distinctive peculiarity
of religion."[1]

(2) "*Regarding piety*," says Kaftan, "*we say in attaching*

[1] Kaftan's *Das Wesen der christlichen Religion*, pp. 83-94 ("The
Essence of the Christian Religion").

*ourselves to Schleiermacher, that before all else it is ex-
perienced in peculiar emotions, that it has therein its core and
centre."* " It is true that there is no piety without representations and theoretical judgments, but only on account of
the practical feelings combined with them do these representations and judgments belong to piety "; and " to every
form of piety some kind of action belongs," but " pious
feeling is the soul of piety." [1] But what does Kaftan mean
by feeling? He holds, as a result of psychological
analysis, that it is correct " to reduce the number of the
fundamental elements which are to be assumed to two.
These may be provisionally called Representations and
Feeling "; and " their difference is this : *representation is a
picture of another, in feeling we become conscious of ourselves
as living beings* "; or " first we grasp the world as it offers
itself to us, and next we take up a position to it as living
beings with the interest always active in us." [2] What interest
of ours as living beings does religion express ? " To put it
briefly," he says, " the concern of all religion is life, and not
—at once to name the contrary—perfect life goods or a
highest good, and not ethical ideals." [3] It is this that
distinguishes religion from morality. But what distinguishes
it from the other desires of life ? " Need," he says, " always
becomes the special motive of religion, but not need alone,
but even also the universal feeling which in need is most
bitterly experienced, *the feeling of man regarding the
insecurity of his life and of the goods which he values highly*,
the consciousness drawn from experience of the limits of
his own capacity to secure this life and these goods." The
distinctive religious impulse in man accordingly is this,
" *that he finds no desirable satisfaction in his earthly
enjoyment of life in the goods which the world offers him.*" [4]
The religions of the world may be distinguished from one

[1] *Op. cit.* pp. 29, 30.   [2] *Op. cit.* pp. 39-41.
[3] *Op. cit.* p. 52.   [4] *Op. cit.* pp. 65, 70.

another in two respects. (1) "*Either it is the manifold goods of the world, the maintenance and the increase of which is sought in religion, or it is a highest supramundane good, in the enjoyment of which with the resignation of all other goods blessedness is found.*" (2) The other difference is, "*whether in any religion the possession and enjoyment of natural or moral goods is chiefly striven for.*" [1] The religion that combines a supreme desire for a supramundane good with the dominant pursuit of moral goods is to be regarded as the highest ; and Christianity does this. "It teaches us to seek and find our highest good in the *supramundane* Kingdom of God, it gives us in our participation by means of faith in this Kingdom the blessedness of eternal life, a blessedness which cannot be enjoyed without a zealous striving for the mundane realisation of the Kingdom of God." [2]

IV

(1) Such are the views of Ritschl, Herrmann, and Kaftan. The criticism of Ritschl and Herrmann by Kaftan must be regarded as valid. (*a*) The consciousness of a contradiction between personality and nature is one possible only in our own age, when human thought has reached an advanced stage as regards both the idea of personality and the idea of nature. To ascribe such a consciousness to all religions is an anachronism. (*β*) If Ritschl and Herrmann were

[1] *Op. cit.* p. 77. Natural goods are life, health, wealth, pleasure, power, fame. "Moral good are such goods, as the correlate of which certain duties are known to us," such as family and state.

[2] *Op. cit.* p. 81. The German term *ueberweltlich* literally means overworldly, but as English is losing its power to form such compounds, the term supramundane has necessarily been used instead ; it would be more correct to render the contrasted term *innerweltlich* by intramundane, but the simpler term mundane will convey the meaning with sufficient accuracy. The meaning of the German terms *ueberweltlich* and *innerweltlich* very nearly, if not quite, corresponds with the sense of the English terms supernatural and natural.

interpreting to us the ideal religion, this charge would not be justified, but another would take its place. We might justly maintain that the ideal was altogether inadequate, first as regards the prominence given to man's relation to the world, and secondly as regards the subordinate and secondary character assigned to the relation to God. God cannot be conceived as a means towards man's ends, as making man's ends His own ; but man must be conceived as a means towards God's ends, but not as merely a means, but as a means in such sense that he fulfils his own ends in realising God's. The world cannot be conceived as having a more immediate relation to man than God, so that man can be thought as falling back on his relation to God when he fails to find satisfaction in the world. The conception is altogether too subjective and utilitarian. In their desire to deliver the idea of religion from the exaggerated intellectualism assigned to it by the Hegelian school, Ritschl and Herrmann have gone to the opposite extreme of an inadequate practicality. (γ) These two objections might be set aside on the ground that this description is not intended to be a general definition, or an ideal presentation of religion, but something more definite than the former and less developed than the latter ; but even from this standpoint it must be urged, that the element in religion on which stress is laid has too little in common with the universal characteristics of religion, and does not faithfully represent the tendency which in the ideal religion finds its perfect result. In their definition of Christianity both are led by the evidence of history to a more adequate conception, and yet both are compelled by their view of religion to give, as we shall see more clearly afterwards (chap. viii.), an undue prominence to the idea of the Kingdom of God. To this narrowness of outlook may we not also ascribe the unsympathetic attitude which is assumed towards all other religions except Christianity ?

(δ) While Herrmann more emphatically than Ritschl lays stress on the ethical content of the personality which finds nature a hindrance to its self-realisation ; yet in assigning to morality an *à priori* origin, while for religion he seems to claim only an empirical derivation, he subordinates religion to morality, and so does not reach a satisfactory conception of their relation. Religion must be regarded as just as essential and original an element in man as morality ; and morality must be viewed as the expression in social human relations of a necessary relation of finite to infinite personality, to which religion gives a still more definite and adequate expression.

(2) As regards Kaftan's own view of religion, it cannot command an unqualified assent. In the first place, his method seems to be too empirical ; the religious impulse finds too indefinite and imperfect an expression in most religions to allow us by a consideration of what is common to them all to get any definite idea of religion. Ritschl is so far right that we must interpret the imperfect stages by the perfect result. But secondly, the mere desire for, or dissatisfaction with, life is not a sufficient motive of religion ; nor even is the recognition that the world cannot yield permanent or adequate satisfaction. Is not man's failure to find in the world what he seeks a proof rather of a real though latent consciousness of relationship to a God beyond and above the world ? A result of man's destination for religion is mistakenly regarded as the cause of his capacity for it. While stress is rightly laid on the practical rather than the theoretical character of religion, yet it seems a mistake to isolate one element of man's consciousness as of primary importance. Even if feeling be used as the appropriate term for man's reaction on his environment, it must be maintained that undue prominence is given to the influence of environment in religion. The complete separation of religion and morality is a further proof that religion

has not been conceived in its essential nature as the bond that, binding each man to God, binds all men to one another.

(3) The Ritschlian account of religion might be generally described as a pathology and not a biology. Religion is not a function of man's health as a spiritual personality, but rather a remedy for his disease. Without denying that the view is seasonable, as it proposes religion as a relief from a burden that weighs on many modern minds, it must still be held that a temporary phase of religious thought and life distinctive of a small class should not be described as though it were the permanent and universal character of religion. In very many cases it may be true that religion begins with a sense of need and an assurance of relief, but it does not and should not end there. As soon as the consciousness of satisfaction of desire and dominion over the world in God is reached, the centre at once, so to speak, shifts from man, who seeks satisfaction and dominion, to God in whom that satisfaction and dominion are found. Then religion becomes conscious dependence on, voluntary submission to, and blessed communion with God. God ceases to be in the religious consciousness a means for man's ends, and Himself becomes the absolute end, in which man's finite ends are fulfilled. Yet, on the other hand, it must be admitted that the religion of many men has its centre in self and not in God. The passage from the higher to the lower stage is very clearly and simply expressed in Francis Xavier's hymn—

> "My God, I love thee, not because
>   I hope for heaven thereby,
> Nor because they who love Thee not
>   Are lost eternally.
>
> Not with the hope of gaining aught,
>   Not seeking a reward,
> But as Thyself hast loved me,
>   O ever-loving Lord.

E'en so I love Thee, and will love,
    And in Thy praise will sing,
Solely because Thou art my God
    And my eternal King."

If, however, this be the last stage of religious development, then, on the principle that what is last in execution
is first in intention, we may contend that man's religious
disposition has this relation to God as its end and aim,
and whatever other phases it may assume must be
regarded as provisional and temporary, and this alone as
essential and final. The Ritschlian view of religion
accordingly stops at one of the lower stages, instead of
pressing on to the highest development of religion in man ;
and accordingly it must be pronounced defective and
inadequate. As we shall afterwards see, other faults and
failures in the Ritschlian theology can be directly traced to
its view of religion.

V

(1) Such is the Ritschlian view of religion, in which
great prominence is given to knowledge, not because the
other factors in religion, feeling and willing, are ignored,
but because theology as the intellectual exponent of
religion must necessarily give special consideration to this
factor. Religion implies knowledge, a view of the world in
relation to man on the one hand, and to God on the other.
This knowledge all the Ritschlians are agreed has a distinctive character of its own. It consists of value-judgments. As was shown in the third chapter (see p. 73),
Ritschl at first sought the distinction between religious
and philosophical or scientific knowledge in a difference of
object, the former dealing with the world as a whole,
the latter with the world in its parts ; but he afterwards
found the difference in the intellectual functions of the
subject. " Now," he says, " to seek the difference in the

sphere of the subject, I recall the double way in which the
spirit further appropriates the sensations excited in it.
These are determined in the feelings of pleasure and pain,
according to their value for the ego.   On the other hand,
the sensation is in the representation judged in respect
of its cause, of what kind it is, or what is its relations to
other causes." The former function of the subject yields
value-judgments (*Werthurtheile*), the latter theoretical judgments; in the one case the object is regarded solely as it
affects the subject, in the other as it exists in its own
nature and relations.   But one cannot altogether separate
feeling from representation, or representation from feeling.
Even in theoretical judgments there is an accompanying
feeling of interest in knowledge as such.   "Accordingly
one must distinguish between *accompanying* and *independent*
value-judgments."   The former are found even in science,
for the man of science delights in the observation of
phenomena and the induction of laws.   "But independent
value-judgments are all *knowledges* (*Erkenntnisse*) of
moral purposes, or hindrances to such purposes (*Zweck-
widrigkeiten*), in so far as they excite moral pleasure or
pain, especially as they set the will in motion to appropriate
goods, or to protect itself against what is hostile."   When
an action is judged good or bad, a person praiseworthy or
blameworthy, this is an independent value-judgment; this
however, is in the moral sphere, and the range of value-
judgments is still wider.   "Another class of independent
judgments of value is formed by religious knowledge.
This, namely, cannot be derived from the conditions of the
knowledge of the moral will, as there is religion which
actually exists without reference to the moral order of
life."   As there is a distinction between morality and
religion, and as in human history the two are not always
found in alliance, nay even are sometimes found in
antagonism, the value-judgments of religion must have

another content than the value-judgments of morality. "Religious knowledge moves in independent value-judgments, which refer to the position of man in regard to the world, and excite feelings of pleasure or pain, in which he either enjoys his dominion over the world accomplished by God's help, or grievously lacks the help of God for that end."[1] Whatever proposition either affirms or contradicts man's faith in God's help over against the world is a religious value-judgment. Such is Ritschl's account.

(2) We may now turn to Herrmann. "The interest of religion," he says, "does not attach itself to the representation of the actually given existence of the world as a connected intelligible unity," but "rather the concern of religion is to regard the multiplicity of the world as the orderly whole of means, by which the highest value of the pious man, which is expressed in feeling, is realised." In religion man "makes himself with his purposes the standard" of judgment, and so in religion "there is involved a value-judgment in which man is compared with the nature surrounding him, and the latter is defined as the means for the former as the valuable end." Objects are not regarded in their relation to one another, but solely in their relation to man, who has "a sense of his own dignity," and accordingly makes himself "the centre round which the world closes as a circle." But inasmuch as man knows himself to have an absolute value as the subject of an unconditional moral law, this judgment of objects in their relation to himself is not an arbitrary or fictitious process, but expresses the conviction that "the inmost essence of the world is in harmony with his own demand for self-preservation," and so the determination of objects as means to himself as an end does correspond with the

[1] Ritschl's *Rechtfertigung und Versöhgung*, iii. pp. 194, 195 ("Justification and Reconciliation").

essential purpose of these objects.   Here Herrmann
indicates, as Ritschl does not, an objective basis for the
value-judgments, which otherwise might appear to rest on
a merely subjective foundation.   To put the subject in
another way, the theoretical judgments are concerned with
causes, the value-judgments with purposes.   Accordingly,
the former relate each object to its conditions in the
world-whole, the latter relate it to the ends which man sets
before himself; the former answer the question how, the
latter the question why; the former end in a metaphysic,
the latter in a theology.   "When I seek to represent a
world-whole," says Herrmann, "because I wish to comprehend the multiplicity of things in a never-failing context
of law, then I go in the way of metaphysics.   When I
seek to represent a world-whole, because I do not wish to
lose myself as a person conscious of my highest good in
the multiplicity of things, then I receive the impulse to
religious faith.   Whether the world-whole sketched for
this purpose is regarded as theistic, pantheistic, or
materialistic, does not alter its universal religious character.   Religion remains the conviction of such a world-
whole in all these forms."   Of course, Herrmann does not
mean that it is a matter of indifference what form this
representation of the world-whole from the religious standpoint assumes ; all he means is that a religious as well as a
scientific impulse may lead to any of these theories.   While
no religion can be indifferent to the view of the world-whole
which belongs to it, it may be altogether indifferent to any
metaphysical theory, for "that unity of the world, which
has only a religious interest, is altogether indifferent to the
order established by the scientific explanation of the
world"; [1] and "it is a matter of indifference to us as

[1] Herrmann's *Die Religion im Verhätlniss zum Wetterkennen und
zur Sittlichkeit*, pp. 80–82, 85. 36 (" Religion in Relation to our Knowledge of the World and to Morality").

theologians whether philosophy is deistic, pantheistic, or theistic, or anything else." [1]   This does not mean, however, that the mind may or must entertain two contradictory theories of the world-whole on the conclusion of metaphysics, the other the conviction of religion ; for on closer investigation it is discovered that along the path of theoretical judgments no valid conclusion regarding the world-whole, such as metaphysics assumes, can be reached while the valuable conviction of religion alone holds the field.   "Only on the highest stage of religion is this demand with which the dogmatic metaphysic seeks to comply satisfied by a religious judgment.   And, in fact, this satisfaction takes place in such a way that not only the occasion for the mixture of dogmatic metaphysics with religion is removed, but that even the former straightway appears as an altogether vain sport of fancy, which can assert a higher value only for the crowd which is irreligious or does not understand the significance of religion." [2]   The investigation of causes can never lead to the discovery of the secret of the universe, but the interpretation of purposes may.   The theoretical judgments cannot give an intelligible unity to the world-whole, but the value-judgments can.   Herrmann does not leave us in the end with an unreconciled dualism in knowledge, but with a subordination of theoretical to value-judgments. ✓

(3) From Herrmann we now pass to Kaftan, who states, that "*all our simple judgments are of a double kind. Either they express a state of fact which we represent, or they express a relation which we as human beings assume to the represented*   *The theoretical judgments express a fact ; the value-judgments give expression to our attitude to the same.* A more accurate consideration shows at once that the

---

[1] Herrmann's *Die Metaphysik in der Theologie*, p. 21 (" Metaphysics in Theology ").

[2] Herrmann's *Die Religion*, u.s.w., p. 85 note (" Religion," etc.).

theoretical propositions of religious faith are of another kind than the usual theoretical judgments. They are distinguished from these just in this, that they are the result not of an objective comprehension of the events and changes in the world, and just as little of an intelligent manipulation of the judgments so gained, but rather that value-judgments are their basis." [1] This last sentence expresses an important difference between Kaftan and Ritschl. Ritschl holds that "religious knowledge is constituted by value-judgments." [2] Kaftan, on the contrary, asserts, to put the distinction as briefly as possible, that religious knowledge consists of theoretical propositions which are based on value-judgments. "Nowhere have I affirmed," he says, "that the religious judgments *are* value-judgments, but I hold this expression itself at least open to misunderstanding; nay, value-judgments are their basis, but they themselves *are* theoretical propositions, are this so essentially that even the judging of the worth of the world in connection with religious faith, while it is attached to the thought of God, is constituted by theoretical propositions of objective validity, which are derived or demonstrated from the conception of God." [3] At the same time, however, he strictly maintains the distinction between the theoretical propositions, based on value-judgments, which are characteristic of religion, and the theoretical judgments of science or philosophy. "They historically arise in another way, the

---

[1] Kaftan's *Das Wesen der christlichen Religion*, pp. 42, 45, 46 ("The Essence of the Christian Religion").

[2] Ritschl's *Rechtfertigung und Versöhnung*, iii. p. 201 ("Justification and Reconciliation").

[3] Kaftan's *op. cit.* p. 49. Attention may be called to the German terms used in this passage. "Value-judgments" is a translation of *Werthurtheile*; "theoretical propositions," of *theoretische Sätze*; "judging of the worth," of *Werthbeurtheilung*; "theoretical judgments," of *theoretische Urtheile*. As *Werthurtheile* is so distinctly a technical term in the Ritschlian school, it seems desirable to render it as literally as possible "value-judgments" rather than "judgments of value."

conviction of their truth is otherwise founded subjectively, objectively too they have another measure of truth. And when we investigate this their peculiarity, then we find it based on this, that they are not the result of observation of facts and reflection on them, but have as their foundation value-judgments."[1] Without anticipating the fuller discussion which will follow, it may be remarked that the difference seems to be this. According to Ritschl, religious knowledge never gets beyond the consciousness of its subjective certainty, whereas according to Kaftan it may attain a consciousness of objective validity, although reached only by subjective evidence; or to adopt a traditional distinction, according to Ritschl πίστις remains πίστις to the end, while according to Kaftan πίστις may become γνῶσις, which, however, can never disown its beginning in πίστις. It is to be understood, of course, that as used above, the terms subjective and objective are not equivalent to imaginary and real respectively, but are intended to distinguish the knowledge in which we have a personal interest and that to which we are individually indifferent. Accordingly, in Ritschl's view our religious knowledge must always be accompanied by a more or less intense feeling of the relation that the objects of that knowledge bear to us as either helping or hindering the end of all religion. Knowledge must never advance further than this feeling can go. If there be aspects of an object of religious knowledge which excite an intellectual curiosity, but do not arouse a practical interest of this kind, these aspects lie beyond the range of the knowledge that can claim to be religious. In Kaftan's view it would seem, however, that while the starting-point must always be acknowledged in which this personal interest is present, yet the relation of the objects of knowledge to individual ends may fall altogether into the background, and what may be called

[1] *Op. cit.* p. 50.

the scientific impulse to know the objects, so to speak, for
their own sake, in their distinctive features and general
relations, may be allowed free play.   Herrmann, who speaks
of our positing "objects as real, exclusively on the ground
of their value," [1] appears to be nearer Kaftan than Ritschl.
Kaftan's view, however, has been strenuously contested by
Ritschl's son, who has dealt very fully with this subject in
a pamphlet *Concerning Value-Judgments*, which may now
claim our attention.

VI

(1) In this pamphlet Otto Ritschl first of all gives a
historical sketch, in which he traces the origin of this
conception to Luther, who "discovered the characteristic
feature of religious knowledge or faith in this, that the
objects of the Christian religion, which are to be known or
to be believed, necessarily are at the same time the objects
of an incomparable interest for the religious subject." [2]   He
confirms this statement by a quotation from Luther, which
deserves to be reproduced.   "It is not enough that a man
believes, that God is, that Christ has suffered, and such-
like; but he must steadfastly believe, that God is his God
for his blessedness, that Christ suffered for him, died, was
crucified, rose again, that he bore his sins for him."   The
name "value-judgments," however, must be traced to
another source, even to Kant, who distinguished "relative
value, that is, a price," from "inner value, that is, worthiness"; and declares that "talent has a commercial price,
temperament an emotional price, character 'an inner
worth, and is raised above all price'": for "any man calls
agreeable what delights him; beautiful, what simply pleases
him; good, what is esteemed, approved, that is, in which

---

[1] O. Ritschl's *Ueber Werturtheile*, p. 12 ("Concerning Value-
Judgments").

[2] *Op. cit.* p. 1.   "Objects" is unavoidably used to render two
different German words, *Objecte* and *Gegenstände*.

he places an objective value." Although he coined the
term "taste-judgment," he did not use the term "value-
judgment," for the good reason that "moral judging, and
the good conduct determined by it, are for Kant not complicated, but thoroughly simple psychical processes," that
is, do not imply any feeling whatever.[1] Herbart distinguished "theoretical representations" from "æsthetic
judgments" "He called those representations theoretical,"
says O. Ritschl, "the subject of which is regarded as an
indifferent one; æsthetic, on the contrary, are, according to
his view, the judgments which, in virtue of a 'spontaneous
involuntary preference or rejection,' 'add the predicate of
preferableness or rejectableness to the subjects immediately
and spontaneously, that is, without proof, and without
partiality or repulsion.'" Herbart, according to O. Ritschl,
also declared that "religion makes an æsthetic impression in addition to the moral, and that is so essential to
it, that if it did not act at all æsthetically it could not
act at all morally. For behind the moral conceptions
there necessarily lie hidden, as the first fundamental presuppositions, æsthetic conceptions."[2] Kant's ideas about
the true worth and worthiness of man were familiar to
Schleiermacher; and he too laid great stress on the distinction, which has already met us in Kaftan's account of
value-judgments, between man's receptivity and activity; but
he made no use of these ideas in his theory of religion.
De Wette developed Kant's thoughts. "We recognise," he
said, "not only the existence of things, we also assign them
a value, and it is this assigning of value that drives us on to
action, inasmuch as the value becomes our purpose. This
judging of things according to value and purpose is of different

[1] *Op. cit.* pp. 2, 3.
[2] *Op. cit.* pp. 6, 7. The word rejectableness in one of the translations
must crave the indulgence of the reader as expressing more accurately
than any phrase could the sense of the German term.

kinds, and rises in stages or different feelings of pleasure
and impulses from the sensuous to the spiritual.   Only in
combination with the highest and purest feeling of value is
faith complete and perfect, and can be separated from it
only by an abstraction."   Although De Wette went beyond
Kant in combining feeling with " this assignment of value
by reason," and " formed the expressions feeling of value
and judging by value," yet he did not hit on " the term
value-judgment." [1]   Rothe was for a moment drawn into
this advancing current of thought when he acknowledged
that " we also know with our feeling, that the function of
feeling is also a knowledge," especially with regard to
" these things without the knowledge of which an existence
worthy of man is not at all possible." [2]   Lotze carried this
development a stage further.   " There is," he says, " no
value or valuelessness which could belong to a thing in
itself; both exist only in the form of pleasure and pain,
which a spirit, capable of feeling, experiences."   " In the
feeling for the value of things," so O. Ritschl continues
the exposition of Lotze's view, " reason possesses " (here
exposition passes into quotation) " ' a revelation as seriously
intended as it has in the fundamental propositions of
logical inquiry an indispensable instrument of experience.'
Accordingly, Lotze finally distinguishes the world of figures
or of forms from the world of values, which he once also
identifies with the world of ends." [3]   Although use of these
ideas, and even of the term " value-judgment," has been
made in more recent philosophical literature, yet it has not
generally affected theological thought.   Ritschl, in the first
edition of his great work, uses this point of view in two
ways,—with reference to " the distinctive value which the
Christian subject assigns to itself in its religious judgment
of self," and with regard to " the representations of the
divinity of Christ," which " have their religious character in

[1] *Op. cit.* pp. 8, 9.   [2] *Op. cit.* p. 9.   [3] *Op. cit.* p. 10.

this, 'that they define the value of Christ in the world-view introduced by Him, and for the self-judgment that attaches itself to this.'"[1]   In the third edition, as we have already seen, Ritschl expresses definitely the theory of value-judgments, but not he, but Herrmann, introduced the term into contemporary theology.   What O. Ritschl says about Herrmann's and Kaftan's views need not be reproduced, as the subject has already been dealt with, but it may be noted that he states that Scheibe, attaching himself to Kaftan, regards " the judgments of religious knowledge " as " postulates on the basis of value-judgments."[2]

(2) This historical sketch is followed by a psychological analysis of value-judgments, the main points of which are these. (a) The unity of the soul involves that none of its functions, thinking, feeling, or willing, is ever exercised in absolute isolation. (b) Most men are not called to, or fitted for a purely intellectual activity, to the exclusion, as far as possible, of feeling and will. (c) Children do not begin with theoretical judgments about the objects around them, but with judgments that express the pleasure or pain they experience with regard to these, that is, convey their value for them. (d) Familiarity with objects lessens our sensibility regarding them, and so what may be called customary judgments supersede the value-judgments. (e) Theoretical judgments are formed from these customary judgments by a further process of abstraction, which involves a considerable self-discipline in the exercise of the intellectual to the exclusion of all other functions. (f) The loss of sensibility is, however, compensated for by the gain in moral self-control; the change from value-judgments to theoretical judgments indicates not only that the mind is being taught, but also that the will is being trained.[3]

---

[1] *Op. cit.* pp. 10, 11.   [2] *Op. cit.* p. 12.

[3] *Op. cit.* pp. 13–18.   The German term translated " customary judgments " is *Gewohnheitsurtheile.*

(3) This psychological analysis leads to a closer consideration of the value-judgments of religious knowledge. O. Ritschl starts with Luther's statement that " whatever the heart clings and trusts to, that is really God," faith and God being inseparable correlates. He then shows that " no one directs his confidence to any object from the activity or method of operation of which he does not also anticipate a justification of his confidence"; and that " that confidence is by no means only the content of a theoretical judgment, but there is assigned to one's own intellectual capacity, on account of one's feelings, a definite value." To put it in other words, the expectation of help from God which faith cherishes gives to that faith a value for the person exercising it. " This value-judgment," he continues, " is now the actual foundation on which the further expression of confidence are raised to become knowledge and ability." [1] Whatever I know or whatever I can do as a religious subject depends ultimately on the value I attach to my faith as justifying the expectations of help from God which I cherish.

As in the psychological analysis it was shown that " the facility to form value-judgments is found " in the closest connection with the first and original susceptibility for new impressions," so now it must be noted that " such a susceptibility is, as is well known, an essential condition for the beginning of religion in any subject"; [2] for the words of Jesus regarding the children, " of such is the kingdom of heaven," indicate this, and it is also proved that a disproportionate development of the intellectual faculties lessens the capacity to receive religious impressions. Hence it may be concluded that value-judgments are the appropriate form of religious knowledge; for its basis must be faith, and its characteristic must be an accompanying emotion, a personal interest, and not an indifferent intellectualism.

[1] *Op. cit.* pp. 19, 20.   [2] *Op. cit.* pp. 20, 21.

(4) But the important question remains, Has "this knowledge gained by value-judgments any objectivity?" O. Ritschl condemns the distinction of value-judgments from existence-judgments. "To set in opposition to one another value-judgments and so-called 'existence-judgments,' and now to identify the theoretical judgments with the so-called 'existence-judgments,' as if the value-judgments expressed a non-existence, is a quite senseless misrepresentation of the mental process which really takes place"; for "all human beings regard as also genuine and real the objects they perceive, which they in fact first recognised in value-judgments," inasmuch as these objects meet all the practical tests of reality. Man will not and cannot cease to exercise religious faith, and to affirm in value-judgments the objects on which it is fixed. The progress of theoretical knowledge in science cannot disprove the reality of these objects, for "science as such is not at all competent to judge or to decide regarding the existence or non-existence of the supersensuous magnitudes of Christian faith"; and, on the other hand, "religious knowledge in Christianity is self-sufficient and independent of every legislation foreign to it. And for this reason also the reality which it assigns to the objects of its faith, is not to be controlled by the signs of actuality, by means of which things belonging to quite different realms of being are recognised as real or unreal." Christian faith does not need any theoretical evidence of the reality of its objects, for the Christian experience is always verifying and vitalising the evidence which is expressed in its judgments of value. Hence it is a mistake to separate, as Kaftan does, the content of religious knowledge, as expressed in theoretical propositions (see p. 177), from the evidence as given in the value-judgments; for these religious-judgments "are always a direct synthesis of faith with the object recognised by it and trustfully grasped, accordingly always synthetical

judgments." To put it in other words, personal conviction is not only a preliminary condition of religious knowledge, but its distinctive form. Hence this personal conviction can never be so transformed as to become universally valid evidence, intelligible to and authoritative for those who have not themselves this personal conviction. "The inference from the value to a reality of the object declared valuable could never compete in universal validity with the scientific objectivity." [1] But we can get a step further if we turn from the religious subject to "the values objectively given" in history.

(5) What, then, is the testimony of history? "Of all spiritual values it is just religion, or what in some individuals apparently is a substitute for it, which is that value which consciously or unconsciously is recognised by all men as the highest." But of all the religions, which can claim the supremacy? "It is that religion the objects of faith of which will of necessity prove themselves as the only genuine and real ones." "We Christians anticipate, if only provisionally for reasons of subjective validity, that highest standard of objectivity in our faith, in so far as this not only shows itself in the practice of life for every pious man as power and truth, but also teaches us to hope for the final victory of our religion." [2] It lies in the very nature of the Christian religion, which justifies its claim and verifies its truth only in experience and practice, that only an experimental and practical proof of the reality of the objects of its faith can be offered. There would be less demand for theoretical evidence of the truth of Christianity if the life of Christians exercised a more convincing power over others.

(6) One other misunderstanding O. Ritschl seeks to remove. "That finally the Christian view of the world and human science, which according to the previous ex-

[1] *Op. cit.* pp. 22, 24-27.   [2] *Op. cit.* pp. 31, 32.

positions are apparently to go alongside of one another, but not any more to interfere with one another, must just on that account form a double truth, that is a conclusion for which neither in the one nor in the other there exists a sufficient reason. The other religions and world-views, but not science, which confines itself to the provinces of nature and history which belong to it, are the rivals and opponents of Christianity." [1] Religion and science may be, on the contrary, mutually helpful,—religion to science in enforcing and encouraging the moral qualities which its pursuit demands, science to religion in supplying the Christian with a knowledge and a skill that enables him to discharge his moral task in the world. As science can neither confirm nor contradict the world-view which is distinctive of Christian faith, and as that world-view does not interfere with any conclusions of science, there is for the Christian only one truth.

VII

(1) So full an account of O. Ritschl's pamphlet has been given, as it answers many questions that may be asked about the value-judgments. It disproves, first of all, an objection that has been very generally brought against the Ritschlian position. Ritschl and his followers do not mean, as some of their critics suggest, to distinguish the value-judgments as less from the theoretical judgments as more certain. They do not hold that while science and philosophy are dealing in their theoretical judgments with objective reality, theology is dealing in its value-judgments with subjective illusion. It is not their intention to suggest that man by his thinking makes God and all other objects of Christian faith, because for his life he needs them. If we are to deal fairly with Ritschlianism, we must fully and frankly admit that its advocates are as con-

[1] *Op. cit.* p. 33.

vinced of the existence of the objects of Christian faith as
of the reality of physical phenomena.   The value-judgments are as true as the theoretical judgments ; as Kaftan
expressly says : " The truth of the propositions of faith
means nothing else, and can mean nothing else, than that
they are _objectively_ true." [1]   Yet this is what a critic thinks
himself justified in stating without any qualification.
" Though Jesus," says Professor Denney, expounding the
Ritschlian position, " has for the Christian consciousness
the religious value of God, He has for the scientific consciousness only the common real value of man.   He is, in
truth and reality, to the neutral consideration of science,
mere man like any other ; it is only the _Werthurtheil_,
the subjective estimate of the pious Christian, that gives
Him the value of God." [2]   Here is a double misconception.
In the first place, the Ritschlian would deny, and rightly,
that " the scientific consciousness " can affirm or deny anything as regards the divinity of Christ.   That truth lies in
a region which cannot even be reached by the methods
and with the instruments of science.   Sensuous perception
or observation, logical induction or deduction, are quite
useless here.   In the next place, the Ritschlians would
deny, and again rightly, that " the neutral consideration of
science " corresponds more closely with " truth and reality "
than " the subjective estimate of the pious Christian."
They do not respect science less than Dr. Denney, but
they recognise the limits of its province.   They respect
" the pious Christian " more than Dr. Denney seems to do,
and regard his " subjective estimate " not as an illusion,
but as a revelation, to use Herrmann's phrase, " of the
Living to the living."   When it is said that divinity is
predicated of Christ by a value-judgment, what is meant is

---

[1] Kaftan's _Das Wesen der christlichen Religion_, p. 102 (" The Essence
of the Christian Religion ").

[2] Denney's _Studies in Theology_, p. 14.

not that Christ is merely imagined God, but that the evidence of His divinity is such that it can be appreciated only by one who has a personal relation of faith to Christ. Other instances of the same misconception of the Ritschlian position abound in recent theological literature, but this may be regarded as the most flagrant, and so most demanding correction.

(2) Another objection is this, that the value-judgments alongside of the theoretical judgments involve a dualism of knowledge.   This has been stated very moderately by Professor Orr.   " We cannot have two kinds of truth with no sort of relation to each other.   The mind cannot be divided into compartments, with its theoretic knowledge on the one side, and its religious knowledge hermetically sealed off from contact with the theoretic on the other." [1] Professor Wenley, however, lets his wit run riot in ridiculing what is but a caricature of his own creation.   " From Monday to Saturday, knowledge dances among its phenomena, which it knows are not knowledge ; on Sunday the other power moons among its realities, which cannot fail to impress it, but which may or may not exist.   The knower of the lawful days doubts and cannot dream ; the dreamer of the Sabbath believes and can never know.   There is no possible appeal from Philip sober to Philip drunk.   For this classical gentleman is now so constituted that he cannot but be always drunk and always sober at one and the same time." [2]   There is a great deal more in the same strain.   Now, while it may be frankly conceded that some statements in the Ritschlian literature may afford some justification for this objection, yet a closer study will, the writer is persuaded, disprove it.   The Ritschlians are not dividing the mind of man against itself.   All that they seek to do is to make clear that there are different

[1] Orr's "Albrecht Ritschl," *Expository Times*, v. p. 537.
[2] Wenley's *Contemporary Theology and Theism*, p. 119.

modes of knowing appropriate to and corresponding with different objects. Material objects are known by sensuous perception, irrespective of moral character or religious condition. Kant's *Critique of the Pure Reason*, or Hegel's *Logic*, can be understood only by a man with some aptitude for metaphysical inquiry, and are unconvincing to many men of keen perception, and even good reasoning power. Beauty is not equally appreciated by all men, but appeals strongly only to those of some æsthetic sensibility. Moral ideals even are authoritative only as the conscience is developed. The perception of spiritual realities is not as common as sensuous perception. The confidence with which a man accepts as true the statement that God is good, that duty must be done, or that death does not end all, depends on individual conviction, and that is determined by personal character. The higher the object of knowledge, it may be said confidently, the more does the personal factor affect the mode of knowing it. In art, morality, religion especially, the personal interest is important. Ritschlianism has laid hold on a valuable truth when it thus distinguishes the kind of evidence on which our common experience of the world rests, from that which underlies our moral and religious beliefs in goodness, God, immortality. This theory of value-judgments is but a new way of putting the truth, that if a man does the will he will know whether the doctrine be of God or not, that the pure in heart shall see God, that what is spiritual is spiritually discerned. The organ of science, sensuous perception and logical demonstration, can never reach the unseen and the eternal. The organ of philosophy, analysis of human consciousness and synthesis of its elements, cannot give certainty of the existence of those ultimate principles of existence and intelligence that it is led to assume by a more or less stringent mental necessity. In the organ of religion, faith, the value-judgments, the object and the subject of knowledge, are in such close contact, in so inseparable relation with one another, that faith can soar where science cannot follow, and where even philosophy can essay only a fluttering flight. As the objects and the purposes of knowledge vary, so must the organs and methods and to recognise this is not to divide the mind, but to enlarge man's consciousness of the varying possibilities of his thought. These modes of knowledge are complementary, and not contradictory. While Herrmann and Ritschl in the abstract admit a possibility of the opposition of theoretical and value-judgments, yet when we examine the theory of the former and the practice of the latter more closely we shall see that the admission is superfluous. Ritschl meets science and philosophy on its own ground; and either disproves conceptions of the universe opposed to the Christian, such as materialism and pantheism, or shows the insufficiency of the evidence for, or the inadequacy of the idea of, God, offered by metaphysics. Herrmann too shows that metaphysics, in offering a solution of the problem of the universe, forsakes the firm and sure ground of science, and has less claim to be believed than the religious consciousness. Kaftan so limits the sphere of science, and so defines the task of philosophy, as to subordinate both to the religious consciousness. We shall afterwards see how the Ritschlians deal with the relation of the theoretical and of the value-judgments respectively to the one province of reality, which is common ground for them, namely, the historical facts of the Christian revelation ; but let it now suffice to say that they do not hold that what is false for the theoretical judgment is true for the value-judgment. It could have been desired that Ritschlianism had made plainer than it has attempted to do, that, as there must needs be unity in existence for the believer in a God as ultimate cause and final purpose of the universe, so unity must be the ideal of

knowledge, and that accordingly the theoretical judgments
of science and philosophy by their necessary limitations not
only leave room for, but even show the need of, the value-
judgments of religion, the contents of which complete and
certify our knowledge.   The world-view which science may
suggest, or which philosophy may infer, may appear at
first sight inconsistent with or contradictory of the world-
view, which is distinctive of Christian faith.   What Christian
theology has to do is to show that science and philosophy
have either altogether ignored or only partially recognised
the most important data, the testimony of conscience and
the witness of religion ; and that as morality and piety are
the supreme interests of man, so no world-view can be true
that does not accord them their due recognition.   By distinguishing theoretical from value-judgments, Ritschlianism
does appear to shirk this task ; it does seem to withdraw
religion into a small province of its own, and abandon to
irreligious science or philosophy the wider realm of human
knowledge.   This is, however, not its intention, nor even as
we have seen is it its practice, although its terminology
does lay it open to this objection.

(3) This theory, that religious knowledge consists of
value-judgments, involves in the theological method of
Ritschl and some of his followers a limitation of the range
of theology.   The objects of religious knowledge are not
as completely defined and described as to gratify the
desire of knowledge to be full and thorough ; but only
those aspects are dealt with to which a distinct religious
interest attaches.   Thus as we shall see, much is affirmed
in the New Testament which the Ritschlian dogmatics
practically ignores.   But if, as Ritschl admits, the theoretical
judgments of science even are not altogether disinterested,
that is, there is pleasure in the pursuit of knowledge for its
own sake, then why should there not be the theoretical
impulse in religious knowledge, that is, why should not the

objects of faith be investigated as thoroughly as the conditions will allow? In his deduction of God's love from His personality, and of the Kingdom of God from God's love, Ritschl himself, it seems to me, goes beyond the narrow bounds he sets the value-judgments of religious knowledge in, for instance, his treatment of the person of Christ. When Herrmann narrows the range of divine revelation to what a man has himself actually experienced, he is pressing unduly this theory of value-judgments. Let it be recognised that the value-judgments of religious knowledge may have for their content not only what a man has individually verified in his own experience, but all that is verifiable for him in the typical and normative experience that is presented to us in the New Testament. Nay, let there be included also in religious knowledge all those further inferences which offer an explanation of, and give certainty to, the contents of the value-judgments. Theology may obey a theoretical impulse as well as gratify a practical interest.

(4) Lastly, now we face the question, Does religious knowledge lose in truth and certainty by being thus confined to value-judgments? Is personal conviction, in which the conscience and the spirit in man assert themselves, less trustworthy than sensuous perception or logical demonstration or metaphysical necessity? A writer, who does not acknowledge any indebtedness to Ritschl and his school, yet shows likeness to and kinship with the Ritschlians, answers this question admirably. " Personality is, as a matter of fact, our tacitly acknowledged standard of reality ; and other things are accounted real in proportion as they are related to, and so embraced within, the sphere of personality. . . In a word, what affects me personally, and thereby becomes part of myself, is real for me ; while what affects me most persistently and most powerfully is most real." [1]   Accordingly, as the value-

[1] Illingworth's *Divine Immanence*, pp. 53, 54.

judgments of religious knowledge express most clearly and fully the relation between the object and the subject of knowledge, relate most closely the existence of these objects to the existence of this personality, they express reality not with the least, but with the greatest certainty and truth.

CHAPTER VII

THE HISTORICAL CHARACTER OF REVELATION

I

(1) THE value-judgments of religion indicate only the subjective form of religious knowledge, as the Ritschlians understand it. But it is not to be supposed that this subjective form accounts for, or explains, its objective content. Faith does not imagine or invent its contents; it does not practise a deceit upon itself for its own satisfaction: it simply apprehends, appreciates, and appropriates revelation, the historical character of which describes the objective content of religious knowledge, even as the value-judgments define its subjective form. Historical facts, composing this revelation, exist actually and really, quite independent of the wishes or the hopes of the individual believer; all that in his value-judgments he does is to claim for his own need and trial the help and the comfort that are offered to him in the revelation presented in these facts. With justice has the Rev. William Morgan, in the most appreciative article in the English language on Ritschlianism which the writer has yet seen, described "Faith and Revelation" as "the two fundamental principles of Ritschlianism"; and said of the relation of these two conceptions in Ritschlian thought, that "the correlative of faith is revelation. Each supposes the other; and our conception of the one will necessarily determine our conception of the other." [1]

[1] *Expository Times*, ix. pp. 485, 537.

(2) Just as the Ritschlians, then, have an original and independent conception of faith which is expressed in their doctrine of value-judgments, so correspondingly have they their own distinctive presentation of revelation, the characteristic feature of which is the exclusive emphasis laid on its historical character. The historical person Jesus Christ is the divine revelation; this sums up their position. The negative consequences of this treatment of the subject we have already had occasion to notice. They will hear nothing of a natural revelation; they reject not only as inadequate, but as injurious to Christian faith, all the traditional arguments for the existence of God, hitherto discovered in nature or in man's conscience and reason; they regard any attempt to bring into continuity and harmony of thought the results of metaphysical speculation, and the contents of Christian revelation as an obscuration and distortion of the distinctive features of Christian faith; they oppose themselves to any form of piety that even in appearance claims to be independent of the historical revelation in Christ. It is well always to recall the fact that the whole of their negative criticism has as its positive motive this estimate of the absolute and exclusive value of the Christian revelation.

(3) The positive contents of their treatment of the subject of revelation now invite our attention. While all the Ritschlians are led to indicate their views on this subject in the course of their theological labours, it is Herrmann more than any of the others who has dealt with it, not only with greater clearness and fulness, but also with keener feeling; and it is to him we must now turn, although we cannot fix our gaze on him alone, but may here and there glance at some of the others. The nature of religion determines the *object* of revelation, and the object fixes the *limits*. If the motive of religion were an intellectual curiosity merely, a verbal communication would

suffice; as it is a practical necessity, it must be met by actual assistance in the sphere of history, in which man experiences this necessity.   The revelation must be sufficient for, but need not extend beyond, what is demanded by religion.   On the *object* and the *limits* of revelation depends the *evidence* for its truth which needs to be produced.   As the revelation is intended to do something for man, the proof of it is this and this only, has it done its work?   On each of these subjects Ritschlianism has its own independent contribution of thought to offer.   To sum up in a few words what it will be the aim of this chapter to show at length, the object is practical, to make men " wise unto salvation "; the limits are historical, Christ and all that explains and interprets Christ historically; the evidence is experimental, the experience possessed when the revelation is received, and not arguments external to that experience.   We shall deal then in order with the objects, limits, and evidences of revelation.

II

(1) " If we want to see what revelation is," says Herrmann, " then we must give heed to this, how the revelation becomes certain to us, and helps us.   It is not difficult to say what is to be generally understood by revelation, by the biblical terms ἀποκαλύπτειν and φανεροῦν, the uncovering of something hitherto covered, the bringing out of something hitherto hidden.   But the true sense of such words we first grasp only when we experience in ourselves, how that which we have long called revelation changes for us out of something old and familiar into something incomprehensibly new." [1]   Thus from the outset of Herrmann's treatment of the subject

---

[1] Herrmann's *Der Begriff der Offenbarung*, p. 4 (" The Conception of Revelation ").

attention is fixed on the subjective individual experience;
and the objective universal revelation comes into consideration only in so far as it directly and potently affects
this experience.   What is the occasion of this contact of
revelation and experience?   "Accordingly," he continues,
"we must for ourselves look at the struggle of temptation
in us, if we want to know what revelation is.   The essence
of temptation lies in this, that we feel ourselves unhappy." [1]
But man is not only miserable, he is sinful as well.
Accordingly, "to temptation from need there is in the
Christian allied temptation through the inner self-judgment
of guilt; to disgust with the world there is in us added
disgust with ourselves.   If anything whatever were to
bring us out of this state of death, then we could greet
that truly with the prophetic word: 'the people that
walketh in darkness seeth a great light.'   Whatever
should appear to us in such a situation and in such
a manner as something never experienced, that we
could with sincere truthfulness call revelation." [2]   The
individual subjective experience of passing "from darkness
into God's marvellous light," together with its objective
historical cause, but not that cause itself, is called revelation, even as Paul speaks of the time of his conversion in
the words "when it pleased God to reveal His Son in me."
Revelation is thus conceived, not as a historical event of
the distant past, but as a personal experience in the
immediate present.

(2) Granting, however, for the present the legitimacy
of so using the term revelation, what is the relation of the
personal experience to the historical event?   'When we
now wish to bring into the frame of this universal con-

---

[1] *Op. cit.* p. 4.   The word rendered temptation is *Anfechtung*; no
more accurate or appropriate term could be thought of; but the word
temptation must be taken in its wider sense, as in Jas. i. 2.

[2] *Op. cit.* p. 5.

ception of revelation that which is offered to us as
revelation, then the difficulties begin, and perhaps the
differences. Daily one may hear among us the following :
the Holy Scriptures embrace the fulness of revelations,
which are given to us ; their doctrines and narratives are
the means whereby God desires to enlighten our darkness." [1] To this, which may be described as the traditional
attitude, Herrmann very strenuously opposes himself.
" These narratives are naturally something new to us when
we read them for the first time, but the newness of
revelation they do not have. They increase the circle of
that which we regard as real, but they do not transplant
us into a new reality. For we ourselves remain the same,
whether we accept them or reject them " ; and " woe to the
Christian who imagines that the sum of these scriptural
ideas composes the revelation, which could make all new
for him " ; for " those scriptural ideas do not form the
content of the revelation, but they are the thoughts which
a man is first enabled to grasp in the right way by
this, that revelation allows him everywhere to see something new." [2] While this protest is useful and lawful
against the view that the mere belief of the facts and the
truths recorded in the Holy Scriptures can save a man, it
surely ignores the fact that the Holy Scriptures are the
writings of men who themselves experienced a revelation
of God, and are on that account not at all unlikely, if
sympathetically and reverently studied, to bring a man
just into that spiritual condition in which he may have
that experience which Herrmann chooses to call revelation.
As we shall afterwards see, Herrmann himself is compelled,
as regards the picture of Christ in the Gospels at least, to
recognise this dependence of Christian experience on the
Holy Scriptures.

(3) If the Holy Scriptures are not the revelation of

[1] *Op. cit.* p. 6.   [2] *Op. cit.* pp. 7–9.

God, as is currently believed, where is the revelation to be found? " All revelation is the self-revelation of God. Any communication whatever we can call a revelation only when we have found God therein. But we find and have God when He so undoubtedly touches and seizes us, that we are compelled to submit ourselves entirely to Him. We experience the revelation of the Almighty in the moment in which we bow ourselves with deep joy under His power," which " is His love." [1] Is revelation, then, merely an individual experience frequently repeated, yet having no permanent value or universal validity?   It would so appear at first sight ; but Herrmann, as soon as he has duly insisted, as he thinks it needful to do, on the relation of God to each soul in revelation, is careful to explain that he contends for a historical manifestation of God, and not a mystical communication from God as the universal cause of this experience.   " Revelation is there as an undeniable element of our world.   It is the historical appearance of Jesus, which belongs to our own reality as the coat which we put on, or the house in which we dwell."   But if we were to press strictly the language that Herrmann has just used, then we should not allow him to speak of Jesus as the revelation of God, but only, to imitate Mill's phrase about matter, as " the permanent possibility " of revelation ; for it is only in the actual experience of the believer that He becomes to each one individually the revelation of God.   What, then, is the character of this experience?   A man " gets into circumstances in which he thinks he can discover nothing but an irrational violence which crushes his happiness ; or to the sinner his unfaithfulness, which he has long hidden from himself, becomes suddenly uncovered." [2]   Can he help or save himself by believing in God's providence or Christ's salvation?   If he could, then he would already be out of

[1] *Op. cit.* pp. 10, 11.   [2] *Op. cit.* pp. 16, 17.

his trouble and misery; for the very capacity to believe
implies already deliverance and relief. Again, is he to
wait for the spirit that shall enable him to believe to be
given to him, and to pray for that gift? But prayer needs
faith, and it is that he lacks. Yet "the man struggling
with temptation becomes aware of Jesus Christ as something real," without any effort to believe or attempt to
pray. What is the effect upon him? While "to the
man hardened in sin, who would be glad if God were not,
the thought forcibly presents itself that there might, in fact,
be a God in whom the good has power and by whom the
evil is judged," yet "to the unfortunate man who would
gladly escape from sin and become blessed in goodness, in the
appearance of Jesus there draws near the God who takes
pity on him. One must have experienced this in Christ,
then one can speak about God's revelation." Thus God
finds a man and makes Himself known to him in "the
appearance of Jesus, which touches us as a real fact in the
world, whether by the Gospels or by the Christian life of
saved men around us."[1]

(4) This revelation in Christ has in itself such vitality
and vigour, that it inspires and sustains the very faith
which apprehends, appreciates, and appropriates it. A
strenuous effort to believe need not be made; there needs
to be simply submission to a potent influence. Let us see
how Herrmann describes this process. Jesus "becomes" a
revelation of God to us "through all whereby He compels
us to trust Him"; and "all that can be traced back to
two facts. Jesus reveals to us the Good, and makes the
claim that He makes the Good real in the world; that is
one fact. The other fact is: He lives in undisturbed
confidence in the love of a God whom He has recognised
as the holy power of the Good." In proportion to the
perfection of His moral ideal was the sensitiveness of His

[1] *Op. cit.* pp. 20, 21.

conscience; and "nevertheless there does not fall on this soul a shadow of guilt no memory of transgression puts itself between Jesus and His God, whom He has yet learned to know as the consuming omnipotence of the Good." "He said that all men after Him, in looking back on His person, would discover the knowledge, that by His death the new covenant of grace and forgiveness was provided for them." [1] These are the plain facts of the revelation of God in Christ. How are we brought to believe them? "The image of Jesus we have received can act upon us as something indubitably real. We need not make any effort to regard it as true, in order that we may grasp it as something historically real. Neither do we need any apologetic arts to protect these facts against doubt. But the simple matter is, whether we wish to pass the real, or to remain standing before it. And God be praised that it is so. For a revelation which is to save us cannot be first established as a revelation by our own exertions." [2] What is assumed in this statement must be carefully noticed. The man to whom Jesus thus becomes the revelation of God for salvation is assumed to be a member of a Christian society, in which not only the Scriptures have been preserved, but in which also are found "living epistles known and read of all men," so that Christ meets him as a reality in its literature and its life. But if this man were of a critical or sceptical turn of mind, inclined to question whether the Christian society were right in accepting this literature as at all historical, or to suggest other reasons for the lives of Christians than that which they themselves assign, would the image of Christ necessarily present itself to him as "something indubitably real"? For many an earnest inquirer it would seem even a treason to truth to yield himself unhesitatingly to such an impression before certain questions that doubt-

[1] *Op. cit.* pp. 22, 23.   [2] *Op. cit.* pp. 23, 24.

less would force themselves on his attention had got some sort of an answer. It is to be feared that there are some men at least for whom a preliminary process of inquiry and argument is an intellectual necessity. For those, however, for whom no such necessity exists, this consciousness of Jesus as a reality involves, according to Herrmann, further consequences. " The certainty of God is established and maintained for the Christian by Jesus Christ," and " thus Jesus becomes to us a redeeming revelation of God." This position, he holds, is much more satisfactory than that which could be reached by the traditional method, for " we are now in a position to give witness to our brethren of a reality which makes us happy and free, not only of doctrines, which we laboriously support with proofs from Scripture and reason." [1] It is by this process, Herrmann holds, that the historical event becomes the personal experience of revelation.

(5) The characteristic feature of this view of revelation is this, not only that the historical facts of the life and work of Jesus are regarded as the revelation of God, but that the experience of each individual believer, as Jesus appears to him and saves him, is also included in the revelation. Thus Christ is brought into the same relation to every believer as He bore to His first disciples. As He revealed God to a Peter or a John, so He reveals Him to each one of us. Although the medium of revelation is the life and work, which belongs to the past, yet the process of revelation is continued into the present. God does not, so to speak, finish His self-revelation, and then leave us as best we can to make it our own; but He so carries on that revelation, that our faith is not of our own making, but the response to His presence, the result of His power. There can be no doubt that two very valuable truths in this view find due recognition: (1) that, inasmuch as the object

[1] *Op. cit.* pp. 24, 25.

of revelation is to save and bless each man, that object has
not been attained in the case of any man until he has been
thus saved and blessed; (2) that the revelation of God
which thus saves and blesses must be presented to each
man with such convincing and converting power, that not
by his own works, but by faith, and faith alone, he is saved
and blessed; not by his independent activity, but by his
obedient receptivity does the revelation become real to
him.   But nevertheless it is altogether doubtful whether so
ambiguous a use of the term revelation is at all desirable.
Confusion can only result, if we do not distinguish what
may be called the objective presentation of the mind, heart,
and will of God in Christ, from the subjective appropriation
by the faith of man; and do not reserve the term revelation
for the former instead of applying it, as Herrmann does, to
the latter also.   One result of this confusion especially
demands a few words of caution.   In Herrmann's treatment
of the subject there is a tendency to limit revelation by
individual experience, and so make every man a measure
of revelation.   But every believer ought to recognise that
not only what he has already himself appropriated by faith
is God's revelation for him; but that in Christ there is a
fulness of revelation, beyond the measure of his experience
hitherto, which others have been enabled to appropriate in
larger measure than he as yet has, and which it should
be his aim to appropriate ever more and more fully for
himself. √

III

(1) As the object of revelation is so practical, the limits
of revelation must be determined not by any theoretical,
but only by utilitarian considerations, and therefore very
differently from the current method of traditional theology.
Christ is the revelation of God; but is it every word and
deed, every doctrine and event, that is recorded regarding

Him? Herrmann very clearly and firmly says that it is
not. The limits of revelation are to be more narrowly
drawn than the bounds of Christ's life on earth. "The
way of salvation for a Christian," he says, "is to learn to
see Christ. But we do not help men to do this, if on the
strength of the reports and doctrines of the New Testament
we relate about Jesus, that He was born as the Son of God
of a virgin; that He taught this and that, wrought many
wonders and also raised the dead; that He Himself rose
again, and now after His ascension to the Father reigns
almighty. Such a tale, however impressively presented, is
not a Gospel:" for "in our time by this means a hindrance
is, as a rule, prepared for men, most of whom cannot take
these things for granted any longer in childlike simplicity."[1]
These things, it is true, are not to be ignored or denied;
but "one should communicate them as part of the New
Testament witness regarding Jesus, but one should not put
them before men with the demand that they should, above
all things, assent to them"; for we must not try to persuade
ourselves that "what acted on the disciples as indubitably
real must also so act upon us." The true method is this:
"We are to allow ourselves, as the disciples did then, to be
seized and uplifted by that which in our position touches us
as something indubitably real. That is, in the first place,
the testimony of the disciples to the power and majesty of
Jesus. The second is the inner life of Jesus, which from
the testimony of the disciples meets us as something real
and active in the world. In this we have Jesus Himself as
the source of our salvation."[2] While in the subsequent
discussion Herrmann limits himself to the second of the
two realities, the "inner life of Jesus," it is here worth
noting that he does recognise that there is a significance

[1] Herrmann's *Verkehr des Christen mit Gott*, p. 63 ("The Communion
of the Christian with God," pp. 65, 66).

[2] *Op. cit.* Ger. p. 64; Eng. pp. 66, 67.

and value for us in the impression Jesus made on, and the influence He exercised over, His first disciples ; but to this point we must afterwards return.

(2) What, then, are the contents of this inner life of Jesus which is God's revelation to us ? " The fact is undisputed, that the Christ of the New Testament shows a firmness of religious conviction, a clearness of moral judgment, and a purity and force of will, as these are not found united in any other figure in history." He claims to be Messiah, and yet He is humble, does not push Himself forward, is modest in speech. While He claimed to establish the kingdom of God, yet " by the kingdom of God He understands God's dominion in the inner life of personal beings, and in their intercourse with one another. To the kingdom of God, as He understands it, belong the men who are fully surrendered unto God in boundless trust in Him, and unbounded love to their neighbours." While He comes in conflict with pious Judaism in regard to its Messianic hopes, He cherishes a wonderful confidence in the face of this opposition, and the ruin with which it seems to threaten Him. He " shows us the image of a man who is conscious that He does not fall short of the ideal for which He offers Himself" ; and that, not only in isolated sayings about sinlessness, but most convincingly in the claim He puts forward for Himself at the Last Supper. Not only is He conscious of His own innocence and perfection, but what is still more wonderful, " He has the confidence that He can lift men to such a height that they will partake of the highest good in their full surrender to God, and therefore in a life of love." Thus He offers Himself to mankind as Saviour. " It is a fact for us that within history stands Jesus with the claim that He exclusively is Himself salvation for all men," for He " founds in us by the fact of His personal life a certainty of God which lies beyond all doubt," inasmuch as in our " con-

fidence in His Person and Cause there is contained the thought of a power over all things, which takes care that the Jesus who has gone under in the world gets the victory over the world. The thought of such a power gets as firm a hold of us as the overpowering impression of the person of Jesus. It is the beginning of the consciousness of a living God, the only real beginning of an inner surrender to Him.' But how does this God, who we are convinced cares for Jesus, become our God caring for us; for is there not this great difference between us and Him, that He is perfect, we sinful? Here is the answer. "The same man through whom the reality of God becomes comprehensible and certain to us, deals in a friendly way with the men who are conscious of their distance from God," and "this personal bearing of Jesus raises us to the confidence that His God is our God, and therewith into the reach of the love of God." In this experience "God enters into communion with us in such a way as that He thereby forgives our sins at the same time," for the restoration of personal relations between God and man is the forgiveness of sins. "The attitude of Jesus towards us lifts us to the confidence that the divine power, which must be with Him and His work, actually accepts us and makes us sharers in His work, the sole aim of which is the realisation of the moral purpose in a kingdom of God. Therefore the impression that God has intercourse with us in Christ transplants us into the inner disposition, in which we overcome the contradiction between our natural life and the moral demand. Now there becomes possible to us the faith that whatever in our surroundings and in ourselves resists the good, by God's power becomes serviceable to the good." [1]

(3) It is clear at first sight that what Herrmann aims at is to bring to the front those elements in the life of Christ that are likely to prove most effectual in meeting the need,

[1] *Op. cit* Ger. pp. 57–79; Eng. pp. 70–81.

and so winning the faith of the men of our own age, and to
cast into the background those that are likely to awaken
doubt, and so to be a hindrance to the soul's approach to
God. Although in a practical interest he draws thus
sharply a line of distinction between what will and what
will not prove a revelation of God to the present age, yet at
the same time it must not be taken for granted that he
does not recognise the value and significance of much that
he desires should at first be held back.   (a) He maintains,
to give a few instances, that no man can confess Jesus as
God until he has come to know Jesus in his own living
experience, and until in Jesus he has come to know God.
" The true teaching of the Church about the meaning of the
person of Jesus," he says, " can be made his own, it goes
without saying, only by the man to whom Jesus Christ
means everything." [1]   (β) In the same way the doctrine of
the Atonement, as taught by the Church, can be only a
hindrance to the man whom Christ has not yet saved.   But
the man who has found salvation in Christ can understand
it.   " When the believer,' says Herrmann, " has once seen in
the message from God which comes to him in Christ the
divine forgiveness as made his very own, then his faith has
a presentiment that God could again enter into communion
with sinners only through the fact of the moral personality
of Jesus as made perfect in suffering.   Yes, still more.   The
believer says to himself, involuntarily looking back on the
life of Jesus, what we should have suffered, He suffers." [2]
The contrast which Herrmann draws between his method
of presenting God's revelation in Christ to save and bless
men, and that of others, is worth noting.   " *According to the
Socinian and rationalist teaching, Christ proclaimed the
divine forgiveness of sin ; according to the orthodox doctrine,
He made it possible, in truth He carried it out in us.*"   In

[1] *Op. cit.* Ger. p. 102 ; Eng. p. 102.
[2] *Op. cit.* Ger. p. 107 ; Eng. pp. 106, 107.

other words, while, according to the orthodox doctrine, Christ by His sacrifice secured forgiveness for us, leaving us by faith to claim the gift He has thus won for us (we need not now pause to consider whether this is a fair statement or not); according to Herrmann, Christ by our faith in Him restores us directly into that personal communion with God which is the actual forgiveness of sin. This difference in the representation of the work involves a difference in the conception of the Person. " For the first," continues Herrmann, " it is sufficient to see in Jesus the man who proclaims a divine truth ; for the second, it suffices to represent a divine essence as united with Him which is something else than Himself ; the third we experience only, because we, as a fact, look at God Himself in the historical Christ." [1] Only when forgiveness has in this way been realised can any doctrine of its possibility have any meaning or worth. (γ) Again, a man can get to the exalted only through the historical Christ, " One finds the true Christ, and experiences the direct working of the exalted Christ, while one understands the historical Christ." [2] (δ) Once more, " for the birth from the virgin, surely none among us, who uses his words with care, can come forward as a witness. He can only report it. It forms a part of the tradition, in which the power of salvation is for all of us enclosed. He who has found Jesus Himself will also find the right attitude to this." But that " the spiritual life of Jesus has not proceeded from the sinful race, but that in Him God Himself has stepped into the history of this race, of that we can be witnesses, for this knowledge forms a part of that which we have ourselves experienced." [3] (ε) That Herrmann accepts a real

[1] *Op. cit.* Ger. pp. 110, 111 ; Eng. p. 110.
[2] *Op. cit.* Ger. p. 151 ; Eng. p. 146.
[3] Herrmann's *Worum handelt es sich in dem Streit um das Apostolicum*, p. 13 (" What is involved in the dispute about the Apostles' Creed ").

pre-existence of Christ will afterwards be shown (see Chap.
IX.); now a sentence may be added to prove his belief in the
resurrection.   " It is certainly incomprehensible to me how
the faith, that His Person in its whole existence and activity
is the revealed action of God for our eternal salvation, and
along with this the revelation of the essence of God Himself, can surrender the conviction that He actually rose
from the dead,—a conviction on which the community, after
He had parted from it, was raised up, and which is placed
in the way even of the indifferent by historical evidences
of undoubted, impressive weight." [1]   As frankly are the
miracles of Jesus accepted.   Only it is maintained that
belief in them is a consequence of faith in Christ, and must
not be regarded as a condition of membership in the
Christian Church.   To sum up briefly the general position
indicated in these special cases : the Christian believer,
starting from his experience of salvation through Christ,
gradually comes to understand and make his own the facts
and truths offered for his intelligence and appropriation in
the New Testament ; but not the whole New Testament
as such is a revelation to him, only what his faith can
make its own nourishment.   It may be acknowledged that
Herrmann has put in the forefront of the Christian revelation what undoubtedly is most likely to commend Christianity to most modern men, and has thrown into the
background what might at first be a hindrance to faith.
Of course any estimate of, so to speak, the irreducible
minimum in the object of faith, which is to be insisted on,
will depend ultimately on individual subjective conditions.
Probably not a few modern men could begin with more
than Herrmann insists on.   He is right, however, in maintaining as he does, that all that is believed should be

---

[1] Herrmann's *Die Religion im Verhältniss zum Welterkennen und
zur Sittlichkeit*, p. 387 (" Religion in Relation to our Knowledge of
the World and Morality ").

14

brought into vital, organic relation to the personal experience, whatever be its beginning, or however it may develop.
From the fixed centre in Christ the gradually expanding
circumference of revelation must be drawn.

(4) That the Christian revelation has very much wider
relations than the life and work of Jesus, Herrmann fully
recognises in a passage so noteworthy that it deserves to
be quoted in its entirety. " Jesus is certainly historically
possible only at the place where He is historically real. He
came when the time was fulfilled. That means that the
history of Israel belongs to His existence. The history of
this people. the eternal right of its law, and the knowledge
of God of its prophets, nourished Him. There belongs
thereto in smaller measure also Greek culture, which, besides
all other products of a spirit of astonishing freshness and
liveliness, included as its best the moral consciousness, which
has been reached in the Socratic school—above all, in
Plato's *Gorgias*. Although many seek to discover in the
natural grace of the words of Jesus something of the Greek
spirit, yet it is still more important that the work of Jesus
found a humanity raised by the power of this spirit.
Lastly, there belongs to the historical existence of Jesus
also the organisation of society by the Roman State. For
the new life that is awakened by Him needs for its unfolding an environment so set in order : in a horde its seeds
would have been choked."[1] We may call all this revelation
if we will, he admits ; but what we must beware of is giving
it the same value or significance as the original, supreme,
and unique revelation in Christ, and thereby dimming its
glory. The Church, he holds, has erred in putting the Old
Testament alongside of Christ, instead of keeping Him
apart and above all ; for in Him alone all that is true meets,
and finds perfect expression. Yet revelation at a lower

---

[1] Herrmann's *Die Gewissheit des Glaubens und die Freiheit der Theologie*, p. 33 (" The Certainty of Faith and the Freedom of Theology ").

stage, and so of lesser worth, there has been, not only in
Israel before Christ, but even outside of Israel.   " We by no
means wish," says Herrmann, " to deny altogether that the
savages of New Holland have a knowledge of God and the
stirrings of real religion, accordingly a communion with
God.   But how that is brought about for them we do not
know.   We cannot even transplant ourselves into the
religious life of a pious Israelite with a complete understanding.   For the facts which acted on him as the revelation of
God have for us this power no longer." [1]   This revelation,
he elsewhere strenuously maintains, is not to be explained
as a purely subjective process.   " The bearers of revelation,"
he says, " who in a definite moment of their life receive the
certainty that God has worked on them, and through them
on others, in order to regulate the communion of men with
Him, distinguish this event of their inner life, to which their
religious certainty is referred as to a revelation, from themselves, in so far as they desire such a message from God.
The inner experience, if it is more to them than a pleasant
hour, for the repetition of which they carry the conditions in
themselves, if it really means a revelation of God to them,
becomes for them also an outer event." [2]   Accordingly,
while almost exclusive attention is given by Herrmann to the
revelation in Christ, he does not deny a revelation to Israel,
and even beyond Israel, as an objective communication from
God, and not merely a subjective consciousness of God.

(5) The positive significance and supreme value of the
New Testament for Christian faith has been stated more
definitely by Ritschl than by Herrmann, and we may therefore turn for a time from the disciple to the teacher.   With
Jesus as the founder of the Christian religion, we must,

[1] Herrmann's *Verkehr der Christen mit Gott*, p. 49 (" The Communion of the Christian with God," p. 53).

[2] Herrmann's *Die Religion im Verhältniss zum Welterkennen und
zur Sittlichkeit*, p. 365 (" Religion in Relation to our Knowledge of the
World and Morality ").

according to Ritschl, associate the apostles as the oldest representatives of it, if we are to get the Christian revelation in its original and so authoritative form.   The life and the words of Jesus are not a sufficient source of the Christian revelation ; for " the full compass of His historical reality one can reach only from the faith in Him of the Christian community, and even His intention to found the same cannot be understood historically in its completeness if one does not subordinate oneself to the Person as a member of that community."   For this reason " it would be a falsely understood purism, if one were to prefer the less developed indications of Jesus in this respect to the forms of the apostolic representations.   Further, one will be justified not to level down the most developed forms of the Pauline structure of thought, but to maintain them erect in their theological use, because they serve the purpose of expressing most distinctly the contrast of Christianity and Judaism.' [1]   In this statement there is offered a necessary correction of the position of Herrmann, who at least appears to represent Christ as in historical isolation, having relations only to the individual believer.   Here it is recognised that Christianity is not only a historical person, but through His instruction and influence a historical movement, the earliest stages of which must be known and understood, if its significance is to be duly appreciated ; the earliest representatives of which as nearest to the founder must be regarded as typical, and so normative in their thought and life.   The consequence of this estimate of the apostolic age as regards the authority of the New Testament is accepted by Ritschl.   In his handbook of Christian doctrine he formally accepts " the fundamental principle of the Evangelical Church, that Christian doctrine is to be drawn *only* from the Holy Scriptures " ; and explains that " this

[1] Ritschl's *Rechtfertigung und Versöhnung*, iii. p. 3 ("Justification and Reconciliation ").

fundamental principle refers directly to the original sources
of Christianity gathered together in the New Testament, to
which the original sources of the Hebrew religion in the
Old Testament are related as indispensable auxiliaries for
their understanding." The meaning and worth of the New
Testament is thus explained. " These writings afford a
foundation for the appropriate understanding of the Christian
religion from the standpoint of the community for this
reason, because the Gospels let us recognise in the work of
its founder the nearest cause and destination of the religion
of the community ; but the letters, the original state of the
common faith in the community, and that, indeed, in a form
which is not yet troubled by the influences which already
in the second century put Christianity into the Catholic
shape."[1]   These influences were Greco-Roman, and these
the Ritschlian school agrees in condemning as foreign to
the genius of the Christian religion.   The Hebrew influences
which through the Old Testament moulded the religion in its
infancy, are recognised as legitimate, and Ritschl even uses
agreement with the religious ideas of the Old Testament as
a test of the canonicity of the New Testament writings.
This acceptance of the Holy Scriptures as the historical
witnesses of the Christian revelation is in Ritschl's use of
them qualified in two ways.   First of all, Ritschl accords to
the apostles a very much limited authority, and freely claims
the right to differ from them.   To give only one illustration :
he says, for instance, that " certainly Paul traced the validity
of the universal destiny of death to the sin of Adam.
Nevertheless, just for this reason that the apostle has formed
this idea, it is not yet suited to be a theological rule."[2]
In the next place, Ritschl's exegetical method is often

[1] Ritschl's *Unterricht in der Christlichen Religion*, p. 2 (" Instruction
in the Christian Religion ").

[2] Ritschl's *Rechtfertigung und Versöhnung*, iii. p. 341 (" Justification
and Reconciliation ").

very arbitrary.   With good reason Pfleiderer gives the
following description of it : " But I miss in it one thing
which I certainly hold as an indispensable condition of
every sound exegesis, the unbiassed objectivity which, without squinting to right or left, looks simply on the text and
allows the biblical writers to say what their words according to the plain grammatical sense are intended to express.
Ritschl's exegesis stands throughout in the service of his
dogmatics, he twists and trifles at the passages of Scripture
so long, until they yield a result which fits his purpose." [1]
These defects, however, are unfortunately not peculiar to the
theology of Ritschl.   To the attitude towards the traditional
doctrine of inspiration held by the Ritschlian school we must
later return; here be this noted that the limits of the Christian
revelation are so drawn as to include the Holy Scriptures.

(6) With the pre-eminence in the Christian revelation
which is accorded by Herrmann (to return again to him) to
Christ, no Christian can have any desire to quarrel.   We
cannot but share his zeal for the glory of Christ, his suspicion of aught that would in anyway hide that glory.
But even if we start, as he does, from the inner life of Jesus,
His perfection and His grace, as the centre of God's revelation, and valuing that as highly as he does, we should be
less exclusive in our appreciation and reverence than he
seems to be.   In the first place, the life of Christ is an
organic unity, and therefore no feature of, no factor in it,
can be insignificant and valueless.   The evangelical testimony should therefore command a greater reverence, and
allow a narrower liberty than Herrmann admits.   In the
second place, the preparation for Christ in the Old Testament, especially in the faith and hope of the godly, and

---

[1] Pfleiderer's *Die Ritschl'sche Theologie*, p. 37 (" The Ritschlian Theology "). The second of the three essays in this book deals with " the
Theology of Ritschl according to its biblical foundation," and very
effectively exposes the defects of Ritschl's exegetical method.

the activity of Christ by His spirit in the typical religious experiences which are presented to us in the New Testament, stand in more vital relations to Christ Himself than Herrmann seems to acknowledge, and therefore both belong to God's revelation in Christ in a fuller sense than he is ready to admit. From Herrmann's own historical standpoint, without assuming any doctrine of inspiration, these criticisms seem both necessary and legitimate.

IV

(1) Since Christ is recognised as the revelation of God in individual experience, it may be asked whether this confession of Him may not be merely a subjective illusion without any objective validity. While, as far as the writer has been able to make himself familiar with Ritschl's writings, he does not attempt to prove the reality of the Christian revelation, and occupies himself with it as one who writes within, and for the Christian community, as he expressly says, " One can know and understand God, sin, conversion, eternal life in the Christian sense only in so far as one includes oneself consciously and intentionally in the community which Christ has founded " ;[1] Herrmann and Kaftan, both of whom recognise clearly and fully the apologetic function of Christian theology, attempt proofs of the *truth* (*Wahrheit*) of the Christian religion as well as statements of its *essence* (*Wesen*), to adopt the distinction which Kaftan has expressed in the titles of his chief works. Kaftan devotes the first division of his book on the *Truth of the Christian Religion* to a criticism of ecclesiastical dogma in order to show that the traditional method of apologetics has proved a failure. That method, briefly put, was this, to render by means of the general knowledge and thought

[1] Ritschl's *Rechtfertigung und Versöhnung*, iii. p. 4 ("Justification and Reconciliation").

of each age each article of the Christian creed intelligible
and credible ; and was possible only as long as the Church
could so control secular culture as to make it serviceable
for its purpose; but the independence, nay, authority, now
claimed by science and philosophy has necessarily terminated
this alliance.   A new method of apologetic, better adapted
to this age, must be adopted.   After indicating the necessary limits of *human knowledge* (chap. i.) on the one hand,
and the *primacy of the practical reason* (chap. ii.) on the
other, *the traditional speculative method* (chap. iii.) is rejected
on the ground that it assigns too great importance to knowledge, and does not sufficiently recognise the practical
purpose of man's existence, whereas " the guiding idea of
speculative philosophy must be an idea of the chief good."
Instead of it there is offered this *proof of Christianity* (chap.
iv.).   (1) " Only *the Christian idea of the kingdom of God
as the chief good of humanity,* answers to the requirements
which must be made of the true, rational, absolutely valid
idea of the chief good."   (2) There has been " *a special
revelation of that kingdom of God in history.*"   (3) As these
two *postulates* of the practical reason have been fulfilled in
the Christian revelation, " *the reasonableness and the absoluteness of the faith reposed in it*"[1] have been proved.   He
admits, on the one hand, that " if it can be demonstrated
by means of historical investigation beyond the possibility
of doubt that the Person of Jesus Christ is not of that
nature which is assumed in the Christian faith, the faith
must be held in that case to be refuted, to be *untrue*"; but
he maintains, on the other hand, that " that case will

---

[1] Kaftan's *The Truth of the Christian Religion*, ii. pp. 325, 383, 384.
This work, Harnack's *Christianity and History*, and Stählin's *Kant, Lotze,
and Ritschl*, are the only German works quoted in this volume which
have not been consulted in the original, and the quotations from which
are not independent translations.   As very little use has been made of
this work of Kaftan's, the writer has thought himself justified in referring
only to the English translation.

certainly not occur, since from the nature of the subject the argumentation in question can never take the form of that which involves compulsion ; and the inward certainty of faith itself appears as decisive evidence against its correctness" : and further concludes that " he who cannot allow himself to despair of the highest ideals of humanity and of the reason in history, will have to decide for faith in *the revelation of God in Christ*." [1]   To sum up in a few words the whole argument, Christianity is so inseparably involved in all that has any ideal significance or absolute value for man in his history, that if the race gave up Christianity it must give up its most precious possession, it must entirely change all its standards of worth.   In the name of historical truth that demand can never be made, as historical science is under no necessity of denying the reality of the Christian revelation.   This argument suggests several comments. First, it has been objected that this proof is in a circle, as the idea of the chief good which is realised in the Christian revelation as the kingdom of God is itself a product of Christianity.   But even if the form of the argument be defective, its substance is true, and it is briefly this, that the Christian revelation is the highest, truest, and best satisfaction of man's religious need as approved by the reason and conscience of man in history.   Secondly, the criticism of the speculative proof illustrates what has already been noted, the one-sided practicality of the Ritschlian position, with its disregard of the due claims of the intellect. Thirdly, the possibility of a double truth, with the assumption of which Ritschlianism has been charged, is expressly excluded in the recognition of the validity for the religious consciousness of the theoretical judgment of history, even if it destroyed the supreme object of faith.

(2) Herrmann puts the argument in a somewhat different form.   " There are," he says, " *two objective bases*

[1] *Op. cit.* pp. 405, 407.

on which the Christian consciousness of communion with God rests. *First, the historical fact of the Person of Jesus.* This fact is a part of our own reality. *Secondly, the fact that the moral demand lays claim to ourselves.* Christ brings it about that the Good ceases to be a grievous problem for us, and begins to be the element in which we live. Other objective bases there are not for the truth of the Christian religion."[1] The moral law, on the one hand, presents itself to us with an absolute authority, regardless of our wishes; Christ, on the other, presents Himself to us with the positive assurance that He can put us in accord with this moral law. The moral law is timeless; Christ is in time. How can a historical person meet the demands of an eternal law? This problem Herrmann deals with in one of his pamphlets, *What need has our Faith of Historical Facts?* His answer is briefly this. While in the moral law, on the one hand, "the eternal law of our will takes possession of us"; yet, on the other hand, we are living in time; we belong to history, and it is in time and through history that this eternal law must be realised in our temporal existence. "God is for us the power which joins the temporal with the eternal, which makes it possible for man who lives in time to cleave to the eternal law, which turns to him as the law of his own inner life." As the moral law is to be realised in history, so God, who makes that realisation possible, must be manifest in history. "In the history of mankind there is one event" that so manifests God; "that is the appearance of Jesus Christ as it is handed down to us in the books of the New Testament."[2] This argument is a good one so far as it goes. Christ is His own self-evidence; and conscience does

---

[1] Herrmann's *Verkehr des Christen mit Gott*, pp. 80, 81 ("The Communion of the Christian with God," pp. 82, 83).

[2] Herrmann's *Warum bedarf unser Glaube geschichtlicher Thatsachen*, pp. 24, 28, 30.

respond to His appeal, and finds its satisfaction in Him. But Kaftan's argument, too, is good, while neither can be said to exhaust the possibilities of proof. Christ meets man's needs, and so commends Himself to man's faith in other ways than these. Each of these writers has borne witness to what it is in Christ that claims his faith ; but it would be folly and wrong to claim that either or both of the statements give all the evidence for the truth of the Christian revelation. ✓

V

(1) According to both writers the revelation of God, because it is in Christ, is inseparable from human history. It is necessary at this point, then, to ask how in the Ritschlian view historical criticism affects the evidence for revelation. Harnack, himself one of the foremost historical critics, has answered this question in a lecture on *Christianity and History*. First of all, he states the connection. " The whole substance and meaning of religion, life in God, the forgiveness of sins, consolation in suffering, —the Church couples with Christ's person; and in so doing she associates everything that gives life its meaning and its permanence, nay, the Eternal itself, with an historical fact, maintaining the indissoluble unity of both." [1] Against this connection these objections are brought by modern thought. (1) " It is just because the Christian religion is a part of history, and consequently of that *development* of which all history consists, that it is no more than a link in that development, and therefore its founder cannot be allowed any peculiar or unique position." (2) " Even though the founder of the Christian religion may have been an incomparable man, He lived many centuries ago ; and it is therefore impossible to go to Him with our

---

[1] Harnack's *Christianity and History*, pp. 17, 18. This work also has been consulted only in the English translation.

troubles and sorrows, and to lay hold of Him as the rock of our life. It is not the *person* which we have any longer to consider, but the *doctrine*, the *principle*." (3) "We may speak of Jesus Christ as we will, and He may have been all that we say, but we cannot be certain of it; for where our idea of Him has not been destroyed by historical criticism, it has been rendered doubtful; and, even though it were more trustworthy than it is, still the facts of history can never be known with a certainty that would entitle us to make them the foundation of our religious belief." [1] After showing, in answer to the first objection, the part that personality has played in human development, and the absolute uniqueness of the part played by Jesus, he concludes that "this fact, which lies open to the light of day, is unique in history; and it requires that the actual personality behind it should be honoured as unique." [2] The second objection is met by an appeal to Christian experience, which testifies that "the personality of Christ may save us" from doubt, darkness, despair. "As surely as everything depends on the soul finding God and becoming one with Him, so surely is He the true Saviour, Guide, and Lord who leads the soul to God." [3] As regards the results of historical criticism, Harnack makes this reassuring confession: "It is true that His clothes—the outward form of His doctrine—were part of the heritage; but the great and simple truths which He came to preach, the personal sacrifice which He made, and His victory in death, were what formed the new life of His community; and when the Apostle Paul with divine power described this life as a life in the Spirit, and again as a life in love, he was only giving back the light which had dawned upon him in and through Jesus Christ his Lord. This is simple matter of fact, which no historical criticism can in anyway alter." [4] He adds, as regards the external

---

[1] *Op. cit.* pp. 26, 27.   [2] *Op. cit.* p. 38.
[3] *Op. cit.* pp. 47, 49.   [4] *Op. cit.* pp. 57, 58.

details of the life of Jesus, that "much that was formerly rejected has been re-established on a close investigation, and in the light of comprehensive experience" He also asks: "Who in these days, for example, could make such short work of the miraculous cures in the Gospels as was the custom of scholars formerly?"[1] Even what cannot be proved as a fact may be valuable as a lesson, significant as a symbol.

(2) Harnack, be it remembered, represents probably the most advanced critical opinion in the Ritschlian school, and his critical views are not to be regarded as in any sense necessary consequences of his Ritschlian tendency. Another Ritschlian, Reischle, has in a short pamphlet, *Faith in Jesus Christ and the Historical Investigation of His Life*, dealt with the same problem. He states that "it is not alone the *result* of this historical investigation which can make faith anxious, but the *whole attitude* which this assumes." He maintains, however, that faith is independent of historical investigation, for "we feel how God draws us to Himself through Him, and imparts divine life to us"; and "it is this that makes faith quite certain that this Jesus Christ is not a human invention."[2] Nay, while faith maintains its independence, it may even make this historical investigation subservient to its desire to know Christ more fully and clearly; and the Christian theologian, in dealing with the life and the teaching of Christ, requires its assistance. Only if historical investigation attempt so to draw Jesus into the limits of human history as to exclude His absolute uniqueness, will faith be bound to protest against its pretensions.

(3) These writings show that the Ritschlian school is not so blindly confident in its value-judgments as to be foolishly indifferent to the theoretical judgments of historical

[1] *Op. cit.* p. 63.
[2] Reischle's *Der Glaube an Jesus Christus und die geschichtliche Erforschung seines Lebens*, pp. 8, 19.

criticism, as it is often represented that it is.   One great
question that cannot at this stage of the discussion be
entirely passed over, is what the Ritschlian school has to
say about miracles and the supernatural generally.   Professor Denney very confidently informs us that " it is doing
no injustice to the whole school of writers to say that in
point of fact they reject miracle altogether, in any sense
which gives it a hold on man's intelligence or a place in
his creed."[1]   In a note he quotes a passage from Ritschl,
in which Ritschl states the dependence of belief in miracles
on faith in God's providence ; denies any necessary opposition between this belief and " the probability of a continuity of the whole world according to natural law ";
maintains that " when certain records of miracles in the
biblical books appear to come into conflict with this rule,
it is neither a scientific task to remove this appearance or
to establish it as fact, nor is it a religious task to recognise
these recorded events as divine actions against the laws of
nature " ;[2] and concludes, finally, that as each man will have
experience of miracles himself, he need not be always dwell-
ing on the miracles which others have experienced.   On
this statement Professor Denney bases the criticism, " Then
comes the virtual surrender of the biblical facts."   In another

[1] Denney's *Studies in Theology*, p. 10.   Two clauses have been
omitted in the sentence quoted which have no bearing on the subject
immediately under discussion.   Notes, pp. 253, 259, 262.

[2] Ritschl's *Unterricht in der christlichen Religion*, p. 15 (" Instruction
in the Christian Religion ").   The important sentence may be here given
in the original, " Wenn jedoch gewisse Erzählungen von Wundern in
den biblischen Büchern gegen diese Regel zu verstossen scheinen, so
ist es weder eine wissenschaftliche Aufgabe, diesen Schein zu lösen
oder ihn als Thatsache festzustellen, noch ist es eine religiöse
Aufgabe jene erzählte Ereignisse als göttliche Wirkungen gegen
die Naturgesetze anzuerkennen."   With regard to this last clause, be
it carefully noted that Ritschl does not say that " it is not a religious
task to accept these recorded events " as having actually happened, but
" as divine actions against the laws of nature," which is not a matter of
fact, but a question of theory.

note he draws from this assumption the further conclusion, that " to admit Christ's resurrection as the New Testament teaches it, would, of course, be inconsistent with his teaching on miracle." Before producing the proofs that Ritschl accepts not only the resurrection of Jesus, but also the miracles wrought by Him, the writer cannot refrain from pressing the question whether Ritschl's statement affords justification for the far-reaching conclusions that are so confidently drawn from it. All that the statement, when carefully examined, can be held to prove about Ritschl's position is this. He refuses to commit himself to any theory about the relation of miracles to the order of nature. It is quite possible that they are consistent with such an order. There are events recorded in the Scriptures which we cannot see the way to reconcile with that order ; but it is not necessary for science, so that it may be justified in its assumption of such an order, either to prove that these events are quite consistent with the order of nature, or that they are inconsistent. Religion, in accepting these events, is under no obligation to regard them as divine interferences with natural laws. " The continuity of the whole world according to natural laws " is a " probability " (*Wahrscheinlichkeit*) ; it is a " scientific assumption " (*wissenschaftliche Annahme*). That continuity has not been so exhaustively and absolutely demonstrated as to necessarily exclude the possibility of such events as from the religious standpoint are described as miracles. Science with its present limitations can say nothing either for or against such events. If, then, science cannot claim to have given any such demonstration of the inconsistency of miracle with natural order, it is by no means necessary for religion so to define miracles as to assert this inconsistency. Surely other Christian thinkers, who had no thought of denying the biblical miracles as facts, have, before Ritschl, refused to describe them as breaches of natural law or interferences with natural order.   Have not some Christian thinkers even gone so far as to suggest that miracles are revelations of higher laws, operations of latent forces in the universe?   Without in anyway committing oneself to any of these positions, it is surely mere justice not to charge Ritschl with the denial of miracles as facts, when all he does is to refuse to accept a particular theory of miracles. But there is positive evidence to disprove this charge.   He describes " the Christian view of the world " as of a " teleological and especially miraculous character"; he shows the insufficiency of " the mechanical view of the world " which excludes purpose and miracle; lastly, he claims that " a teleological, and in single features even miraculous, view of the world, which corresponds with man's need of religion, which guarantees him his position as a spiritual and moral whole in his connection with nature and human society, is anything but irrational in comparison with the knowledge of nature and its laws."[1]   In answer to the charge that this religious view of the world is subjective, he goes on to argue that it is not more subjective than the scientific view, which equally involves the exercise of man's own faculties.   Of the resurrection of Christ, Ritschl says that " it is the completion of the revelation made in Him, which not only absolutely corresponds with, but necessarily results from (*folgerechte*) the worth of His Person."[2]   The miraculous cures of Jesus are taken for granted, when Ritschl explains that these did not imply " that Jesus had the whole continuity of nature, according to its laws, at His arbitrary disposal"; that He Himself in " His sensible existence was dependent on all the regular conditions of man's life "; that " His miraculous power did not extend so far as to make

[1] Ritschl's *Rechtfertigung und Versöhnung*, iii. p. 582 (" Justification and Reconciliation ").

[2] *Unterricht in der christlichen Religion*, p. 21 (" Instruction in the Christian Religion ").

trial of itself in the alteration of the great mechanism of the world"; but that "the exercise of the miraculous power, of which He was conscious (Mark vi. 5, 6), and which He reckoned as part of His equipment in His calling (Matt. xii. 28), has a far narrower scope." He goes on to argue that we have insufficient material in the records to allow us to form any theory as to "the extent of the power of the will of Christ over external nature," or, in the absence of any analogous experiences, as " to the psychical and physical conditions of the miraculous power of Christ."[1] This surely is sufficiently distinct testimony; but as it seems to be a rule in the interpretation of Ritschl by some of his critics that he can never mean what he appears to say, one more passage may be added. " Meanwhile *our insight into the matter is so limited that one cannot even affirm that God is fettered by the laws of nature,* of which we know the smallest part. In this respect it is to be noted that *our whole view of Christianity assumes the recognition of the resurrection of Christ as a fact in which is most directly proved the prerogative of God to create, and to create life out of death. We would surrender the whole Christian view, if we were to surrender this key to our whole mental attitude with the argument that the restoration of a dead man to life contradicts natural law."* He makes still more definite what he means by the resurrection when he says: "*It is self-evident,* according to analogy, with what Paul expresses in 1 Cor. xv., *that Christ made Himself known to His disciples in the body."*[2] Herrmann's acceptance of the miracles of Jesus generally, and of His resurrection particularly, has already been indicated; but the following further explanations may be with advantage added. He says that "we do not share

[1] *Rechtfertigung und Versöhnung,* iii. p. 43c ('Justification and Reconciliation").

[2] Quoted from Ritschl's *Lectures on Dogmatics* in Ecke s *Die Theologische Schule Albrecht Ritschls,* pp. 198, 199 ("The Theological School of Albrecht Ritschl')

15

the belief common to the apologists and their opponents, that nature for our knowledge is a closed whole. For our representation it is endless manifoldness, and that belief in a cognisable whole of nature, by which one allows oneself to be confused on the question of miracles, is nothing more than the sediment of a dogmatic metaphysic, which has no concern with Christianity. For this reason every miracle of God is for us in immeasurable degrees naturally mediated. God works through nature, which He has created as a means for His final purpose. But we must decline it as a superstitious undertaking, when one wishes distinctly to give a decision regarding the possibility or impossibility of any recorded events on the ground of any representation of the whole of nature for which the results of knowledge of nature have hitherto furnished the materials. If the life of Jesus, according to the account of the Gospels, shows a series of miraculous facts, then it is dogmatic prejudice to declare these impossible on account of their surprising character." [1] Ecke, who is by no means a partisan of the Ritschlian school, sums up the matter convincingly when he declares that "*all the representatives of the Ritschlian school are of one mind with their master in their acceptance in principle of the belief in miracle*, whether they assume a more positive or more critical attitude to the single miracles recorded in the Holy Scriptures. In any case *the resurrection of Christ* is recognised by all the theologians of this tendency as a *fact* of religious faith, and the conviction of the disciples that they had seen the Lord is *universally traced back to real miraculous appearances of Christ*; by some it is true according to Ritschl's example to *attestations of the bodily Risen One*, by others, Harnack for instance, to *objective visions* in which the exalted Lord

---

[1] Herrmann's *Die Religion im Verhältniss zum Welterkennen und zur Sittlichkeit*, p. 386 ("Religion in Relation to our Knowledge of the World and Morality").

made known to His disciples His continued life in glory." [1]
The extreme importance of this question, and the almost
universal misconception of the Ritschlian position upon
it, have necessitated this long statement. It is evident
that, recognising the legitimate uses of historical criticism,
the Ritschlians will not surrender to an assumption which it
sometimes makes the miraculous element in the Christian
revelation. ✓

VI

(1) One other question, important not from the Ritschlian standpoint, but from the point of view of the traditional
theology, still remains to be dealt with.   It is the subject
of the inspiration of the Holy Scriptures.   On this subject
Herrmann expresses himself very frankly. " When faith
receives the first revelation of God from historical events, it
does not allow itself to be sundered from them in anyway.
But that happens through that dogma.   For the Scripture,
which on account of its inspiration claims to be the revelation, thereby hides the work of those events, and lets us
forget that the historical continuity, which unites us to
them, produces the divine deed of our salvation. We do
not build on the inspired Scripture, but on the Scripture,
which is the original source of the revelation which has
been operative in the Christian community since its beginning." [2]   As against the traditional theory of inspiration
this is a sound position; God has not merely dictated a
book, He is a living and a working God.   In the facts of
history, pre-eminently in the Person of Christ, He reveals
Himself.   It is still He who reveals Himself to us because
He lives and works in us, when through the impression

[1] Ecke's *Die Theologische Schule Albrecht Ritschls*, pp. 199, 200
(" The Theological School of Albrecht Ritschl").

[2] Herrmann's *Die Bedeutung des Inspirationslehre für die evangelische Kirche*, p. 30 (" The Significance of the Doctrine of Inspiration
for the Evangelical Church").

these facts make upon us, and the influence that they exercise over us, all things become new for us. The record of the historical revelation which has come to us in the Holy Scriptures must always be dependent on, and subordinate to, the revelation itself. The traditional doctrine practically reverses this relation. Pushing that doctrine to its ultimate consequences, Jesus need never have lived, or wrought, or spoken; for God might have composed and dictated a revelation if the verbal communication is all important. If, however, facts are essential to a real revelation to men, then the history is more than the record. It is this view that Herrmann is rightly contending for. By the revelation of which the Scriptures are the record, he means an objective communication from God, not a subjective product of human development. A passage has been already quoted in which Herrmann asserts that for the bearers of revelation, the revelation is always something distinct and distinguishable from their inner life. He opposes himself entirely to the position of those who "desire to transfer revelation entirely into the subject, in that they allow the same to be contained in the subjective process of religious exaltation."[1] Accordingly, he asserts what is equivalent to an inspiration of the persons, if not of the writings. If, however, the writings are, as he holds them to be, trustworthy and authoritative as regards the contents of this objective divine communication to the human persons, who are the bearers of the revelation; if, as he maintains, Christ Himself meets us, and acts on us in the image of Himself presented to us in the Gospels : then it seems to the writer in this admission there is the basis of a doctrine of the Holy Scriptures which Herrmann himself, however, does not develop, but which, from the historical

[1] Herrmann's *Die Religion im Verhältniss zum Welterkennen und zur Sittlichkeit*, p. 365 ('Religion in Relation to our Knowledge of the World and Morality").

standpoint, which Herrmann rightly holds, would be entitled to affirm that the means for perpetuating and diffusing this historical revelation must needs be included in the same divine operation. If the record of the revelation is to be at all adequate and authoritative, it cannot be a merely human product. Along such lines of thought a more satisfactory doctrine of the Scriptures might be reached.

(2) While Ritschl also rejects " the dogmatic doctrine of verbal inspiration," which he describes as "a perilous means " of establishing the authority of the New Testament, yet he insists as strongly as he can on the distinctive character of the New Testament as the sole means of " an authentic knowledge of the Christian religion and revelation," inasmuch as it consists of " the original sources which are near to the period of the foundation of the Church," when the " spiritual power gives expression clearly and completely to its peculiarity at the beginning of its operation," which is not to be confined to " the personal activity of Christ," but includes also " the first generation of His community."[1] If, then, the New Testament belongs to this initial movement of the Christian religion, distinguished by its fresh vitality and full vigour, it may again be urged, it will display qualities that set it apart from all subsequent literature. From this historical point of view again we might work out a doctrine of inspiration, which, recognising fully the historical character of the Christian revelation, would at the same time justify the estimate of the Holy Scriptures, which is not merely advanced in the interests of theological dogmatism, but actually expresses the demands of religious experience. The Ritschlian school has not reached such a doctrine of the Holy Scriptures, but such an advance is in no way forbidden by its distinctive teaching of the historical character of revelation. ✓

---

[1] Ritschl's *Rechtfertigung und Versöhnung*, ii. pp. 11, 13 (" Justification and Reconciliation ").

CHAPTER VIII

The Regulative Use of the Idea of the Kingdom of God

I

(1) ALTHOUGH, as we have seen, Ritschlianism condemns ecclesiastical dogma as an illegitimate mixture of heathen metaphysics and Christian faith, yet it is very far removed from the undogmatic Christianity which has its advocates in this country as well as in Germany. It maintains not only the legitimacy, but even the necessity of a systematic exposition of the value-judgments of religion in which the contents of revelation find expression, so as to exhibit their organic unity as related to one principle. Before we pass on to inquire what this principle is, let us pause to consider very briefly the defence of dogmatics offered by the Ritschlian theology. As far as the writer is aware, Harnack stands alone in giving the restricted sense to the term dogma, which we have already had occasion to discuss. The other Ritschlians are not unwilling to use the term in its wider sense for any definite statement of Christian truth which finds general acceptance in a Christian community.

(2) Using this term in the wider sense, Kaftan has published two small books, *Faith and Dogma*, and *Do we need a new Dogma?* which in this connection will repay closer study. The first of these books is directed against Dreyer's *Undogmatic Christianity*, and the second

justifies against criticisms positions maintained in the first.

(*a*) In the former work Kaftan states first of all what can be said against Dogma. He shows that the development of positive science has resulted in a growing antagonism to dogma, which has consequently become a hindrance instead of a help to the Church. While he admits that this opposition to dogma is in some cases due to a habit of mind to which even faith is an offence, and maintains that the Christian Church must not attempt a compromise with this intellectual mood by sacrificing any distinctive feature of the gospel; yet, on the other hand, he argues that the Church must do what it can to heal the wound from which not only our culture, but our whole spiritual life even is suffering, and reminds us that the dogma from which modern thought is so estranged was in its own origin an attempt to reconcile faith and knowledge. "The same need," he says, "which we now represent in advocating the necessity of an accord between science and faith, even this and no other need led to the origin of dogma."[1] His conclusion is that as the antagonism of science and dogma exists, there is nothing else to be done but to give up the dogma.

(*b*) But he does not stop here. He goes on next to show all that can be said in favour of dogma. By dogma he understands a doctrine which is to be valid in the Christian Church; and affirms (1) "that the Christian faith of itself and necessarily leads to a doctrine; (2) that the church-community cannot dispense with a doctrine which is to be valid, accordingly a dogma in the proper sense; (3) that the evangelical Church also, and it exactly with its condition, is directed to such a dogma."[2] The first position he proves by showing that faith always involves knowledge;

[1] Kaftan's *Glaube und Dogma*, p. 20 ("Faith and Dogma").
[2] *Op. cit.* pp. 21, 22.

that this knowledge is knowledge of God; that faith knows
God as the personal Spirit transcending the world; that
what faith knows it must acknowledge in a doctrine.   The
second position, that in the Church doctrine becomes dogma,
is maintained on the following grounds, that what keeps the
Church together by binding its members to one another is
its common faith, and that this common faith must needs
find expression in a doctrine, the validity of which is
generally recognised, and which, therefore, becomes a
dogma of the Church.   The third position, that dogma
is of special importance for the evangelical Church, follows
necessarily from the contrast between Roman Catholicism,
in which the sacramental cultus and the ecclesiastical polity
are of primary importance; and Protestantism, in which
" cultus and ecclesiasiastical organisation fall into the background," and " faith, and therefore doctrine, and therefore
dogma, is all." [1]   As the members of the evangelical
Churches are kept together by their common faith, the
expression of that common faith in a doctrine which
commands general acceptance and exercises general
authority, or, in other words, in a dogma is of supreme
importance.   The Protestant Churches must have a
dogma.

(c) In the third part of his book Kaftan shows what is
the reconciliation of his antagonism to, and his advocacy
of, dogma.   " What we need is *a new dogma*."   How are
we to get it?   This is his answer.   " One cannot *make* a
dogma, it must *come into being* (*werden*).   God preserve
us from the folly of wishing to *make* something in this
realm!"   " We do not want," he continues, " any other
dogma than such as corresponds with the faith of the
Reformation." [2]   This faith, he argues, did not, in the
theology of the Protestant Churches, come to a direct and
an adequate expression, for that theology never fully freed

[1] *Op. cit.* p. 28.   [2] *Op. cit.* pp. 30, 31.

itself from the fetters of Roman Catholic dogma. The dogma we need must not be a mere compromise with science, but a pure confession of faith; and this, he maintains, will in nowise come in conflict with science, for "it does not meet with science on its own ground." There is only one point at which science and faith do come into contact, and so may be brought into conflict. We must admit the possibility, although we need not anticipate the reality, "that historical research may destroy the living image of the Saviour to which the faith of the Christian clings."[1] Many of the ideas which are supposed to be in conflict with Christian faith are not the results of science proper, but are conclusions due to a view of the world, which finds support at some points from science, but which can be shown to be not strictly scientific, but philosophical; and no philosophy can claim for its conclusions greater certainty than faith can for its contents.

(*d*) In the last part of his book, Kaftan expresses himself as in no way concerned to maintain the term dogma; but what he does desire to put beyond all doubt is that what we are dealing with in the knowledge of faith, in doctrine, is *truth*, and *the only truth* about the objects with which faith is concerned; that there is no other way, by science or philosophy, to a knowledge of God, but the way of faith; and that as there is only one God, so there is only one truth about Him. This knowledge of faith, however, is not of the same character as the knowledge of science; for it is a law of our knowledge that the more important its object, the more does our knowledge assume the character of personal conviction, the certainty of which depends on our interest in the object, its value for us. "Quite simply," he says, "*the highest can be got only at the highest price.* Thou canst not know God unless thou givest thy whole manhood as the pledge." Hence, "our faith and our

[1] *Cp. cit.* p. 42.

confession of it always has something of the character
of *obedience*."[1]   It is not merely intellectual assent to a
proved proposition, it is always moral consent to an
acknowledged authority.   But a truth which meets faith
as an authority, to which submission is due, is a dogma.   If
such a truth has not yet presented itself to the faith of the
present age, yet it is being surely, if slowly, formed ; and
there must be no impatience with the delay of its coming,
and no premature effort to hasten its approach, for "*the
truth can wait.*"   In this statement of the contents of
Kaftan's book, a subject already dealt with, the value-
judgments of religion, has again been brought to our notice,
but from a fresh point of view, which may prove useful in
enabling us to understand better this distinctive feature
of the Ritschlian theology.

(3) In his second small book, *Do we need a new
Dogma?* Kaftan comes back to the subject, in order to
remove misconceptions of, and objections to, his position
by indicating the directions in which the new dogma he
desires will move.   First of all, it will make plainer than
ever the distinctive character of Christian knowledge, that
it is *the obedience of faith.*   Secondly, it will show more
clearly than has been shown before that Christian life is
essentially *a life "hid with Christ in God."*   Thirdly,
it will bring to full growth the living germs of the
Reformation, the true doctrine of the Holy Scriptures, and
the sole sufficiency of faith.   Fourthly, it will face the
question, *What think ye of Christ?* and, in its answer,
will have regard only to the essential and necessary contents of Christian faith.   " Faith," he says, " moves about
these two points, about the glorified Head of the community
and the historical life of the Lord.   It rounds itself off in
affirming and confessing the origin of Jesus from God."
"*The evangelical faith*" he continues, "*and the old dogma*

[1] *Cp. cit.* pp. 54, 57, 60.

have no internal connection." [1]   This new dogma, by the
very nature of the objects with which it deals, need fear no
conflict with science, and so meets the greatest spiritual
need of the age.

(4) The size of these works is no measure of their
significance and value ; and before going any further in our
inquiry, we may pause briefly to note some considerations
immediately suggested by Kaftan's statements, and then to
glance at the subject he deals with generally.   That the
old dogma of the Church and modern science are in
conflict on several questions needs no proof, nor does the
grievous effect of this in the spiritual life of many men
in the present day.   The need of an intellectual expression
for faith, on which Kaftan insists, must be fully admitted,
even although one may be inclined to maintain that
genuine religious sympathy may exist where there is very
little intellectual agreement in matters of belief.   That
Protestantism especially needs a common understanding
of the contents of faith in the absence of the other bonds
of unity which Catholicism possesses, is a position that
seems unassailable.   The need of a new dogma which will
not come into conflict with science will be generally
admitted ; but there remain not a few theologians who
still so define the contents, and so determine the limits of
this new dogma, that it seems an impossibility to avoid
a conflict between science and even the new dogma.   So
long as science, on the one hand, claims the right to
pronounce a judgment on the possibility or impossibility
of certain supernatural events recorded in the Holy Scriptures, which Christian faith must, by necessity of its very
nature, maintain to be facts ; so long as, on the other, Christian
faith attaches to all the statements of Scripture, even when
dealing with the subjects of common knowledge, which

---

[1] *Brauchen wir ein neues Dogma?* pp. 59, 63 ("Do we need a new
Dogma?").

have no immediate connection with the religious life, an
authority which demands an unquestioning intellectual submission: so long will there be a wide field of common
possession, which will again and again be the occasion of
mutual conflict.   But if it be recognised that certain
assumptions of science regarding natural law and order,
which are useful in the very highest degree in the investigation and explanation of our common experience, are not
universal principles to be applied beyond the range of that
experience, if it be acknowledged that certain tendencies
and habits of mind, that are of the greatest possible value
in scientific inquiry, may become positive hindrances to the
exercise of other spiritual faculties in their respective
spheres, then much of the conflict, in so far as it is provoked by science, will be avoided.   On the other side, too,
the lust of battle may be restrained, if Christian faith can
be brought to admit that all the contents of the Holy
Scriptures are not the truth of the living God, are not
essential or necessary to the life and growth, health and
strength of faith.   Even on what, with all due self-restraint
on both sides, remains common ground of science and faith,
it does not seem impossible to come to a mutual understanding.   Kaftan's confidence that the new dogma may
avoid conflict with science, does not appear at all unwarranted.   The last part of the first of his works, now
under examination, puts in a new light the theory of value-
judgments, and shows how unjustified is the objection of
Ritschlian critics, that the theory involves a double truth, or
suggests the untrustworthiness of our religious knowledge.
In the indications Kaftan gives in his second book of the
character of the new dogma he desires, he is for the most
part in agreement with the other members of the Ritschlian
school.   His positive position, that the germs of the
Reformation need, and will find development in the new
dogma ; and his negative position, that the ecclesiastical

dogma of the Person of Christ must, in the interests of
faith itself, be superseded by a new doctrine of the
divinity of Christ, the interests of which shall be
distinctively religious,—both are common to Ritschlianism.
So also is the general principle that religious knowledge is the obedience of faith. Only when he insists
that the Christian life must be exhibited distinctively as
a life hid with Christ in God, he betrays a mystical
tendency which distinguishes him from Ritschl and Herrmann. With his contention generally, that we need a
new dogma, the writer in his first chapter has already
expressed cordial agreement. With his more special
conviction that this new dogma, if science and faith
severally observe the limits of their spheres, need not
come into conflict with science, he finds himself also in
thorough accord ; but he would add, conflict can be
avoided only if the old dogmatic use of the
Scriptures as infallible oracles on all questions be
abandoned. ∨

II

(1) If the Christian faith needs a Christian dogmatics
as its expression, what is to be its regulative principle
that it may appear, not as a sum of separate doctrines,
but as a system of truth possessing organic unity ? As
the Ritschlians are agreed that we need a new dogma,
so they are agreed as regards the truth that is to bind all
its parts into one whole. This is the idea of the kingdom
of God. So prominent is this idea in the Ritschlian
theology, that one of its critics ventures to affirm that,
" should it appear that one of the adherents does not
assign its full value to the idea of the kingdom for the
teleological construction, and accordingly does not accord
to it the central position in the system, then he has separated
himself from Ritschl, and has no claim to belong to his

school"[1]   To this statement it must, however, be added, that as all the Ritschlian writers have not given us a systematic theology, we cannot with equal distinctness in all indicate the application to all Christian doctrines of this regulative principle.   In this case, as in others, general statements about Ritschlianism require modification and qualification in individual instances.

(2) Herrmann, in his book on *The Communion of the Christian with God*, gives almost exclusive prominence to the "inner life" of Jesus as the revelation of God individually to every believer, and makes only casual mention of the kingdom of God.   Yet this is due to his special apologetic purpose, and not to any formal dissent from this distinctive position; for in his work, *Religion in Relation to our Knowledge of the World and Morality*, he says: "An invaluable moment of Christian faith is the idea of the kingdom of God, the universal moral community, the aspect under which humanity is included in God's purpose for Himself.   The reality of the kingdom of God must in some way or another have seized a man, and positively influenced his thinking, if he is to be capable of trusting God in the Christian sense.   In this moment of Christian faith itself there lies for us both the point for the organisation of the Christian view of the world, and the germ of the dogmatic proof of the same."   "The circumference," he says again, "of the truly legitimate and soluble dogmatic problems is described by the question, how is it possible that man, sinful and subject to the power of nature, can seek his blessedness in the form of personal life, expressed in the moral law, or in the moral community of the kingdom of God, and can be sure of the same?   Dogmatics takes the answer from the historical revelation of God; if this had not such a content, then

[1] Wegener's *A. Ritschls Idee des Reiches Gottes*, p. 122 ("A. Ritschl's Idea of the Kingdom of God").

neither our faith nor dogmatics would exist." [1] This involves a limitation of the range of dogmatics. "The dogmatics demanded by us will, in the first place, turn out shorter than the traditional," for "the biblical representations will be utilised in it only in so far as we can honestly say to ourselves, that, as belonging to the solution of the fundamental question of dogmatics as defined above, they have already become intelligible to us." [2] The regulative principle is thus seen to involve a formal method. Theology is concerned only with the solution of a practical problem, how sinful man may be saved in the kingdom of God. Only he who has personally experienced this salvation is in a position to understand the terms of the problem and its solution. The statements of the Bible are to be used by dogmatics only as they are clearly understood to relate to the personally experienced solution of the practical problem.

(3) In neither of the small books which we have been considering does Kaftan, in his indications of the content of the new dogma, give any prominence to the idea of the kingdom of God ; but it will be remembered that in his work, *The Truth of the Christian Religion*, he offers, as a proof of the reality of the Christian revelation, the agreement betwen the Christian idea of the kingdom of God and the Practical Reason's Postulate of a Chief Good. In his other large work, *The Essence of the Christian Religion*, he begins the discussion of Christianity with a chapter on the Kingdom of God, followed by chapters on Reconciliation and the Revelation of God in Jesus Christ. The essence of a religion he states is to be discovered in one feature, " *What is the character of the good which it desires to offer to its adherents ?* " The answer

---

[1] Herrmann's *Die Religion im Verhältniss zum Welterkennen und zur Sittlichkeit*, pp. 431, 432 ("Religion in Relation to our Knowledge of the World and Morality").

[2] *Op. cit.* pp. 439, 440.

to this question for Christianity is to be found in this way:
" We must take the preaching of Jesus regarding the kingdom
of God as our starting-point, and with the knowledge that
this offers approach the apostolic writings, and search out
in them the corresponding propositions." [1] Jesus, according
to Kaftan, preached the kingdom of God "*as our highest
good and as our supreme ideal*," and as a heavenly, not an
earthly good, the possession of which, however, depended
on human moral activity in the world.   He admits that
"*the preaching of the kingdom becomes in the mouth of the
apostles the proclamation of the risen and glorified Christ*";
and that in the case of Paul "*the glorified Christ fills the
place which in the teaching of Jesus the supramundane
kingdom of God holds, which has appeared in His Person,
and has become accessible for possession by His disciples
through faith in Him*." [2]   While he does not venture with
Harnack to describe this difference between Christ's and
the apostles preaching as a mistake on the part of the
apostles, yet he does not seem to recognise that this change
may make the theologian pause before accepting the idea
of the kingdom of God as the regulative principle of
Christian dogmatics; for surely there was a good reason
why the apostles, Paul especially, ceased preaching the
kingdom of God, as Christ Himself had done, and began
instead preaching Christ Himself.   But this remark is an
anticipation of subsequent criticism.

(4) In the introduction to the third volume of his
Justification and Reconciliation, Ritschl lays down the rules
by which the Christian theologian must be guided. (*a*)
First of all he must be himself a believer, one who has
claimed for himself the good Christianity offers, and who
is discharging the duty to which it calls.   " The full range

[1] Kaftan's *Das Wesen der Christlichen Religion*, pp. 226, 229 (" The
Essence of the Christian Religion ").

[2] *Op. cit.* pp. 235, 251, 253.

of the historical reality of Jesus can be learned only from the faith of the Christian community in Him, and even His intention merely to found the same cannot be completely understood from the historical standpoint, unless one subordinates oneself to His person as a member of this community"; and again, "one can know and understand God, sin, conversion, eternal life in the sense of Christendom only in so far as with consciousness and intention one includes one's self in the community which Christ has founded." [1] (b) In the next place, as we have already seen, from this standpoint "the authentic knowledge of the Christian religion and revelation can be drawn only from the original sources, which stand near to the period of the foundation of the Church, and from no others," and "the original sources are the books of the New Testament," and not any oral tradition.[2] (c) In the third place, however, even from this standpoint in the Christian community, and with these original sources in the writings of the New Testament, the theologian's method needs to be further defined, for he must possess some *regulative principle* in the comprehension, the selection, and the construction of his dogmatic material." [3] Expressing this principle in general terms, Ritschl affirms that "in the Christian religion Jesus Christ is the standard in the view of the world, and the judgment of themselves, which marks believers," and accordingly "in dogmatics His Person must be taken into account as the standpoint of knowledge, from which the limits of every doctrine are regarded." [4]

(5) But as Jesus is both redeemer from sin and founder of the kingdom of God, further definition of the principle

---

[1] Ritschl's *Rechtfertigung und Versöhnung*, iii. pp. 3, 4 ("Justification and Reconciliation ").

[2] *Op. cit.* ii. p. 13.

[3] Steinbeck's *Das Verhältnis von Theologie und Erkenntnis-Theorie*, p. 27 ("The Relation of Theology and Epistemology").

[4] Ritschl's *op. cit.* iii. pp. 313, 314.

16

is necessary. It is curious that in Ritschl himself we do not find the same certain sound in his statements on this subject as we find in his disciples. His great work is called, *The Christian Doctrine of Justification and Reconciliation*, and treats all the Christian doctrines as presuppositions, or evidences, or consequences of this one leading doctrine. Nevertheless, in the Introduction he criticises Schleiermacher's definition of the Christian religion as " the monotheistic mode of faith belonging to the teleological tendency, in which all is referred to the redemption effected by Christ," in the following terms : " The position of this particular attribute as the specific definition of this religion lacks the desirable distinctness. For if the divine final purpose is expressed in the kingdom of God, then it should be anticipated that, besides, the redemption through Jesus would be also brought into relation to this final purpose as a means. As this relation does not come to expression, it results that Schleiermacher brings all Christian consciousness of God in relation, at one time with the redemption through Jesus, at another time with the idea of the kingdom of God, without coming to a decision about the mutual position of this purpose and that attribute. It corresponds with this indistinctness, therefore, that in the exposition of the doctrine of faith, justice is done to anything but the recognised teleological character of Christianity." [1] This passage shows that Ritschl subordinates the doctrine of redemption to the doctrine of the kingdom of God on account of " the teleological character of Christianity," by which he means that Christianity is not only a good already gained, but still more an ideal to be yet realised. He justifies the place he gives to the doctrine of the kingdom by an appeal to Jesus Himself. For him there is no doubt that " the purpose recognised by Christ of the universal moral kingdom of

[1] *Op. cit.* p. 9.

God evoked in Him the recognition and the resolution for
the kind of redemption which He accomplished by maintaining His fidelity to His vocation, and His blessed
communion with God in suffering unto death." It is
important for us to grasp just what this means. To put
the antithesis strongly, so as to bring into bold relief just
what is implied in Ritschl's words, the redemption of
Christ was determined in its form and character, not by man's
actual condition as sinner, but by his possible destination
as citizen of the kingdom. Evangelical theology, he asserts,
has not kept to the right standpoint, for " all that concerns
the redemptive character of Christianity has been the
subject of the closest consideration ; and accordingly one
finds in the redemption by Christ the centre of all Christian
knowledge and conduct, while at the same time the ethical
conception of Christianity under the idea of the kingdom
of God fails to get justice. But, so to speak, Christianity
is not to be compared to a circle which should run about
one centre, but to an ellipse, ruled by two foci." [1] Here
he himself abandons his own position, and co-ordinates
the two doctrines, instead of, as formerly, subordinating the
one to the other. This is not a casual lapse, for in the
subsequent argument he in varied forms asserts this co-
ordination. " Assuredly," he says, " all in Christianity is
' brought into relation ' with the moral organisation of
humanity by conduct from the motive of love, but in the
same way and at the same time all is ' brought into
relation ' with the redemption through Christ, the spiritual
redemption, that is, the freedom from guilt, and over the
world which is to be won in the relation to God as Father.
For the lifework of the founder of this religion is at the
same time to redeem and to establish the kingdom of
God." [2] Yet in the first chapter, when he comes to define
the conception of justification, he distinguishes it from the

[1] *Op. cit.* pp. 10, 11.   [2] *Op. cit.* p. 13.

idea of the kingdom of God, only at once to deny the
distinction, and to assert that the two sets of ideas are of
the same kind, for human activity is included in divine
grace, and divine grace implies human activity. As the
conception of justification expresses the one aspect—the
divine grace,—and the idea of the kingdom of God
expresses the other aspect—the human activity—of the
one spiritual process, both are of the same kind. Without
now seeking an answer to the question whether we can so
identify divine grace and human activity, we must now
note that here again a further modification of his position
emerges. First of all, the one doctrine is subordinated to
the other; next, the two doctrines are co-ordinated; and,
thirdly, they are declared to be practically identical.
These changes show that his own mind was moving from
one standpoint to another, and yet was not fully conscious
of this movement. He starts from the traditional position
of Christian theology, for which the doctrine of redemption
is of primary importance; he is drawn by influences which
cannot now be discussed towards the new position, for
which the doctrine of the kingdom is of supreme interest;
and he does not altogether abandon the old before he
assumes the new standpoint. Here as elsewhere his mind
is still passing through a crisis.

(6) When we turn to his small book, *Instruction in the
Christian Religion*, we find that the new position has been
finally assumed; and the idea of the kingdom of God has
become without qualification the regulative principle of his
theology. It has, however, been enriched in its content,
and has absorbed much that belonged formerly to the conception of justification. "The kingdom of God," he says,
"is the highest good assured by God to the community
founded by His revelation in Christ; yet it is regarded as
the highest good, only inasmuch as at the same time it is
reckoned as the moral ideal, for the realisation of which

the members of the community bind themselves to one another by a definite mode of reciprocal action."[1] The religious aspect as contrasted with the moral is here put in the forefront of the definition, whereas in his great work the moral aspect of the Christian life is specially included in the idea of the kingdom of God, and the religious in the conception of justification. The fact, however, that this more complex idea gets the name of the kingdom, is not without effect in giving the moral element a predominance over the religious, in putting in the forefront human activity instead of divine grace.

III

(1) It may be seriously questioned whether our Lord's use of the term kingdom of God in His public preaching, according to the Synoptists, warrants the prominent position and the dominant function in Christian theology which the Ritschlian school assigns to it. Whether the term itself sufficiently indicates the contents of Jesus' teaching may even be doubted; even although so suggestive and sympathetic an interpreter of His words as Professor Bruce declares that "no higher idea can be formed of salvation than to make it consist in citizenship in the divine commonwealth, nor can Christ's importance as Saviour be more conspicuously magnified than by representing Him as one to whom citizens owe their admission to the privilege'; and therefore, he adds, "I have no hesitation in regarding the kingdom of God as an exhaustive category."[2] Even if the term be an adequate description of the contents of Jesus' gospel, it must nevertheless be remembered that, on the one hand it was necessary for Jesus to adapt His teaching to the religious

---

[1] Ritschl's *Unterricht in der christlichen Religion*, p. 3 ("Instruction in the Christian Religion").

[2] Bruce's *The Kingdom of God*, p. 41.

needs of those to whom He spoke, by using the language
that was familiar to them ; and that, on the other hand,
until He had finished the work that His Father had given
Him to do, in His death, rising again, and reign in grace
and glory, the whole gospel could not be spoken to men.
When we find, further, that, according to Kaftan's own
statement, the idea of the kingdom, except in its eschatological aspects, falls into the background in the apostolic
testimony, and Jesus Himself as Saviour and Lord is
preached instead of it, we cannot but think that the idea of
the kingdom of God is a provisional conception, not universally significant. Lastly, here, by way of general
criticism, it may be noted that where the attempt has been
made to construct a system of theology with this as the
exhaustive category, the result has been, to use Professor
Orr's words, " *either* the doctrines are viewed only in this
relation, in which case many aspects are overlooked which
belong to a full system of theology ; *or* a mass of material
is taken in which is only connected with this idea in the
loosest way." [1]   The use of the idea of the kingdom of God
as the regulative principle of theology is not justified
either by theory or practice.

(2) Setting aside these objections, however, although
the Ritschlian school which claims to accept the Reformation principle of the authority of the Holy Scriptures as
the sole source of Christian doctrine cannot reject the
testimony of the New Testament on this subject, we shall
find our doubts about the lawfulness and profitableness of
this use of the idea confirmed by considering further the
results as presented to us in the Ritschlian theology.   To
the use of the idea of the kingdom of God in this way may
be traced, first of all, what may be described as the *teleological* character of the Ritschlian theology, in other words,
the prominence given to the conception of *purpose*.   To

[1] Orr's *The Christian View of God and the World*, p. 404.

this also, in the second place, we may attribute what for want of a better term we may call the *communistic* aspect of many Ritschlian doctrines, the emphasis put on the Christian *community* in contrast to the Christian individual. On the same grounds, too, may we explain the very defective and inadequate exposition of the *nature and action of God* found in Ritschl's writings. Each of these results demands separate treatment. ✓

IV

(1) In one of the passages already quoted, Ritschl himself speaks of ' the teleological character of Christianity." Not many words are needed to indicate what is meant by this. Christianity has a forward as well as a backward look ; it looks backward to the revelation of God in Christ, and the redemption of man by Christ ; it looks forward to the realisation of a moral ideal through man's duty, and of a divine purpose for man's destiny. Christianity has hitherto looked backward more than forward. Ritschl and his followers bid it look forward. But this looking forward may mean, either that the glance is fixed on the divine purpose for man's destiny, or that it is turned to the moral ideal for man's duty. The former, which may be called the *eschatological* view, was characteristic of the early Church; and it still survives in sometimes very grotesque forms in the *futurist* interpreters of *Daniel* and the *Revelation*, and those who blindly follow their leading ; while, apart from such morbid growths, in every genuine and intense Christian experience there must be *hope* as well as faith and love. The latter, which may be described as the *teleological* view, is a distinctive feature of the Ritschlian theology, although it is by no means an exclusive possession of the school. It looks to the τέλος or end which has been appointed to the human race in Christ. Accordingly, in dealing with the objects of the

Christian consciousness, the Ritschlian theology does not
ask what is their nature or their origin, or their relation
each to the other, but what purpose do they serve—how
do they further this τέλος or end, the kingdom of God?
The position and the function assigned to the kingdom
of God involves a distinct theological method, or probably we should be more correct in saying that the
idea is adopted in order to justify that method. It may
here be remarked in passing that this method is right and
fit in Christian *ethics*, where human duty is the subject of
inquiry, and all else may be regarded as means to enable
and impel man to do his duty; but in Christian *dogmatics*
which deal with what God has done for man, the necessary
and appropriate questions are *what* and *how*, not, exclusively or even predominantly, *why*.

(2) One of the critics of the Ritschlian theology,
Wegener, has made *A. Ritschl's Idea of the Kingdom of God*
the subject of an exhaustive examination "in the light of
history." He shows that in the eighteenth century this
idea was brought into prominence for three reasons: (1)
it was Jesus' own teaching; (2) it served to combine in a
unity moral and dogmatic ideas; (3) it could be represented as proving the harmony of reason and revelation.
It stood in close relation to other ideas favoured in the
thought of that century, such as purpose and development, providence as an education of the human race, and
revelation as a means of that education. Use was made
of the idea more or less tentatively by several Christian
theologians; but to Kant was due the assured position
that it gained, and the important function that was
assigned to it. "The kingdom of God," writes Wegener
in stating Kant's position, "as the highest good which is
revealed by the legislative reason in the doctrine of the
will (Critique of practical reason) as the final purpose for
the moral will, is described in 'the doctrine of religion' as

historical revelation, how it arises in Jesus Christ out of
the billowing war of the hostile principles of good and evil
as the victory of the good in principle, and how it completes itself at last as the dominion of the good in an
endless process of becoming. This ethical state, this
kingdom of God, is the invisible Church." This idea was
utilised in various forms by several thinkers; but it was
Theremin who in 1823 attempted "to shape a dogmatic
according to this idea," for "in his doctrine of the divine
kingdom he made the attempt to represent the kingdom of
God as a union of all good men both with Christ and His
Father, and also among themselves. It exists already complete in heaven, incomplete here on earth through the bond
of love." This attempt, according to Wegener, is not
successful, for the kingdom of God is used to express two
distinct ideas, the combination of which under one name
serves only to produce confusion. It is, on the one hand,
"an ideal state, of which each individual is to become a
citizen"; and it is, on the other hand, "the right condition
of the subject, in whom love works as the highest principle."[1] This confusion is the more serious, because it is
unavoidable in the use made of the idea. History thus
shows that the idea of the kingdom of God is employed as
a regulative principle of theology only when teleological
conceptions dominate.

(3) This teleological method has been described by
Wegener pointedly and briefly. "Such a way of looking
at nature and history, which fixes its gaze on, not the
being but the becoming of things, not their truth but their
worth, not their explanation but their destination, not their
ultimate cause but their final purpose, we provisionally call
a teleological."[2] What this involves may be indicated by

[1] Wegener's *A. Ritschl's Idee des Reiches Gottes*, pp. 32, 33, 57, 58
("A. Ritschl's Idea of the Kingdom of God").

[2] *Op. cit.* p. 71.

a few examples.   Creation is to be considered only in so
far as it is a means towards God's final purpose, the kingdom of God.   Revelation is the historical realisation of the
kingdom of God.   Christ's Person and Work are to be
investigated only in so far as He is founder of the kingdom
of God, and by His redemption makes it possible for men
to become citizens of the kingdom.   God Himself is not
to be otherwise thought of than as the love which makes
the world's end, the kingdom of God, His own self-end.
The value-judgments of religion are not simply confined to
the objects that have value for the religious subject, but
are, as we have already seen, limited to those relations of
the objects to the subject which give them value.   While
the mind aims at a complete determination of the objects
of its knowledge, and as thorough an account of its relations to other objects as possible, this teleological method
would restrict it to a consideration only of those relations
of the objects in which they appear serviceable.   The theoretical judgment, according to the Ritschlian school, deals
with *causes*, the value-judgments with *purposes* ; and religious knowledge is excluded from the former, and
restricted to the latter.   But this seems to be an absolutely
arbitrary assumption, for one fails to see how purposes can
be accurately and adequately determined, unless the objects
to which these purposes are assigned are investigated as
thoroughly as can be, that is, as regards their causes.
We shall have occasion again and again to notice the
insufficiency of the Ritschlian treatment of the objects of
the religious consciousness ; but what at this point demands
attention is the close connection between this teleological
method and the value-judgments on the one hand, and
the use of the idea of the kingdom of God as the regulative principle of theology on the other hand.   There is
unity and consistency in human thinking, and we shall
therefore find that the distinctive features of the Ritschlian

theology are not accidentally combined, but organically united.

V

(1) While the kingdom of God is conceived by Ritschl as not only a moral ideal, a social organisation of mankind from the motive of love, but as also a religious good, an individual possession assured to faith ; yet the immanent logic of the term is stronger than its formal definition, and what we practically find is that the moral duty pushes itself to the front, and the religious good falls into the background. The individual's religious position is made dependent on his moral function ; his value is not in himself, but in his service to society ; he enjoys his religious good as he discharges his moral duty. A man is not justified by God, and as a result he loves his neighbour. It is as he loves his neighbour that he is justified by God. This is, as far as the writer can judge, what is involved in a number of Ritschl's statements, which have caused not a little perplexity to his exponents and critics. The object of God's love is not individual man, but humanity as organised in the kingdom of God from motives of love ; the forgiveness of sins belongs to the community, and is appropriated by each believer only as a member of it ; the purpose of the Christian missionary should be, not to win isolated persons for Christ, but to convert nations to Christianity ; God does not know men singly, but in their relations to others in family and people.[1] This way of regarding the individual man not as a person, an end in and for himself, but as a member of society, a means towards its end, has been described by Wegener as a " species-individualism," as contrasted, on the

---

[1] See, for instance, Ritschl's *Rechtfertigung und Versöhnung*, iii. sec. 20, pp. 104–109, and sec. 22, pp. 115–132 (" Justification and Reconciliation ").

one hand, with "pancosmism," which denies all distinctions, and on the other with "personal individualism," for which each man is a distinct unity.[1]   He maintains, and rightly, that personal individualism alone is consistent with the Christian view of man ; for we need not go further than the twin-parables of the Lost Sheep and the Lost Coin to learn the value to God of each soul.

(2) This "species-individualism" is, however, quite consistent with the place assigned to the idea of the kingdom of God in the Ritschlian theology.   If God's final purpose is a society, then individuals are of account only as they are serviceable to that society.   Here the value-judgment in its restrictive form again presents itself. Man is to be considered only as he is of value for the realisation of the kingdom of God.   There is a legitimate socialism which insists on man's duty to his fellows, as there is a legitimate individualism which asserts man's debt to himself; or rather there is a commendable ethical idealism, in which man's debt to himself and his duty to his fellows are seen to be an organic unity, for "man dies to live.'   But this Ritschlian position, although it corresponds with dominant tendencies of the age, is an exaggerated communism, in which the individual is absorbed in the society.

(3) Such being the origin of the Ritschlian statements about the relation of the individual to the society, it becomes evident that Ritschl cannot be charged with *churchliness*.   The society for which he makes these claims is the kingdom, and not the Church, which he sharply distinguishes from it.   The Christian community as worshipping is the Church ; as acting from the motive of love, and so producing the social organisation of humanity, is the kingdom of God.   To this conception of the Church

---

[1] Wegener's *op. cit.* p. 101.   "Gattungsindividualismus" is the word which is translated "species-individualism."

we must again come back; but meanwhile it may be said, without doing Ritschl any injustice, that the Christian community as kingdom of God is of far greater interest and importance for him than as Church, even as his tendency is to subordinate religion to morality, the good to be gained to the duty to be done. √

VI

(1) While the discussion of other doctrines in subsequent chapters will afford us illustrations of the injurious influence on the theology of Ritschl of the use of the idea of the kingdom of God which we are now dealing with, there is one doctrine, that of *God*, which may now be noticed in order to complete the argument; both because in this doctrine the evil effects are most strikingly shown, and because the idea of the kingdom of God itself in this connection receives a fuller and clearer exposition than in any other part of Ritschl's system. While rejecting metaphysics from theology, Ritschl himself here gives us a speculative deduction of the kingdom of God from the love of God; and deals with the personality of God not as a biblical or an experimental theologian, but altogether as a philosopher under an impulse imparted, and with the guidance afforded by Lotze. This lapse into speculative philosophy Ecke describes as "a foreign element in the Ritschlian theology,"[1] irreconcilable with the method of Ritschl; and points out that none of his disciples has followed him in this course. Whatever opinion one may hold as regards the success or failure of this attempt of Ritschl's, it must be pronounced an inconsistency in him. But, as has already been remarked, such an inconsistency neither needs to excite great surprise, nor deserves to incur

---

[1] Ecke's *Die Theologische Schule Albrecht Ritschls*, pp. 44–46 ("The Theological School of Albrecht Ritschl").

severe condemnation, if it be remembered that in many respects Ritschl's own mind experienced the transition from old to new principles and methods in theology, which he sought to effect in the thought of his age.

(2) Refusing to begin with the conception of God as "infinite, inceterminate existence," he asserts that "theology begins, as with the fundamental truth, with the full conception of the personal God, who establishes the kingdom of God as the final purpose of the world, and therein guarantees to everyone who trusts in God his position over the world." He concedes, however, what according to his own principles it was not necessary for him to concede (and this is the first step on the slippery path of speculation) that "the scientific right of theology is, however, yet to be grounded on the proof that the conception of *personality* is applied *to God* without contradiction." [1] In seeking to prove that God and personality can be combined in one conception, he first of all argues against Strauss' aesthetic pantheism, that the Universe cannot be its own ultimate cause and its own final purpose, but that we must infer a legislative and purposeful author; and in the next place against Strauss' objection, that personality and absoluteness are mutually exclusive predicates, he develops his own conception of personality, which he maintains is being progressively realised in men, but can be thought without any contradiction as perfect in God. While our human personality develops in dependence on our environment, and accordingly is not self-existent or self-sufficient, the divine personality contains in itself all that is necessary to its existence. "Nothing," he says, "that acts on the divine spirit is originally foreign to Him, and He does not need first to make anything His own, to be self-sufficient; rather is all that the world means for Him

[1] Ritschl's *Rechtfertigung und Versöhnung*, iii. p. 217 ("Justification and Reconciliation").

fundamentally an expression of His own self-activity ; and what reacts on Him from the movement of things He knows as the circular course of the reality which is through Himself possible." This is the ideal of personality, and " we by it as a standard recognise whether and in how far the same predicate belongs to us." [1] Without now discussing the more general question whether our human thought is capable of forming such a conception as that which Ritschl presents to us in the words quoted, or the more special question whether his definition is as good as such a statement could be made, let these two points alone be meanwhile noted, first of all that Ritschl here practises a speculative method with a thoroughness and boldness that is in marked contrast to the limitation in dealing with the objects of faith which he elsewhere not only rigorously imposes on himself, but vigorously demands from others ; and, secondly, that he practically admits here all that theologians have contended for when they insist on the application of the predicate "absolute" to God and accordingly his polemic against Frank is due to a not altogether blameless, because in some measure wilful, misunderstanding of his opponent's position.

(3) As Ritschl's method is to construct as he criticises, the next step of his argument is an attack on the Socinian and orthodox conceptions of the moral order of the world, which we have already had occasion to notice (see page 89), and which, therefore, need not now detain us. Having, as he believes, disproved the error in regard to the relation of God to the world, he seeks next to exhibit the truth. The question that must first of all be asked is, " What purpose has God in common with the human race, or can He have in common ? " The answer given is that " if the destination of the human race includes spiritual and blessed communion with God, then this purpose cannot stand

[1] *Op. cit.* pp. 224, 225.

out of relation with the purpose of God for Himself; between the creation of men for that purpose and the creative will of God there cannot be thought an accidental, but there must be thought a necessary relation." [1] This is the first step in the speculative deduction of the kingdom of God from the love of God, and ultimately from the personality of God. The starting-point of theology along this path can be only "the conception of God, in which the relation of God to His Son our Lord is expressed, and by His mediation is also extended to His community." This conception is expressed in the name "the God and Father of our Lord Jesus Christ," and this means nothing else than that "God is revealed to the Christian community as love." But this does not mean that to the general conception of personality there is added the special conception of love, but that, unless "the formal conception of the personality of God is just as useless as a pantheistic formula," personality must be predicated of God "only as the form of the particular content of love." [2] At this point we must pause to notice, first of all, that Ritschl does not do justice to his own conception of personality in thus reducing it to be a mere form of which love is the sole content, for personality means self-possession as well as self-communication distinction from as well as union with others; secondly, that he does not treat seriously his own statement that the love of God is directed primarily and originally to His Son our Lord, and only secondarily and mediately to the Christian community; for had he done so, he would have been necessarily led to a more adequate recognition of the significance and the value for Christian thought of the doctrine of the Trinity, and to a less ambiguous statement of the difference between the filial relation to God which belongs to Christ by nature, and the filial relation which the Christian gains by grace; and, thirdly,

[1] *Op. cit.* pp. 257, 258.　　　　[2] *Op. cit.* pp. 259–261.

that in his haste to get from God to the kingdom of God in his speculative deduction he neglects and ignores all that is not at once serviceable for his immediate purpose, however important and even necessary it may be for Christian theology.

(4) Having thus leaped rather than walked from personality to love, Ritschl next tries to get from love to the kingdom of God. The will of God can be the source of any reality only as it receives a particular determination. The purpose of God determines the direction of the will of God. The purpose of God expresses the love of God. Hence the love of God is the ultimate cause and final reason of the world. But this love of God needs closer definition, and this definition may be given in four particulars. (1) " *First of all*, the objects of love are necessarily of the same kind as the loving subject, that is, spiritual persons. (2) *Secondly*, love is a will steadfast in its direction. (3) *Thirdly*, love is directed for the furtherance of the recognised or surmised purpose which another sets himself. (4) *Fourthly*, love will only then be a steadfast will, and there will be no separation and alternation between the appropriation and the furtherance of another's purpose for himself, but a union in every act, if the will of love assume into its own personal purpose for itself the other's purpose for himself." [1] As regards the first and second features of love, according to this description no objection need be made; but as regards the third feature a qualification, which we shall yet see is of utmost importance, must be insisted on ; and it is this, that the recognised or surmised purpose of another can be furthered only if the loving subject is able to regard it as consistent with the end he sets himself; or, in other words, love is not the surrender of one's own personal ideal to another's purposes, but in all self-communication there must also be self-

[1] *Op. cit.* pp. 263, 264.

17

maintenance. This qualification must be applied to the fourth feature as well. The purpose of another can be assumed into one's own purpose for one's self only if the one be consistent with the other, for the latter must not be sacrificed to the former. No personality is at liberty to surrender its individual independence and its moral responsibility, even for the sake of furthering another's purposes. Keeping before us this necessary qualification, let us note how this definition of love is applied to God. " Only in one or in many spiritual persons can we represent the object, which corresponds with His essence as love." But while " reflection on the world offers the thought, that a number of spirits united in a genus can be the correlate of the love of God," yet so united as a genus, subject to natural conditions, humanity lacks the affinity to God that is necessary in love; and therefore the correlate of the love of God, in which all the necessary conditions are met, can be only " the Christian community, which makes the kingdom of God its task." As this community, however, owes its existence to the fact that " the Son of God is its Lord, and it is obedient to Him, the community of Christ is consequently only the point of reference of the love of God, because the love in which God embraces His Son, and assures to Him His uniqueness (Mark i. 11, ix. 7; John xv. 9, xvii. 24; Col. i. 13; Eph. i. 6), through Him becomes operative for those who belong to Christ as His disciples or as His community." The conclusion of the argument may be summed up in the words, " God is love, inasmuch as He reveals Himself through His Son to the community founded by Him, in order to develop it into the kingdom of God, so that He realises in this supramundane purposeful destination of men His honour, or the fulfilment of His purpose for Himself.' The argument, thus briefly indicated, provokes

---

[1] *Op. cit.* pp. 264–268.

two questions : (1) First, if God be God, that is existence by, in, and for self, how can an ideal for the human race which has a local and temporal existence, an ideal, too, which is being only progressively realised, be identified with God's purpose for Himself? This is to bring God into dependence on, nay, even subordination to, His creature. Hegelianism appears at least to represent God as coming to self-consciousness in the intelligence of finite man ; and so Ritschl seems (although probably he does not mean) to present to us God as reaching the goal of His own being only in the social organisation of finite mankind. It is true that the conception of God as love suggests the necessity to His very existence of the objects of His love ; and the deduction from His love of the being and end of mankind, if carried out with any logical rigour, raises the problem of what God was or did before man was made.   In seeking thus to show the dependence of man on God, the thinker is prone to insinuate into the mind the idea of the dependence of God on man.   While this difficulty must be fully admitted, yet it must be frankly added that Ritschl has not been as careful as he might have been in stating distinctly the limitations which must necessarily be imposed on any such argument as he employs ; and the result of the discussion is simply that God is identified in thought with the kingdom of God. (2) Secondly, there is a way of escape from the difficulty which is involved in this mode of argument from which Ritschl turns aside, even although he has taken the first step along it. In recognising that the Son of God is the immediate object of the love of God, and the Christian community only mediately through His dominion over it, and its dependence on Him, Ritschl admits an object for the love, a purpose for the will of God, which if construed as in the doctrine of the Trinity, is not external to God Himself, and so does not represent God as dependent

on any created existence. Why, we may well ask, if
Ritschl will soar into these sublime heights of speculation
regarding the nature and purpose of God, and His relation
to the world and man, why does he not soar just a little
higher into the more open sky and clearer light of this
doctrine, based on scriptural testimony, and confirmed by
religious experience? Ritschl has gone too far to turn
back without imperilling the logical consistency of his
thought.

(5) Unfortunately, however, Ritschl is in thorough
earnest in limiting the doctrine of God by the idea of the
kingdom of God. All the attributes of God are confined to
their relation to the kingdom of God. (*a*) The *righteousness*
is the consistency with which in spite of all hindrances he
carries out His purpose in the kingdom. " By righteousness," he says, " there is described in the Old Testament the
consistency of the guidance of God unto salvation, which
is partly proved in the case of the pious and upright
adherents of the old covenant, and partly anticipated for
the community, in which the dominion of God will be
completed for its salvation. In so far as the righteousness
of God for this purpose is carried through, in spite of all
the hindrances caused by the Israelites, in accordance
with His guiding purpose to save, it is *fidelity*. For this
reason also is the righteousness of God also recognised in
the New Testament as the measure of the distinctive action
by which the community of Christ is brought into existence, and is led on to its completion ; accordingly it cannot
be distinguished from the grace of God." [1] (*b*) Again, no
attempt is made to do justice to the conception of *holiness*,
but it is dismissed from consideration in a few words.
" Beside love," he declares, " no other conception of equal
value comes into consideration. Especially is this the case

[1] Ritschl's *Unterricht in der christlichen Religion*, pp. 13, 14
(" Instruction in the Christian Religion ").

in regard to the conception of holiness, which in its Old
Testament sense for various reasons is not valid in Christianity, and in its New Testament use is indistinct."[1]
(c) The *wrath of God* he holds to be an eschatological conception, and to mean God's intention to destroy those,
if there be any such, who persistently oppose themselves to
the realisation of the purpose of God in the kingdom of
God. "According to the authority of the New Testament," he says, "the wrath of God means the resolve of
God to annihilate those human beings who finally set
themselves against salvation and the final purpose of the
divine kingdom."[2] The term, accordingly, has no application whatever to the sinners, whom God has appointed
to share in the kingdom of God, and the salvation from
sin which it includes. The consciousness of the change
of divine wrath into divine mercy of which the sinner
is often the subject, is a human representation, but not
a divine reality. To this very important subject we
must, however, again come back at a later stage of the
discussion. (d) The *omnipresence* and *omnipotence* of God
mean that "the providence and gracious presence of God
is assured to pious men for this reason, that the world-
creating and sustaining will of God is directed to the
highest good of men."[3] (e) The attribute of God which,
however, suffers most distortion, with wide-reaching and
serious results for other parts of Ritschl's theological system,
is *eternity*. Rejecting the conception of eternity as
"existence without beginning or end," he defines it as
"the steadfastness and the sameness of the intention of
God's will in itself." As "the steadfast and unchangeable

---

[1] Ritschl's *Rechtfertigung und Versöhnung*, iii. p. 260 ("Justification
and Reconciliation").

[2] *Op. cit.* p. 306.

[3] Ritschl's *Unterricht in der christlichen Religion*, p. 13 ("Instruction in the Christian Religion").

direction of His will to His purposes for Himself and within the same to the kingdom of God," it presents a contrast to "the changing activity of God in time, of the assumption of which one can as little get rid in theology as in religion."[1] This admission of a changing activity of God in time, without which our relation to God because our consciousness is conditional by time, would lack reality, is, however, practically ignored; and God is represented as if He had exercised His freedom only in one choice of will, in adopting the kingdom of God as His own purpose, and were henceforth bound by that purpose, so that He could not vary His method of dealing with men according to their attitude to Himself. The atonement of Christ, the forgiveness of sin, the sense of guilt of the sinner, the punishment of sin by God, all these doctrines are affected very injuriously by this narrow conception of God's eternity. All God's relations to men are ignored or denied practically except His destination of them for the kingdom of God. To sum up briefly, the highest object of Christian theology is not dealt with in order that man may as fully as his powers allow know God in His infinite and eternal perfections, but always and only as a means towards an end. God's value for the kingdom of God, that is the exclusive standpoint from which the being of God is regarded. Justly does Wegener say in regard to the use by Ritschl of the idea of the kingdom of God, that "the worst is this: all urges on to this to unite kingdom and God by a sign of equation."[2] If the *worth* of a religion depends on the *truth* of its conception of God, then the theology that does not give an adequate and satisfactory conception of God, so far as human powers allow, is not

---

[1] *Rechtfertigung und Versöhnung*, iii. pp. 282–284 ("Justification and Reconciliation").

[2] Wegener's *A. Ritschls Idee des Reiches Gottes*, p. 126 ("A. Ritschl's Idea of the Kingdom of God").

likely to exercise the best possible influence on religious
faith and life.   For this reason, most of all, must one
deplore that Ritschl (for it is against Ritschl alone that
the criticism is here directed) has fallen so far short in
the supreme task of theology, to set forth the grace
and glory of "the God and Father of our Lord Jesus
Christ." √

CHAPTER IX

THE DOCTRINE OF THE PERSON AND THE WORK OF CHRIST

I

(1) As the name itself shows, the central fact and the determinative truth in the *Christian* religion is the person and the work of *Christ*; and, therefore, the significance and the value of any theology that claims the acceptance of the Christian Church must be tested by the accuracy and the adequacy of its *doctrine of Christ*. This test we must now apply to the Ritschlian theology. To anticipate in a few sentences the results of the discussion on which we are entering, it may be stated that at first sight the doctrine of Christ as expounded by Ritschl himself appears very defective but that a closer view shows that it does not deserve the unmeasured condemnation that it has sometimes received. Some of the charges brought against it cannot on a thorough examination be justified, although they may be explained by isolated statements of Ritschl's. The difference of *principles* and *methods* between the Ritschlian and other schools of theology must always be taken into due account in estimating any of its positions. What appears from another standpoint even foolish or false, may from the point of view of the school have some meaning and truth. This general consideration must be insisted on. It is not the intention of any member of the Ritschlian school to depreciate the person or the work of Christ, to lessen His glory, or lower His position, or weaken His claim. All

are as jealous for His honour and dignity, as zealous for His cause and dominion, as the most orthodox champion of the ecclesiastical dogmas. It may be argued rightly that the principles and methods of the school do not allow it to offer us an accurate and adequate doctrine; but when we are estimating this doctrine itself we must not ignore, as has been done, the distinctive position of the school, in relation to which primarily the doctrine must be judged. It may be added that, as will afterwards be shown, the disciples in their writings advance beyond Ritschl's positions in many respects, and some even show a tendency to approach very nearly the Church's confession concerning Christ.

(2) "Christianity as a universal religion," says Ritschl, "is so constituted that in *its view of the world, a place is made for its historical founder.*" The two other universal religions, Islamism and Buddhism, do not accord the place to their founders which the Christian religion does to Christ; but Christianity is fulfilling its founder's intentions in assigning to Him a unique value. "Without doubt," he continues, "Jesus experienced a religious relation to God that had not previously existed, and demonstrated it to His disciples; and it was His intention to introduce His disciples into the same religious view of the world and judgment of themselves, and under this condition into the universal task of the kingdom of God, which He knew to be assigned to His disciples as to Himself." Jesus constituted a new relation between God and man in His own person, and by His own action on His disciples He reproduced it in them. This new relation was, on the one hand, a fresh estimate of themselves and of the world; and on the other, a fresh task, the fulfilment of the divine purpose of the kingdom of God. He was not only the organic type, but also the vital principle of the new religion. But not only is religion realised in Him and reproduced by Him. "He founds," says Ritschl, "His religion with the claim to reveal God

fully, so that beyond it there is no further revelation thinkable, and to be expected." In Him, then, the absolute revelation and the perfect religion are united; and this union is described by the predicate of divinity which is assigned to Him. This connection between the predicate of divinity and the functions of Christ as regards His Church is expressed in the Greek formula that " God became man (the absolute revelation) that man might become God " (the perfect religion); but, although this formula was accepted in the Latin Church also, yet it was always so construed as to separate and distinguish Christ from the members of His community. The *worth* of Christ Himself seemed to be made greater by making His *work* in and for man less: an exclusive was preferred to a communicative divinity. Luther, while accepting the traditional doctrine of the two natures in the one person, attempted to restore the religious valuation of Christ, which is expressed in the predicate of His divinity. Faith or confidence in Christ is regarded by Luther as the true confession of His divinity; and thus " His divinity is introduced" into theology " as a value-judgment." Christ is God to us because He does for us what God alone can do. " This religious valuation of Christ as God, Luther attaches really to the significance of the work of Christ for the Christian community. and to His position, which is determined thereby, at the head of the kingdom of God." This religious valuation of Christ as God is not a denial of His divinity; for while " it does not belong to the province of disinterested scientific knowledge as the Chalcedonian formula," yet it is a value-judgment, since " all knowledge of a religious kind is direct value-judgment," and " we must be able first to prove Christ's manifest divinity before we can reflect on His eternal divinity." [1]

---

[1] Ritschl's *Rechtfertigung und Versöhnung*, iii. pp. 364, 365, 367, 368, 370, 372, 376, 377 (" Justification and Reconciliation ").

(3) At this point in the exposition some words of further explanation are required. (*a*) First of all, let it be said again, although were it not for persistent misconception of Ritschl on this point repetition would be quite unnecessary, the description of the application of the predicate of divinity to Christ as a value-judgment does not mean that Christ is not God in reality, but that we imagine or represent Him to be God, either to cheat ourselves or to flatter Him. This predicate of divinity is not a fancy born of our need or of our love. It is the only adequate explanation we can give of a fact of our religious experience. Had we not this experience of what Christ has done for us, for us at least the fact would not exist demanding this explanation. This dependence of the genuine confession of Christ's divinity on the actual experience of His grace is all that is meant, neither more nor less, by describing it as a value-judgment. Christ has for us the worth of God, and therefore we call Him God. The critics of Ritschlianism assume, it is true, that Christ may have the *worth* of God for us without *being* God ; but this distinction between the *value* and the *existence* of God is one of those logical subtleties for which they alone can claim the credit, for the Ritschlian school is quite innocent of it. When Ritschl says that Christ has the *worth* of God, he is neither so much the fool nor the knave as to mean that Christ *is not* God ; but as a sincere and intelligent thinker he means that Christ is God. (*b*) In the next place, Ritschl's distinctive method claims careful consideration. To reach the worth of Christ he starts from the work of Christ. This is the inductive method of modern science. He starts from facts, what Christ is and does in the community that bears His name, and thus he reaches the truth, which alone explains the facts, of what Christ is in His own Person. Christian theology hitherto has usually started from the self-witness of Christ, or the apostolic testimony to Christ ;

but this method may be charged with two defects. In the first place, it must at the beginning of the investigation assume the entire and constant trustworthiness of the scriptural records and reports; and such an assumption, unless it be the conclusion of a previous searching and thorough critical process, cannot be made the foundation for such a structure as the ecclesiastical dogma of Christ's Person. But this method suffers from a still more serious defect. It is not experimental; it does not start from the religious consciousness itself; the confession of Christ's divinity rests on external authority, not personal conviction. Ritschl's method seems provisionally at least to be the better of the two.

(4) Ritschl, having thus stated his own method, does not shrink from comparing it with the traditional method. How does the value-judgment of Christ's divinity stand related to the ecclesiastical dogma of the two natures in the one person? This is the question which Ritschl next faces. Luther assumed the ecclesiastical dogma, while going beyond it in the direction of the value-judgment; but this Ritschl reckons as one of his inconsistencies, for he holds that "the historical and religious view of Christ finds no place in the framework of the doctrine of the two natures." In his criticism of this doctrine he first of all denies that "any uniform *doctrine of the divinity of Christ* is to be discovered exegetically in the New Testament." Secondly, he asserts that the predicate Κύριος, "which, according to Jewish custom, is equivalent to God, is attached by the majority of the apostles to the dominion over the world into which Christ by His exaltation to God's right hand has entered," Paul especially connecting "God's bestowal of the same with the exaltation." Thirdly, he attempts to explain all the passages in which Christ's cosmic relations as cause and as purpose of the world are mentioned, as referring to Him in His exaltation, inasmuch as that exaltation, though last in exe-

cution was first in intention with God; for it is not Christ's ✓
priority to the world in time, but His superiority to the world
as "the image of God and as the head of the community"
which is expressed in the phrases πρωτότοκος πάσης κτίσεως
and πρὸ πάντων. Fourthly, he denies that any help in ex-
plaining these passages can be found in the conception of
Christ's pre-existence, "for the exalted Lord alone can be
thought as the purpose of the creation of the world"; but
from the standpoint of God these conceptions "are intelligible without special difficulty," for "if God before the
making of the world foreknows and foreordains his Son as
the perfect Lord of the right community, with reference to
whom the world also is made, then the Son of God stands
over or before the world in the intention of God as the
mediating cause (*Mittelgrund*) of the world." Fifthly, he
maintains that John's two statements regarding "the Word
who became flesh," and "the glory of the only-begotten of
the Father, full of grace and truth," must be understood as
solely the result of "the experience of the community of
disciples," for "both forms of the representation of the
divinity of Christ (the Pauline and the Johannine) are of a
religious kind for this reason, that they describe the value
of Jesus in the world-view introduced by Him, and in the
judgment of self connected with it." Lastly, he holds that
the state of Christ as exalted can be described only by
means of the content of His historical activity; for "if the
representation of His present dominion cannot be filled up
by the distinct features of His historical activity, then it is
either a worthless form, or the occasion of all kinds of
fancies possible."[1] It must be acknowledged that in
Ritschl's treatment of the New Testament there is not
a little arbitrary and artificial exegesis. The conception of
a personal pre-existence of Christ, whatever may be its
obscurities and difficulties, cannot be got rid of in the New

[1] *Op. cit.* pp. 378, 380, 381, 382, 384.

Testament. Yet, on the other hand, Ritschl does well in calling attention to the formative influence on apostolic doctrine, both of the knowledge of the historical Jesus and of the faith in the exalted Christ, for doctrine in the New Testament is the expression of experience.

(5) Passing now from New Testament doctrine to ecclesiastical dogma, Ritschl charges the traditional Protestant Christology with beginning with " the divine nature with all the attributes of God, especially omnipotence and omniscience, which are the principal concern in regard to the creation of the world," instead of the historical person; and accordingly with being unable so to combine with this divine nature a true humanity, as to present to us the living unity of the person of Jesus as it is known to us in history. The Kenotic doctrine, which, to preserve the historical person must divest the divine nature of its distinctive attributes, is the necessary consequence of this traditional Christology, but it is also its sufficient refutation, for " it confesses openly that we cannot express the humanity and the divinity in the same relation and in the same time regarding the person of Christ; that is, that both predicates mutually exclude each other." " It is nothing else than mythology," he adds. " which is taught under the name of the Kenosis of the divine Logos." In opposition to this traditional Christology he maintains that we must begin with the historical person of Christ, as revealer of God and redeemer of men " The religious valuation of Christ, which finds only a specially conditioned expression in the predicate of His divinity, must be maintained from the connection of His evident action with His religious conviction and moral motive; it does not refer, however, directly to the assumed endowment of His person with innate capacities. For not in this respect Christ acts on us, but in that." His activities, so regarded, are not merely human, but fundamentally divine; " and accordingly the theological solution of the

problem of the divinity of Christ must be based on an analysis of the activity of Christ for the salvation of humanity in the form of His community." [1] With Ritschl's judgment of the traditional Christology and its *reductio ad absurdum* in the Kenotic theories the writer can cordially express his agreement. The lesson of that failure, to begin with the work of Christ, he has also for himself learned.[2] By the positive consideration of the experimental character of our religious knowledge, and by the negative consideration of the failure of the traditional theological method, we are led by Ritschl to what it is hoped will prove a safer path.

II

(1) In dealing with the work of Christ, Ritschl again starts from the orthodox Protestant theology. " This subject," he says, " is treated in dogmatics under the heading of the three *functions or offices of the God-man."* The

---

[1] *Op. cit.* pp. 384, 386, 388, 389, 393.

[2] These, the writer may be allowed to add, are not hasty judgments, but conclusions forced on him by a close and careful study for a number of years of the problem of Christology. The ecclesiastical dogma seems to him to sacrifice, on the one hand, the unity of the Godhead ; and, on the other, the unity of Christ's Person. The Kenotic theories are commendable as attempts to do justice to the historical personality of Jesus, while assuming the ecclesiastical dogma ; but are unsatisfactory in putting an undue strain on the passages in the New Testament which are supposed to teach the doctrine, and in venturing on bold assertions about the constitution of deity, which go far beyond the legitimate compass of our intelligence in these high matters. The writer confesses God as Father, Son, and Spirit, and Christ Jesus our Lord as Son of God and Son of Man, and maintains that God is as He reveals Himself, and Christ is what He claims to be ; but he holds that the doctrines of the Godhead and Christ need theological restatement, in which our more adequate modern conceptions of " personality," " development," " liberty " will gain full recognition, and the less adequate ancient conceptions of " nature," " substance," " person" will be superseded. Meanwhile he is content to search ever more deeply into the meaning of the New Testament representations ; and is convinced that such a study is the best preparation for a theological restatement.

rule that ought to be observed in this treatment, that the functions He exercises for us He also transfers to us, so that we, too, become prophets, priests, kings, is not faithfully observed in the dogmatic systems; as stress is laid rather on the difference than on the similarity between Christ and the Christian. There is also some confusion as regards the relation of the three offices to the two states of humiliation and exaltation, as some theologians place the offices in a temporal succession,—teaching first, sacrificing next, and reigning last,—and others, without expressly denying the kingship in the state of humiliation, practically confine it to the state of exaltation. Ritschl holds that this traditional treatment of the doctrine must be modified in several respects: (1) the term personal vocation should take the place of the misleading word office; (2) the likeness between the Founder and the member of the Christian community as regards calling and work should be clearly recognised; (3) the kingly function or activity of Christ should be regarded as primary, and the priestly and prophetic as secondary, being only complementary aspects of it—the one expressing the kingship in relation to man, the other to God; (4) the prophetic and the priestly kingship should be asserted equally of the state of humiliation and the state of exaltation. (i.) As regards the term to be used, he says that " in these relations one can only speak of the personal vocation of Christ," and " it commends itself to one to abstain from giving to the activity of Christ the title of office." The former description corresponds with the ethical and spiritual content of the work of Christ, whereas the latter title has too pronounced and fixed legal and hierarchical associations. (ii.) He maintains, with reference to the likeness of the Founder and the members of the community, that " what Christ is for us must be verified in the transfer of His work to us." This means that Christ transfers us to the relation to God which He Himself occupies, that He communicates to us the consciousness of God, which He Himself possesses. What He realised in Himself (His work for us) He reproduces in us (His work in us). Our Christian life is completed only as we become in all points even as He is. In thus laying stress on the similarity between Christ and the Christian, Ritschl does not intend—as we shall afterwards see—to bring Christ down to the common human level and limitations; for he expressly recognises that Christ was not only "the firstborn among many brethren" in point of time, but that all His brethren are absolutely and continually dependent on Him for the existence and continuance of the relation to God which is His originally. (iii.) Instead of ascribing to Christ three distinct functions, Ritschl seeks to represent the work of Christ wholly from the standpoint of His Kingship. "Jesus," he says, "is called the Anointed only to define His royal dignity. If along with this He is also called prophet and priest, then it is clear that His prophetic activity produces the material for His royal action; and it is to be expected, according to the previous explanations, that His priestly activity in His voluntary sacrifice of His life must be understood as a proof of His Kingship, which was conditioned by the circumstances." This statement affirms three important considerations. Inasmuch, firstly, as, on the one hand, Jesus claimed to be the Messiah of the Jewish expectations, and thereby presented Himself to His disciples as a King; and as, on the other, whatever He did He did as head of the community, the kingdom of God, the royal function must be regarded both historically and theologically as primary. Inasmuch, secondly, as the aim of Jesus' teaching was the establishment of the kingdom of God in His own person, His prophetic function can be included in His royal function. Inasmuch, thirdly, as Jesus in His active and passive obedience, in His sacrifice, was the representative of His community as its head, His

18

priestly function, too, may along with His prophetic be subordinated to His Kingship. But these subordinate aspects of the Kingship cannot without confusion be identified; for " the former (the priesthood) moves in the direction of man to God, the latter (the prophetship) in the reverse direction of God to man." In other words, Christ as priest is identified with the Christian community as its *representative*, but as prophet is identified with God as His *agent*; or the former distinguishes Him from God in uniting Him to man, the latter unites Him to God in distinguishing Him from man. (iv.) The relation of the two states of Christ to His vocation must, according to Ritschl, be otherwise conceived than in the orthodox Protestant theology, the defect of which in this respect has already been noticed. " These two states," he says, " form a contrast only logically; actually all that falls into the state of exaltation must be represented as a continued action of the corresponding members of the state of humiliation, if it is to be brought into a clear representation at all "; for " if Christ has founded His community through His royal prophetship and priesthood, then one can judge its present preservation by the continuance of these functions of the exalted Christ only according to that which one recognises as the content of these in the historical manifestations during His life." [1] A misconception of Ritschl's meaning must here be carefully guarded against. Ritschl does not mean that the exalted Christ is merely a *spectator* of the posthumous influence of the life and work of the historical Jesus, although that has been represented as his meaning; but he does mean that the exalted Christ is still an *actor* in human history, whose action, however, we have no other means of knowing and understanding except the words and works of the historical Jesus. The royal prophetic and priestly functions He exercises now are of the same kind as those which He

[1] *Op. cit.* pp. 394, 409, 410, 395, 404, 405, 407, 408.

exercised in the days of His flesh ; and our understanding of the former depends on our knowing the latter. With these four modifications—the use of the term personal vocation instead of the word office, the recognition of the likeness of Christ and Christians in their functions, the inclusion of the prophetic and the priestly in the royal function, and the interpretation of the state of exaltation by the state of humiliation—Ritschl is willing to accept the doctrine of Christ as prophet, priest, and king.

(2) Ritschl has undoubtedly rendered Christian theology a service in the stress that he lays on the conception of personal vocation instead of the conception of office as descriptive of the work of Christ. Many false and misleading associations attach themselves to the latter term, while the former suggests many significant and valuable considerations, bringing into clearer view the spiritual and ethical elements in Christ's work. The term also has from Ritschl's standpoint the advantage that it brings Christ's work under the same rules as the common moral and religious task of mankind. While there are some theologians still who object to the recognition of any likeness whatever between Christ and Christians in their high and holy calling, and refuse to interpret the sacrifice of Christ by any human analogies ; yet not only, on the one hand, are we likely to gain a clearer understanding of what Christ has done for us if we use our own experience in the interpretation of His work ; but also, on the other, in the work of Christ we may surely expect to discover a perfect application of the absolute principles of duty, which are to be " the light of all our seeing." But this consideration has already led us to the second modification in the traditional doctrine on which Ritschl lays stress. While asserting this similarity of Christ and Christians, he does not, as we have seen, intend thereby equality. Yet he has laid himself open to misconception by the unqualified way

in which he asserts this similarity; for our absolute dependence on Christ for our filial consciousness of, and filial confidence in, God demands that in reverent and adoring gratitude we always recognise that it is in virtue of His unlikeness to us that He in His grace can raise us into such likeness with Himself as may become ours. Yet the correction of this exaggeration of a truth by Ritschl may be found in Ritschl himself. In insisting, as he does, on the Kingship of Jesus as the adequate and exhaustive category for the description of His work, he expressly affirms Christ's superiority to us, and our subordination to Him. If He is prophet and priest as the head of the community, then equality between Him and His members is out of the question, and even any similarity that may be affirmed can be only a relative one. It is evident that Ritschl's use of the idea of the kingdom of God as the regulative principle of dogmatics has led him to prefer the category of Kingship to either of the two other categories. The question may be raised, however, whether if any modification is to be made in the traditional doctrine, the three categories alike should not be set aside; for all alike carry with them misleading associations, and are insufficient to express all that Christ is and does. Although used in the Holy Scriptures, do they not belong to the temporary forms of expression, and not to the permanent contents of our Christian faith? Are not the moral and spiritual facts which they express more fully and truly expressed in the categories of Son and Brother, which are not taken from the Old Testament, but are Christ's own terms? However, accepting Ritschl's own term King as descriptive of the work of Christ, he does well in insisting on the fact that in the state of humiliation Christ already exercised a moral and a spiritual dominion over the world and mankind, and that we are to expect the same genuinely moral and spiritual features in His dominion in the state of exaltation. Not

only is the Jesus of history the interpretation of the Christ
of faith, but He is the only interpretation ; but the Christ
of faith is *actor* in as well as *spectator* of Christian history,
a truth Ritschl fails to state with the clearness which would
save him from being misunderstood.

III

(1) Approaching the Person of Christ more closely
through His vocation, Ritschl, on the one hand, distinguishes
the religious from the ethical estimate of Christ ; yet, on the
other hand, maintains that the ethical estimate of Christ
according to His vocation involves His religious recognition as the revealer of God.   As man perfectly realised (the ·
ethical estimate), He is also God perfectly revealed (the ·
religious recognition).   Jesus, according to Ritschl, distinguished Himself from the prophets, and regarded His life
as " *the perfect self-revelation of God,*" not withdrawing " any
of the relations of His spiritual life and work from this
standard," as Paul does, when he distinguishes Christ's life
in him from his own life of faith in Christ.   For this fact,
that the total content of Christ's " spiritual life and work "
was divine revelation, John finds the appropriate expression
when he states that " the Word became flesh," that is, " the
divine revelation is a human person."   But this expression
can be taken in either of two ways : either the divine Logos
is the form and the human person the content, or the
human person is the form and the divine grace and truth
the content.   The earlier verses of John's Prologue (1—13)
suggest the former view, the later verses (14—18) the latter.
Both views are necessary, and are complementary and not
contradictory.   " When our religious judgment asserts that
God is not only with Him (Acts x. 38 ; John viii. 29) but
in Him (John xiv. 10, xvii. 21), that His characteristic
activities are God's activities, His love to man as the motive ·

of His whole action is identical with the love of God, then it is necessary for us to vary this with judgments, in which the ethical independence of Christ is expressed in the form of human freedom." To put this contrast more briefly, Christ must be regarded as a *divine organ* and as a *human agent*. The moral point of view must first be taken, and then the religious can follow. This is Ritschl's method, but the traditional is the very reverse. If Ritschl's method allows the moral somewhat to obscure the religious view, the traditional method quite hides the moral view behind the religious. It is true that in its emphasis on Christ's obedience the Protestant theology of the past assumed the moral point of view, but in representing that obedience as the discharge of an office, and not the fulfilment of a personal vocation, it again abandoned it. According to Ritschl, the moral point of view is maintained throughout, only if what Christ did for others is regarded as the fulfilment of His own end. To give an illustration to make this point clear : when the writer of the Epistle to the Hebrews declares that it " became Him, from whom are all things and by whom are all things, in bringing many sons unto glory, to make the Captain of their salvation *perfect through sufferings* (ii. 10)," this might mean either that Christ in His death discharged His *official task*, or that He fulfilled His *personal calling*; the former view excluding, the latter including a moral process of development, self-realisation. Ritschl insists on the latter view. " The fundamental condition of the *ethical judging* of Jesus is contained in this, that whatever He was or did, that He is in the first place for Himself. Every spiritual life is included in the form of the personal end for self." The older theologians, according to Ritschl, " so exclusively claim Him for their salvation, that they are unwilling to concede to Him the honour of an existence for Himself (proseity), without which, in fact, no man renders to others anything worthy." " In opposition to this," he continues, " it is certain that the human life of Christ must be included in the framework of the end for Himself of which He was conscious, and of the right of His existence for Himself, in order that His actions and intentions towards man may be understood as such." [1] In other words, Christ as a person is an end in Himself; He realised His own ideal, He developed His own personality, He reached His own perfection in His work for man. He is not, as theology has too often represented Him, merely a means towards the end of man's salvation. In insisting so strongly on this point, Ritschl is obeying a sound and healthy impulse of reverence for the person of Christ; but his position here is in marked contrast to his treatment of the doctrine of God, where he fails to represent God as an end in Himself, and instead deals with Him as a means towards the kingdom of God as end.

(2) Jesus' living for Himself did not, however, exclude His living for others, for His own end was the realisation of the purpose of God for mankind. " While Christ realises His own purpose for Himself by His orderly dealing and speaking, it results from the peculiar content of the same that He in this form also realises the purpose of others, namely, has served the purpose of man's salvation." Christ's sufferings, too, in virtue of the patience with which He endured them, become a kind of action, and so acquire a moral significance. His action and passion alike can thus be embraced in the idea of a moral vocation. Of this vocation Jesus regarded the term Messiah as an appropriate expression; and to this He absolutely subordinated every relation of His life; it exclusively claimed His interest and devotion; He maintained His fidelity in it by His patience in the sufferings unto death which in its fulfilment He brought upon Himself. In thus fulfilling His vocation He was always conscious of fulfilling the will of God: His

[1] *Op. cit.* pp. 412, 414, 417, 418.

action and passion was the work of God Himself. Thus the moral passes over into the religious estimate of Christ; and be it specially noted that this religious estimate of Christ rests on His self-testimony regarding the identity of His work with God's. "The personal purpose of Christ for Himself has the same content as is included in God's purpose for Himself, which Christ knew and willed as such; and accordingly He as the bearer of the divine purpose-for-self is in anticipation also known and loved by God." To this last thought of the pre-existence of Christ in the mind and will of God we must again return; but what meanwhile is to be noted is this, that Christ's consciousness of the perfect accord of His will with God's corresponds absolutely with God's consciousness of Him. God's thoughts regarding Him are as His own thoughts regarding Himself. The religious estimate of Christ which results from the moral is this: "As He as the founder of the kingdom of God, or as the bearer of the moral dominion of God over mankind, is the only one in comparison with others who have received from Him the same final determination, so He is that magnitude in the world in whose self-end God makes His own eternal self-end in an original manner operative and manifest, whose whole activity in His vocation accordingly forms the matter of the complete revelation of God present in Him, or in whom the Word of God is human person."[1] Christ is unique in the human race as perfectly realising God's purpose, and as perfectly revealing God's nature. What this involves as regards the relation of Christ to God, Ritschl forbids us further to inquire, as the problem is insoluble, the solutions attempted are valueless, and Christ is offered to faith and not our understanding. While the writer has followed this exposition with cordial sympathy so far, he cannot, however, accept this prohibition, to go no further; but to this question we must return at a later stage of the discussion.

[1] *Op. cit.* pp. 418, 425, 426.

IV

(1) While Ritschl thus bars our onward path, yet he allows us to take note of those features in the revelation of God in Christ which warrant our assigning to Him the predicate of divinity. (i.) First of all to be noted is the "grace and truth," the love, with which He sought man's highest good in the kingdom of God; and in this He revealed God. "In the distinctive activity of Christ in accord with His vocation the essential will of God as love is revealed, because the final purpose of Christ, the kingdom of God, is identical with the final purpose of the Father." Such a revelation of God is possible, since "the essence of God, as it is spirit and will and especially love, can become operative in a human life, as man, in fact, is constituted for spirit, will, love." (ii.) In the second place, Jesus claimed dominion over the world, "not an inherited omnipotence," "not an arbitrary control of the whole law-governed continuity of nature" (His miracles, Ritschl holds, do not prove any such power); but "an independence of His religious self-consciousness in opposition to the world," which it is His aim to confer on the members of His community also. What was involved in this independence one illustration will show. "Although Jesus could live for His vocation only as a born Israelite, and in connection with His people, yet He raised Himself above these particular or secular limits of His existence, not only by the universally human horizon of His activity, but also by the religious independence of His self-judgment as regards all distinctively Old Testament standards." Of Him it can be said as of God, that "His thoughts are not man's thoughts, neither His ways man's ways." His independence, originality, and authority in word and deed are one proof of His dominion over the world. A still more striking proof of His "distinctive power

over the world is His patience in suffering," in which He
was conscious of meeting and overcoming "the tempting
resistance of the world." The world could not turn Him
away from His fidelity to His vocation either by its pleasures
or by its pains. Its temptations to secure success or to
evade suffering, had no power over Him. (iii.) To these
two features a third must be added : His complete success
in the fulfilment of His purpose. "To the complete determination of the divinity of Christ belongs the circumstance
that His grace and truth and His world-ruling patience have
reached their result in this, that the community of the kingdom of God exists under the analogous attributes." Christ's
success in reproducing His attributes in His community
does not involve, however, that its members are placed on
an equality with Him ; for " Christ as the historical author
of this communion of men with God and among one another
is necessarily *the only one of His kind.* For if a second could
be shown, who were materially equal to Him in grace and
truth, in world-ruling patience as in compass of intention and
result, yet he would stand in historical dependence on Christ,
would accordingly be formally unequal to Him." There is
always a difference of origin between Christ and Christians,
" for the members of the community of Christ come thereto
such as originally had in them another direction of their
will ; the figure of Christ, however, is not to be understood
at all, if it is not His original peculiarity, that He finds in the
self-end of God His personal final purpose." To the charge
that, as this explanation of the divinity of Christ places it
in the will and not the essence, it is not a recognition, but a
denial, Ritschl answers that " everywhere one judges men
according to their character, so that one recognises their
essence in this form of their will." To go behind the character for an explanation to the nature is to ignore the fact
that "the good will is never the simple mechanical action
of the natural combination, within which it comes into exist-

ence." If it is maintained that Christ is not to be explained as any other personality, then, Ritschl asserts, "one makes Christ unintelligible."[1]

(2) While the explanation of the character is not to be sought in the nature of Christ, yet at the same time we must go beyond His historical appearance to give the predicate of divinity its full content. The speculative deduction by which Ritschl seeks to reach this necessary enlargement of the idea must be given fully. "The unity and the similarity with God, which the kingdom of God must command in order to be understood as the point of attraction for the love of God, belongs to that magnitude only in that it is evoked by the Son of God, and subordinates itself to Him as its Lord. Accordingly, the love of the Father is in the first place directed to the Son of God, and only for His sake to the community of which He is Lord. If these relations, further, are eternally posited in the loving will of God, then it results from this our knowledge, that the specific significance of Christ for us is not already exhausted in this, that we value Him as a revelation temporally limited. But it belongs to this, further, that He as the founder and as the Lord over the kingdom of God, is in the same way the object of the eternal knowledge and volition of God as is the moral union of men, which through Him becomes possible, and which possesses in Him its type, or rather that He, too, in the eternity of the divine knowledge and volition precedes the community." But as this statement might appear to admit only an ideal preexistence, it is to be carefully noted that Ritschl himself goes a step further. While he maintains, on the one hand,

---

[1] *Op. cit.* 428, 429, 430, 431, 433, 434, 435, 437, 438, 439, 440. The last sentence has been quoted as proving that for Ritschl Christ was "mere man," as explicable by the terms of our ordinary experience as any other; but all Ritschl means is that, inasmuch as Christ is a person, the category of personality must be applied to Him in the same way as to any other person.

that "the eternal divinity of the Son of God is altogether transparent for God Himself alone"; yet, on the other hand, he asserts that "while we set aside at the same time the difference between willing and fulfilling in God, we get the formula, that Christ exists for God just such as (als derjenige —als der) He is revealed to us in temporal limitation. But this only for God; for as pre-existing Christ is hidden for us." [1]

(3) To sum up Ritschl's teaching on the divinity of Jesus as briefly as can be, be it noted that he maintains that the essence of God's love is fully and clearly revealed in Christ; that He in His teaching and life was independent of the world, owing nothing to it, and fearing nothing from it; that He was wholly successful in His work of re-producing in the members of His community His own consciousness of, and confidence in, God as Father; that, however, His relation to God was direct, whereas that of all others is mediated by Him; that His distinction from all others was in the original identity of His will with the purpose of God; that His life and work can be understood only as He is regarded as primarily, while His kingdom is regarded only as secondarily, the object of the eternal know-ledge and volition; that, consequently, as He is historically revealed to us, so He eternally exists for God. Ritschl, it will be evident from this summary, rejects the orthodox doctrine of the two natures in the one Person of Christ, and of the three Persons in the one substance of the Godhead. What he seeks to substitute for the former is an original direction of the will of Christ, in virtue of which God's final purpose was constantly and completely accepted by Him as His own self-end. What he tries to put in the place of the latter is a real object of the eternal knowledge and volition of God. Both these explanations illustrate his theological method, to fix attention on the phenomenal aspects of

[1] *Op. cit.* pp. 441, 443, 444.

reality, and to neglect consideration of the noumenal.   As
the reality of Christ's person lies for him in His spiritual
activities, so also the reality of God's existence in His
knowing and willing.   Accordingly, from his standpoint the
relation of Christ to God, and of God to Christ which he
affirms, is not less, but more real than identity of nature
would appear to him.   His intention, therefore, is not to
doubt or deny the divinity of Christ, but to give to it the
most adequate expression, and to offer of it the most convincing evidence, that from his point of view are possible.
Nevertheless, his exposition cannot be regarded as satisfactory.   An object of God's knowing and willing, especially
a personal object (for as such Christ is revealed to us
historically) which exists for God eternally, as soon as we
try to form a rational conception of it, forces us to recognise
that a necessary truth about God's being is expressed,
however imperfectly, in the orthodox doctrine of the Trinity,
although we may still question whether so precise a definition
of the nature of God is within our mental capacity.   An
original direction of the will, which results in a perfect
identity in action of divine purpose and human volition,
demands a further explanation, as, although nature does not
exhaustively explain character, yet the compass of individual
liberty is defined by the range of personal capacity, and the
empirical actuality of any person depends on the essential
possibility.   The doctrine of the two natures has already
been admitted to be unsatisfactory, but it at least recognises
a necessity for our thought which Ritschl's view ignores.
While in these respects seriously defective, Ritschl's
teaching has this merit, it begins the proof of our Lord's
divinity where it ought to begin, with the historical life and
work.

(4) As Ritschl devotes one section of the chapter of his
book, with which we are now dealing, to Christ's priestly
work, his conclusions may be here briefly mentioned,

although it will be necessary to discuss these more fully in dealing with His doctrine of *Sin and Salvation*. He denies absolutely that the sufferings of Christ were a vicarious endurance of the penalty of sin, inasmuch as Christ in His suffering had no sense of guilt, did not judge His sufferings as punishment, did not think of them as endured instead of others, or as intended to make men afraid of sin. He affirms confidently that the two features of His priestly action were the maintenance of His own personal religious relation to God, and the reproduction of that same relation in the members of His community. Having thus dismissed the common view of Christ's work as priest, and having limited it to the maintenance in Himself and reproduction in others of communion with God, He is thus enabled to subordinate the priestly to the kingly function of Christ. How far he is untrue in so doing to Christian experience will afterwards be shown at the stage of the discussion at which the subject can most appropriately be dealt with.

V

(1) Professor Denney, in his *Studies in Theology*, brings against the Ritschlian school the following sweeping charge : " We must," he says, " as rational beings try to clear up to our minds what is necessarily involved in the existence among men of a person who has the religious value of God. Theologians who refuse to go beyond this are invariably found to cover, under the guise of a religious indifference to metaphysics, a positive disbelief of everything which gives Christ's Godhead an objective character. They do not admit the supernatural birth, they do not admit the pre-existence taught by St. Paul, they do not admit the doctrine of the Incarnation of the Logos, at least as taught by St. John." [1] He then goes on to contrast " the Christian

[1] Denney's *Studies in Theology*, p. 14.

consciousness " and " the scientific consciousness " in regard
to Christ, and describes the forms as " the subjective
estimate," while ascribing to the latter " the neutral consideration." This part of his charge has, however, been
fully dealt with already (see page 187), and it is therefore
unnecessary to devote any more attention to it. As has
already been noted in dealing with the place of miracles in
the Christian revelation (see page 222), he further accuses
Ritschlianism of a denial of miracles, and especially of the
resurrection ; but this charge also has been shown to be
without justification. In a note on the passage in which
Ritschl is charged with denying the resurrection, it is also
stated that " Ritschl refuses to connect Christ's kingship
with His exaltation after death." [1] This statement has not
yet been dealt with, and therefore now claims consideration
along with the charges made in the passage quoted here.

(2) With the insinuation of insincerity made against the
Ritschlian school the writer need not pause to deal, as in all
courteous, not to say Christian controversy, it is quite out
of place. The suggestion, that the value-judgment by
which the predicate of divinity is assigned to Christ is a
merely pious fancy, shows that the critic has not come to
understand what the Ritschlian " value "-judgments are.
But enough has already been said on this subject to show
this without any further proof now. What demands our
immediate scrutiny is the assertion that " the supernatural
birth," " the pre-existence taught by St. Paul," " the Incarnation of the Logos, at least as taught by St. John," are the
things that give " an objective character " to " Christ's Godhead." One would think that any theologian who weighs
and measures his words with care, would certainly hesitate
about confining the " objective character " of " Christ's Godhead " to these things. It may be remarked, to begin with,
that this contrast between " objective " and " subjective " is

[1] *Op. cit.* pp. 261, 262.

a tempting, but also a perilous one. What is exactly meant by the term "objective" here? Does it mean furthest removed from, least dependent on our own religious consciousness of what Christ is and does for us, which in contrast is to be regarded as "subjective." In that sense certainly these things are more "objective" than the other evidences usually relied on, for they make the least direct and potent appeal to our personal experience. In comparison with these other evidences we have assuredly, in the Ritschlian sense, least interest in them, they have least value for us. Can the term "objective," however, mean most convincing as evidence? This at least would appear to be the meaning intended. But can this be seriously maintained? First of all let it be considered that the first thing is one for which less adequate evangelical testimony exists than for the words and works of the Lord Jesus Christ during His ministry. Every candid scholar must admit that "the virgin-birth" is less fully attested than the other facts of our Lord's life. Next be it noted that Paul's doctrine of pre-existence and John's doctrine of the Logos were not original elements in their Christian faith, and were not part of the common teaching in the apostolic Church, but were individual interpretations of their Christian consciousness. In view of these two considerations it may be remarked, lastly, that, if we are to regard these things as the most convincing proof of our Lord's divinity, we must assign to the New Testament Scriptures an absolute authority, which the Christian may accord to it after having been led to find in Christ his Saviour and his Lord, but which Christian theology cannot for apologetic purposes put forward as the foundation on which faith in Christ must begin to build. It is interesting to note, however, that Professor Denney in his book throughout makes what may be in all fairness described as a *dogmatic* use of the Holy Scriptures, for which his own doctrine of their inspiration does not afford adequate justification. To avoid misunderstanding, the writer may say frankly that he, for reasons that seem to him good, does accept all these things; but what he does object to is, that what is least certain and convincing, what least directly and potently appeals to religious experience (for he holds that the things under consideration are "objective" in the first, but not in the second sense indicated), should be put forward as the only foundation of our faith in Christ as God. On the contrary, he holds that the sinless perfection of Christ, His consciousness of God's Fatherhood, His relation of grace towards sinners, His own self-testimony, stand in the first line of evidences for His divinity; and that it is only those who accept these evidences who can be led on by their reflection on their experience to recognise the truth of the evangelical testimony to the virgin-birth, or of the apostolic interpretation of Christ's Person.

(3) If we endeavour to translate into current speech Ritschl's statements of the features in the revelation of God in Christ which warrant our assigning to Him the predicate of divinity, we find that they are practically the evidences on which modern apologetics has been led to lay most stress. The essence of God as Love is expressed in His person. He is in His teaching and work inexplicable by the world into which He came, and in His action and passion alike shows Himself superior to it. He has been able to establish and maintain in that world a community, the members of which have His own filial consciousness of, and confidence in, God. There is an absolute identity between His activity and the fulfilment in the world of God's purpose for mankind. These are self-evidencing moral and spiritual facts; and Ritschl is justified in putting forward these as the proofs on which the recognition of Christ's divinity for men of the present day at least must rest. In his method he shows a thorough

19

appreciation of the intellectual situation of the present age
(see p. 19), of which, it must be said with regret, his critic
fails altogether to give proof.

(4) These things, which, according to Professor Denney,
" give Christ's Godhead an objective character," the Ritschlians are charged with not admitting.   But this assertion
without any qualification goes far beyond the evidence.

(i.) As far as the writer is aware (but on this point he is
open to correction), Ritschl does not expressly deny the
virgin-birth.   It is probable, however, that as he denies, as
we shall see, original sin, and refuses, as we have seen
(see p. 282), to find in nature an explanation of character,
he would treat the fact of the virgin-birth as having no
religious significance.   His generally distrustful attitude
towards modern historical criticism forbids our taking for
granted, however, that he would have denied the fact, as
some members of his school have done, on the ground of
insufficient evidence.   As the sinlessness of Jesus and the
virgin-birth have by some theologians been brought into
necessary connection, it must be carefully noted that Ritschl
affirms the sinlessness of Jesus, although he regards it as
a fact that is in no way inconsistent with His humanity.
" The sinlessness of Jesus (John viii. 46; 1 Pet. ii. 21;
1 John ii. 5 ; 2 Cor. v. 21; Heb. iv. 15) is only the negative
expression for the steadfastness of His disposition and
method of action in His vocation (obedience, Phil. ii. 8;
Heb. v. 8), or for the positive righteousness in virtue of
which Christ sets Himself over against all other human
beings (1 Pet. iii. 18)."   Nevertheless, " the sinlessness of
Jesus is not in contradiction with His human nature." [1]
If Harnack denies the fact of the virgin-birth, it must
be remembered that he goes further than Ritschl ever did
in applying historical criticism to the New Testament.

[1] Ritschl's *Unterricht in der christlichen Religion*, pp. 19, 20, 26
("Instruction in the Christian Religion").

" Ritschl," says Ecke, " from the year 1857 assumed an essentially conservative attitude in relation to the biblical canon, and almost altogether denied the incursion of Hellenistic views into the confession of the first community "; while " Harnack," he continues, " has made concessions to modern criticism, by which the personal life of faith of the Christian is painfully affected, and the foundation offered by Ritschl for the dogmatic structure is shaken." " It is worthy of note," he adds, " that according to Frank's communication, Ritschl was very much displeased by a remark of Harnack's which made this difference distinct." [1] It is not fair to regard Harnack's critical opinions as results of the Ritschlian position.

It has already been shown (p. 208) that Herrmann does not deny the fact of the virgin-birth, although he refuses to accept it as a necessary article of faith ; and that he finds its significance in the confession " that the spiritual life of Jesus has not issued from the sinful race, but that in Him God Himself has entered into the history of this race." [2] Although some of the Ritschlians, then, may deny this fact, and others pass it over as having no distinctive value for faith, this is not a position that is peculiar to Ritschlianism, but is shared by theologians of other schools. The denial or the neglect of the fact is not a consequence of their alleged " religious indifference to metaphysics," as here we are in the region of physical facts, not metaphysical conceptions. There are theologians who hold as firmly as Professor Denney does the divinity of our Lord, who have nevertheless their doubts and difficulties about the virgin-birth. This first count of the indictment may therefore be dismissed as partly unproven, partly irrelevant.

[1] Ecke's *Die Theologische Schule Albrecht Ritschls*, pp. 117, 118 (" The Theological School of Albrecht Ritschl").

[2] Herrmann's *Worum handelt es sich in dem Streit um das Apostolikum*, p. 13 (" What is involved in the controversy about the Apostles' Creed ?").

(ii.) As regards Paul's doctrine of Christ's pre-existence, Ritschl seeks to do justice to it in discussing a number of passages from Paul's letters. What he insists on is, that Paul conceived of Christ as pre-existing as the Head of the kingdom of God, as the exalted Lord ; and explains this conception by the principle that what is last in divine execution is first in divine intention. That he means something more than an ideal pre-existence we have already seen ; for he maintains that Christ exists eternally for God as we know Him really in history, although that pre-existence is hidden from us. Harnack, who is led by his acute critical impulse rather than by any essentially Ritschlian tendency, does explain the pre-existence as taught in the New Testament by Jewish modes of thought. But Herrmann gives no uncertain sound on this question. " I certainly," he says, " hold the conviction, which I need not here more closely justify, that faith in Christ is led in a natural advance to the representation of a pre-existence of Christ, and indeed a personal and not an ideal. The assumption of a so-called ideal pre-existence seems to me unjustified. It is surely manifestly the *Person* of the exalted Lord, the worth of which for the community and for the kingdom of God is expressed in this, that it did not come to be within earthly conditions as we, but is independent of the world, which represents the fully dependent province of its dominion. This thought finds in the representation of a personal pre-existence of the Lord, it is true, a contradictory expression, and yet the only one that might be at our command, which, therefore, will have its saving truth. The contradiction will be removed when once the riddle of time has been solved for us, in which we now view our existence." [1]

Kaftan in dealing with New Testament Christology

[1] Herrmann's *Die Religion im Verhältniss zum Welterkennen und zur Sittlichkeit*, p. 438 (" Religion in Relation to our Knowledge of the World and Morality").

includes the doctrine of the pre-existence and the doctrine of the virgin-birth as alternative "speculations regarding the divine dignity of Jesus," which attached themselves to "the knowledge of the community."[1]   There is accordingly in the Ritschlian school at least so much difference of opinion on this question as forbids such a sweeping statement as that made by Professor Denney.

(iii.) Again, as regards John's doctrine of the Incarnation of the Word of God, Ritschl undoubtedly rejects the ecclesiastical development of the doctrine, as emphasising the rational instead of the religious aspect of it; but he claims to explain it when he is dealing with Christ as the perfect revelation of God, when he asserts that the divine revelation and the human person are in such organic unity that we may, from the moral point of view, regard the human person as the form and the divine revelation as the content, or, from the religious point of view, regard the divine word as the form and the human life as the content.   Ritschl's objection to the traditional doctrine of the two natures is that it does not give adequate expression to this organic unity; and Herrmann, too, maintains that we want to find God more immediately in Christ than such a doctrine allows.   "Whoever," the latter says, " still shares the desire for salvation of the Reformers, cannot explain to himself the most important object of faith, the presence of God in Christ, in this way, that the divine substance was united with human nature."[2]   Kaftan, while recognising a speculative element in John's as in Paul's Christology, nevertheless declares that "at least it is also according to my view an irrefutable consequence of faith in the divinity of the Lord, that He, that His historical

---

[1] Kaftan's *Dogmatik*, p. 372 ("Dogmatics"). Although the writer has not thoroughly studied this volume, he has allowed himself a few references to it when this seemed specially desirable.

[2] Herrmann's *Verkehr des Christen mit Gott*, p. 141 ("The Communion of the Christian with God," p. 136).

person stands in a connection of nature with God which
is altogether unique, and cannot be repeated. We cannot
say to a human being *God*—the word is too great and
too weighty, if we do not truly mean that the eternal God
Himself in Him has come to us, and in Him has communion with us."[1] That Ritschl, Herrmann, and Kaftan
do full justice to the theological data of the New Testament as regards the doctrine of Christ, the writer does not
for a moment maintain; for he is convinced that an adequate
and satisfactory Christology can be reached only by a very
much fuller use of, and very much greater reliance on,
the evangelical testimony and the apostolic interpretation
than as yet is discoverable in the Ritschlian school. Yet
he ventures to hold that such a phrase as is used by
Professor Denney, "positive disbelief," does not express
justly their attitude to the Johannine Christology, or to the
teaching of the New Testament generally upon this question,

(iv.) Ritschl does not, as is alleged by the same critic,
"refuse to connect Christ's Kingship with His exaltation
after death." What He does is to assert that the Kingship
in its priestly and prophetic aspects was exercised even in
His humiliation, and is not confined to His exaltation, as
the traditional theology inclines to maintain. This Kingship
is continued in His exaltation, and maintains the same
ethical and spiritual character throughout. While he does
maintain that " Christ as exalted is hidden from us " (and
one would like to know who since the appearances of the
Risen Lord to His disciples has seen " Christ as exalted ";
or who can make any affirmations regarding the precise
conditions of His exaltation in addition to what the
historical manifestation suggests, if this position is to be
denied); yet he affirms that the Church founded by
Christ's royal prophetship and priesthood " is at present

[1] Kaftan's *Brauchen wir ein neues Dogma?* p. 58 ("Do we need a
new Dogma?").

maintained" by the continuation of these functions of the exalted Christ.[1] It may be admitted that Ritschl does obscure the truth of Christ's continued presence and activity by his insistence on the historical media,—the Scriptures, the Church, and the Christian society,—but he never really intends to deny that Christ is actually present and active in these. The charge in the connection in which it is made is evidently intended to suggest that Ritschl altogether disbelieves in the exaltation of Christ. For that suggestion, it may be said confidently, there is no warrant whatever, unless Ritschl is to be regarded as one of the most confused thinkers or dishonest writers with whom theology has been afflicted. While he does not in the same degree as Kaftan dwell on the thought of the exalted Lord, yet he again and again speaks of the exalted head of the Christian community. To sum up now very briefly the defects of Professor Denney's criticism of the Ritschlian school, he misunderstands the value-judgments ; he charges, on very slight grounds and in spite of strong evidence on the other side, the Ritschlians with a denial of miracles generally, and the resurrection especially ; he does not justly represent their attitude to the virgin-birth, the pre-existence, and the incarnation of the Logos, while his own position that these alone give "objective character" to "Christ's Godhead" is one which, in the interests of a theology that seeks to cast its roots deep into the soil of Christian experience, must be seriously questioned. One other charge which he makes, that "Ritschl has no eschatology," will be disproved in the eleventh chapter of this volume. As the great popularity of Professor Denney's work has given to his criticisms a very wide currency, the writer has felt himself bound, in the cause of truth and justice, to deal so very fully with these charges.

[1] Ritschl's *Rechtfertigung und Versöhnung*, iii. p. 407 ("Justification and Reconciliation").

(5) Turning back now from Professor Denney's criticism to Ritschl's own teaching, a brief summary may, in closing this chapter, be attempted. Ritschl seems right in insisting at the start on the necessarily religious character of our knowledge of Christ's divinity, which can be confessed only by Christian faith. In dealing with the New Testament teaching he is not altogether just to it, and seeks to force its statements unduly into the mould of his own thought. That the ecclesiastical dogma is inadequate and unsatisfactory he maintains with right and reason. If his treatment of the doctrine of the two states and the three offices looks like an attempt to pour " new wine into old bottles," yet it also shows how the older view in some of its features already suggested the newer. One must always be grateful when the continuity of theological thought is so far as possible maintained. We cannot escape the double estimate of Christ, first from the standpoint of His personal perfection, and then from the point of view of His divine revelation ; and Ritschl's treatment here is of very great value. His representation of the " manifest " divinity of Christ, if not altogether adequate, yet does lay stress on the features of primary importance. His prohibition of any deeper investigation of the problem must be, however, set aside ; and his own essays in that direction, inconsistently made, must be pronounced as altogether inadequate.

CHAPTER X

THE DOCTRINE OF SIN AND SALVATION

I

(1) ALTHOUGH Ritschl's doctrine of sin is altogether distinguished from the doctrine of sin current in the speculative philosophy which has an inclination to pantheism, inasmuch as he denies the necessity of sin and affirms the reality of guilt; yet, on the other hand, he differs from orthodox theology in developing his conception of sin, not in comparison with an absolute standard of righteousness valid for God and man, but in contrast to God's final purpose for the world, the kingdom of God; and he still more provokes opposition by (1) his denial of original sin; (2) his refusal to connect the wrath of God at present with sin, and so to regard the evils of life as penalties; (3) his description of sin as sin of ignorance, and so pardonable. In dealing, however, with these negative aspects of his doctrine, in which he does appear to fall short of Christian truth, it will always be necessary to keep in view the positive aspects which distinguish his teaching from the pantheistic position.

(2) It is advisable that we should begin with these positive aspects, and should give them their full value, instead of seeking to minimise their significance, as Professor Orr seems to do.[1] For Ritschl sin is no necessity, and therefore guilt is a reality; and he does not seek

[1] See Orr's *The Ritschlian Theology*, pp. 140, 141.

to explain them away as pantheistic thinkers even within the Christian Church have endeavoured to do. "Guilt," he says, " in the moral sense is the expression of that disturbance of the normal reciprocal relation between moral law and freedom which results from the abuse of freedom in opposition to law, and is signalised as such by the accompanying discomfort of the sense of guilt." By sin a man's relation to the moral law is changed, and he is conscious of that change. This is the general moral result; but what is the specifically Christian view of this change? "In the Christian world-view God is regarded as the author and the active representative of the moral law"; and, consequently, "guilt in the Christian sense signifies the contradiction against God into which the individual man, even as the totality of men, has entered by non-fulfilment of the moral law, which is recognised as existing by the consciousness of guilt, in which the individual experiences with discomfort the worthlessness of his own sins as also of his share in the common guilt." In this passage, then, are distinguished *guilt* as a moral and religious fact, and the *sense of guilt* as an individual knowledge of that fact. Guilt is a *moral* fact in so far as the contradiction is between freedom and law; a *religious* fact, inasmuch as the contradiction is between man and God. But this passage, it is important to notice, affirms that not only is guilt an *individual*, but it is also a *racial* fact; and the consciousness of guilt in the individual man includes discomfort on account of the latter as well as the former fact, or, in other words, the sinner grieves not only because he himself has sinned, but because he belongs to a sinful race. This contradiction between man and God involves "a separation of men from God, which takes the place of the community which is according to their destination." Men were made for union and communion with God; as guilty they are separated from God. Accordingly, "the *contradiction against God* and against one's own moral destiny, which is expressed in the conception of guilt, and is experienced with discomfort in the consciousness of guilt, is marked by this accompanying circumstance as a real disturbance of man's being"; for "he experiences the logical contradictions of his will against God, which is contained in guilt, as a real contradiction and as a real defect of the will." The disturbance of the relation of community between God and man, which is signified by guilt, of which man is conscious in his sense of guilt, has as its immediate result that the will of man itself suffers injury. Guilt being thus a reality, sin of which it is the effect is a reality also. "Accordingly, in the province of the will, sin as the disturbance of the ideal relation of the will to its final purpose, or to God as the representative of the same in the world-order, is a real contradiction." [1] Sin as the *act* of opposition of freedom to law, and guilt as the *state* of disturbance of man's relation to God, are both to be regarded as realities.

(3) While thus asserting the reality of sin and guilt as the moral consciousness of man testifies, he carefully abstains from any explanation of the origin or purpose of sin in the world which would in anyway invalidate that testimony. "Speaking generally," he says, "one is kept within very narrow limits in one's knowledge of the relation of sin to the divine order of the world. One must beware of describing it as an operation of God, and as a purposive member of His world-order; for it is in all cases the opposite of the good, and that which goes contrary to the recognisable moral final purpose of the world. It is an apparently unavoidable product of the human will under the given conditions of its develop-

[1] Ritschl's *Rechtfertigung und Versöhnung*, iii. pp. 56, 57 ("Justification and Reconciliation").

ment, and yet it is imputed by us as guilt in our
consciousness of freedom and independence.   Between
the two lines of thought, not even with Schleiermacher
does one dare to find a reconciliation in this way, that
God judges sin not as a contradiction of the Good, only
as the moral perfection not yet attained, while we must
judge our imperfection as sin in order to awaken in us
the longing for redemption and perfecting.   For as our
theological insight (*Ansicht*) surely dares not separate
itself from, or put itself in opposition to, our religious
view (*Anschauung*) of Christianity, therefore our judgment concerning sin must agree with the divine." [1]
While in this passage it is admitted that sin *appears*
inevitable, yet the condemnation of conscience is frankly
and fully accepted as convincing evidence that it is not
a necessity ; and the voice of conscience in this matter
is regarded as the voice of God.   "A universal necessity
to sin," he says elsewhere, "cannot be inferred either
from the equipment of the human being or from any
accordance with the purpose of his moral development,
to say nothing of a recognisable intention of God." [2]
Inasmuch as the affirmation of the *necessity of sin* is
being forced upon modern thought from two usually
opposed quarters, scientific naturalism which tends to
materialism, and philosophical idealism which tends to
pantheism, it ought to be regarded as a merit in Ritschl
that he so distinctly repudiates this conclusion, and in
his treatment of the two conceptions of sin and guilt
holds fast by the testimony of the moral conscience and
the Christian consciousness.

(4) We must now consider what is his conception of sin,
of which he affirms the reality and denies the necessity.

----

[1] *Op. cit.* p. 360.
[2] Ritschl's *Unterricht in der christlichen Religion*, p. 26 ("Instruction in the Christian Religion ").

THE DOCTRINE OF SIN AND SALVATION 301

Theology has usually represented sin as the violation of an absolute moral law, valid for God and man, which expresses an essential righteousness of God; but Ritschl refuses to follow this course. (i.) " If it follows from the assumed personality of God that God is real only in the form of will, then it is bad metaphysics to attribute to Him righteousness as a latent (*ruhende*) attribute, which should belong to Him apart from the form of will "; for (1) "the representation of a latent attribute springs only from a self-deception, when our continuous observation is arrested by the form of a steadfast activity "; and (2) " a necessity for God, which is not understood from the standpoint of His will, but is inferred from a latent ' natural' attribute, describes Him as finite and developing personality." [1]   To put this in simpler language, Ritschl refuses with orthodox theology to contemplate God *at rest*, and to describe the attributes of His nature.   He thinks that it is more conformable to the confession of God as personality to regard Him *in motion*, and to define the characteristics of His action.   He rejects the *static*, and prefers the *dynamic* method as more appropriate to the consideration of a living, acting God.   If God be not δύναμις merely, but ἐνέργεια also, his method is not without its justification ; although, at the same time, as has been already indicated (pp. 46, 47), *will* implies *nature*, the *phenomenal* the *noumenal* aspects of reality.   Accordingly, what is expressed as a form of the will is also possessed as an attribute of the nature ; and this is true of God, whose will and being correspond in a far higher degree than of man, for whom there are many unactualised possibilities.   Ritschl's statement is inadequate owing to the imperfection of his method ; but it is not in so absolute contradiction to the orthodox doctrine as his critics assume.   As for Ritschl, will is the reality of personality ; righteousness, as a characteristic of

[1] Ritschl's *Rechtfertigung und Versöhnung*, pp. 237, 238 (" Justification and Reconciliation ").

God's action, is not an accident for, but of the essence of God. (ii.) Righteousness as a characteristic of the will of God is expressed, not as an attribute of the nature would be in a *law*, but in a *purpose*. Here the teleological character of the Ritschlian theology again shows itself. But as Ritschl views God predominantly as love, and does not, as we have already seen (p. 260), do justice to any of the other divine attributes, it is not righteousness that finds expression in this purpose, but love, and righteousness only as subordinate to love. It is not with this righteousness as subordinate to love that sin is to be compared so that its nature may be known, but with the purpose, in which the love of God finds its expression. Not an absolute moral law valid for God and man is the standard of judgment, but a purpose which God chooses as His own self-end, and to which He calls mankind as to its self-end. This purpose is known to man only in the Christian revelation of the kingdom of God. Accordingly, " as we have *to comprehend the fact of sin from the standpoint of the community of reconciliation*, so exactly is the gospel of the forgiveness of sin the ground of our knowledge of our sinfulness." He admits that " the fact of sin was known also outside of Christendom "; but maintains that " the determination of its nature and the estimate of its compass and worthlessness is expressed in Christianity in an original manner, because here other representations of God, of the highest good, of the moral destiny of man, of redemption are valid than in any other religion." As " a representation of sin can be formed only by comparison with a representation of the good," and " as the compass and the binding significance of the good become first fully recognisable in the task of the kingdom of God, even as the same was faultlessly discharged in the life-course of Jesus, so also sin can be fully understood first as the contradiction of this highest moral good."[1] Instead of following this

[1] *Op. cit.* pp. 310, 311, 312.

right method, the traditional method, Ritschl holds, measures sin by an assumed original righteousness prior to sin; but this procedure denies Christ His rightful place as the determinative conception of all Christian theology. With Ritschl, we may agree that as we knew nothing of this original righteousness of man prior to sin, we cannot use it as a standard; with him, too, we may agree that the teaching and example of Christ is the ultimate, perfect, absolute standard, and that it is only in the consciousness of His salvation that men attain the adequate and certain conscience of their sin. Christian theology in its conception and estimate of sin should always assume the standpoint of the Christian consciousness. But to affirm the absolute standard is not to deny the relative standards. God was in the preparation of mankind for the kingdom of God as in the realisation of that kingdom in Christ. Men had a conscience of sin because they had a consciousness of God even before Christ came. Hence sin in any age or people may be conceived and estimated in relation to the best moral standards and the truest religious ideas possessed and confessed. In thus refusing to recognise facts, Ritschl here shows the same exclusiveness which has already been noticed in dealing with his views of revelation.

(5) Applying the standard of the kingdom of God, however, sin assumes for our thought a twofold aspect, a *religious*, as indifference to and distrust of God, as well as a *moral*, as selfish action towards men. "Sin is the contrary of the good, in so far as from indifference or distrust towards God it is self-seeking, and turns to the goods of lower rank without intending their subordination to the highest good." But sin in this double form is in contrast with the kingdom of God, not as the sin of each individual man, but as the sin of the whole race. "The subject of sin," says Ritschl, "is *humanity as the sum of all individuals*, in so far as the selfish conduct of each, which puts him into innumerable

reciprocal actions with others, is directed in some degree or another to a contradiction of the good, and leads to a combination of individuals in common wickedness." Thus "we form the conception of a *kingdom of sin*," [1] in which our evil actions affect others to encourage and develop their sinful inclinations, and we in turn are affected by the sinful action of others. As the kingdom of God is a community of men in goodness, so there is opposed to it a community of men in sin. Christian theology ought not, therefore, as it has hitherto done, to fix its attention exclusively on the individual sinner, but ought to recognise that the sin of every individual is conditioned by, and conditions the sin common to all the members of the society to which he belongs. The channels of intercourse between men, and the opportunities of influence, become the means of the confirmation and the extension of sin. This idea of "a kingdom of sin" opposed to "the kingdom of God" does correctly interpret facts, and so is to be warmly commended.

II

(1) From the positive aspects of Ritschl's doctrine we now turn to the negative; and first of all we have to consider his denial of original sin. He will not accept the doctrine of original sin as an explanation of this community of men in sin, which he calls "the kingdom of sin." "Even if this idea were distinct and necessary, yet it could not express the highest possible sense of sin"; for "the active sins are more than appearances or accidents of original sin," but "according to the direction of its actions the will acquires its kind, and develops to a good or a bad character." Active sins are the results of character, but character is formed by the direction which the free actions have given to the will. If this were not the case (1) we should not be

[1] *Op. cit.* pp. 317, 318, 320.

responsible for our actions; (2) education would be impossible; (3) differences of character would be inexplicable. The idea of original sin, which relieves us of responsibility, excludes the possibility of education, and makes all alike guilty, is due to that theory of knowledge which distinguishes "essence and appearance, substance and accident"; and must be regarded as "both an exaggeration and a diminution of the idea of sin,"—an exaggeration, inasmuch as it ascribes to sin a change in the constitution of mankind; and a diminution, because we are less responsible for a result of our nature than for a resolve of our will. Heredity is not a proof of original sin, for it is only as certain inherited dispositions are exercised in definite directions that any guilt attaches to them. The personal inclination to sin in every individual is, as far as our observation goes, adequately explained by "the self-determination of the individual will," for "'the law of sin' in the will follows from the necessary reaction of every act of will on the direction of the power of will." Paul does not, Ritschl maintains, "either express or suggest anywhere the inheritance of sin by generation," and "he offers no other ground for the universality of sin, or for the kingdom of sin, than the sinning of all individuals." Accordingly "it is not to be denied that there may be a sinless development of life, either *à priori* or according to the conditions of experience."[1] It must be frankly conceded that Ritschl in this position carries his prejudice against any theory of knowledge which recognises features and factors of existence that are not given immediately in experience to an extreme. As a question of fact merely, most keen observers and thorough reasoners would agree that there is a bias towards evil which belongs originally to, and is not gradually developed in, each individual human being; and that this bias is to be explained by the very close connection between parents and children. But ex-

[1] Ritschl's *op. cit.* 319, 322, 331, 330, 358.

20

aggeration of this fact must be carefully avoided; and
Ritschl is right in insisting as he does on individual liberty
and personal responsibility, on the formation of character
by the reaction of the will, and therefore on the importance
of education. Traditional theology has not been always
innocent of such an exaggeration. If we take into due
account the literary character which is now generally
assigned to the narratives in Genesis, and the subordinate
position in the Holy Scriptures accorded to all questions as
regards the origin and diffusion of sin, the place which the
traditional theology has given to the doctrine of original sin
will appear a far more prominent one than all the facts
warrant. Ritschl, by his denial of original sin, does not
minimise the extent or the potence of sin, but seeks to
explain it by an acquired tendency instead of an inherited
bias. In so doing he supposes himself to be bringing only
into greater prominence the distinctive character of sin, as a
voluntary violation of moral law, by an abuse of personal
freedom. In denying original sin he believes himself to be
defending man's individual liberty and personal responsibility.
If we are able to recognise, as he failed to do, that there is
no necessary contradiction between the several truths which
he sets over against one another, all we need charge him
with is defective mental vision. This is not shared by the
members of his school; for this denial is a peculiarity of
Ritschl, and is not distinctive of his school. Harnack, to
give only two illustrations, gives a most sympathetic account
of Augustine as a reformer of piety, and mentions as a debt
we owe to him that "we believe that it is necessary to pay
much greater heed to the essence of sin than to the forms
in which it is manifested—fixing our attention on its roots,
not on its degrees or on sinful actions." [1] Kaftan declares,
" sin reigns over us by nature, not we have sin, but sin has

---

[1] Harnack's *History of Dogma*, Eng. trans. v. p. 73 ; *Lehrbuch der Dogmengeschichte*, 2 A. iii. s. 64, quoted by Ecke, p. 249.

us," and "our nature is sinful from youth up, and yet we feel ourselves in our conscience responsible for the evil that we do." [1]

(2) The second feature of Ritschl's doctrine of sin which is opposed to the general teaching of the Christian Church is his refusal to connect the wrath of God at present with sin, and so to regard the evils of life as penalties. (i.) The transmission of sinful tendencies and inclinations by heredity has been commonly regarded as part of the penalty of sin ; and Ritschl accordingly has, besides his insistence on individual liberty and personal responsibility, another reason for denying this, inasmuch as he maintains that the wrath of God against the sinner is only an eschatological possibility, but not a present reality. He affirms that the representation of God's wrath belongs only to the standpoint of the Old Testament, and has no meaning whatever for the Christian. "All reflections," he says, "about God's wrath and mercy, His patience and forbearance, His severity and pity, rest on the religious comparison of our individual situation with God in the form of time." In other words, subjective changes in our own spiritual state, which is conditioned by the lapse of time, are explained by us as due to objective changes in God's relation to us, although God is not Himself subject to the condition of time. In this matter theology must correct religious reflection. "From the theological point of view, accordingly, the wrath of God and His curse on the sinners to be reconciled has no meaning ; all the less does there appear from this point of view as needful or as thinkable a special mediation between the wrath and the love of God, in order to explain the reconciliation of sinners with God." For inasmuch as "according to the

[1] Kaftan's *Das Evangelium des Apostel Paulus in Predigten*, s. 7, 12 ("The Gospel of the Apostle Paul in Sermons"), quoted by Ecke, p. 250.

authority of the New Testament the wrath of God means the resolve of God to annihilate those men who finally oppose themselves to redemption and the final purpose of the kingdom of God"; as regards the redeemed " we can infer their redemption theologically only directly from God's love, even although just these redeemed in their temporal mode of representation have the experience of the change of divine wrath and pity." According to this statement God has only one relation to humanity in His present dealings with it, and that is love. He holds in reserve for His future action an intention to deal in wrath with those individual men, be they many or few, who finally refuse to accept that relation to Himself which at present controls all His actions towards them. Thus He does not now change from wrath to love, nor is there any means necessary or possible to effect such change. Ritschl is well aware that his theology here cannot appeal to experience, and therefore he now seeks to show reason why experience may be disregarded. " It is of the greatest importance," he says, " for the systematic method of theology that the difference between our individual religious reflection and the form of theological knowledge *sub specie æternitatis* should never be left out of account." Accordingly, whatever changes there may be in our experience, we must not " introduce any change in the essential relations of the divine will." [1] On this argument several comments must be made. (*a*) And first of all Ritschl's view of the teaching of the New Testament on this subject will at first sight appear altogether unwarranted, as it runs counter to current conceptions ; but a closer consideration of the subject may at least compel us to pause before we dismiss it as one of the eccentricities of which his exegesis is not altogether free. In the *Inter-*

[1] Ritschl's *Rechtfertigung und Versöhnung*, iii. pp. 305–308 (" Justification and Reconciliation ").

national Critical Commentary on Romans there is a note on the phrase "ὀργὴ Θεοῦ" (i. 18) which substantially supports Ritschl's position, and at the close of which a reference is made to Ritschl's treatment of the subject as deserving consultation. Without transcribing the numerous references, the important parts of the note may be given. "(1) In the Old Testament the conception of the Wrath of God has special reference to the Covenant relation. It is inflicted either (*a*) upon Israelites for gross breach of the Covenant, or (β) upon non-Israelites for oppression of the Chosen People. (2) In the prophetic writings this infliction of 'wrath' is gradually concentrated upon a great Day of Judgment, the Day of the Lord. (3) Hence the New Testament use seems to be mainly, if not altogether, eschatological."[1] This is not the place for the discussion of this exegetical problem, but this note shows at least that biblical scholars, of whose knowledge and skill there can be no doubt, incline to take the same view as Ritschl. (*b*) But even if he be right in his exegesis, we may with good reason question his theology. God in his view is "crib'd, cabin'd, and confined" in one purpose,—and not only in one purpose, but even in one method of fulfilling that purpose. The fixity of His purpose is assumed to exclude variety in His method. Nay, even the very personality of God is deprived of all fulness and manifoldness, and is exhausted in one resolve. God's eternity is conceived not as identity in variation, but as fixity without change. God appears as free in the moment, so to speak, when He makes the world's last end, the kingdom of God His self-end, but as bound from and by that choice. Placed thus in His changeless eternity apart from, outside of the changes of history, how can He have any reciprocal relations

---

[1] *A Critical and Exegetical Commentary on the Epistle to the Romans*, by the Rev. William Sanday, D.D., LL.D., and the Rev. Arthur C. Headlam, B.D., p. 41.

with men, who are subject to these changes? This conception of Ritschl's strikes at the very roots of a living and growing communion between God and man. (*c*) Lastly, here, in the distinction Ritschl makes between the theological point of view and the religious, he introduces confusion into our religious thoughts, and deprives them of all certainty. But he is inconsistent with himself; for, arguing against the necessity of sin, he declares " our judgment must agree with the divine." Even so our religious experience reports to us not what God's relation to us *appears*, but what it is.

(ii.) If there is no wrath of God against sin, there can be no punishment by God of sin. This conclusion Ritschl expressly draws. He declines to regard the evils of our life as divine punishment, and declares that " the conception of evil (*Uebel*) has no direct relation to the conception of sin (*Sünde*)," for " it is no religious idea as this is." " Evil in general," he maintains, " is not recognisable as divine punishment of sin in the individual or the whole race," for " the interpretation of evils as punishments is rather conditioned by the specifically religious consciousness of guilt." A man conscious of gilt regards the evils that befall him as punishments. Here, then, we are concerned with a subjective representation, not an objective reality. Death as the last evil must be regarded from the same point of view. Even although Paul connected death with sin, his authority is not such as to compel the Christian theologian to adopt the same view. For the Christian, whatever view he may take of its origin, " to die is gain." Christian theology is concerned only with this view of death, as it is limited to the ideas that are distinctive of " the eternally chosen community of the kingdom of God."

But if the evils of this life, and even death itself, are not to be regarded as penalties of sin, can man sin with impunity? Ritschl answers decidedly, No. Sin does involve the sense of guilt, and this is not a subjective representation, but corresponds with an objective reality guilt, or separation from God. "The divine punishment" is "an experience of separation from God." "The unremoved sense of guilt is not a penal condition along with others, but this is the thing to which all other penal evils are related only as accompanying circumstances," for "outer evils can be shown to be divine punishments only from the standpoint of the subjective sense of guilt. Accordingly the penal condition of the whole pre-Christian humanity signifies the enforced distance of that humanity from the communion with God which was to be first brought about by Christ."[1] But if guilt means separation from God, exclusion from His communion, then in some sense God separates Himself from man, excludes man from His communion. Guilt must be a reality for God as well as for man, as we cannot, as has been already pointed out, entertain the distinction Ritschl tries to maintain between man's temporal and God's eternal point of view. What man experiences on account of sin, God intends. There is, then, punishment for sin, and that punishment must express God's displeasure with sin, His opposition to sin. Why not call it His wrath against sin, so long as we are careful to exclude from the conception whatever is inconsistent with God's perfection? But need we limit God's punishment of sin to this separation from the sinner? Without attempting to solve the insoluble problem of physical evil, and recognising that the saint suffers as well as the sinner, have we not good reason to affirm that God intends what each experiences in regard to the evils of life, that the saint should find in these a means of discipline

[1] Ritschl's *op. cit.* pp. 335, 337, 342, 345, 346, 347. The term "evil" has been used as rendering most exactly the German term *Uebel*, in spite of its ambiguity in being sometimes used as synonymous with "sin," an ambiguity which does not attach to the German term.

and development, and that the sinner should be compelled by these to recognise his estrangement from God? Man does not simply adapt the constitution of the world to moral and religious ends, but God Himself has made the world for these ends. The truth which Ritschl exaggerates is this, that God's sovereign purpose towards mankind is its salvation and blessedness, that all His present dealing subserves that end; but this does not involve, as he assumes, a uniformity and monotony of method.

As Harnack and Kaftan have been quoted to show that Ritschl's denial of original sin is not a common feature of his school, so Herrmann may now be quoted to show that his view of the wrath of God is not shared by all his followers. "Above all," he says, in describing the experience which leads to Christ, "we must feel in the needs of our moral life that we are forsaken by God." "We cannot," he says, "once more raise ourselves again out of the God-forsakenness of the evil conscience, and find our way back to God, unless when we can see that God in His revelation makes provision for this our need." "The sinner," he says elsewhere, "demands a fact which can be a match for the fact of his inner judgment." "God knows and loathes our sins, but does not wish to let us be lost," and He, "by His holy being keeps the sinner far from Him, and yet reconciles the sinner to Himself," but only in Christ.[1] These are but stray samples of the searching analysis of "man's state of sin and misery" which may be found in this book of Herrmann's, which shows beyond all doubt that to him the gospel means a great deliverance from a great distress.

(3) Ritschl's position regarding the wrath of God is not a necessary consequence of his general principles; but it is

[1] Herrmann's *Verkehr des Christen mit Gott*, pp. 94, 95, 106, 111, 23 ("The Communion of the Christian with God," pp. 94, 95, 106, 110, 26), quoted by Ecke, *op. cit.* p. 247.

due, on the one hand, to a metaphysical assumption of God's
eternity as changelessness of purpose, and, on the other,
to his too exclusive application of the idea of the kingdom of God as the sole regulative principle of Christian
theology; and in this position he has not been generally
followed.   The same reason can probably be given for the
third feature of his doctrine of sin, which has provoked
general opposition, his description of pardonable sin as
ignorance.   The purpose of Ritschl in this statement is not
to deny or to minimise the fact of sin, but simply to prove
the possibility of its forgiveness.   In this attempt he
appeals to the New Testament.   " In all the points of
view of the New Testament there is found the *recognition
of the differences in the value of sin*, namely, that sin which
can be forgiven or made inoperative by change of mind is
to be distinguished from that which is completed in the
form of final decision against the Christian salvation, or in
the form of incurable selfishness."   The former kind of
sin Ritschl describes as ignorance, for " ignorance," he says,
" is, as experience with children teaches, a very important
factor in the origin and development of sin.   Children,
when they enter into the common spiritual life, are neither
equipped with a knowledge of the good, or of the moral
law as a whole and in particulars, nor yet with an
inclination that had decided against the good as a whole."
But, on the other hand, he admits that " ignorance is not
the sufficient reason for the strengthening of the will in
evil, for will and knowledge are not altogether com-
mensurable."   Nevertheless, we must distinguish those
degrees of sin in which ignorance is an important factor
from that degree of sin " which can anticipate only
exclusion from God's world-order"; for if some men
are " reckoned by God as capable of salvation, then there
follows the judgment that God regards their sin as
ignorance."   This sin, however, " as enmity against God,

excludes the relation of grace between man and God."
As, however, "the possibility of love is in no way bound
to responsive love," "God loves the world, the sinners who
are possessed with enmity against Him with this intention,"
that "He may exercise towards them respect as moral
personalities by the maintenance of their existence and the
desire for their return." As such a return to God is possible
only where a final choice of evil has not been made, God's
will of love embraces only those whose will is not yet finally
determined, to whom the predicate of ignorance may be
applied, but excludes those whose "will intentionally sets
its own purpose in evil." But "whether there are such
men, and who they are, does not fall under our practical
judgment or our theoretical knowledge." Ritschl does not
intend, by calling attention to this fact that sin as we
know it, in most men at least, has not yet assumed the
form of fixity in evil, does not yet exclude the possibility
of repentance and reform, and therefore can be forgiven by
God, to affirm that the forgiveness of sin is a matter of
course ; for he says expressly "the forgiveness of sin is not
to be inferred from any of itself universally established
idea of God," but "its validity is attached to the unique
action of Christ."[1] That ignorance is a potent factor in
the development of sin cannot be denied. Even he who
does wrong when his conscience prohibits first and then
rebukes, is generally unconscious of all the moral issues of
his wilful choice. It is untrue that he who falls through
the weakness of his own nature, or the strength of the
temptation that assails him, deliberately and determinedly
makes evil his good. The sinner generally tries to evade,
rather than dares to defy the moral law. Most men, at
least, are not finally fixed in evil, finally opposed to good.
So far we may agree with Ritschl that a distinction is to

[1] Ritschl's *op. cit.* pp. 357–363, and *Unterricht in der christlichen Religion*, pp. 35, 36 ("Instruction in the Christian Religion").

be recognised between the sinner for whom there can be no
help or hope, and the sinner still capable of recovery; and
and that the latter in choosing evil is not fully conscious of
all that his choice means, while the former acts against the
clearest light.   Surely our Lord asserted these facts when
He spoke of the sin against the Holy Ghost which cannot
be forgiven, and distinguished it from all other sins as
pardonable, and when in His prayer for His murderers He
used their ignorance as a plea.   Paul, too, speaks of the
times of ignorance which God winked it; and John of a
sin that is not unto death.   But then Ritschl himself
admits that the development of sin in any individual
man is never fully accounted for by his ignorance; for in
all sin there is more or less wilfulness.   In fact, a man
may be gradually growing confirmed in wickedness, and
may be certainly approaching very near to that moral
state which is beyond help and hope; and yet the downward course may be arrested, the direction of the will may
be changed, and the diseased moral nature may be restored to health by the grace of God.   As man's condition
before God may be far worse than Ritschl's term ignorance
would describe it, so the possibility of forgiveness, which
means more than God's excusing sin, which means even
God's undoing in man of what sin had wrought, is a far
greater mystery of divine love than in Ritschl's theology
it appears.   God saves even the man who may be on the
point of denying Him.   Ritschl's use of the term ignorance
in this connection is very unfortunate, as it does suggest
a denial or a depreciation of the reality of sin, which he
surely does not intend.   What he means is that as
pardonable, sin has not assumed its final form as absolute
rejection of the good.   Yet one cannot but admit that
his treatment of the subject shows that he lacked an
understanding for the deepest Christian experiences of
abounding sin and superabounding grace. ✓

III

(1) These positions of Ritschl's as regards man's sin and guilt, and God's wrath and punishment, do very seriously affect his view of the work of Christ. As we have already seen, he affirms that there is no mediation necessary between God's wrath and mercy, and that man's capacity for moral and religious recovery and return to God explains the possibility of the forgiveness of sin. There is thus no hindrance in God, and no hindrance in man ; but the positive motive of the forgiveness of sin is the intention of God to form a kingdom of God, in which men should be united to one another in love. "If the reconciliation of sinners by God is to be thought, then it is thinkable without contradiction from the love of God, as the means of the establishment of the kingdom of God." [1] Sinners as the possible subjects of the kingdom of God are the objects of God's love and not His wrath ; sin is pardonable in so far as it is not a final opposition to the kingdom of God. God loves sinners, and forgives sin, not because He is morally indifferent, but because this love and this forgiveness are necessary as a means of establishing the kingdom of God, which God has chosen as His own final purpose. We must pause to consider the full significance of this position as compared with the position generally taken in the Christian Church. God so hates sin that He must punish sin. God so loves the sinner that He must save him from the punishment of his sin, and from his sin itself. In Christ, who suffers on account of sin, and on behalf, nay, even instead of the sinner, God's love fulfils its will to save. God in Christ does or suffers something, and so meets the necessities alike of His hate

[1] Ritschl's *op. cit.* p. 309.

of sin and love of the sinner.   This, apart from distinct
theories, is what Christian faith has hitherto commonly
affirmed.   All this, however, Ritschl denies.   Nothing
needs to be done or to be suffered on account of God's
hatred of sin.   God's righteousness is not to be thought
of as an inherent attribute, but as an operative purpose.
The kingdom of God is what God lives and works for.
He does not vindicate His righteousness by punishing
sin ; He realises it by establishing the kingdom of God.
He does not look backward on the sinner's past, but
forward to the sinner's future; He does not regard him
as an actual transgressor of His law, but as a possible
citizen of His kingdom.   He cancels the sinner's past, so
to speak, takes no account of it, in order that the sinner
unburdened with, unfettered by his sense of guilt and
his sin, may be capable of realising his future.   The
sinner needs, and yet does not deserve forgiveness ; but
the sinner cannot begin even to become a citizen of the
kingdom unless he is forgiven, that is, unless his separation
from God, due to sin, is changed to communion with God.
For this reason then, and this alone, that he may begin
to realise God's moral purpose as expressed in that kingdom, is the sinner forgiven.   That he may be encouraged
and enabled to keep the law, his breaches of the law are
not reckoned any more against him.   Thus forgiveness
is not in contradiction of the law, but is granted as a
necessary condition of its fulfilment.   To put the antithesis of the two positions thus outlined as briefly as
possible, leaving the necessary qualifications of the statement to be afterwards supplied, one may say, that while,
according to the orthodox view, the sinner is forgiven
for the sake of what Christ has done, according to
Ritschl's view he is forgiven for the sake of what he
may become as a citizen of the kingdom.

(2) This antithesis, however, would not be fairly stated

if it were said that, according to Ritschl's view, we are
forgiven, not for Christ's sake, but for the kingdom's sake,
inasmuch as the establishment and maintenance and completion of the kingdom are inseparably attached to Christ,
for the kingdom of God and the community of Christ
are identical. Christ, however, is not founder and ruler
of His kingdom because by His sacrifice He has made
atonement for sin. As priest, Christ "*is in the first place
priest for Himself*." "If Christ is to be represented as
priest, then the basis of this activity is contained in every
element of His consciousness that He as the Son of God
stands in an incomparable community with God as His
Father, which is present for Him in His knowledge of
God, in His submission of His will to God's appointment,
in the security of His accompanying mode of feeling."
It is in His religious relation to God in thought, feeling,
will, that Christ fulfils His priesthood for Himself. His
sacrifice must be looked at from this point of view, and
not as in the traditional theology. "Not the '*occurrence*'
of the death of Christ conditions its sacrificial value; but
His *submission* to this decree of His opponents as an
appointment of God and highest proof of His fidelity in
His vocation makes this decease significant for others.
Accordingly one cannot accept the interpretation of the
sacrifice of Christ in death which, under the title of
satisfaction, only superficially connects it with the active
life, but fundamentally assigns to the death of Christ a
different reference, namely, that of substitutionary punishment." Against this doctrine Ritschl appeals to Christ's
consciousness. "Christ did not experience along with
His sufferings a sense of guilt, accordingly He could not
have judged them as punishment, not even as the punishment which He suffered to pass over Him instead of the
guilty, or as a means of frightening men away from sin."
He maintains, however, that there is a close connection

between the death of Christ and the forgiveness of sins.
" The Socinian assumption of a universal order of divine
forgiveness which should be independent of Christ, is
out of all relation to experience, and is altogether unsub-
stantial.   On the contrary, the single cases in which
Christ communicates the forgiveness of sin arise from
His consciousness that He Himself stands in the closest
relation to God we can think of, and that He is called
also to receive others into the same, in order that their
sins may not produce any hindrance of their confidence
towards God and their communion with God." Forgiveness of sins is not explicable apart from the mission of
Christ, which consisted in reproducing in others the same
consciousness of God as He had realised in Himself.   But
this mission finds its culmination in His death.   " With
this personal dealing it is certainly not in contradiction,
that the representatives of the Christian community attach
the universal validity of the forgiveness of sin to the death
of Christ, especially as the thought regarding it was evoked
by Christ's own discourse at the Supper.   For the death of
Christ, as it must be understood by means of His previous
obedience, is in the view of the apostles the summary expression of the fact that Christ maintained His religious
unity with God and His position as a revelation in the
whole course of His life." [1]   To sum up, the forgiveness
of sin is inseparable from the Person of Christ, for He
puts men into the same relation to God as He holds.
His priesthood consists in His maintenance of that relation throughout His life.   His submission in death is
the clearest expression and most convincing evidence of
His maintenance of that relation.   Hence the forgiveness
of sin especially attaches itself to His death.

(3) How does Christ, however, put men into the same
relation with God as He Himself holds?   First of all, He

[1] Ritschl, *op. cit.* pp. 446–450, 511, 512.

places His community into that relation, and individual believers only as members of that community. This forgiveness of sins " is to be understood as the common fundamental *attribute of the community to be founded by Christ*," for " Christ as priest is the representative of the community which He leads to God in the complete fulfilment of His personal life." But " the meaning of this thought is not, that what Christ does as priest the community does not also need to do, but rather that what Christ as priest in the place of and as the representative of the community does before, that same position must accordingly be taken by the community itself." In relation to the forgiveness of sin, Christ as prophet on behalf of God declares it, as priest on behalf of man secures it ; " for in so far as we are concerned with understanding the forgiveness of sin from the loving will of God the Father, who suffers sinners to come near to Him, then this is manifest as grace and truth, in which Christ represents God for men. On the contrary, when we are concerned with seeing how the forgiveness of sin as the attribute of a community becomes operative, then it is in this respect guaranteed by the representative of the community, whose inviolably-maintained position towards the love of God, which signalises Him, is imputed by God to those who are to be computed as His." Christ as prophet reveals the relation in which God as Love wills that men should stand to Him ; but as priest He realises that relation in Himself. Inasmuch as, however, He is the representative of a community, that community is reckoned by God as standing in the relation to Himself which Christ realised for Himself, but also on its behalf. How is the connection between Christ and this community, of which the consequences are so advantageous, to be conceived ? " The judgment of justification or forgiveness of sin is not to be formulated that to the community is imputed its belonging to Christ, but that to the community belonging to Christ is imputed the position of Christ to the love of God, in which He maintained Himself by His obedience." This is a distinction of great importance. The connection of the community with Christ is not any merit on account of which it is rewarded with forgiveness. This would be justification by works. It is Christ's relation to the community that secures for it this blessing. Justification is all of grace. But why, it may be asked, put the community before the individual? Is this not a lapse from Protestantism to Roman Catholicism? "It is not," answers Ritschl, "for also for the evangelical Christian the right relation to Christ is conditioned historically as logically by the community of believers; historically, because one always finds the latter in existence, when one attains to faith, and when one does not reach this goal without its influence; logically, because no action of Christ upon men can be represented unless in accordance with the standard of the preceding intention of Christ to found a community." For "in the intention of Christ the guarantee of universal forgiveness of sin for humanity, and the founding of the community, whose members recognise in God as His Father their Father, are thoughts of the same significance." But the forgiveness of sin thus guaranteed to the Christian community is not otherwise appropriated than by "individual faith in Christ"; and this faith is "the permanent direction of the will to the final purpose of God and Christ which the believer for his own sake maintains."[1]   Individual faith is social loyalty.

(4) The individual appropriates for himself the good that belongs to the community by accepting the task which God has assigned to the community. This task—the kingdom of God—is the ultimate end of the Christian

[1] Ritschl's *op. cit.* pp. 512, 514, 516, 517, 519, 558, 560.

community; this good—the forgiveness of sin—is the proximate means for its discharge. In Christ's intention the task and the good were, according to Ritschl's representation in one passage already quoted, co-ordinated; but we should rather have expected him to say that the good was subordinated to the task; for we have already seen that the motive of the forgiveness of sin is God's purpose to establish the kingdom. Christ gets for men this good, because He sets to men this task. Only those gain from Him the good who take the task. He Himself enjoyed the good as He fulfilled the task. As the task is not only set to a community, but is itself the realisation of an ideal community, we can understand why the Christian community has the place it holds in Ritschl's thought, and why Christ is most frequently and prominently presented to us as the representative of a community. There is, when we thus think Ritschl's thoughts together, a consistency and unity in them which, when we view them separately, we should not discover. This view, taken as a whole to be judged, and not looked at only in its parts to be found fault with, has excellences as well as defects. (i.) God's righteousness has a reproductive as well as a repressive function. God seeks to make men good as well as to keep them from evil. He has a beneficent purpose to fulfil as well as a punitive law to maintain. The traditional theology has, there can be little doubt, laid undue stress on the negative aspects of God's righteousness. Ritschl does redress the balance by the weight he gives to the positive aspects. But the two aspects are not mutually exclusive, and, therefore, one cannot but feel that, while Ritschl's affirmations are often for the most part right, his denials are generally wrong. (ii.) Again, Christ did, in His work and suffering, "fulfil all righteousness." He realised in Himself the moral and religious ideal; and He by

His Spirit reproduces His own mind, heart, and will in believers in Him, followers of Him. He, the only-begotten and well-beloved Son, seeks in all respects and relations to be "the firstborn among many brethren." Here, too, Ritschl wisely and rightly emphasises an aspect of Christ's life and work often neglected by the traditional theology. But, on the other hand, he sets himself in opposition to apostolic testimony and Christian experience generally, when he denies that Christ endured, we must not say the penalty, for only the guilty can be punished, but the miseries and sufferings that are the necessary consequences of sin, and that by His endurance for all who believe the curse of sin is removed. His denials are not at all necessary for his affirmations. Nay, the submission of Christ to the divine law in its opposition to sin may be regarded as an essential element in His fulfilment of all righteousness; and it is a simple fact that the knowledge of Christ's suffering on account of sin and on behalf of sinners has been one of the most potent motives of opposition to sin and devotion to goodness. Here again Ritschl's tendency to exaggeration in his antagonisms has made him blind to the right proportions of the truth. (iii.) Lastly, here Ritschl is right in making much of the moral task of the Christian community; but the religious good of the individual believer cannot be so entirely subordinated to it as in his representation. His other views, dependent, as has been shown, on this dominant one, are accordingly in need of correction.

(5) A few sentences must again be added at this point to show that in this teaching about the death of Christ Ritschl does not represent his school generally. Kaftan says that " we regard *the death of Christ as the removal of our penalty, as a vicarious suffering of penalty for us*," and that "*more than hitherto, this doctrine will henceforward*

stand in the foreground of the Christian consciousness." [1]
Herrmann, as has already been mentioned, while refusing
to demand acceptance of this doctrine as the first step in
Christian experience, holds that Christian experience will
itself bring a man to confess this truth. " The believer
then says to himself, involuntarily looking back on the
work of Christ, *What we should have suffered He suffers."*
This is his reason, " He will then see that Jesus in dis-
pensing forgiveness at the same time did all to confirm
the immovable authority of God's moral order." [2]   Harnack
even in dealing with various theories of the atonement,
makes remarks by the way which show that he too in
this respect is nearer the New Testament standpoint than
Ritschl. [3]   It may be remarked generally that Ritschl's
views which separate him most from orthodoxy are least
generally held in his school. √

IV

(1) We have, in dealing with the work of Christ in
relation to man's forgiveness, assumed the conception of
forgiveness without any closer or fuller definition of it.
Now we must learn how Ritschl defines it.   Ritschl
himself sums up the chapter in which he gives his definition in the following propositions : " (1) Justification or
Forgiveness of sins, as the religious expression of the fundamental action of God in man in Christianity, is the acceptance of sinners into communion with God, in which their
salvation is to be realised, and to be carried out unto

---

[1] Kaftan's *Das Evangelium des Apostel Paulus in Predigten*, s. 87,
88 (" The Gospel of the Apostle Paul in Sermons "), quoted by Ecke,
op. cit. pp. 260, 261.

[2] Herrmann's *Verkehr des Christen mit Gott*, pp. 107, 108 (" Communion of the Christian with God," p. 107), quoted by Ecke, *op. cit.*
p. 264.

[3] See Ecke, *op. cit.* pp. 261–263.

eternal life. (2) Justification can be thought of as the removal of guilt and the consciousness of guilt in this respect, that in the latter the opposition to God completed in sin and expressed in guilt, works on as distrust, and brings about a moral separation from God. (3) In so far as justification is represented as effective, it must be thought of as reconciliation in such a manner, that, while in fact the memory preserves the dissatisfaction felt with the sin that had been committed, at the same time there enters in the place of distrust of God a positive concurrence with the will of God and His saving purpose." [1] A brief statement of the contents of this chapter will make this summary quite clear.

[1] Justification and Reconciliation are religious ideas, applicable, not to the individual believer, but to him as a member of the community, and expressive of not only a relation to God, but also a relation to the world corresponding to the relation to God. [2] These religious ideas, and the more ethical idea of the kingdom of God, are practically identical. [3] Justification is not making righteous, but declaring righteous; not the Roman Catholic, but the Protestant doctrine is right. [4] There is no difference between justification and the forgiveness of sins; both mean the restoration of the sinner to communion with God. [5] The forgiveness of sins is not deliverance from divine punishment, as the traditional theology maintains; for physical evils, even death itself, are not punishments of sin, the only actual consequence of sin being the sinner's separation from God. [6] The forgiveness of sin is the removal of the separation of the sinner from God, which is expressed in the sense of guilt. [7] Consequently the sense of guilt is removed by forgiveness. [8] This, however, would be no benefit, but an injury, unless with the sense of guilt there is also taken

[1] Ritschl's *op. cit.* p. 83.

away the guilt, which is a real contradiction by man of
God, and of his own moral destiny. As this contradiction
is real, else man's sense of guilt were an illusion, so the
removal is real, else man's feeling of forgiveness were a
deception. [9] This forgiveness is to be thought of in
the same way as pardon among men. "While God
forgives sins, or pardons, He exercises His will in this
direction, that the contradiction expressed in guilt, in
which sinners stand to Him, is not to be allowed to
hinder that communion of men with Himself which He
for higher reasons (the establishment of the kingdom of
God) interds."[1] [10] This forgiveness as negative, as
the remission of man's penalty on account of Christ's
substitutionary suffering, is not to be distinguished, as in
orthodox Protestant theology, from justification as positive,
as the result of the imputation to man of Christ's righteousness. For as has been already shown, Christ's suffering
has not the character of a substitutionary suffering of sin's
penalty; and righteousness as a moral quality is inseparable from the person to whom it belongs, and thus
cannot be transferred to those who have not their own.
Nevertheless, believers as belonging to Christ are for His
sake received into the same relation with God as was
His. [11] In this relation their enmity against God,
the opposition of their wills to God's, is at the same time
removed as their separation from God; that is, justification, involves reconciliation, which is to be understood
exclusively as the taking away of man's distrust and
hatred of God, and not in any sense as any change in
God's feeling. [12] Justification must not be regarded
as an analytic judgment, God's recognition simply of
what the sinner is actually or potentially; but as a
synthetic judgment, an act of will, by which God treats
the sinner as other than he is, receiving him, in spite

[1] Ritschl's *op. cit.* pp. 61, 62.

of his sin, to fellowship with Himself; in other words, justification is not of law, but of grace. The features of Ritschl's treatment of the subject that claim special attention are—(1) his identification of justification and the forgiveness of sin; (2) his denial of any punishment of sin except the separation of the sinner from God; (3) his rejection of the ideas of Christ's imputed righteousness, and His substitutionary suffering; (4) his subordination of the idea of reconciliation as a subjective human state, and not an objective divine act in the sacrifice of Christ, to the idea of justification; (5) his ascription of the attribute of justification to the Christian community; and (6) his inclusion in the idea of justification of a reference to man's relation to the world. To the last two features, as most characteristic, we shall return. Of his other ideas some command assent, others provoke dissent. To be commended is the stress he lays on justification as a synthetic act, as a *declaring* righteous and not a *making righteous*, on the reality of the removal of guilt and the sense of guilt, on separation from God and consequent antagonism to God as that which in the Christian salvation is removed, on the mediation of Christ for believers. Worthy of attention, at least, is his criticism of the doctrine of imputed righteousness, and the consequent distinction of justification from the forgiveness of sin. Doubtful, however, is his practical identification of the conceptions kingdom of God and justification, as it is well to distinguish the religious good which is offered in Christ from the moral task set by Him. The denial of Christ's substitutionary suffering, and of the penal character of physical evil, and consequently his limitation of reconciliation to man alone, are positions open to very serious attack; but with these the writer has already had the opportunity to deal. Although Ritschl's definition of justification is not likely to meet with general agreement yet the knowledge and skill displayed in the discussion of the subject make it worthy of close study.

(2) After the definition of Justification in the first chapter of his work, Ritschl in the second deals with " the universal relations of justification," and sums up its contents in the following propositions: "(1) Justification, or the reception of sinners into the relation of children of God, must be traced back to God under the attribute of Father. (2) Justification of sinners by God takes place on condition of faith; or inasmuch as justification as reconciliation evokes in sinners faith, which as the direction of the will to the highest final purpose which is represented in God and as confidence towards God does not in itself include love to men, and as freedom from the law in like manner also excludes all ceremonial conditions, and the assumption perhaps operative along with it of a claim against God. (3) Justification or Reconciliation, as it is positively attached to the historical appearance and activity of Christ, refers in the first place to the whole of the Christian community, which maintains in integrity the gospel of the grace of God in Christ as the immediate means of its existence, and to individuals in accordance with this rule, that these through faith in the gospel enrol themselves into the community." [1]

Of this chapter thus summed up the contents are these: [1] Justification cannot be regarded as an act of God as Judge or as Lawgiver; for in law duties and penalties cannot be transferred from one to another; and God can with a view to His final purpose, the kingdom of God, forgive sins without any hindrance from His law. [2] Justification must be recognised as the act of God as Father, and as such is equivalent to adoption, or the reception of eternal life. [3] In accordance with the

[1] *Op. cit.* p. 132.

estimate of sin in the Christian religion as separation
from, and distrust of, God, the condition of justification is
faith, which is the direction of the will to God as confidence in Him as the highest end and the highest good;
but faith does not include love to one's neighbour directly,
but it does indirectly, inasmuch as it results from the
recognition of God as Father, and the valuation of the
kingdom of God as the highest moral end. [4] This
justification is attached to the community as the sphere in
which the gospel of God's grace is preached, and in which
alone it can by individuals be appropriated; mysticism is
thus excluded. [5] Freedom from the law results from
justification, because the possession or the increase of
grace is in no way dependent on human merit, or on
obedience to ecclesiastical rules. [6] The compass of
the divine intention of justification is to be otherwise
determined than by either Calvinists or Lutherans.
The contradiction between the Calvinistic doctrine of an
individual election and the Lutheran doctrine of a divine
intention to save all, which is, however, carried into effect
only in the case of those who believe, and who in anticipation of their faith are eternally elected, this contradiction is
explained as due to two errors—(1) the contrast assumed
between God's limited purpose and the universal offer
of the gospel, and (2) the conception entertained of
humanity or the Christian community as a sum of individuals. In opposition to these errors, Ritschl holds
that we must not think of a number of isolated acts of
justification, " but these are only the temporal appearances
of the one eternal resolve of justification for mankind for
Christ's sake." "There is," he continues, "one divine
predestination according to which, out of the totality of
the human race the totality of the new creature will be
evoked." [1]   In the realisation of this purpose nations

[1] *Op. cit.* p. 123.

rather than individuals must be taken into account; and even of the nations only the historical nations of the West seem capable of its appropriation. As the community precedes the individual in the divine mind, it is the immediate subject of justification. Thus by limiting the divine intention to the community the contradiction of the Calvinistic and the Lutheran views is avoided. To comment on this last position in this chapter first of all, the writer would remark that, while one cannot but agree with Ritschl that the individual as such, apart from family, nation, race, is an abstraction; yet, on the other hand, one cannot but be very suspicious of a view which dismisses, as his does, the greater part of the human race as at least apparently incapable of appropriating the Christian salvation (a judgment which, it may in passing be remarked, shows very little knowledge of, and very slight sympathy with, missionary enterprise throughout the world); and which represents God as caring only for the establishment of a community without seeming regard for each individual of the human race. If we may use the terms in this connection, this is an aristocratic and not a democratic view. To the writer, at least, it seems beyond all doubt that the New Testament teaches the universality and individuality of grace. Historically the individual is dependent on the community, yet God cares directly for the individuals as well as the community.

That a truer view of the doctrine of justification, and indeed of all Christian doctrines, is gained by always thinking of God as Father, and that the forensic conceptions of God's relations to men could not possibly do justice to God's purpose of grace, are conclusions with which cordial agreement must be confessed. But as has already been quite sufficiently insisted on, the work of Christ has a relation to the law as well as the love of

God; and one cannot follow Ritschl in his antithesis of love and law.

Faith is rightly defined as an act of will, which includes not only confidence in God, but acceptance of the final purpose of God consequent on that confidence, for trust in God involves surrender to God; but why, if this is all implied in faith, separate love to our neighbour from faith in God? The only reason one can think of for this dualism, to which Professor Orr gives great prominence, is Ritschl's anxiety to distinguish the religious good and the moral task of Christianity, and by so doing to avoid even the appearance of teaching justification by works. What Ritschl says about the believer's freedom from the law is evidence of his intention to maintain the genuinely Protestant position, although in even more important respects he abandons it.

(3) The third chapter treats specially the subjective side of justification, and seeks to answer the question how the individual believer can be sure of his salvation. Here is Ritschl's own summary of his position: "(1) The question of individual certainty of salvation remains insoluble, if it is put in a form in which the subject should maintain a passive attitude. (2) The individual certainty of salvation will not be secured either by the active effort of penitence, or even by the observation of the accompanying moral activity. (3) The individual certainty of salvation through justification will be experienced in confidence in God in all the situations of life, especially in patience, by the man who, by his faith in Christ, includes himself in the community of believers."[1] After discussing the relation of justification to individual certainty of salvation in its historical aspects, and after rejecting all the recognised methods of securing this certainty (waiting on the gift of assurance, exercising oneself in penitence on

[1] Ritschl's *op. cit.* p. 183.

account of sin, devoting oneself to good works) as in-adequate, Ritschl states his own distinctive position, which he complains has not found any adequate recognition in the traditional theology. What, then, is this distinctive position? " Justification cannot express a relation of man to God and Christ without at the same time including a distinctive *position of the believer to the world* based thereon " ; for " the sinner who in his previous distrust of God shows himself dependent on the world, can, in his confidence in God's forgiveness of his sins, be proved to be changed only inasmuch as the new dominion over the world through confidence in God's universal providence is combined with it." [1]   This dominion over the world, which means indifference to its frowns or favours, because independence from t for any good, is the result of faith in God's providence, and as such is the evidence of salvation, and so affords the individual certainty of it ; for the man who seeks nothing from the world, and trusts God for all things, is a saved man, and can know himself as such. This consciousness of the Christians is by God's grace, as for it he is always dependent on the community of believers, in which the promises of grace are always present for individual appropriation. One may with very good reason doubt whether this idea of Ritschl's possesses the importance or deserves the pro-minence which he gives to it. For the Christian his relation to God is what most concerns him, and his relation to the world matters very little. Nor is he at all likely from his security in the latter relation to derive the evidence of his satisfaction in the former. Ritschl has not discovered any essential element of the Christian faith which has been hitherto neglected or ignored, he has simply laid stress on a phase of Christian experience which is undoubtedly seasonable. The modern scientific

[1] *Op. cit.* pp. 161, 167.

view of nature involves a denial of divine providence; and Ritschl has, in the interests of the moral and religious life alike, been forced to lay hold on this truth, which is in danger of slipping from the grasp of men in this age. In this he has done well; but he has overlooked the temporary and limited need that this truth meets, and so has fallen into an exaggerated emphasis. The belief that the physical order of the world serves a moral and religious purpose of God, is one which in the present day needs to be asserted. The belief in miracles as a particular application of this principle, still more needs to be maintained. The belief that we may so use the circumstances of our earthly lot as to further the progress of our heavenly life, is one that Christians always need to exercise. Ritschl is to be commended for insisting on this truth, although the place he gives it is not according "to the proportion of faith."

CHAPTER XI

THE DOCTRINE OF THE CHURCH AND THE KINGDOM

I

(1) THE believer is justified, as was shown in the last chapter, in reckoning himself a member of the Christian community. The Christian life, then, may be regarded as a life in the community. But this community has a double aspect; it is both Church and kingdom of God, and these must be carefully distinguished. "In order that the right connection of the Christian world-view may not be missed, it is necessary to make clear the distinction, in accordance with which the same followers of Christ are combined, on the one hand, under the conception of the kingdom of God, on the other, under the conception of the *worshipping congregation* or church." The distinction between Church and kingdom is this. "Those who believe in Christ are the Church, in so far as they express in prayer their faith in God the Father, or present themselves to God as the men well-pleasing to Him through Christ. Those who believe in Christ are the kingdom of God, in so far as they, regardless of the differences of sex, calling, or people, act mutually from love, and so produce the community of moral dispositions and moral goods which extends in all possible degrees to the limits of the human race." While the Church "enters into sensible appearance," the kingdom of God "is revealed only for Christian faith." While the Church "needs for its own sake an authoritative organisation

(*rechtliche Ordnung*)," the kingdom of God is "in its existence altogether independent of authoritative forms." While Ritschl rejects the Roman Catholic identification of the kingdom of God with the papal Church, he also regards the views of the leading Protestant theologians upon this question as unsatisfactory. While thus emphasising the difference between Church and kingdom, he also asserts their intimate relation to one another. "Christians must learn to know one another as such in their worshipping functions in order to secure for themselves the motives for their combination by mutual action from love. On the other hand, the whole compass of this activity serves the purpose of giving help to the maintenance and the extension of the worshipping community." [1] Thus, then, are Church and kingdom of God distinguished from, and yet related to, one another. What first of all strikes one in considering Ritschl's treatment of this subject is that he altogether ignores the New Testament teaching on the subject. In dealing with the kingdom of God in Chapter VIII. this was pointed out in regard to one of the conceptions. It must now be briefly noted in regard to the other. As all students of the New Testament know, the term Church is used of each local assembly of believers, of all these local assemblies regarded as a unity, although not externally united in one organisation; and by Paul, of all true believers in heaven and on earth, who form a body, of which Christ is Head, and which serves as His πλήρωμα or complement. The term is nowhere restricted, as by Ritschl, to an external organisation in the one function of worship. But, in the second place, surely the Church serves even in relation to the kingdom of God a more important function than merely to enable believers to

---

[1] Ritschl's *Rechtfertigung und Versöhnung*, iii. pp. 270, 271, 275 ("Justification and Reconciliation").

become acquainted with one another, so that they may come to love one another? Surely its worship includes communion with God, which inspires devotion and loyalty to His kingdom, and which affords them the wisdom and power which they need in its service.

(2) While this is all that Ritschl has to say about the Church in his work on *Justification and Reconciliation*, in his smaller book, *Instruction in the Christian Religion*, the last section is devoted to "the doctrine of the common worship of God." "Prayer," he says, "is not only an exercise and a necessity of the individual believer, but it is also intended to be practised in common with others." Prayer, as "the most spiritual form of the worship of God," is primarily adoration and praise, and only secondarily petition; for, as the Lord's Prayer shows, every request must assume gratefully and submissively the relation to mankind in which God stands in Christ. "All Christians," as able to approach God with the sacrifice of prayer, "are priests." As religion rests on revelation, so in the Christian Church worship must be controlled by the word of God, the preaching of Christ and God as revealed in Him. The two sacraments, the Lord's Supper and Baptism, are, as administered in the Church, acts of worship, and so like prayer; but inasmuch as the one refers to "the sacrificial death of Christ, on which the foundation of the Church rests," and the other to "the revelation of the Father by the Son and by the Holy Spirit granted to the community," they are also pledges of the divine grace, and so like the word of God. As "an object of faith" the Church is "the communion of believers in the Holy Spirit, the sphere which is marked out by the forgiveness of sin";[1] and the external organisation of the Church, although in some

[1] Ritschl's *Unterricht in der christlichen Religion*, pp. 72-87 ("Instruction in the Christian Religion").

form or another necessary for the existence of the Church in the world, is indifferent to faith. In the historical development of the Church, polity, doctrine, and discipline have assumed prominence and importance; but none of these is of primary significance and value for faith. Infant baptism is justified, inasmuch as the moral and religious education of children is to be conducted within the Christian community; whereas the assumption of those who insist on adult baptism is that Christian personality can be developed outside of the community. The Lord's Supper was given by Him as a means of uniting His followers, not as an occasion for division, as it has become. Although Ritschl does not here remedy the defect in his treatment of the subject already noted, yet he does give a genuinely evangelical Protestant account of the Church. To what he here says about prayer we must return in another connection.

II

(1) The Church and the kingdom of God are the spheres of the Christian life. But how does this life begin? Ritschl rejects the elaborate analysis of the older theology, which sought to distinguish exactly the successive stages of the spiritual process, and to separate accurately the two factors, the action of divine grace and the activity of human freedom. The believer "who is no longer guided by the natural, that is, both self-seeking and world-loving motives, which in indifference or distrust towards God bear in themselves the chief mark of sin, finds himself in the *state of regeneration*." But this state "cannot as a predicate of the individual believer be substantially distinguished from effective justification or reconciliation or adoption," and must not be regarded as its antecedent. The traditional theology

22

represents according to Ritschl, the regeneration of man by the Spirit, as if "this divine factor set man in motion with a kind of natural necessity"; and, in separating regeneration from justification as distinct from it, or as antecedent to it, makes it impossible to regard it otherwise than "as a substantial transformation." To this view he objects that "the Holy Spirit cannot be understood as a substance, nor is He represented in the New Testament as the divine means of the regeneration of the individual in limitation to the beginning of the new religious life." The account he gives of the Holy Spirit, and His action in the Church, deserves quotation in full. "The Spirit of God or the Holy Spirit, who in reference to God Himself is the knowledge which God has of Himself, is at the same time an attribute of the Christian community, because the same in accordance with the completed revelation of God through Christ has that knowledge of God and His counsel towards men in the world which corresponds with God's self-knowledge. As the power of the common exhaustive knowledge of God belonging to believers in Christ, the Holy Spirit is at the same time the motive of the life of all Christians, which as such is necessarily directed to the common aim of the kingdom of God (1 Cor. ii. 10–12; Rom. viii. 2–4; Gal. v. 22–26). When, accordingly, in accordance with this representation of Paul, the state of regeneration or of the new life is in the doctrine of the Reformation put in the closest relation with the Holy Spirit, then that is not to be so understood as that each individual is changed by the specific power of God in the form of a power of nature, but that he is moved to penitence and humility as to moral activity in the service of the kingdom of God by the confidence, common to all Christians, in God as the Father of our Lord Jesus Christ. For this reason it is forbidden that anyone should assert his relation to the Holy Spirit by an observation of himself in which he should isolate himself from all others ; " for " regarding the justification and the regeneration of the individual nothing else can be objectively taught," and " how this state is brought about is as much withdrawn from all observation as the development of the individual spiritual life generally." [1] This important statement may be translated into the following propositions : (1) The Spirit of God is God's knowledge of Himself. (2) As God is fully revealed in Christ, the Christian community shares God's knowledge of Himself, even His Spirit. (3) This Spirit is in the Christian community not only as *knowledge,* but also as the *motive* of action directed to the realisation of the kingdom of God ; or, putting it in another form, the *will* as well as the *mind* of God is in the community. (4) The individual Christian participates in this *knowledge,* and experiences this *motive,* that is, possesses the Spirit who belongs to the community. (5) But this possession is his only in the community, and cannot be claimed by him apart from it. (6) The process by which the individual becomes a member of the community, and so claims for himself its knowledge and its motive, is hidden from us. The last proposition is of special importance as it is a distinct recognition of the fact that there is more in the individual religious experience than has been stated in the preceding propositions.

(2) To offer now the necessary criticism, there is some measure of truth in Ritschl's censure of a theological subtlety that undertakes to distinguish each stage, to separate each factor in a spiritual process, for the process is continuous and organic. Again, there can be no doubt that traditional theology has often used categories of thought and terms of

---

[1] Ritschl's *Rechtfertigung und Versöhnung,* iii. pp. 566, 567, 570, 571, 572, 573 (" Justification and Reconciliation ").

speech which are appropriate in physics but not in morality or religion. The Spirit has been spoken of as if He were a physical cause, and regeneration as if it were a physical effect. Ritschl is right also in his desire to explain the spiritual life by what lies within the range of human consciousness, instead of by processes and factors which lie wholly beyond it,—a tendency only too common in theology. But what he fails to recognise is that we cannot within our own consciousness adequately explain even its contents; that to the objects of our consciousness, if they are to have any objective reality for us, we must assign an existence distinct from and independent of our consciousness. (*a*) Accordingly, to apply this general consideration to the subject immediately before us, the conscious change of justification or regeneration cannot be sufficiently accounted for by any of the thoughts, feelings, wishes, or resolves of the person who is the subject of it; and, therefore, we have a right, nay, even we are under the necessity, of inferring from this actual effect in consciousness an adequate cause which may lie more or less beyond our consciousness. (*b*) Once more this change, as experienced by many Christians, has been so thorough a transformation, the mind has been so enlightened, the heart has been so quickened, the will has been so strengthened, that it must be conceived of as affecting the whole man; not a new content for his consciousness only, but a fresh capacity in all his functions, and so may be described as a renewal of the personality. (*c*) Further, although the relation between cause and effect differs in many respects in the physical and in the spiritual sphere, equivalence in the former case, difference in the latter case, inasmuch as there is a new factor—personal freedom, which either co-operates with or opposes itself to the operative cause, and thus decisively modifies the effect; yet we are not giving a complete account of even spiritual facts, if, because of the importance of this new factor, we recognise only the effects, and refuse to inquire into the causes. Yet this is Ritschl's method. (*d*) Especially in so decisive a change as regeneration, in which this factor of freedom, while being fully recognised, cannot be regarded as in itself a cause adequate to the effect, must there be frankly admitted a cause distinct from and independent of the personality which it so transforms. (*e*) Without intending to abandon this method of exclusive attention to the human activity in the spiritual life, Ritschl, in his statement about the Holy Spirit's presence and operation in the Church, admits the dependence of the individual believer on the religious community. But this relation must allow the application of the category of causality. The community, by its common knowledge of God, and common motive of action for the kingdom of God, acts on the individual believer. Its instruction and influence, by means of which he comes to share this knowledge and this motive, is the cause, and his experience is the effect. (*f*) Now, we must ask, What exactly, on Ritschl's showing, is this cause? It is a consciousness, intellectual and volitional (for it is knowledge and motive), common to a society, "it is an attribute of the Christian community." But can the Christian community, which consists of a number of persons, be intelligibly or credibly represented as a subject of which this consciousness is an attribute, for surely consciousness can be found only in a person? In order to be seriously regarded as the subject of this attribute, the Christian community must be, not merely *poetically personified*, but even *metaphysically personalised*. Escape from this intellectual difficulty presents itself along two paths; and it will make a very serious difference in our estimate of Ritschl's doctrine which of these two paths we feel ourselves compelled to follow. (*g*) We may hold that all Ritschl means is that this common consciousness is simply the sum of the thoughts, feelings, wishes of the individual members of the Christian society. We are not to think of one subject of this common consciousness, but of as many subjects as there are members in the Christian community. If that were his meaning, then the individual believer would be dependent wholly on his fellow-men for his religious life ; he would need to recognise only human agency in his spiritual experience. Even if the Christian society were traced back to its historical origin, and it were admitted that the original members stood in a direct dependence on God, and had received divine instruction and influence, still that fact for the present-day believer, separated by so many generations from that earliest age, would be " one far-off divine event," which could give him little confidence that the work being wrought in him now was really of God. In that case, Professor Orr's charge against Ritschl (see p. 143), that he denies any " immediate action of the Spirit in the soul," even in the sense of the term " immediate " indicated at p. 144, would be amply justified ; for the Spirit would here and now be absent and inoperative. (h) Are we, however, shut up to this explanation ? It seems to the writer that we are not, and that Ritschl's own words carefully considered point to another path. In the first sentence of the passage now under discussion the Spirit is described as " in reference to God Himself the knowledge which God has of Himself." Thus even viewed merely as an attribute, the Spirit has not human individuals united in the Christian society as its subjects, but God Himself. The possession of this attribute by the Christian community is due to the relation to God into which that community is brought through " the completed revelation in Christ." The community is made a sharer in God's self-knowledge. That self-knowledge is in the present, and does not belong merely to the past. There is nothing in Ritschl's language to indicate that the knowledge of God which the community now has, and " which corresponds with God's self-knowledge," was once divinely communicated, but has since been humanly preserved. On the contrary, it seems more reasonable to interpret Ritschl's words as meaning that God Himself is the subject of this common consciousness of the Christian society, He Himself as Spirit continuously communicates this knowledge and this motive. (*i*) This explanation, which would disprove the charge made against Ritschl, nevertheless is still open to two objections. First of all, the Spirit, so far as one can draw any inferences from his words on a subject which he would have pronounced beyond the legitimate compass of theological inquiry, is represented as *a mode* of divine presence and operation in the Christian community. The doctrine of the Trinity does not find any recognition whatever. But if it be admitted, as the writer believes Ritschl's language admits, that God Himself is present and operative in regeneration, using the Christian community as His medium, not His substitute; then, however significant it may be for theological inquiry, it is not important for religious experience whether this presence and operation be described as a "mode" of the one God's being and doing, or as a distinct "Person" in the Godhead. Nevertheless, as has already been indicated in dealing with the Person of Christ (Chapter IX.), theological inquiry would in this case as in that lead to the recognition of the truth about God which is expressed in the doctrine of the Trinity. Ritschl's method here, as elsewhere, may be blamed with "a voluntary humility." (*j*) The second objection is this, that Ritschl goes beyond any lawful inference from acknowledged data of Christian experience, when he so very decisively confines the Spirit's sphere exclusively to the Christian community. It may be frankly and freely acknowledged that the Spirit's general method of operation is through the instruction and influence of the Christian community, and that even in many cases where the dependence of the individual on the community is not evident, it can be on closer inquiry ultimately traced; yet, nevertheless, we have no right to confine the Spirit's movements or to limit His liberty. Beyond the range of Christian teaching and training there have surely been souls in whom God by His Spirit has witnessed, and wrought for Himself; and even the members of the Christian community themselves may surely claim a light and a leading from God that their relation to the community does not fully explain. The progress of the community itself depends on such original individual development by the Spirit's own presence and operation. In this respect Ritschl has exaggerated a truth so far as to deny plain and certain facts of Christian experience. (k) To draw this discussion to a conclusion, attention must again be called to Ritschl's last proposition as inferred from the passage quoted. He admits that his account is not a completed account; for he expressly maintains the ultimate mystery of the process of individual regeneration. Surely we must agree with him that there is a sacred and solemn secrecy about God's Presence and Operation in the soul; and that the spiritual dissection of some theologians is, to say the least, an impertinence, one could even say an irreverence; for we cannot so measure and weigh God, or even the soul. But admitting this as fully as truth demands, yet Ritschl has failed in the account he gives, not only to discover and describe what is quite within the reach of our knowledge and our speech, but even to recognise and confess what on closer study is necessarily involved in his own statement. The analysis of that statement which has been given has, it is hoped, not only shown wherein Ritschl's defects lie, but also how, from his own standpoint, it is possible by casting aside the illegitimate restrictions he imposed on his thinking, to advance to a more satisfactory position. (l) It is profitable as well as interesting to trace his defects to their roots. This has been correctly done in the following statement by Ecke: "Quite a number of circumstances has contributed to this, that the teaching about the Holy Spirit exactly in Ritschl has not received justice; the inductive method followed by him, which led him first of all and above all to fix his attention on the *active* functions of the *human* spirit; then an erroneous understanding of relatively assumed results of *psychology*, which caused him to banish the mystical element from his *theological* standpoint; further, his inclination to sharp *antitheses*, in consequence of which he formulated his opposition to errors of mysticism and pietism more bluntly than he had surely originally intended; finally, one must add his *aversion to the expression of inner experiences*, which has already been mentioned, and which was connected with Ritschl's critical disposition, in order to understand his far-reaching reserve in this doctrine."[1] As these characteristics are not common in his school, we may expect that his disciples will not repeat the errors of their master. That this expectation is well-grounded may next be shown.

III

(1) Herrmann expressly disowns the interpretation of Ritschl's doctrine of the Spirit which has been suggested as an alternative to that which has been here adopted. "A Holy Spirit," he says, "that should be nothing else than the spiritual life of the community, would certainly not be the Holy Spirit of the New Testament. This Holy Spirit the believer has not before his eyes, when he presents to himself only an earthly magnitude. The Christian, who becomes conscious of the Holy Spirit, is under the impression of a power which is fully raised above earthly capacity." Regeneration and conversion, he maintains, cannot be separated

[1] Ecke's *op. cit.* p. 292.

from an understanding of the gospel; and the means of
grace must be regarded as "the grounds of conscious
faith," and not "exclusively as secretly operative causes
of salvation." "*Faith*," he continues "can and ought
to say to itself that *they are also the latter*; but for
theological investigation they can come into view only
in the significance which is made known to us, and
offers a foundation for faith. When we, on the basis
of our knowledge of their significance in this respect,
express the judgment, *that they are the causes of salvation*, then we are at the limit beyond which there is
nothing for us to know."[1] While theological investigation is primarily concerned with conscious faith, it may
secondarily admit inferences from the content of conscious faith to operations and agents beyond consciousness,
but it ought not to give, as scholasticism tended to do,
exclusive attention to the latter. Herrmann, it is true,
ascribes to the direct action of Christ Himself what in
the traditional theology has been usually assigned as a
function to the Spirit; but as there is no division in
the Godhead, his method is theologically correct, and
what is still more important, it corresponds with the
New Testament representations. That man is changed
by a Power above, and greater than himself, is clearly
stated in the words, "*It must be our experience, just as
the child's, that we allow ourselves to be entirely determined
by a stronger personal life, and to be carried above what
we of ourselves are.*" Again, "if we only remain united
to the inner life of Jesus as the Power which raises us
to God, then the impression will ever anew arise within
us that a new content is coming into our life which

[1] Herrmann in *Theologischer Litteraturzeitung*, 1891, s. 263 ("Theological Literary Journal"); and in "Rezension von Franks System der
christlichen Wahrheit" in *Theologischer Litteraturzeitung* ("Review
of Frank's System of Christian Truth" in the "Theological Literary
Journal"), quoted by Ecke, *op. cit.* 295, 296.

we cannot master, because it is inexhaustible, but which transforms us." Lastly, here "every man must himself experience that the spiritual power of Jesus destroys his self-confidence, and creates in him a confidence in God which makes him anew. A man becomes inwardly transformed when he finds and understands the communion of God with his soul in the inward operation of the Person of Jesus on him."[1] While Herrmann holds, as Ritschl also does, that we cannot explain the change so as to be generally intelligible; yet he makes distinct what Ritschl obscures, the thoroughness of the change, which is described by the terms regeneration and conversion, and the cause of the change, not in the exercise of any human faculty merely, but in the potent operation of a spiritual Power, distinct from, and superior to any human capacity.

(2) Kaftan is even more explicit regarding the work of the Holy Spirit. "In the New Testament community," he says, "it is said of *all*, that they through faith can become partakers of the Spirit of God." "The revelation through the Holy Spirit," he continues, "takes place in *the hidden inner life of the human spirit*. Here the Spirit of God seizes man, and only for him who has had such an experience is the revelation in Christ present as it wills and ought to be; that must accordingly be described as a continuation, and in a certain sense as a completion of it. God has not appeared in Christ, and then follows the appropriation of salvation as a process in the subjective spirit, which comes to revelation as something altogether other and new. Rather has this process the *two sides*, that it is on the one side the concluding moment of the revelation itself, and on the other side the subjective appropriation of the same through faith." Man receives the revelation by the same spirit

[1] Herrmann's *Verkehr des Christen mit Gott*, pp. 97, 92, 98 ("Communion of the Christian with God," pp. 97, 93, 98).

as reveals. This is how the Spirit works in each soul. " Where a Christian is, there is a new creature of God. According to his old man he belongs to the world, which is perishable, and the province of sin ; according to his new man he is the work of God and of His Spirit, born of Him to imperishable life, as God Himself is eternal and imperishable. In the old humanity there is a new humanity, It is this activity of the Spirit, to which every Christian is conscious of owing all that has worth in him, and that does not deserve death, which is the continuation of the revelation in Christ." He rightly and fitly asserts the dependence of the work of the Spirit on the revelation in Christ. " While it is true that the Spirit of God is the indispensable concluding moment of the divine revelation, yet it has never the meaning, that it joins the perfect revelation in Christ as *something new, which completes it or even transcends it.* The Spirit of God, which there illumines, is the Spirit of the Lord, and the enlightenment is according to its content nothing else than *the saving knowledge of Jesus Christ*, that is, not of a principle, which he brought into the world, but of His historical person. If, accordingly, these two moments coincide, the perfect knowledge of Jesus Christ and the enlightenment by the Spirit of God, then indeed they are logically related to one another in such a way *that the enlightenment springs out of the knowledge of Jesus Christ*, not in the reverse way, that a man might have in the enlightenment of the Holy Spirit, which might occur independently of Christ the principle of the knowledge of Christ. And this is a point of *fundamental significance.* If it were otherwise, then it would not be true that Christ is the perfect revelation of God ; the revelation in Him would be superseded by the principle of the Spirit placed above Him." [1]

[1] Kaftan's *Das Wesen der christlichen Religion*, pp. 343-345, 346, 347 ("The Essence of the Christian Religion").

While Kaftan thus insists on the truth which Ritschl states with such undue emphasis as to appear, at least, to deny the indwelling and inworking of the Spirit, yet he at the same time recognises, as Ritschl, in his language at least, fails to do, the Presence and the Power of God's Spirit in the individual Christian experience. A rigorous analysis of the spiritual process by which a man becomes a Christian, in its stages and factors, such as was attempted in the old theology, is not to be commended; but what must be required is an adequate recognition of God's action as well as man's activity, and a sufficient estimate of the magnitude of the change which is thus effected. In both these respects Ritschl's shortcomings are not found either in Herrmann or in Kaftan. While we have no right to say that Ritschl's Christian life was less real and sincere than that of his followers, yet we are forced to notice that Ritschl's religious experience was more limited in its range, and less varied in its content than theirs from their writings appears to be. The common saying, " Pectus facit theologum," is applicable here.

IV

(1) The first of " the religious functions " which results from reconciliation with God is dominion over the world, by which is meant, not such a dominion over nature as science, industry, or commerce seeks to obtain, but a spiritual capacity of making all circumstances sub-servient to the highest purpose of life. " By the thought," says Ritschl, " that to those who love God, and are loved by Him, all things must serve for good, the experience of all natural and social evils is changed into the disposi-tion in which one exercises dominion over these experi-ences." But this dominion over the world is not a denial of the world or an ascetic abstinence from its use, or a

Stoic indifference to its sufferings. The source of this sovereign relation to the world on the part of the believer is his faith in the fatherly Providence of God, which is made possible only through the revelation of Christ. " The confidence with which one relies, in favourable as in unfavourable situations in life, on the guidance and help of God while one sees oneself directed by Him to a highest purpose of dominion over the world in the community of the kingdom of God, is the result of the Christian religion. For the God, who is the Lord over the world and our Father, who cherishes no envy or wrath against His children, guarantees to them that all things serve them for good. The truth is valid also only on the basis of our reconciliation with God." (a) By way of comment on this statement first of all, let all that is implied in it be very carefully noted. (1) The sinner has been forgiven, and his estrangement from, and enmity to God has been removed. (2) He has accepted as the end of his life and work, not any earthly goods, but the highest good, the kingdom of God. (3) He trusts in God's care, and surrenders himself to God's will. (4) As having his portion not in this world, the circumstances of his earthly life are significant to him only as the means of spiritual discipline and development; he has dominion over the world, because its favours do not allure him, and its displeasure does not dismay him. As thus interpreted, the phrase " dominion over the world " expresses a true and worthy element in Christian experience, and one which one could earnestly desire to be more prominent and potent in the lives of Christians, which too commonly are still far too closely attached to this present world.

(b) But, in the next place, when Ritschl speaks of God's Providence, he means what he says. He does not believe in an inevitable course of nature, independent of a Personal Will, which does not do its worst with us, because we make the best we can of it. He does not give a stern fact, submission to fate, a sweet name, faith in God's Providence, by a "poetic licence," which some thinkers seem to regard as the distinctive feature of religious thought. He himself compares this religious function with the efforts of science. "The theoretical knowledge of universal laws and authoritative truths is in itself indifferent to the worth of the individual, and does not suffice to exhaust the world-whole; in the knowledge based on faith in Providence the individual desires to be master of his position in relation to the whole of the world, in which he himself as a Christian reaches the worth of a whole." Science does not exhaustively interpret nature, and it ignores personality; it leaves room for an interpretation that recognises personality, and completes the interpretation of nature. "The feeling of self, which expresses the incomparable value of the person over against all other persons, and the whole connection of nature, is also the basis of all scientific observation of nature, and cannot be neutralised by its results, of whatever kind they may be." We observe nature as self-conscious persons, and no results of that observation can disprove that we are self-conscious persons. But belief in human personality is inseparable from, and dependent on, faith in God's Providence. Man as a part of nature can believe himself a whole distinct from and supreme to nature only as he believes in God, who maintains his worth as a person over against nature. "The characteristic of the religious view of the world is this, that all natural events are regarded as at God's disposal, when He desires to help man."[1] Miracles are

---

[1] Ritschl's *Rechtfertigung und Versöhnung*, iii. pp. 577, 590, 584, 587 ("Justification and Reconciliation"); *Unterricht in der christlichen Religion*, p. 14 ("Instruction in the Christian Religion").

thus inseparably associated with God's Providence; and belief in the former depends on faith in the latter. It has already been shown (Chapter VII.) that Ritschl does not deny the possibility or the reality of miracles, as has been sometimes alleged by his critics. But if it can be proved that he admits the occurrence of miracles, then there is no reason for denying that God's Providence, or use of nature for His own ends, is for him a fact and not a phrase.

(c) The position that he assigns in his treatment of the religious functions to this " dominion over the world," placing it in the very forefront, is in no way justified by religious experience; as in most Christian lives other elements of the Christian faith are much more evident and important. Surely the consciousness of the forgiveness of sin and of the call to holiness is much more to many Christians; to others fellowship with the living Christ, or the indwelling and inworking of the Holy Spirit, gives their experience its distinctive significance and value. Ritschl is, there can be no doubt, expressing his own religious peculiarity in this undue emphasis on this one element of Christian experience, and at the same time, as has been already suggested, he is potently affected by one of the distinctive tendencies of the age. Nevertheless, while one desires theology to be always sincere and seasonable, yet one also demands from it sympathy and permanence. While Ritschl's theology certainly possesses the former characteristics it is often found conspicuously lacking in the latter attributes. The recognition of this fact will help to explain very much in his theology that otherwise might perplex.

(2) The faith in God's fatherly Providence shows itself in patience and in humility. *Patience*, which is different from apathy, deprives all evils that befall us of their sting, enables us to regard these sufferings, which our

sense of guilt would represent as punishments, as means of discipline, and is the result of submission to the will of God. Patience may be exercised not only "in the subordination of the private life under God's guidance, but also in the cautious judgment of the history of the present age." *Humility* is the subordination of oneself to God in all things, and is the complement of patience. "Patience is the religious disposition as dominion over the opposing world, which humility as the disposition of subordination to God completes." As the former is specially needed in suffering, so the latter in success. "It is quite a distinctive proof of Christian piety, to maintain patience in lack of success, humility in fulness of success."[1] The appropriate expression of humility towards God is *modesty* towards men, which expresses our esteem of others, as engaged along with us in the same higher task, and as possessing on that account a moral value for us.

(3) Besides patience and humility, prayer is to be regarded as an expression of faith. "Prayer in the Christian sense is, on the one hand, a specific manifestation of the faith in the fatherly providence of God which springs out of reconciliation; and, on the other hand, a specific manifestation of the resolve of humility, which is distinguished from the regular course of this virtue in this way, that the resolve, which is present in the indistinct representation or in the mood of feeling, is brought to distinct expression." As "in each of these religious acts the spiritual functions all participate, it is not the case that faith in the divine providence is a kind of knowledge, humility a kind of feeling, and prayer a kind of resolve of the will"; but "only this can be affirmed, that in each of these religious functions, knowledge, feeling, and willing respectively assume the leading and preponderating position." Prayer expresses primarily gratitude and submission, and

[1] *Op. cit.* pp. 597, 601, 602.

23

only secondarily petition. " For the Christian community *thanksgiving* is *the recognition of God which is placed over petition*; thanksgiving is not a kind of prayer beside petition, but is the universal form of prayer ; and petition is only a modification of the prayer of thanksgiving to God." Further, as regards Christians, " the range of petition is more narrowly limited by the certainty of reconciliation which is to be assumed, than is the case in the religion of the Old Testament " ; for all Christian desire is subject to gratitude and submission, and selfishness and wilfulness can have no place in it. " Prayer is the manifestation of humility and patience, and the means of confirming oneself in these virtues."[1] This limitation of prayer to thanksgiving, and this practical exclusion of petition from it, is contrary to religious experience. It is due, on the one hand, to Ritschl's recoil from some extravagances in which pietism has sometimes indulged, in using prayer as a kind of charm to be worked on God, that He may be made to meet man's wishes, selfish and wilful though they may be ; and, on the other hand, to the false assumption, which we have already had occasion in other connections to condemn, that God's eternity means not only fidelity to His purpose, but even fixity in His method of fulfilment. This view of prayer, which forbids a man's seeking humbly and submissively, yet trustfully, a fulfilment of his desires at the hands of God, narrows and impoverishes the faith in God's fatherly Providence, of which Ritschl makes so much, for it makes it little more than acceptance of whatever God may choose to send us, without any expectation whatever that our desires will in anyway be taken into account. Submission to God is good, but even in relation to God liberty has also its claim ; and this the prayer of petition maintains, without disowning

[1] *Op. cit.* pp. 606, 607, 608, 609, 610.

submission. In this respect, however, Ritschl has not been followed by his school generally.

(4) Herrmann, in dealing with the relation of the scientific category of causality and the Christian belief in miracles, declares that "in spite of this epistemological necessity (that is, of applying this category to all events), from which actually no man withdraws himself, it is possible for the Christian to recognise thankfully in events, which vitally affect him, miracles of God on his behalf, and to trust for an answer of his prayers." The last clause of this sentence implies that the Christian may legitimately offer definite petitions for other than purely spiritual benefits or deliverances. Still more distinctly does he express himself on this question in the following sentences : " It is quite certain that it is not due to faith that the Christian altogether abandons petitions for natural goods. This assumed purification of prayer would be an emptying of it. What really burdens the soul, so that it is thereby threatened in its peace, is to be brought in prayer before God with the confidence, that the love of the Father also understands our anxious cleaving to natural things." To try and free ourselves from these burdens, instead of seeking relief from God, " injures us doubly. First of all, our prayer becomes on that account lifeless and untrue ; it is then, in truth, not at all our own prayer, but, perhaps, the possible prayer of a man in quite another situation. Secondly, we in so doing do not really place ourselves before the God who wishes to be sought for as our helper and deliverer. For in this we imagine to ourselves a God who, it is true, loves the ideal of man, but has no sympathy for our need." [1] In a very

---

[1] Herrmann's *Die Religion im Verhaltniss zum Welterkennen und zur Sittlichkeit*, p. 384 (" Religion in Relation to our Knowledge of the World and Morality "); *Der Verkehr des Christen mit Gott*, pp. 267, 268 (" The Communion of the Christian with God," pp. 247, 248).

interesting address by Kaftan on " The Christian Doctrine
of Prayer," it is stated that " prayer is petition "; that " to
pray to God means to beg God "; that while " the seat
of prayer is our Christian inner life, the man hid with
Christ in God," yet " prayer has to do with all that we
experience,' for " one can think of a Christian as perfect
only if all that moves him is also in prayer moved before
God by him." Prayer is to be distinguished from reverent
contemplation; in the latter " God comes to us on the
ground of His revelation in Christ," in the former " we
come to God with our needs." " The one goes from
above downwards, the other from below upwards." The
first presupposition in prayer is that " what happens comes
from God, and the future stands in His almighty hand."
The second is " the revelation of God in Christ," for in it
alone God is known as " the living God who rules the
world according to the holy will of His eternal love," and
in it alone we learn " to know the ends God follows in
the world.' [1] The Lord's Prayer as the typical prayer
teaches us to pray for (1) the fulfilment of God's purpose,
(2) the perfecting of God's work in ourselves, and (3)
earthly gifts and goods. The prayer for temporal benefits
may be offered confidently, if submissively.

(5) In these three religious functions the *Christian's*
perfection finds expression. It consists in " humility, faith
in, and submission to God's Providence, appeal and thanksgiving to God in prayer, and fidelity in the moral vocation
which is useful to the community." This claim "strikes a note
which sounds strange in the ears of evangelical Christians,"
for " we can never assert a perfection of our moral actions ";
and this is thought to be even an advantage, as it delivers
us from " self-righteousness "; nevertheless disbelief in the
possibility of our perfection must inevitably have as its
result, that " the power of our will is enfeebled, its effort

[1] *Die Christliche Lehre vom Gebet*, pp. 4, 6, 7, 13.

ceases, and our zeal slackens." Accordingly "the representation of moral perfection in conduct as in the formation of
our own character is necessary for us not only to establish
our imperfection, but has its value in this, that we believe
in our destination to the same." The possibility of perfection is assumed in the New Testament. Jesus describes
love as perfection ; James speaks of patience in suffering as
a perfect work ; Paul knows perfect Christians, to whom he
can speak wisdom. But this Christian perfection must be
carefully distinguished from the perfection aimed at by
monasticism. " This attribute has not a quantitative, but a
qualitative significance it is the sign of this, that man in
Christianity is destined and qualified to be a whole in his
spiritual kind " ; that is, he is to have a value for and in
himself as a person, distinct from and independent of the
world, of which he is not to regard himself as merely a part.
" Accordingly, because each one of us in Christianity distinguishes his own personal worth from the whole world,
the task is also set to us as Christians each one to become
a whole in his kind." " With this qualitative sense (of
perfection) it does not stand in contradiction, that one is
conscious of quantitative incompleteness and defectiveness
even in those functions in which one exercises the Christian
religion. For every organic being, which in its kind forms
a whole, can endure a certain measure of defects without
being destroyed in its kind." Even " the faith which breaks
out in the prayer, Lord, help my unbelief, is perfect of its
kind." [1] Other perfection than this, secured on the bases of
justification and reconciliation by the exercise of faith in
patience, humility, and prayer, together with fidelity in the
personal vocation, the Christian cannot claim and need not
seek. It does not mean infallibility of judgment, sinlessness

[1] Ritschl's *Die Christliche Vollkommenheit*, pp. 3, 4, 5, 8, 11 (" The
Christian Perfection ") ; and *Rechtfertigung und Versöhnung*, iii. pp. 615,
616 (" Justification and Reconciliation ").

of life, moral completeness ; but it does mean that in his
relation to God man is conscious of his own worth as a child
of God, of his own claims on the grace of God, of his own
independence of nature and society. His life is a unity
subordinate to, yet recognised in God's final purpose. This
conception of Ritschl's is a very valuable one, and deserves
our grateful recognition.

(6) The Christian life is not, however, completely
described in its religious functions. As has already been
mentioned in the last paragraph, there also belongs to it
" moral conduct in the civil calling." On this the Reformers
laid stress in opposition to the monastic ideal, and included
it in their representation of Christian perfection. No man
is called in " every moment of time in all possible relations
of life to fulfil the Good "; but " one limits obligation by
the universal moral law to the distinctive sphere of the
vocation in which one renders, not good works, but a
connected, organic lifework, and, in fact, as a whole, which
has its value, even although one says to oneself, that one
should have rendered always yet more in one's calling than
one accomplishes." While " all the moral organisations
which Christianity finds in existence, family, station, people,
are limited on the bases of our spiritual community, which
are naturally conditioned, and therefore always refer to only
parts of the human race " ; and " while the universal task
of the kingdom of God and the law of universal love to
man, which Christ has made operative, bind us to an all-
embracing supernatural union of men with one another " ;
yet " the universal is only always real in the particular,"
and " the whole is a multiplicity, which, by subordination
under a universal purpose, is articulated according to its
laws in a distinctive manner "; and, therefore, the realisation of the kingdom of God, and the fulfilment of the law
of love, is sought and found by meeting the obligations of
the particular relationships. " From Christ Himself no

other special moral pattern is to be borrowed, except perfect fidelity in His vocation." This limitation of moral perfection to the vocation involves that "there is excluded every moral necessity to good conduct towards such ends as are not appropriate to the individual vocation," and "this determination of good conduct by the vocation makes the apparent demand invalid, that one has in every moment of time in all possible directions to be acting well." This conception gives a unity and completeness to character and conduct that they would otherwise lack. The danger of narrowing the sympathies and so impoverishing the experience is to be avoided by the constant recognition of the obligation, that "in the distinctive sphere of his regular activity every man is to act not only for his own, but also for the common good in the widest sense," and "that one should round one's life to a whole in faithful service in one's own moral calling, whether it be exalted or limited." This fidelity in the vocation has its reward; for "in the doing of the good one becomes blessed, and the performance of the moral vocation secures for a man his position in the kingdom of God, also inasmuch as that is the community of blessedness." [1] In this section of his system Ritschl has also rendered good service to Christian theology; as his ideal of fidelity in one's vocation is much more useful for the practical guidance of life than that of conformity with the universal moral law.

(7) In this statement by Ritschl of the religious functions, there appears what most Christians will regard as a serious omission. While the law of love to man is recognised as the guiding rule of all moral action, nothing is said about love to God or Christ. We must turn back to an earlier section of Ritschl's great work for the explanation. "Love to Christ," he says, "is less definite

---

[1] Ritschl's *Die christliche Vollkommenheit*, pp. 11–14 ; *Rechtfertigung und Versöhnung*, pp. 630, 633.

than faith in Him. In that formula it is not decided whether one places oneself on an equality with Christ, or subordinates oneself to Him. Faith in Christ, however, includes the confession of His divinity and His lordship, refuses accordingly the possibility of placing oneself on an equality with Him."[1] The mediæval familiarity with Christ as the bridegroom of the soul is rightly condemned; and attention is called to the stress that the Reformers laid on faith in Christ, as reverence and confidence, excluding such familiarity. In this opposition to mysticism, Ritschl has, there can be no doubt whatever, ignored an essential element of Christian experience, as love to Christ as well as faith in Christ necessarily and permanently belong to it. Herrmann and Kaftan alike recognise, as has already been shown (pp. 153–160), the communion with Christ in which love to Christ seeks and finds expression and satisfaction.

V

(1) Of the three Christian graces, *faith*, in Ritschl's view, as regards man's relation to God, is the chief; and *love* in his relations to his fellow-men alone holds the same place; of *hope* he has very little to say. Along with the denial of the Resurrection, with which we have already dealt, Ritschl is charged by Professor Denney with rejecting "all the eschatological elements in the teaching of Christ Himself, on the ground that on such points we cannot separate the authoritative words of Jesus from the Jewish commonplaces put into His mouth by the apostles";[2] and this charge is evidently intended to be of very serious import. It is desirable, therefore, to remember that many scholars have felt that no part of the report of the teaching

---

[1] Ritschl's *op. cit.* p. 560.
[2] Denney's *Studies in Theology*, p. 49.

of our Lord is so beset with difficulties as that which deals with the last things. Professor Stevens states in a work that is marked by the sobriety of its tone, that "to determine precisely the form of Jesus' teaching concerning His parousia and the consummation, is not possible in the present state of our sources"; and "a candid criticism must admit that it is almost as difficult to be sure of the exact words of Jesus respecting the 'day of judgment' as to determine what He said concerning His second advent."[1] This, then, is a question on which a latitude of critical judgment must be freely and frankly allowed in the Christian Church. Ritschl's attitude on the subject is one of reserve. He elsewhere maintains that 'no connected theory of the last things can be reached by the use of the data of the New Testament"; and that " the indications in the New Testament which refer to the condition of the blessed and the damned lie beyond the possibility of a distinct representation.'[2] If it be remembered that at least three theories of the hereafter claim with show of reasons the support of the Holy Scriptures, namely, those of conditional immortality, eternal punishment or blessedness, and universal restoration, this statement cannot be unhesitatingly condemned. Principal Salmond has devoted a volume of nearly seven hundred pages to *The Christian Doctrine of Immortality*, and he confesses in his preface that the result he has reached " has not been reached without an acute sense of the attractiveness of other views of man's destiny which are held by many earnest men, and of the limitations which the God of Revelation has placed upon our knowledge of the future life."[3] Professor Orr states still more definitely that " we have not the elements of a

---

[1] Stevens' *The Theology of the New Testament*, pp. 162, 165.

[2] Ritschl's *Unterricht in der christlichen Religion*, p. 71 (" Instruction in the Christian Religion ").

[3] Salmond's *The Christian Doctrine of Immortality*, third edition, Preface, p. x.

complete solution, and we ought not to attempt it." [1]   This
is the attitude that is more and more commending itself to
those who have a due sense of the gravity of the problem,
and of the insufficiency of our data for its solution.   Nor is
it at all necessary that the problem should be theoretically
solved.   Very wisely Ritschl concludes that "we are not
here concerned with the satisfaction of curiosity, but with
this, that no man is blessed unless in union with all the
blessed in the kingdom of God."   While he maintains that
"the perfection," of which mention has already been made,
"is necessarily accompanied by the sense of blessedness"
here and now ; yet he admits that "the Christian faith,
which s sure of eternal life on the ground of the reconciliation through Christ, and keeps hold of this good in
righteousness as in sanctification, sustains itself with the
hope that the completion of the kingdom of God as the
highest good, lies before it under conditions which lie beyond
the world-order of our experience." [2]   In the course of an
argument he mentions with, so far as one can judge, cordial
assent, "the Christian hope of the continuance of the
spiritual life in a corresponding body." [3]   This statement
acquires greater significance if it be remembered that
Ritschl, as has been already shown (see p. 225), holds that
"Christ made Himself known to His disciples in the body"
after His resurrection.   To sum up, then, Ritschl holds
in prospect for believers immortality, resurrection, perfection,
blessedness, the completed kingdom of God, the community
of the blessed.   For those who persist in unbelief he expressly reserves the wrath of God (see p. 261), which will
destroy them.   While it is true that Ritschl does not give
to the Christian hope the prominence that it not only holds

[1] Orr's *The Christian View of God and the World*, third edition,
p. 345.
[2] Ritschl's *op. cit.* pp. 71, 70.
[3] Ritschl's *Rechtfertigung und Versöhnung*, p. 575 ("Justification
and Reconciliation").

in theology, but even in Christian experience ; yet it is surely an overstatement, which one is tempted to describe as altogether unjustified, when Professor Denney asserts that " Ritschl has no eschatology." [1] It may be frankly admitted that this comparative neglect of the Christian hope in Ritschl's theology does show a defect in his piety as tested by the standard of the New Testament, which does undoubtedly bid us live under " the powers of the world to come," as " strangers and pilgrims on the earth."

(2) This defect is, however, not characteristic of his school. Kaftan's definition of religion, which has already been dealt with, is itself a clear proof of this. He maintains that the origin of religion is due to man's discovery that " *he finds no permanent satisfaction in the enjoyment of life, in the goods which the world offers to him* " Christianity alone meets man's craving for a lasting and satisfying good ; for " divine revelation shows man such a good in the supramundane kingdom of God, in the calling of individuals to eternal life in the same." This good is not an earthly one, but a heavenly. Its full realisation lies in the future, but " is *organically* connected with the moral development of the kingdom of God in the world." [2] These two characteristics of the kingdom of God, on which Kaftan lays stress, that it is *supramundane* in character, and that it is *future* in its realisation, indicate on his part a more positive attitude to the Christian hope than Ritschl's. Greater definiteness may be given to these indications by the quotation of a passage in which a reviewer (Rev. Professor W. P. Paterson, D.D.) gives an account of the last section of Kaftan's recently published volume on *Dogmatics* : " The eschatology," he says, " is meagre, being dismissed in twelve pages. The reason for this slight treatment is that, in Kaftan's view, a

---

[1] Denney's *Studies in Theology*, p. 261.

[2] Kaftan's *Das Wesen der christlichen Religion*, pp. 70, 153, 244 (" The Essence of the Christian Religion ").

THE RITSCHLIAN THEOLOGY

large body of the biblical material is not an integral part
of Christian faith, but was simply taken over from the
apocalyptic cycle of Jewish thought. What faith stands
sponsor for refers only to the portion of believers, and is
summed up as follows: ' Christian hope expects the consummation of the kingdom of God, and eternal life in the
same as the goal of human history and of the individual
life. In both cases the goal is reached after a catastrophe
involving the destruction here of the outer world, there of
the outward man. Of the final judgment (*Entscheidung*)
the principle is Christ, and to all who have become members
of His body eternal life is assured' (p. 636). Into the
problems connected with the intermediate state and the
fate of unbelievers, Kaftan declines to enter, except to
declare that as there is an eternal life so there is an eternal
death. The immense gulf between faith and unbelief has
its counterpart in the antithesis of eternal life and death,
and the doctrine of universal restoration is untenable. But
over the nature of the death which is everlasting the veil is
left drawn." [1] Many Christians will find no fault with this
reverent reticence as compared with the self-confidence
with which the hidden future is described by some writers.
Kaftan's account of the hope of the future may be supplemented by a passage in Herrmann, where the vision of
Christ is claimed for Christian hope, although it is denied
to Christian experience. " But it is just when we confess
this barrier of our present experience that our hope for the
future gets the content, which can contend against the
dominion of earthly goods over our heart. The personal
life of Jesus has so wrought upon us, that it allows us to see
the love of God in the might of reality, which makes that
on which we seemed to be wholly dependent a means of our
eternal life. If we have experienced this in Jesus, then the
thought that He lives and reigns in perfection fills us with

[1] *Critical Review*, viii. pp. 416, 417.

the longing that we may once see Him other than in the mirror of history, and other than with the eyes of the spiritual struggling upward out of the earthly. That is the content of the Christian hope of the future, which man can already understand. When we have experienced how it delivers us, when the features of the Person as something divinely wonderful become clear to us, then the prospect, that we shall some day experience this power in the un-hindered and immediate intercourse of person and person, can snatch us from embarrassment by earthly needs and enjoyments. Whether the Christian, as in the primitive Christian community, waits for the return of the Lord, or rejoices in this, that he will be taken up to Him, as it will be with us, is indifferent. But every Christian has this intuitive fulness of hope for the future as a necessity for his inner life. In this good on the other side, but in-telligible to us, and seizing our hearts, there lies a power which we cannot do without in the errors and troubles of the earthly Christian life." [1] Giving due weight to all these statements, it must surely be admitted that Ritschlianism cannot justly be charged with " a rigorous exclusion of eschatology from theology." [2] That the treatment of the subject is adequate or satisfactory in all respects need not be maintained; but it is not altogether ignored, and what is most important for the future of the school, the leading disciples in this matter correct the defects of their master.

(3) In concluding this chapter a criticism which can, with apparent justice, be made may be forestalled. It may be said that the contents of this chapter do not correspond with the title. But it may in explanation be pointed out that the secondary position and the subordinate function assigned to the *Church* is very closely connected with the

[1] Herrmann's *Verkehr des Christen mit Gott*, pp. 240, 241 (" The Communion of the Christian with God," pp. 224, 225).
[2] Professor Orr in *Expository Times*, vi. p. 253.

two features of Ritschl's treatment of the religious life which have received considerable attention in the course of the discussion, his inadequate doctrine of *the Holy Spirit's operations*, and his relative neglect of *the communion of the soul with Christ*, and this discussion, therefore, may be justly claimed as a closer definition of his view of the Church.   Again, *the kingdom of God* is appropriated as a *religious good* in the *active functions, patience, humility, prayer* with which so much of our attention has been engaged; and is realised as a *moral ideal* in *fidelity to the personal vocation*, of which a brief account has been given.   Thus the kingdom of God also has throughout this chapter been made a more distinct conception.   May it not then be claimed that title and contents correspond?

CHAPTER XII

CRITICAL ESTIMATE: THE SOLUTION OFFERED

I

(1) WE have passed in review the Ritschlian theology in its negative or critical, and in its positive or constructive aspect. We have been led from time to time to comment on excellences or defects, to admit charges made by its critics, or to defend it against condemnation by its opponents. Now there remains for us the task which can be discharged only in a tentative fashion, to estimate as sympathetically, and yet as justly as we can, its theological significance and its religious value. Any such estimate must be provisional; for, on the one hand, the Ritschlian theology is still in course of development, and has not assumed any final fixity; and, on the other hand, the literature of the movement is so abundant and varied, and its interpretation is often so difficult, that he would be a very foolish and rash man who would affirm that his mind was quite made up about what it meant, and how much it was worth.

(2) The first consideration which must be duly taken into account in dealing with the Ritschlian theology is the religious individuality and the theological position of Ritschl himself, the founder of the school. If we do not know the man and his times, we shall never do justice to his work. Ritschl's was a distinctive personality, which expressed itself even in his mode of thought and his style of writing. (a) Ritschl's was not a self-centred

and self-contained intellectual development, the gradual
exposition of fundamental principles of thought.   But his
mind always moved in opposition to the opinions of others.
His critical antagonism was the impulse to his constructive advance.   As he distinguished and separated his own
thoughts from the thoughts of others, he became conscious of, and gave expression to what was characteristic
of his own mind.   As a man of quite unusual learning,
he had always abundant material at his command on
which to exercise his critical faculty; but that faculty
itself was not controlled in its activity by a predominantly
intellectual interest in any of the objects of his investigation, but by an aggressive practical purpose to keep theology always as a servant of the moral and the religious
life.   Accordingly he treated with impatience any theological speculation, the bearing of which on practical life
was not apparent.   (b) He combined in a very remarkable manner dependence and originality.   Antagonism
to others not only provoked his own efforts, but many
of his distinctive positions had been occupied by others
before him.   It was in the combination of ideas that
had hitherto been found detached from one another,
that he showed his mental grasp.   If he did not always
succeed in giving consistency to this combination, yet
it is not a little surprising how he succeeded in im-
pressing his own individuality even on the materials that
he borrowed from others.   Of this individuality three
features by their prominence arrest attention : first, his
practical tendency ; secondly, his *historical positivism* ; and,
thirdly, his *philosophical scepticism.*   All these features we
have already repeatedly had occasion to mention.   (c)
This practical tendency is not always vigilant and
dominant ; and Ritschl, who had for a time felt the
bewitching spell of the Hegelian dialectic, sometimes
lapses into speculative indulgences, some of which have

already been noticed. This practical tendency, however, is usually prominent and potent. It asserts itself in the subordination of thought and feeling to will in the religious life, in the importance attached to the kingdom of God, in the explanation of the work of Christ by the conception of a moral vocation, in the position in religion assigned to dominion over the world, in the dependence of the individual certainty of salvation on the exercise of the religious functions of patience, humility, and prayer, in the definition of Christian perfection, in the description of faith as obedience,—all distinctive features of Ritschl's theology, which, while often calling attention to neglected aspects of truth, at the same time in a one-sided way exaggerate their significance and value. (*d*) This individuality shows itself further in his inclination to oppose without qualification any type of thought, phase of feeling, or mode of life that was not congenial to him. His opposition to scholastic speculation leads him to deny the legitimacy and even necessity for Christian theology of the causal as well as the teleological point of view. His sense of the absolute value of the Christian religion makes him express himself too unfavourably regarding all other religions, and causes him to ignore practically the preparation for Christianity in the Hebrew religion. In order to assert the voluntary character of sin as an abuse of freedom in opposition to law, he goes as far as to deny in every sense the doctrine of original sin, instead of being content with criticising Augustine's exaggeration of the truth. Dissatisfied with the traditional treatment of the idea of God's justice, he allows himself to be carried away to the affirmation that there is no truth in the almost universal moral conception of rewards and punishments. In rejecting on biblical grounds the old position of Protestantism that God was propitiated by Christ's death, he sets

24

himself against biblical testimony when he denies that
our Lord's sufferings had a vicarious character, or had
any relation to the penalty of sin. Because the idea of
the absolute was a philosophical conception which had
been introduced into Christian theology, he is quite unable
to recognise any truth in it whatever. Inasmuch as the
familiarity and irreverence, which had sometimes character-
ised the intercourse between the soul and its bridegroom
claimed by mystic piety, were an offence to him, he sets
himself in opposition to a sane and healthy piety even
in the limitations he wishes to impose on the communion
of the believer with Christ. Intolerant of sectarianism,
he exaggerates the necessary mediation of the Church
in the individual religious life. Conscious of the super-
ficiality and artificiality of a popular revivalism, he fails
to do justice to the doctrine of conversion. Because the
traditional dogmatics had given too formal and mechanical
an account of the *ordo salutis*, he obscures the truth and
confuses the mind by refusing altogether to distinguish
the stages and the factors of this spiritual process.
Because prayer in the circles of pietism was sometimes
disfigured by a lack of submission to the divine will, and
an undue confidence that any request offered in faith
must be answered, he robs prayer of much of its energy
by excluding petition from it. Because vain and foolish
dreamers indulged their imagination in picturing the last
things, he turns away with aversion from the problems
of eschatology. (*e*) These defects of his theology, however much we may regret them, do afford evidence of
the intensity and the sincerity of his faith. What he
could not himself spiritually appropriate, that he would
not theologically affirm. Yet they also show a lack of
sympathy and patience with others. He would not, or
could not, pause and inquire whether there might not be
a truth necessary to the wholeness of Christian faith

and life, even in errors of opinion and practice, which excited his aversion. His piety in its individuality and independence was of a thoroughly manly sort, reverent, reticent, candid, practical, energetic, and assertive; but it lacked the womanly and childlike qualities that have a necessary and legitimate place in the Christian religion. (*f*) His antagonism to pietism of all sorts (such expressions of religious thought and life as are represented in our midst by Revivalism, the Keswick Movement, the second Adventists, and Plymouth Brethrenism) was so extreme, that he was led to condemn the good as well as the bad in all these movements; and accordingly on the one hand his own theology suffered, and on the other he excited a prejudice and opposition in all the more earnestly and aggressively pious circles of Germany, which have proved a hindrance to the recognition and acceptance of what is really valuable in his teaching. His theology, it must be conceded, was in many features an academic theology, and suffered from his lack of acquaintance and sympathy with the practical piety of the Churches. As, fortunately, theology in this country is usually in vital contact with Church life and work, Ritschl's one-sidedness in this respect is not likely to be a danger to it; but it may even, on the contrary, benefit by learning from him some of the defects of our practical piety. (*g*) In these ways did his personality influence his theology. Of the extent of that influence this does not profess to be an exhaustive statement. Enough has been said, it is to be hoped, however, to enable any student of the Ritschlian theology to be always on the alert to detect any trace of that influence, and so to give due recognition to it in estimating the worth of the theology.

(3) While Ritschl was able to attract disciples to himself, who reverently recognise his worth, and grate-

fully confess their debt to him, yet fortunately for his own reputation and influence, none of them has proved as "clay in the hands of the potter." His disciples are not copies or echoes of himself. Herrmann, Kaftan, Harnack, to mention the most prominent members of the school, are all men of distinct and independent individuality. Their writings show as much their personalities as Ritschl's influence upon them. Hence we often find that the disciples correct the defects of their master. Herrmann's *Communion of the Christian with God* is the expression of an individual piety which is altogether different from the piety distinctive of Ritschl, and which displays features which Ritschl ignores or even suspects. Kaftan's *Essence of the Christian Religion* presents to us a piety which embraces a legitimate mysticism, and gives to the Christian hope of glory and blessedness a larger place than Ritschl allowed to it. Harnack, in his *History of Dogma*, shows himself sympathetic towards religious ideas, for which Ritschl had only condemnation. While all of them allow their sincere and intense piety to influence evidently and potently their theological writings; yet, as none of them is marked by the same one-sided peculiarity of disposition and character as Ritschl himself was, that influence has not the injurious results which we have been compelled to recognise in the case of Ritschl. It may be said with truth, it seems to the writer at least, that none of the disciples is so estranged from pietism as the master was, and that all are in closer touch with the practical piety of the Church than he was. Kaftan expressly acknowledges his deep indebtedness to pietism. Harnack is interested in the practical problems of the Church's life and work. Herrmann displays a fervour in his teaching that shows his kinship with the truly godly in the Church. There is good reason for anticipating, then, that the disciples, by their less individual and more sympathetic personalities, will ultimately relieve the development of the Ritschlian theology of the limitations and exaggerations which Ritschl, owing to his peculiar personality, imposed upon it, and will thus bring it nearer to Christian piety generally.

(4) The considerations which have been now engaging our attention suggest a question of a more general character that deserves to be dealt with briefly. It is this: Should theological writings be marked by the same impersonality as scientific works are? Is such pure objectivity possible or desirable? Must, to use a common phrase, "the personal equation" be as far as can be eliminated? The traditional method of dogmatics, in which the texts of the Holy Scriptures and even the formulæ of the ecclesiastical creeds are treated as the data of the science of theology in the same way as physical phenomena are the data of the sciences of nature, and in which a logical method of manipulating the data thus assumed is regarded as authoritative, demands this impersonality. But if theology be, as seems now to be more generally accepted, an exposition of the essential and vital contents of personal faith, then this pure objectivity is neither possible nor desirable. " To eliminate the personal equation " would be to remove the subject of the experience which is to be expounded. The theologian is not dealing with a theme in which he has no individual interest, but is bearing witness to men of what God in Christ is to his own soul. Of course he is bound, if he wants to be a helper of the faith of others, not to isolate himself in his own religious peculiarity, but to appreciate and appropriate so far as he can sincerely, all that is offered in the Christian revelation for the acceptance of faith; but if there are aspects of truth that do not appear luminous to him, if there are phases of piety in which he can find no satisfaction, if

there are forms of duty the obligation of which his conscience does not enforce, he must be content to write
only about the things that he has proved as the power,
the wisdom, and the grace of God to himself. A systematic completeness, or a logical consistency in theology,
is secured at too high a cost, if the theologian is on
that account not absolutely sincere. We do want less
of this quasi-scientific impersonality in our theology, and
more frankly and fully expressed personal conviction.
For that reason it seems to the writer not a defect, but
a merit of the theology of Ritschl and his followers,
that in their practice they meet the demand which they
make in their theory that theology shall express religion,
personal faith and not traditional opinion.

II

Ritschl's position as a pioneer must also be taken into
account in judging his theology. It is easy for those whose
steps never stray from the trodden paths of traditional
thought and conventional life to find fault with the sometimes uncertain tread of one who is endeavouring to open
up new ways. There are in Ritschl's system elements that
do not really belong to his fundamental principles, and are
even sometimes inconsistent with them; but he is not to be
condemned without any qualification on that account. (*a*)
Among "the foreign elements" in his theology must be
reckoned first of all his attempt to prove the truth of the
Christian idea of God in such a way as will meet the
demands of science. He shows, as we have seen (p. 83),
great uncertainty of mind, as what he at one time includes
in "theoretical knowledge," at another time he confines to
"practical faith." Here he ignores the limitation he has
himself laid down, that all religious knowledge consists of
value-judgments. (*b*) He forsakes the sure and safe ground

of Christian experience again in his speculative construction
of the personality of God; for in it he asks us to combine
elements of thought, which we do not find so combined in
practical experience. Whether such speculation is legitimate
or not is not now the question; what is now being indicated
is that it is not in accordance with Ritschl's empirical
method. In the same way his deduction of the idea of the
kingdom of God from the love of God is a bit of Hegelian
metaphysics, which is very much out of place in a theology
which claims to rest exclusively on Christian experience.
(c) Thirdly, he has introduced only confusion into his own
thinking, and so has exposed his theology to quite unnecessary condemnation by his attempt to expound and to
vindicate a particular theory of knowledge in his theology.
A theory of knowledge is implicit in all knowledge; but
thought is too complex, and too closely connected with its
object to be formally regulated by a theory of knowledge.
Ritschl's intention is undoubtedly to affirm the objective
reality of the contents of Christian faith, but his inclination
to a Kantian epistemology at one time, to a Lotzian at
another, often, at least apparently, defeats this intention.
Stählin's attempt to show the logical consequences of Ritschl's
philosophical principles, as the critic understands them, has
at least this value. It makes very clear that Ritschl did
not actually teach what Stählin affirms he ought consistently
with his epistemology to have taught; and accordingly
proves that either Stählin has misunderstood his epistemology, or that Ritschl's theology did not stand in any
organic connection with his philosophical principles. As a
matter of fact, Stählin does misrepresent Ritschl's epistemology (p. 51), and Ritschl's theology is not always
consistent with his philosophical principles. His theory of
knowledge, however, does sufficiently affect his theological
method (p. 62) to justify in some measure Steinbeck's
objection to Ecke's description of the epistemology as a

"foreign element"[1] in Ritschl's theology in the words, "nevertheless, in opposition to this view, we remark that the philosophy in a very much higher degree than appears from this has laid down rules for the theology of Ritschl."[2] In spite of the undoubted influence of the epistemology on the theology, so that it would be quite impossible to remove the epistemology without a complete transformation of some parts of the theology at least, yet the two facts which must be admitted without any doubt, first, that Ritschl wavers in his epistemology; and, second, that his theology is not always consistent with the one or the other of the two theories of knowledge between which his mind wavers, prove that philosophical principles formed a region in which Ritschl was not thoroughly at home, and that what he borrowed here never became vitally, organically a part of his own mind. In this sense Ecke's term "foreign element" is justified. (*1*) A speculative construction of the idea of the eternity of God, as His consistency in the realisation of His final purpose in time, corresponding to the identity for God as eternal of the willing and the fulfilling of His final purpose, leads Ritschl to deny any possibility of variation in God's relation to men. God's love is an eternal will to save and bless mankind in the kingdom of God. God's wrath is an eternal resolve finally to destroy any man who excludes himself from that kingdom. Sinners, accordingly, are always the objects of God's love; subject to His wrath are only those who ultimately defy His love. So long as mankind is still undergoing probation, God's relation to it must be love and love only. It is not, then, to lessen the

[1] Although the writer has already (p. 38) made acknowledgment of his indebtedness to, and agreement with, Ecke in his book on *The Theological School of Albrecht Ritschl*, he desires with reference to this chapter particularly to confess gratefully, that in the arrangement of his material here he has for the most part followed the order of treatment adopted in Ecke's book.

[2] Steinbeck's *Das Verhältnis von Theologie und Erkenntnis-Theorie*, p. 81 ("The Relation of Theology and Epistemology").

heinousness of sin that Ritschl denies that God's wrath rests
on the sinner, but to maintain this speculative construction
of the idea of God's eternity. His position has one very
serious consequence. Men, as in time, are conscious of a
change in their relation to God. Before, they had feared
God's displeasure; now, they enjoy His favour. But this is
only a subjective impression involved in man's temporal
existence. The objective condition of men as known to
God in His eternal being always and only is that God loves
them. Ritschl demands that theology shall interpret the
religious consciousness; yet here he sacrifices the truth of
the religious consciousness on the altar of a speculative idea.
This foreign element in his theology involves him in still
deeper inconsistency. A prominent feature of his theology
is *the historical character of revelation*; yet the significance
and value of history which is necessarily subject to the
condition of time is brought into doubt by his insistence on
this speculative idea of God's eternity, which affects not
only his doctrine of God's relation to *sin*, but also his idea
of *reconciliation*, making it impossible to recognise in Christ's
life and work a Godward as well as a manward reference,
and his idea of *prayer*, excluding from prayer definite petition
with the trustful expectation of its fulfilment. His idea of
justification as pertaining to the Christian community is due
to the same tendency to keep God in His eternal being and
willing out of the course of time, in which each individual
believer claims for himself that justification. Although he
does not by any means consistently maintain his position, yet
his tendency undoubtedly is to distinguish so sharply between
what is eternally realised for God and what is being temporally realised for man, that it is difficult to recognise the
organic unity of the eternal and the temporal; and so God's
view and man's view fall apart, and what *seems* truth to man
is not truth for God. A contrast, too, and a correction of
this speculative tendency may be found in Herrmann's

pamphlet, *Why does our faith need historical facts?* and Harnack's lecture on *Christianity and History*, in which justice is done to history in time.[1]

(*e*) Another element in Ritschl's theology that is not necessarily connected with its fundamental principles, is the rule he lays down that all the predicates of Christ are necessarily transferable to His community. While it is certainly quite characteristic of the Ritschlian method to insist that the divinity of Christ is to be found in His activity, and that His activity as exalted must be represented in accordance with the forms assumed in His historical action, yet it is not at all necessary for Ritschl to insist, as he does, that every predicate that is applicable to Christ must also, in virtue of their relation to Him, be applicable to believers, and that the doctrine of divinity must never express the difference that separates Him from them. This position may even be affirmed to be inconsistent with the estimate of Christ's person and work that is generally expressed. If Christ be, as Ritschl holds, the unique bearer of the divine revelation, and if all believers are dependent on Him, as Ritschl admits, for their relationship to God, such a difference is recognised, that it seems a wilful attempt to cause confusion to lay down any such rule, which appears rather as an unwarranted intrusion of a speculative pantheism, for which mankind as a whole is the Son of God.

(*f*) While Ritschl does assert the continued Presence and the exercised Power of the exalted Christ with, in, and for His people; while it is his intention only to insist on the necessary representation of that Presence and Power in the forms afforded by the earthly life and work, and on the necessary mediation of the action of the exalted Christ by the Holy Scriptures, the preaching of the gospel, and the

[1] See for an account of the former, p. 213; and of the latter, pp. 219–221 in Chapter VIII.

other means of grace ; yet his analysis of the historical and
psychological conditions of this mediation receives such
prominence, as to suggest at least a denial of the personal
action of Christ in Christian experience. There is, and
must needs be, in all Christian experience a factor which
eludes all psychological or historical analysis, God Himself
present in and active by His Son. Just because Ritschl
attempts what professes to be a complete analysis with
insufficient recognition of this factor, he has exposed himself needlessly to suspicion, as though he intended to represent Christian experience as a purely subjective process
dependent on exclusively historical conditions. Is it not
the scientific temper of the age to measure and to weigh all
reality, which explains this tendency to neglect what by
its very nature is beyond exhaustive analysis? These
" foreign elements " of Ritschl's theology have been thus
fully described, not to relieve Ritschl of responsibility for
them, not to protect him from any censure which he may
rightly deserve for having adopted them, but in order to
promote a more intelligent and sympathetic attitude to his
theology as a whole by distinguishing clearly what is more
or less accidentally and externally attached to it, from what
is essentially and organically a part of its distinctive contribution to religious thought.

III

(1) Having thus briefly indicated the peculiarities of
Ritschl's personality, and the " foreign elements " in his
theology, which explain many of the defects which it
presents, we may now note as briefly what are its distinctive
merits. The first feature of the Ritschlian theology which
claims recognition and appreciation is its method, when
freed from certain limitations that attach themselves to it.
The principles of this method may be formulated in three

propositions. (i.) The *formal* principle of Christian dogmatics is not the Holy Scriptures in their entirety, but
the confession of the first Christian community as recorded
in the New Testament Scriptures.   (ii.) The *regulative*
principle is the Person and Work of Christ as Founder of
the kingdom of God.   (iii.) The *material* principle is the
religious consciousness of salvation through Christ.   We
may, to express these principles in descriptive terms, say
that the method is *biblio-spheric*, *Christo-centric*, and *pisto-
basic*.   (a) As regards the first principle, there are two
tendencies evident and operative in the Ritschlian theology,
of which Ritschl represents the one and Harnack the other.
Ritschl, the systematic theologian, does not confine himself
to the teaching of Jesus as the authoritative source of the
Christian confession, but attaches very special importance to
the development of Christian theology by Paul in opposition
to Judaism, and sets a high value on the Old Testament as
a means of distinguishing the original elements in the New
Testament from later Hellenic influences.   Ritschl, it is to
be remembered, abandoned the Tübingen critical position
for a very much more conservative one.   Harnack, on the
other hand, is a historical critic ; but his Ritschlianism is
not responsible for his free treatment of the records of the
Christian revelation.   Ritschlianism should act rather as a
restraint on the critical tendency, which for many minds is
almost inevitable in the existing intellectual conditions.
Ritschl, however, as has already been shown (p. 213), uses
the testimony of the New Testament Scriptures to the
original Christian faith in an arbitrary manner.   He often
does not submit to its authority, but asserts his own
theological independence.   What is still necessary in the
Ritschlian school is an adequate doctrine of the Holy
Scriptures ; if their authority is to be consistently maintained
there must be an advance beyond the assertion that they are
the literary sources of the historical revelation ; and it must

be recognised that the relation between the literary sources and the historical revelation is essential and organic. It cannot be said, however, that the Ritschlian school has voluntarily abandoned a satisfactory position on this question, as, in candour, it must be frankly admitted that a doctrine of the Holy Scriptures is one of the constructive tasks which Christian theology has as yet failed with success to discharge. There is nothing in the Ritschlian attitude towards the Holy Scriptures necessarily to forbid an advance to a fuller recognition of their significance and value for Christian faith ; and the standpoint assumed, that what we have to seek in the Scriptures is a confession of faith, is, it seems to the writer, that from which alone any safe and certain advance can be made. Ritschlianism stands on the path of necessary and desirable Christian progress. (*b*) The Christo-centric principle of this theology requires a more thorough application and a fuller development than it has as yet received. In the first place, it seems to the writer (and this consideration is closely connected with the preceding statements regarding the Ritschlian attitude towards criticism) that the evangelical testimony and the apostolic interpretation of the Person and Work of Christ need to be more fully utilised in order to get an adequate Christo-centric theology. In the second place, the specu-lative idea of the kingdom of God must be brought into subordination to the historical fact of the Person and Work of Christ. As has already been shown, the image of Christ is less distinct and vivid in this theology than it might be, were the New Testament records more fully and freely used. How injuriously many Christian doctrines have been affected by the prominence given to the idea of the kingdom of God has already been made abundantly evident. The correction that the Ritschlian theology still needs is, first of all, to grasp more firmly the historical reality of Christ, and next to make use of that historical reality in its entirety as the regulative principle of Christian dogmatics. The importance which it does certainly attach to the Person and Work of Christ proves that it is already moving along the lines of a sound and healthy development, and is, therefore, not incapable of such correction as seems desirable. (c) While it is a right and true standpoint which Ritschlianism assumes in insisting that dogmatics has to do with the religious consciousness of salvation through Christ, yet it may be denied that Ritschlianism has correctly fixed the centre of that consciousness, or sufficiently described its circumference. For Ritschl, justification is salvation ; and justification means, if not exclusively, yet very distinctively, dominion over the world. That a subordinate aspect of Christian experience is hereby brought into undue prominence has been adequately proved already. The centre of the Christian consciousness is more satisfactorily and sufficiently described as " the life that is hid with Christ in God," a new relation to God through the mediation of Christ. The range of this Christian consciousness is also unduly restricted in the Ritschlian theology, because its practical ideal and its teleological reference are too limited. The new life includes thought and feeling as well as action, and salvation meets the questions of the mind and the longings of the heart, as well as the needs of the will for liberation and development. There is, therefore, a larger place for the theoretical impulse in the religious consciousness than Ritschlianism allows, and many questions, to which it would refuse to give an answer as remote from any practical interest, are not only legitimate, but even necessary, if intellectual certainty as well as moral security is to be regarded as an element in the Christian consciousness of salvation in Christ, by whom we are delivered from error as well as from sin. That error and sin on the one hand, truth and righteousness on the other hand, are closely related, is a fact which condemns the Ritschlian attempt to limit the religious consciousness to practical interests, to the exclusion of the theoretical impulse. The barriers that Ritschlianism sets up on this and that path of Christian inquiry must be thrown down, if the religious consciousness is to be adequately interpreted by Christian theology; but still Ritschlianism is right in insisting that theology has to deal only with the religious consciousness; not with truth conceived in abstraction, but with truth realised in life. It is this insistence on " the experimental character" of all Christian theology which is the significant and valuable aspect of the theory of value - judgments, which, rightly understood, is neither sceptical nor dualistic (p. 186), although, as applied by the Ritschlian school generally, it unduly restricts the range of Christian knowledge (p. 191).

(2) The second feature in which the Ritschlian theology shows merit, and so deserves praise, is its opposition to " speculative rationalism." Pfleiderer, it will be remembered (p. 76), blames Ritschl for his growing philosophical scepticism and historical positivism. Instead of appealing to reason as represented by philosophy, Ritschl more and more exclusively appeals to revelation as realised in history. We have already seen Ritschl's rejection of metaphysics (Chapter II.), and whatever in theory (Chapter III.) or practice (Chapter V.) may depend on it, and his dependence, accompanied, it is true, with some inconsistencies, wholly and solely on revelation (Chapter VII.). While Christian faith will yet find its full expression in a Christian philosophy, and accordingly the negative attitude of Ritschlianism to all philosophy must be regarded as a temporary phase and not a permanent disposition of Christian faith, yet Ritschl and his followers are altogether right, in the writer's judgment, in refusing to apply to Christian facts and truths the standard of a philosophy which claims to be independent of revelation, and affirms its origin in a universal and

permanent reason. Ritschlianism is opposed to rationalism in the following respects: (*a*) It gives prominence to the forgiveness of sin, justification, reconciliation, or the religious good which by God's grace is offered to man in Christ (Chapter X.); whereas rationalism knows only an ethical process of dying unto sin and becoming alive unto righteousness, which every man has to realise for himself, although Christ is the supreme type. (*b*) It insists on Christ as the historical revelation of God, without the distinction made by rationalism between the Person of Christ and the Christian principle, to which the person stands in an external relation (pp. 7, 220). Christ Himself is the object of Christian faith, and not merely the person in whose consciousness the metaphysical principle of man's divine sonship first reached clear and full expression. (*c*) According to Ritschl, the Christian community is the continuation of the revelation in Christ, and by that community the revelation is mediated for individuals (p. 321). For rationalism, no essential significance attaches to the Christian community, for the individual reason and conscience directly possess God, being independent of Christ, and, therefore, of His community also. (*d*) However defective in some respects Ritschl's doctrine of sin is, yet he does insist that sin is an actual contradiction of the divine will, guilt a real separation from God (p. 299); whereas, for speculative philosophy, sin is a necessary condition of moral development, for "the real is the rational." (*e*) Although the Ritschlian theology has not always expressed itself fully and clearly on the question of miracles, and some of the Ritschlians are led by their critical tendency to take up a negative attitude to some of the biblical miracles, a denial of miracles is not, as it is hoped has been sufficiently shown (pp. 221–227), an essential feature of the Ritschlian theology, as it is of rationalism in its modern forms. On the contrary, Ritschl frankly and fully accepts miracles as having a place and playing a part in God's Providence ; and all his followers accept his position. (*f*) While some representatives of rationalism, such as Pfleiderer, do affirm the personality of God, yet wherever in rationalism there is a pantheistic tendency, this truth is obscured. Whether Ritschl's construction of the personality of God be successful or not, yet the Ritschlian school speaks with no uncertain voice of a personal God.

(3) A third feature in which Ritschlianism may receive commendation is its opposition to, and exposure of, some of the errors and wrongs of an unhealthy pietism. Instances of this criticism, with which we have met in the previous discussion, may be mentioned : the familiarity and irreverence of the mystical intercourse with Christ as the soul's bridegroom, the abuse of the imagination in representing Christ in His exaltation, the curiosity which pries into the last things, the confidence which seeks in prayer to impose its wishes on God's will, all receive deserved rebuke. Ritschl, it is true, carried this polemic very much further than was necessary or legitimate, and injured his own system by his prejudice against pietism. His followers have been more moderate in tone, and so more successful in effort. As the theologian who criticises the excesses and extravagances of an intense and fervent, although ignorant and undisciplined piety, exposes himself to the suspicion of being himself indifferent, even while he is labouring in the interests of true godliness, Ritschl and his followers do deserve credit for their courageous and consistent criticism of all forms of unsound piety.

IV

(1) While Ritschl himself is the most prominent feature and the most potent factor in the Ritschlian theology, yet it must not be forgotten that he is the founder of a school,

25

the members of which while gratefully acknowledging his influence, and loyally accepting his purpose, exercise their liberty, and show their independence. In estimating Ritschlianism, we must consider the significance of their departures from their master, and the value of their contributions to the thought of the school. To treat this subject with intelligence and sympathy, it will be necessary to indicate as briefly as possible the history of the school. Its development may be considered in three stages: (i.) In the first period (1874–1880) Ritschl began to gather disciples. The publication of the second and third volumes of his great work attracted a number of theological thinkers to him, the more prominent of whom were Harnack, Herrmann, and Schürer, who were drawn to him by (1) his return to the historical revelation of the Person of Christ; (2) his claim for the independence of theology from philosophical tendencies; (3) his attempt to set Christian faith beyond the reach of historical criticism; and (4) his practical tendency. The characteristic of this period was the substantial agreement between master and disciples. (ii.) The second period (1880–89) may be said to have begun with the approach to Ritschl of Häring (a theologian with whom, as quite unknown to English students, the writer has not in this volume dealt at all) and Kaftan. Both from the beginning took up a more independent attitude, and so introduced new tendencies into the school. Henceforth it became evident that the agreement of the Ritschlian school was in a theological method rather than in dogmatic propositions. During this period a violent antagonism was excited on the part of other theological schools, liberal, conservative, and mediating. Bender, whom, it seems to the writer, Professor Orr has unfairly represented as the logical exponent of Ritschlian principles,[1] in 1886 separated himself from the

[1] See *Expository Times*, vi. pp. 257, 258, for a brief account of Bender's views.

movement. (iii.) The third period since 1839, the date of Ritschl's death, shows further developments. Harnack, one of the most prominent of the members of the school, is guiding many into theological paths, which Ritschl had carefully avoided, to a more critical and much less dogmatic attitude. But, on the other hand, Kaftan and Herrmann are showing a desire to come to an understanding with the evangelical theology of the Church. Thus already two tendencies are being developed within the school of Ritschl.

(2) In the representatives of the more positive tendency in the Ritschlian school there may be observed a desire to correct many of the defects of Ritschl's own theological statements. (*a*) Ritschl's *doctrine of sin*, involving a denial of original sin, of the reference of God's wrath to sin, and of the perversity of sin, is not accepted by his followers (pp. 306, 312). Herrmann and Kaftan, to mention only the two with whom we have already made some acquaintance, speak with the necessary emphasis of the evil and the curse of sin. (*b*) His *doctrine of the work of Christ*, in which the vicarious satisfaction involved in Christ's death is altogether denied, is expressly rejected by members of his school. Kaftan and Herrmann both affirm Christ's vicarious suffering for our salvation (p. 323). (*c*) The *doctrine of the divinity of Christ* is of all doctrines that in which the Ritschlian position must appear to Christian thinkers most unsatisfactory. But here, too, some of the disciples go beyond their master, while others keep to his position. Kaftan, while declining all speculations upon the question, asserts the incarnation of God in Christ, the unique relation of Christ to the Father, which can never again be repeated in human history, the necessity of the doctrine of Christ's divinity to Christian faith. Herrmann has already been quoted (p. 292) as affirming his belief in a personal pre-existence of Christ. In these positions the disciples are not contradicting their Master by affirming what he denied,

but are rather supplementing him by a frank confession where he maintained a firm reserve. They do not accept the orthodox formulæ of three persons in our substance, or of two natures in one person; but they do desire to recognise Christ's divinity as fully as they can without committing themselves to what they regard as doubtful speculations. (*d*) *The doctrine of the Holy Spirit* was dealt with very inadequately by Ritschl; on the one hand, he declined to examine the spiritual process by which the sinner becomes a believer; and, on the other hand, he laid such emphasis on "the active functions of the human spirit" as to appear practically to exclude the mystical element, the presence and the power of the Spirit of God, which eludes psychological analysis. Herrmann and Kaftan both transcend his limitations, just because, as one can gather from their writings, both have had a religious experience more varied if not more intense than Ritschl's. They both speak more freely of the soul's experience of God's grace, and of the work of the Holy Spirit in man (pp. 345–349). (*e*) Lastly, Ritschl's *doctrine of prayer*, with its practical exclusion of petition for outward things, is not generally held in his school (pp. 355, 356). It is due, as we have seen (p. 377), to his speculative idea of God's eternity; and as his followers do not share that idea, they do not find any difficulty, as he does, in admitting a place in prayer for petition for outward things.

(3) There has been thus a development of Christian doctrine within the Ritschlian school itself, which may be described as an approach to an evangelical theology, which will conserve what is permanently valuable in traditional orthodoxy. For this development two reasons may be given. On the one hand, Ritschl's disciples have used the biblical material for theology more extensively and more consistently than Ritschl himself did, even although he affirmed the Bible as the source and norm of Christian

doctrine. On the other hand, Ritschl's disciples have not stood apart from the practical piety of the Christian Church as he did, and so have been beneficially influenced by the common Christian faith and life. Within the school itself the development has involved growing differences, and these differences may yet lead to divisions. In the one party will be found those who have appropriated and developed the more positive elements of Ritschl's thought; in the other, those who have been attracted by, and have even advanced beyond the more negative elements. It is even possible that we shall not be able much longer to speak of a Ritschlian school.

(4) These four facts, to which attention has been called, that Ritschl's personality has had a very marked influence on his theology; that he has retained in his theology elements not involved in, and sometimes even inconsistent with his fundamental positions; that what is most characteristic of his school is its method, which though imperfect, is capable of correction; and that in his school there has been a development, in which some of his errors have been removed: these facts must all be taken into due account in estimating the significance and the value for English theological thought of the Ritschlian movement in Germany. They forbid a final judgment on its merits or defects, and they allow a confident hope that the future history of the school may yet prove a service and a benefit to the cause of Christian truth in the world.

V

(1) What the Ritschlian theology seems still to lack is (i.) a fuller appreciation of the significance and the value of the Holy Scriptures, as media of revelation to all lands and to all ages ; and (ii.) a more thorough recognition of the necessity for the mind of man of " thinking things together,"

to use a phrase which has been applied as a description of philosophy. Modern theology cannot restore the traditional doctrine of the verbal inspiration and the absolute inerrancy of the Holy Scriptures ; it is not at all necessary for its security, nor is it desirable for its progress, that it should even make any such vain and hopeless attempt. But, neverless, what is necessary and desirable is that the fit place and the right function of the Holy Scriptures be adequately recognised. That they are the literary sources of our knowledge of the historical revelation is not a satisfactory statement ; for if the recorders of the events and the reporters of the truths which constitute that revelation stand in a merely external relation to it, we may with good reason doubt their capacity to understand it, and their accuracy in sending it on to us. The certainty of our faith in that Revelation depends on the vital and organic unity between the facts and the truths of the historical revelation and its literary records and reports. The Revelation is not completed until it is made permanent and universal by means of the Scriptures. The writers of the Scriptures must be regarded as the subjects and the agents of the Revelation, qualified for their task by the Spirit of revelation. When this necessary and essential relation between the Holy Scriptures and divine Revelation is recognised, then the ritual, prophetical and historical preparation for Christ, the evangelical testimony regarding Christ, and the apostolic interpretation of Christ will be accorded an authority over Christian faith and life which will deliver us from the individual limitations, and the subjective impressions, which mark so much modern theological thinking. This authority must, it need hardly be said, be a genuinely spiritual authority — not an arbitrary and external restraint imposed on the mind, but the mind's liberation from error by submission to self-evidencing truth. The experience of the apostolic Church must be relived in order that its doctrine may again be rethought. One must most cordially agree with the Ritschlians, when they maintain that a man must not confess as his creed what he has not experienced in faith ; that our reverence for the apostles should never lead us to pretend and profess that we share and understand their experience, when it has as yet not become a vital reality to us ; that a mere holding-for-true (*Fürwahrhalten*) because others have told us is not living Christian faith. The objects of faith must be real ; the character of faith must be sincere. But then, on the other hand, the Christian Church, in all its branches, offers to the individual believer the Holy Scriptures as a record and report of divine revelation. He must not deny or reject what he himself cannot at once appreciate and appropriate for himself ; he ought not, by a word even, to lessen the worth, or weaken the force, that the Holy Scriptures possess for others. If he treats the Scriptures with reverence and loyalty, comes to the study of them in a trustful and teachable spirit, he will discover that they will nourish and exercise, and so vitalise and invigorate his faith ; his own experience will verify their claim. In this respect Ritschlianism still leaves something to be desired.

(2) Several speculative ideas of Ritschl's have been noted as " foreign elements " in his theology. These have been criticised not because they are speculative, but because Christian experience is not their starting-point and has not marked out their path, and because they contradict instead of completing Christian beliefs. There is a speculation which is quite legitimate, and altogether necessary in Christian theology. Ritschlianism fails to satisfy the mind of the writer, because it refuses to explain fully the objects of faith. It is quite true that what is in the first place most important for us is God's relation to us, Christ's mediation for us, the Spirit's operation in us ; but it is not true that it is altogether indifferent to faith what God as the

eternal and infinite existence is, what Christ in His relations
to God is, how the Holy Spirit is related to God and to
man.   Thought is compelled to attempt a complete
determination of its objects.   Reserve does not, and cannot
escape the suspicion of denial.   If we refuse to show as far
as our thought will allow that Christ comes from God, is in
God, then, whether we intend it or not, we suggest a doubt
about His relation to God.   So much of absolute value and
infinite significance for me, so every believer may argue,
depends on Christ, that I must have as complete and final
a certainty as it is possible for me to have, that in trusting
myself, body, soul, and spirit, for time and eternity to His
grace, "the eternal God is my refuge, and underneath are
the everlasting arms."   The Ritschlian reserve on these
sublime topics is not intended as a doubt or a denial
of any of the great Christian verities, of that the writer
is quite convinced, although it has often provoked such
a suspicion.   It can, however, be only a lodging for
a short time for thought, it can never be its home for any
length of time.   There is, let it be here fully acknowledged,
often an offensive confidence in human speculation on
divine realities, against which the Ritschlian reserve forms
a welcome protest.   There are theories which dissect the
Godhead, which analyse the person of Christ, and which
experiment on the operations of the Spirit, that to the
writer at least seem profane.   Dogmatic scholasticism has
often needed to learn the lesson of reverence and modesty.
Yet this Ritschlian "voluntary humility and poverty" in
thinking may prove injurious to faith, even as intellectual
arrogance and extravagance have been.   That Ritschlianism
is altogether right in its suspicion of, and aversion to, the
traditional metaphysics, the writer has already maintained
(p. 112).   The objection that he strongly feels to that
metaphysics is that it is altogether inadequate to aid in the
interpretation of the Christian verities, just because the world

of which it was the logical abstract did not include Christ, and the life for and in man which has come through Christ. Christ has made such a difference, that Christianity cannot borrow, but must create its own metaphysics. None of the philosophical systems which, within the Christian era, have come into being with more or less conscious dependence on Christianity, seems to him to be so thoroughly Christian as to justify the dependence of Christian theology upon it. The reason of the modern world, it seems to him, must be more thoroughly and soundly converted unto Christ than it has as yet been, ere Christian speculation on the ultimate problems will always prove an assistance, and never a difficulty to Christian faith. It is the merit of Ritschlianism that it has sought to free Christian theology from the traditional metaphysics, but it is its defect that it has not recognised the need for Christian faith of a Christian metaphysics, which from the Christian standpoint will think things together.

(3) There are not, however, two distinct remedies for these two defects of the Ritschlian theology ; there is but one. As Christian faith fully and freely appropriates the contents of the Christian Scriptures, it will both discover the necessity and attain the capacity for that Christian speculation which is necessary to give unity to thought, and so certainty and security to faith. It must not be forgotten that in the New Testament we have not only religious experience, but also the theological speculation that grew out of, and drew its health and strength from, religious experience. The more completely the Person of Christ as presented in the New Testament testimony to His words and works, His character and influence is appropriated by religious experience, the more certainly will theological speculation be compelled to follow in the footsteps of the Christian apostles in their Christological conceptions. The more fully the teaching of Christ regarding God is accepted by Christian faith, the more surely will Christian thought be

led to apply this sublime and splendid conception in the solution of all the problems of existence, that baffle yet arouse intelligence.

(4) If Ritschlianism would accept more fully the *material* afforded by the Holy Scriptures, and would apply more faithfully the *method*, which recognises the noumenal as well as the phenomenal aspects of the objects of faith, the permanent unity as well as the varying differences of spiritual realities, then it would be much nearer being a restatement of the Christian gospel in the intellectual situation of the age, which would deserve and could receive a cordial welcome. Whether the movement will transcend its limitations and remedy its defects the writer is not able to affirm, nor is he ready to deny. But whatever may be its future, whether it fulfils our best hopes for it or our worst fears, yet it deserves a sympathetic study as a theological development that has made Christian faith and life possible to earnest and honest thinkers, whom the intellectual situation of the age, its distrust of philosophy, its confidence in science, its activity in criticism, its social enthusiasm, has estranged from the orthodoxy of the Christian Churches. It has not only explained and justified the existing distrust of philosophy, but has by expounding and vindicating the independence of theology on philosophy, sought to save theology from the suspicion attaching to philosophy. If it has not given any satisfactory solution of the problems regarding which science and theology appear to be in opposition, yet it has so determined the limited scope of science, and so defined the distinctive purpose of religion, as to separate their provinces as far as possible, and as, therefore, to prevent, at least seemingly, their contact and conflict. With criticism it has sought to secure a truce, by showing that on the one hand faith has no vital interest in much that criticism brings into doubt and dispute, and on the other

that criticism has freedom to do its work without assailing what is absolutely essential to faith. The prominence that it accords to the idea of the kingdom of God fits it to attract the social enthusiasm of our times. Although its conclusions in each of these respects are open to criticism, a criticism which in this volume has been freely given, yet it has at least seriously and candidly attempted to deal with the real necessities of living men.

(5) So much of the theology of Great Britain is marked by an undue dependence on ecclesiastical authority, and an excessive timidity in venturing on any independent advance, that a theology such as the Ritschlian with its openness and boldness deserves to be widely known, and carefully studied if only as a stimulant, or even irritant to activity. Even in Ritschlianism there are local features, it brings with it the savour and the odour of its native soil; but that itself is a very good reason why we should study it, because to become acquainted with phases of thought which are unfamiliar to us is a salutary corrective of intellectual insularity, for exemption from which we in Great Britain are assuredly not famed. If the disease of doubt and unbelief in regard to the Christian faith, due to the intellectual situation of the age, has not reached as acute a stage in Britain as in Germany; yet it is an advantage for Christian thinkers to recognise in all their compass and intensity the varied and potent forces which are allied against "the faith once delivered to the saints," of which the Christian Church is the guardian.

(6) As the writer has himself felt very keenly the severe pressure of the problems which Ritschlianism at least recognises, but which traditional theology has for the most part ignored, his attitude towards this school has been more generous and sympathetic than has been hitherto usual in the English literature that has dealt with the subject. He would regret exceedingly, if in

his desire to do full justice to Ritschl and his school he had failed to be altogether just to any of their critics. He has not been able, however, to rid himself of the unwelcome impression that in much of the criticism he has read the offences of Ritschlianism were thrown into bold relief, while its merits were allowed to fall into the dim background.   Perhaps the difference, of which he has been conscious, between other writers and himself might be expressed in this way.   They, remaining in the standpoint of an assured Christian faith, have seen most clearly how far short Ritschlianism falls of an adequate and satisfactory Christian theology.   He, seeking to place himself as far as he could at the standpoint of a faith distressed by doubt and difficulty, has endeavoured to discover how near to a true and full Christian theology Ritschlianism can bring a faith so distressed. Those whom the *dogmatic* task of Christian theology attracts may find very little in Ritschlianism to help them in their definition of the Christian faith.   Those, however, who are most drawn by the *apologetic* aim of Christian theology, will discover not a little suggestion and stimulus in Ritschlianism as they seek not only to defend against attack, but to commend for acceptance, what has been the light of their path, the highest good of their soul.   Surely this apologetic aim in its more gracious aspect as the commendation and not the defence of Christian faith, has a larger claim than is commonly allowed to it on the intelligence, sympathy, conscience, and effort of all Christian believers.   The Christian Churches do not seem to be keeping their hold on many of the cultured and intellectual men and women of the age.   Here is a pressing need and an urgent duty.   Because the Ritschlian theology does lay bare this need and press home this duty, it is here and now commended for study in this Critical Estimate, in which as far as can be " mercy tempers justice."

INDEX

PRINTED BY MORRISON AND GIBB LIMITED, EDINBURGH

LOTZE'S MICROCOSMUS.

Microcosmus: Concerning Man and His Relation to the World. By HERMANN LOTZE. Translated from the German. Cheaper Edition, in Two Volumes, 8vo (1450 pp.), price 24s.

Messrs. Clark have pleasure in announcing this Cheaper Edition of Lotze's 'Microcosmus,' which the 'Athenæum' refers to as 'the greatest philosophic work produced in Germany by the generation just past.' It is issued in two handsome 8vo volumes (1450 pp.), and is in every way complete.

N.B.—A few copies of the 36s. Edition, printed on thicker paper. may still be had.

'The English public have now before them the greatest philosophic work produced in Germany by the generation just past. The translation comes at an opportune time, for the circumstances of English thought, just at the present moment, are peculiarly those with which Lotze attempted to deal when he wrote his "Microcosmus," a quarter of a century ago. . . . Few philosophic books of the century are so attractive both in style and matter.'—*Atheræum.*

'These are indeed two masterly volumes, vigorous in intellectual power, and translated with rare ability. . . . This work will doubtless find a place on the shelves of all the foremost thinkers and students of modern times.'—*Evangelical Magazine.*

Kant, Lotze, and Ritschl. A Critical Examination. By LEONHARD STÄHLIN, Bayreuth. Translated by Principal SIMON, D.D., Bradford. In demy 8vo, price 9s.

'This learned work goes to the very root of the philosophical and metaphysical speculations of recent years.'—*Ecclesiastical Gazette.*

Elements of Logic as a Science of Propositions. By E. E. CONSTANCE JONES, Lecturer in Moral Sciences, Girton College, Cambridge; Joint-Translator and Editor of Lotze's *Microcosmus.* In demy 8vo, price 7s. 6d.

'We must congratulate Girton College upon the forward movement of which the publication of this work is one of the first steps.'—*Cambridge Review.*

The Philosophical Basis of Theism: An Examination of the Personality of Man, to ascertain his Capacity to Know and Serve God, and the Validity of the Principles underlying the Defence of Theism. By Prof. S. HARRIS, D.D., LL.D. In ex. 8vo, price 12s.

'Full of suggestive thought, and of real assistance in unfolding to the mind the true account and justification of its religious knowledge.'—*Spectator.*

The Self-Revelation of God. By Professor SAMUEL HARRIS, D.D., LL.D., Yale College. In extra 8vo, price 12s.

'In "The Philosophical Basis of Theism" Dr. Harris laid the foundation, in the present work he raises the superstructure, and in both he has done good service to philosophy and theology. His is a mind full of knowledge, and rich in ripe reflection on the methods and results won in the past, and on the problems of the present hour.'—*Spectator.*

Modern Pantheism. Essay on Religious Philosophy. Translated from the French of M. EMILE SAISSET. Two Vols. 8vo, price 10s. 6d.

CONCORDANCE TO THE GREEK TESTAMENT. MOULTON-GEDEN.

A Concordance to the Greek Testament: According to the Texts of Westcott and Hort, Tischendorf, and the English Revisers. Edited by W. F. MOULTON, D.D., and A. S. GEDEN, M.A. In crown 4to (pp. 1040. SECOND EDITION, *Revised throughout.* Price 26s. net; or in half-morocco, price 31s. 6d. net.

₊ *It will be generally allowed that a new Concordance to the Greek Testament is much needed in the interests of sacred scholarship. This work adopts a new principle, and aims at providing a full and complete Concordance to the text of the Greek Testament as it is set forth in the editions of Westcott and Hort, Tischendorf (VIIIth), and the English Revisers. The first-named has throughout been taken as the standard, and the marginal readings have been included. Thus the student with any one of these three editions in his hands will find himself in possession of a complete Concordance to the actual text on which he is engaged; while the method employed, it may fairly be claimed, precludes the omission of any word or phrase which, by even a remote probability, might be regarded as forming part of the true text of the New Testament. On the other hand, passages disappear, as to the spuriousness of which there is practical unanimity among scholars.*

Professor W. SANDAY, D.D., LL.D., Oxford, writes: 'There can be no question as to the value of the new "Concordance." It is the only scientific Concordance to the Greek Testament, and the only one that can be safely used for scientific purposes.'

'It would be difficult to overpraise this invaluable addition to biblical study. . . . For all English students of the Greek Testament this great work is indispensable.'—BRITISH WEEKLY.

Prospectus, with Specimen Page, free on application.

DILLMANN ON GENESIS.

Genesis: Critically and Exegetically Expounded. By A. DILLMANN, D.D., late Professor of Theology in Berlin. *Authorised Translation.* In Two Volumes, 8vo, price 21s.

'The most perfect form of the *commentarius perpetuus* to the Old Testament which the 19th century has produced.'—Professor BUDDE, Strassburg.

'Dillmann's commentaries are inimitable works for labour and insight, for the mass of their contents, as for the thoroughness and fineness of their scholarship. They form an indispensable basis for all further works on the same subjects. . . . There is not a living scholar of the Old Testament but follows him to his rest with the deepest reverence and gratitude.'—*Bookman.*

St. Paul's Conception of Christ; or, The Doctrine of the Second Adam. Being the Sixteenth Series of the 'Cunningham Lectures.' By Rev. DAVID SOMERVILLE, D.D., Edinburgh. In demy 8vo, price 9s.

'By its keen and profound insight, by its sanity, and by its fulness of knowledge, the volume will at once take its place as the best authority on that department of New Testament theology with which it deals.'—*Critical Review.*

'This is the work of an honest and careful student of St. Paul's writings. . . . One of the most solid contributions that has been made to the study of St. Paul's Epistles for a considerable time.'—*Guardian.*

The Christ of History and of Experience. Being the 'Kerr Lectures' for 1897. By Rev. DAVID W. FORREST, D.D., Glasgow. In demy 8vo, Second Edition, price 10s. 6d.

'An exceedingly able treatment of a great and important subject.'—The late Professor CALDERWOOD.

'An eminently stimulating and improving book.'—*Glasgow Herald.*

'Displays marked ability, and possesses unusual interest.'—*Manchester Guardian.*

'. . . It is scarcely necessary, however, to specify particular passages in a book which throughout exhibits literary and theological powers of a high order, and which abounds in observations and criticisms which could only have been penned by a masculine and fearless, but reverent, thinker.'—*Literature.*

An Outline of Christian Theology. By Professor WILLIAM NEWTON CLARKE, D.D., Colgate University, Hamilton, New York. In post 8vo, Fourth Edition, price 7s. 6d.

Professor MARCUS DODS writes: ' Has it ever happened to any of our readers to take up a work on systematic theology, with the familiar divisions, " God," " Man," " Sin," " Christ," " The Holy Spirit," " The Church," " The Last Things," and open it with a sigh of weariness and dread, and find himself fascinated and enthralled, and compelled to read on to the last word? Let anyone who craves a new experience of this kind procure Dr. Clarke's " Outline." We guarantee that he will learn more, with greater pleasure, than he is likely to learn in any other systematic theology.'

' Altogether the book, by being always clear and candid, is a surprise in theological literature, and it will charm any reader, as the simply expressed does charm always. If there is to be a resurrection of the doctrinal sermon, which we pray God hasten, this book will be sought on every hand.'—*Expository Times.*

Recently Discovered Manuscripts, and ORIGEN'S COMMEN- TARIES ON MATTHEW AND JOHN. Being an Additional Volume to ' The Ante-Nicene Christian Library.' Edited by Professor ALLAN MENZIES, D.D., St. Andrews University. Containing: Gospel of Peter (by Professor ARMITAGE ROBINSON)—Diatessaron of Tatian— Apocalypse of Peter—Visio Pauli—Apocalypses of the Virgin and Sedrach—Testament of Abraham—Acts of Xanthippe and Polyxena —Narrative of Zosimus—Apology of Aristides—Epistles of Clement (Complete Text)—Origen's Commentaries on Matthew and John, etc. In One Volume, 4to (pp. 540), price 12s. 6d. net.

' It was a happy idea which occurred to the publishers of " The Ante-Nicene Library " to supplement that series with a volume containing translations of the more important discoveries of recent years. A judicious arrangement has been observed in grouping the recovered treasures. . . . It has been compiled with great care, and the Introduc- tions are short and to the point.'—*Record.*

The Ancient Faith in Modern Light: A Series of Essays. By JOSEPH PARKER, D.D., City Temple, London; Principal T. V. TYMMS, Rawdon College; Professor MEDLEY, Regent's Park College; Principal A. CAVE, D.D., Hackney College; SAMUEL G. GREEN, D.D., London; Principal R. VAUGHAN PRYCE, New College; S. NEWTH, D.D. (late Principal), New College; Rev. W. BROCK, Hampstead; J. GUINNESS ROGERS, D.D., Clapham; H. R. REYNOLDS, D.D. (late Principal of Cheshunt College). In demy 8vo, price 10s. 6d.

' These writers have passed their storms and found anchorage. They are the men who do the world's best work; healing work it often is, and will be here; saving work it will even be, for there is no dulness or dissipation that would weary the youngest reader. There is the living mind, fearless in face of the living problems of to-day; and the young minds who come to this volume will find rest to their souls, for they will come to the mind of the Master Himself.'—*Expository Times.*

Theologia Pectoris: Outlines of Religious Faith and Doctrine, founded on Intuition and Experience. By J. M. HODGSON, M.A., D.Sc., D.D., Principal of the Theological Hall of the Congregational Churches of Scotland. In crown 8vo, price 3s. 6d.

' He has written out of the fulness of his heart, and his thoughtful book will doubt- less find a response in the heart of others.'—*Scotsman.*

BY PRINCIPAL A. CAVE, D.D.

An Introduction to Theology: Its Principles, Its Branches, Its Results, and Its Literature. By ALFRED CAVE, B.A., D.D., Principal of Hackney College, London. Second Edition, largely rewritten, and the Bibliographical Lists carefully revised to date. In demy 8vo, price 12s.

'The best original work on the subject in the English language.'—PHILIP SCHAFF, D.D., LL.D.

'Its arrangement is perfect, its learning accurate and extensive, and its practical hints invaluable.'—*Christian World.*

'A marvel of industry, and simply invaluable to theologians.'—*Clergyman's Magazine.*

The Scriptural Doctrine of Sacrifice and Atonement. In demy 8vo, New Edition, Revised throughout, price 10s. 6d.

'Every page in this edition has been carefully revised in the light of the latest relative researches. The literary references have also been brought down to date. . . . More than half of the New Testament portion has been rewritten.'—*Extract from the Preface.*

'Let readers judge—is this not now the best systematic study of the Atonement in the English language?'—*Expository Times.*

BY PRINCIPAL D. W. SIMON, D.D.

Reconciliation by Incarnation: The Reconciliation of God and Man by the Incarnation of the Divine Word. By the Rev. D. W. SIMON, D.D., Principal of the United College, Bradford. In post 8vo, price 7s. 6d.

'A treatise of great value, for its broad philosophical grasp, its subtle spiritual insight, and its apt illustrations. It is a fresh, timely, and independent study of a subject which must ever be to the fore.'—*Baptist Magazine.*

The Redemption of Man: Discussions Bearing on the Atonement. In demy 8vo, price 10s. 6d.

Principal FAIRBAIRN, Mansfield College, writes: 'I wish to say how stimulating and helpful I have found your book. Its criticism is constructive as well as incisive, while its point of view is elevated and commanding. It made me feel quite vividly how superficial most of the recent discussions on the Atonement have been.'

'Its learning, ample although that be, is its least merit: it has the far higher and rarer qualities of freshness of view and deep ethical insight. I hope it will find the general and cordial reception it so well deserves.'—Professor R. FLINT, D.D.

The Bible an Outgrowth of Theocratic Life. In crown 8vo, price 4s. 6d.

Dr. JOHN BROWN, of Bedford, writes: 'I feel sure that such of your readers as may make acquaintance with it, will be as grateful for its valuable help as I have been myself.'

Delivery and Development of Christian Doctrine. By ROBERT RAINY, D.D., Principal, and Professor of Divinity and Church History, New College, Edinburgh. Price 10s. 6d.

'We gladly acknowledge the high excellence and the extensive learning which these lectures display. They are able to the last degree, and the author has, in an unusual measure, the power of acute and brilliant generalisation.'—*Literary Churchman.*

PUBLICATIONS OF

T. & T. CLARK,

38 GEORGE STREET, EDINBURGH.

LONDON: SIMPKIN, MARSHALL, HAMILTON, KENT, & CO. LIMITED.

Abbott (T. K., B.D., D.Lit.)—EPHESIANS AND COLOSSIANS. (*International Critical Commentary.*) Post 8vo, 10s. 6d.

Adam (J., D.D.)—AN EXPOSITION OF THE EPISTLE OF JAMES. 8vo, 9s.

Adamson (Rev. T., D.D.)—STUDIES OF THE MIND IN CHRIST. Post 8vo, 4s. 6d.

———— THE SPIRIT OF POWER. Second Edition. Fcap. 8vo, 1s.

Ahlfeld (Dr.), etc.—THE VOICE FROM THE CROSS. Cr. 8vo, price 5s.

Alcock (Deborah)—THE SEVEN CHURCHES OF ASIA. 1s.

Alexander (Prof. W. Lindsay)—BIBLICAL THEOLOGY. Two vols. 8vo, 21s.

Allen (Prof. A. V. G., D.D.)—CHRISTIAN INSTITUTIONS. (*International Theological Library.*) Post 8vo, 12s.

Ancient Faith in Modern Light, The. 8vo, 10s. 6d.

Andrews (S. J.)—THE LIFE OF OUR LORD. Large post 8vo, 9s.

Ante-Nicene Christian Library—A COLLECTION OF ALL THE WORKS OF THE FATHERS OF THE CHRISTIAN CHURCH PRIOR TO THE COUNCIL OF NICÆA. Twenty-four vols. 8vo, Subscription price, £6, 6s. *Additional Volume, containing MSS. discovered since the completion of the Series,* 12s. 6d. net.

Augustine's Works—Edited by MARCUS DODS, D.D. Fifteen vols. 8vo, Subscription price, £3, 19s. net.

Balfour (R. G., D.D.)—CENTRAL TRUTHS AND SIDE ISSUES. Crown 8vo, 3s. 6d.

Bannerman (Prof.)—THE CHURCH OF CHRIST. Two vols. 8vo, 21s.

Bannerman (D. D., D.D.)—THE DOCTRINE OF THE CHURCH. 8vo, 12s.

Baumgarten (Professor)—APOSTOLIC HISTORY. Three vols. 8vo, 27s.

Bayne (P., LL.D.)—THE FREE CHURCH OF SCOTLAND. Post 8vo, 3s. 6d.

Beck (Dr.)—OUTLINES OF BIBLICAL PSYCHOLOGY. Crown 8vo, 4s.

———— PASTORAL THEOLOGY OF THE NEW TESTAMENT. Crown 8vo, 6s.

Bengel—GNOMON OF THE NEW TESTAMENT. With Original Notes, Explanatory and Illustrative. Five vols. 8vo, Subscription price, 31s. 6d. *Cheaper Edition, the five volumes bound in three,* 24s.

Besser's CHRIST THE LIFE OF THE WORLD. Price 6s.

Beyschlag (W., D.D.)—NEW TESTAMENT THEOLOGY. Two vols. demy 8vo, 18s. net.

Bible Dictionary. Edited by JAS. HASTINGS, D.D. *See page* 16. *Special Prospectus on application.* Vols. I. and II. now ready.

Bible-Class Handbooks. Crown 8vo. Forty-four Volumes, 1s. 3d. to 3s. each. Edited by Prof. MARCUS DODS, D.D., and ALEX. WHYTE, D.D. *Detailed List free on application.*

Bible-Class Primers.   Thirty-four now issued in the Series.   Edited by Princ. S. D. F. SALMOND, D.D.   Paper covers, 6d. each ; free by post, 7d. In cloth, 8d. ; free by post, 9d.   *Detailed List free on application.*

Blaikie (Prof. W. G., D.D.)—THE PREACHERS OF SCOTLAND FROM THE 6TH TO THE 19TH CENTURY.   Post 8vo, 7s. 6d.

Blake (Buchanan, B.D.)—HOW TO READ THE PROPHETS.   Part I.— The Pre-Exilian Minor Prophets (with Joel).   Second Edition, 4s.   Part II. —Isaiah (ch. i.-xxxix.).   Second Edition, 2s. 6d.   Part III.—Jeremiah, 4s. Part IV.—Ezekiel, 4s.   Part V.—Isaiah (ch. xl.-lxvi.), and the Post-Exilian Prophets.   *The Series being now complete, Messrs. Clark offer the Set of Five Volumes for 15s.*

Bleek's INTRODUCTION TO THE NEW TESTAMENT.   Two vols. 8vo, 21s.

Briggs (Prof. C. A., D.D.)—GENERAL INTRODUCTION TO THE STUDY OF HOLY SCRIPTURE (*Replacing the Author's* 'Biblical Study,' *entirely re-written and greatly enlarged*).   8vo, 12s. net.

———— MESSIANIC PROPHECY.   Post 8vo, 7s. 6d.

———— THE MESSIAH OF THE APOSTLES.   Post 8vo, 7s. 6d.

———— THE MESSIAH OF THE GOSPELS.   Post 8vo, 6s. 6d.

———— THE BIBLE, THE CHURCH, AND THE REASON.   Post 8vo, 6s. 6d.

Brockelmann (C.)—LEXICON SYRIACUM.   With a Preface by Professor T. NÖLDEKE.   Crown 4to, 30s. net.

Bruce (Prof. A. B., D.D.)—THE TRAINING OF THE TWELVE ; exhibiting the Twelve Disciples under Discipline for the Apostleship.   Fifth Edition, 8vo, 10s. 6d.

———— THE HUMILIATION OF CHRIST.   3rd Ed., 8vo, 10s. 6d.

———— THE KINGDOM OF GOD ; or, Christ's Teaching according to the Synoptical Gospels.   New Edition, 7s. 6d.

———— APOLOGETICS ; OR, CHRISTIANITY DEFENSIVELY STATED. (*International Theological Library.*)   Post 8vo, 10s. 6d.

———— ST. PAUL'S CONCEPTION OF CHRISTIANITY.   Post 8vo, 7s. 6d.

———— THE EPISTLE TO THE HEBREWS : The First Apology for Christianity.   Just published.   Post 8vo, 7s. 6d.

Bruce (W. S., D.D.)—THE ETHICS OF THE OLD TESTAMENT.   Cr. 8vo, 4s.

Buchanan (Professor)—THE DOCTRINE OF JUSTIFICATION.   8vo, 10s. 6d.

———— ON COMFORT IN AFFLICTION.   Crown 8vo, 2s. 6d.

———— ON IMPROVEMENT OF AFFLICTION.   Crown 8vo, 2s. 6d.

Bungener (Felix)—ROME AND THE COUNCIL IN 19TH CENTURY.   Cr. 8vo, 5s.

Burton (Prof. E.)—SYNTAX OF THE MOODS AND TENSES IN NEW TESTAMENT GREEK.   New Edition.   Post 8vo, 5s. 6d. net.

Calvin's INSTITUTES OF CHRISTIAN RELIGION. (Translation.) 2 vols. 8vo, 14s.

———— COMMENTARIES.   Forty-five Vols.

Calvini Institutio Christianæ Religionis.   Curavit A. THOLUCK. Two vols. 8vo, Subscription price, 14s.

Candlish (Prof. J. S., D.D.)—THE KINGDOM OF GOD, BIBLICALLY AND HISTORICALLY CONSIDERED.   8vo, 10s. 6d.

Caspari (C. E.)—A CHRONOLOGICAL AND GEOGRAPHICAL INTRODUCTION TO THE LIFE OF CHRIST.   8vo, 7s. 6d.

Caspers (A.)—THE FOOTSTEPS OF CHRIST.   Crown 8vo, 7s. 6d.

Cassel (Prof.)—COMMENTARY ON ESTHER. 8vo, 10s. 6d.

Cave (Principal A., D.D.)—THE SCRIPTURAL DOCTRINE OF SACRIFICE AND ATONEMENT. Second Edition, 8vo, 10s. 6d.

———— AN INTRODUCTION TO THEOLOGY. Second Edition, 8vo, 12s.

Chapman (Principal C., LL.D.)—PRE-ORGANIC EVOLUTION AND THE BIBLICAL IDEA OF GOD. Crown 8vo, 6s.

Christlieb (Prof. T., D.D.)—MODERN DOUBT AND CHRISTIAN BELIEF. 8vo, 10s. 6d.

———— HOMILETIC: Lectures on Preaching. 7s. 6d.

Clark (Professor W. R., LL.D., D.C.L.)—THE ANGLICAN REFORMATION. (*Eras of Church History.*) 6s.

Clarke (Professor W. N., D.D.)—AN OUTLINE OF CHRISTIAN THEOLOGY. Post 8vo, 7s. 6d.

Concordance to the Greek Testament—MOULTON (W. F., D.D.) and GEDEN (A. S., M.A.). Crown 4to, 26s. net.

Crawford (J. H., M.A.)—THE BROTHERHOOD OF MANKIND. Crown 8vo, 5s.

Cremer (Professor)—BIBLICO-THEOLOGICAL LEXICON OF NEW TESTAMENT GREEK. Third Edition, with Supplement, demy 4to, 38s.

Crippen (Rev. T. G.)—A POPULAR INTRODUCTION TO THE HISTORY OF CHRISTIAN DOCTRINE. 8vo, 9s.

Critical Review OF THEOLOGICAL AND PHILOSOPHICAL LITERATURE. Edited by Princ. S. D. F. SALMOND, D.D. Quarterly, 1s. 6d.

Cunningham (Principal)—HISTORICAL THEOLOGY. Two vols. 8vo, 21s.

Curtiss (Dr. S. I.)—THE LEVITICAL PRIESTS. Crown 8vo, 5s.

———— FRANZ DELITZSCH: A Memorial Tribute. *Portrait.* Cr. 8vo, 3s.

Dabney (Prof. R. L., D.D.)—THE SENSUALISTIC PHILOSOPHY OF THE NINETEENTH CENTURY CONSIDERED. Crown 8vo, 6s.

Dahle (Bishop)—LIFE AFTER DEATH. Demy 8vo, 10s. 6d.

Davidson (Prof. A.B., D.D., LL.D.)—AN INTRODUCTORY HEBREW GRAMMAR. With Progressive Exercises in Reading and Writing. 15th Edition, 8vo, 7s. 6d.

———— A SYNTAX OF THE HEBREW LANGUAGE. 2nd Ed., 8vo, 7s. 6d.

Davidson, Dr. Samuel. Autobiography and Diary. Edited by his DAUGHTER. 8vo, 7s. 6d.

Deane (Wm., M.A.)—PSEUDEPIGRAPHA: An Account of Certain Apocryphal Writings of the Jews and Early Christians. Post 8vo, 7s. 6d.

Delitzsch (Prof.)—SYSTEM OF BIBLICAL PSYCHOLOGY, 8vo, 12s.; NEW COMMENTARY ON GENESIS, 2 vols. 8vo, 21s.; PSALMS, 3 vols., 31s. 6d.; PROVERBS, 2 vols., 21s.; SONG OF SOLOMON AND ECCLESIASTES, 10s. 6d.; ISAIAH, Fourth Edition, rewritten, 2 vols., 21s.; HEBREWS, 2 vols., 21s.

Dictionary of the Bible, A. (*See page 16.*)

Dillmann (Prof. A., D.D.)—GENESIS: Critical and Exegetical Commentary. Two vols., 21s.

Doedes—MANUAL OF NEW TESTAMENT HERMENEUTICS. Cr. 8vo, 3s.

Döllinger (Dr.)—HIPPOLYTUS AND CALLISTUS. 8vo, 7s. 6d.

———— DECLARATIONS AND LETTERS ON THE VATICAN DECREES, 1869-1887. Authorised Translation. Crown 8vo, 3s. 6d.

Dorner (Professor)—HISTORY OF THE DEVELOPMENT OF THE DOCTRINE OF THE PERSON OF CHRIST. Five vols. 8vo, £2, 12s. 6d.

———— SYSTEM OF CHRISTIAN DOCTRINE. 4 vols. 8vo, £2, 2s.

Harris (S., D.D.)—GOD THE CREATOR AND LORD OF ALL. Two vols. post 8vo, 16s.

Haupt (Erich)—THE FIRST EPISTLE OF ST. JOHN. 8vo, 10s. 6d.

Hävernick (H. A. Ch.)—INTRODUCTION TO OLD TESTAMENT. 10s. 6d.

Heard (Rev. J. B., M.A.)—THE TRIPARTITE NATURE OF MAN—SPIRIT, SOUL, AND BODY. Fifth Edition, crown 8vo, 6s.

———— OLD AND NEW THEOLOGY. A Constructive Critique. Cr. 8vo, 6s.

———— ALEXANDRIAN AND CARTHAGINIAN THEOLOGY CONTRASTED. The Hulsean Lectures, 1892–93. Crown 8vo, 6s.

Hefele (Bishop)—A HISTORY OF THE COUNCILS OF THE CHURCH. Vol. I., to A.D. 325. Vol. II., A.D. 326 to 429. Vol. III., A.D. 431 to the close of the Council of Chalcedon, 451. Vol. IV., A.D. 451 to 680. Vol. V., A.D. 626 to 787. 8vo, 12s. each.

Hengstenberg (Professor)—COMMENTARY ON PSALMS, 3 vols. 8vo, 33s.; ECCLESIASTES, ETC., 8vo, 9s.; EZEKIEL, 8vo, 10s. 6d.; THE GENUINENESS OF DANIEL, ETC., 8vo, 12s.; HISTORY OF THE KINGDOM OF GOD, 2 vols. 8vo, 21s.; CHRISTOLOGY OF THE OLD TESTAMENT, 4 vols. 8vo, £2, 2s.; ST. JOHN'S GOSPEL, 2 vols. 8vo, 21s.

Herzog—ENCYCLOPÆDIA OF LIVING DIVINES, ETC., OF ALL DE-NOMINATIONS IN EUROPE AND AMERICA. (*Supplement to Herzog's Encyclopædia.*) Imp. 8vo, 8s.

Hill (Rev. J. Hamlyn, D.D.)—THE EARLIEST LIFE OF CHRIST EVER COMPILED FROM THE FOUR GOSPELS: Being 'The Diatessaron of Tatian' Literally Translated from the Arabic Version, and containing the Four Gospels woven into one Story. With an Historical and Critical Introduction, Notes, and Appendix. 8vo, 10s. 6d.

———— ST. EPHRAEM THE SYRIAN. 8vo, 7s. 6d.

Hodgson (Principal J. M., M.A., D.Sc., D.D.)—THEOLOGIA PECTORIS: Outlines of Religious Faith and Doctrine. Crown 8vo, 3s. 6d.

Hutchison (John, D.D.)—COMMENTARY ON THESSALONIANS. 8vo, 9s.

———— COMMENTARY ON PHILIPPIANS. 8vo, 7s. 6d.

———— OUR LORD'S SIGNS IN ST. JOHN'S GOSPEL. Demy 8vo, 7s. 6d.

Innes (A. Taylor)—THE TRIAL OF JESUS CHRIST. In its Legal Aspect. [*In the Press.*

International Critical Commentary.

DRIVER (Prof. S. R., D.D.)—Deuteronomy. Post 8vo, 12s.
MOORE (Prof. G. F., D.D.)—Judges. 12s.
SMITH (Prof. H. P., D.D.)—Samuel. 12s.
GOULD (Prof. E. P., D.D.)—St. Mark. 10s. 6d.
PLUMMER (ALFRED, D.D.)—St. Luke. 12s.
SANDAY (Prof. W., D.D.) and HEADLAM (A. C., B.D.)—Romans. 12s.
ABBOTT (Prof. T. K., B.D., D.Lit.)—Ephesians and Colossians. 10s. 6d.
VINCENT (Prof. M. R., D.D.)—Philippians and Philemon. 8s. 6d.
For List of future Volumes see p. 15.

International Theological Library.

DRIVER (Prof. S. R., D.D.)—An Introduction to the Literature of the Old Testament. Post 8vo, 12s.
SMYTH (NEWMAN, D.D.)—Christian Ethics. Post 8vo, 10s. 6d.
BRUCE (Prof. A. B., D.D.)—Apologetics. 10s. 6d.

International Theological Library.
FISHER (Prof. G. P., D.D., LL.D.)—History of Christian Doctrine. 12s.
ALLEN (Prof. A. V. G., D.D.)—Christian Institutions. 12s.
McGIFFERT (Prof. A. C., Ph.D.)—The Apostolic Age. 12s.
GLADDEN (Washington, D.D.)—The Christian Pastor. 10s. 6d.
STEVENS (Prof. G. B., D.D.)—The Theology of the New Testament. 12s.
For List of future Volumes see p. 14.

Janet (Paul)—FINAL CAUSES. Second Edition, demy 8vo, 12s.

—— THE THEORY OF MORALS. Demy 8vo, 10s. 6d.

Johnstone (Prof. R., D.D.)—COMMENTARY ON 1ST PETER. 8vo, 10s. 6d.

Jones (E. E. C.)—ELEMENTS OF LOGIC. 8vo, 7s. 6d.

Jouffroy—PHILOSOPHICAL ESSAYS. Fcap. 8vo, 5s.

Kaftan (Prof. J., D.D.)—THE TRUTH OF THE CHRISTIAN RELIGION. *Authorised Translation.* 2 vols. 8vo, 16s. net.

Kant—THE METAPHYSIC OF ETHICS. Crown 8vo, 6s.

—— PHILOSOPHY OF LAW. Trans. by W. HASTIE, D.D. Cr. 8vo, 5s.

—— PRINCIPLES OF POLITICS, ETC. Crown 8vo, 2s. 6d.

Keil (Prof.)—PENTATEUCH, 3 vols. 8vo, 31s. 6d.; JOSHUA, JUDGES, AND RUTH, 8vo, 10s. 6d.; SAMUEL, 8vo, 10s. 6d.; KINGS, 8vo, 10s. 6d.; CHRONICLES, 8vo, 10s. 6d.; EZRA, NEHEMIAH, ESTHER, 8vo, 10s. 6d.; JEREMIAH, 2 vols. 8vo, 21s.; EZEKIEL, 2 vols. 8vo, 21s.; DANIEL, 8vo, 10s. 6d.; MINOR PROPHETS, 2 vols. 8vo, 21s.; INTRODUCTION TO THE CANONICAL SCRIPTURES OF THE OLD TESTAMENT, 2 vols. 8vo, 21s.; HANDBOOK OF BIBLICAL ARCHÆOLOGY, 2 vols. 8vo, 21s.

Kennedy (H. A. A., M.A., D.Sc.)—SOURCES OF NEW TESTAMENT GREEK. Post 8vo, 5s.

Keymer (Rev. N., M.A.)—NOTES ON GENESIS. Crown 8vo, 1s. 6d.

Kidd (James, D.D.)—MORALITY AND RELIGION. 8vo, 10s. 6d.

Killen (Prof.)—THE FRAMEWORK OF THE CHURCH. 8vo, 9s.

—— THE OLD CATHOLIC CHURCH. 8vo, 9s.

—— TheIGNATIAN EPISTLES ENTIRELY SPURIOUS. Cr. 8vo, 2s. 6d.

König (Dr. Ed.)—THE EXILES' BOOK OF CONSOLATION (Deutero-Isaiah).
[*In the Press.*

König (Dr. F. E.)—THE RELIGIOUS HISTORY OF ISRAEL. Cr. 8vo, 3s. 6d.

Krummacher (Dr. F. W.)—THE SUFFERING SAVIOUR; or, Meditations on the Last Days of the Sufferings of Christ. Eighth Edition, crown 8vo, 6s.

—— DAVID, THE KING OF ISRAEL. Second Edition, cr. 8vo, 6s.

—— AUTOBIOGRAPHY. Crown 8vo, 6s.

Kurtz (Prof.)—HANDBOOK OF CHURCH HISTORY (from 1517). 8vo, 7s. 6d.

—— HISTORY OF THE OLD COVENANT. Three vols. 8vo, 31s. 6d.

Ladd (Prof. G. T.)—THE DOCTRINE OF SACRED SCRIPTURE: A Critical, Historical, and Dogmatic Inquiry into the Origin and Nature of the Old and New Testaments. Two vols. 8vo, 1600 pp., 24s.

Laidlaw (Prof. J., D.D.)—THE BIBLE DOCTRINE OF MAN; or, The Anthropology and Psychology of Scripture. New Edition Revised and Rearranged, post 8vo, 7s. 6d.

Lane (Laura M.)—LIFE OF ALEXANDER VINET. Crown 8vo, 7s. 6d.

Lange (J. P., D.D.)—THE LIFE OF OUR LORD JESUS CHRIST. Edited by MARCUS DODS, D.D. 2nd Ed., in 4 vols. 8vo, price 28s. net.

———— COMMENTARIES ON THE OLD AND NEW TESTAMENTS. Edited by PHILIP SCHAFF, D.D. OLD TESTAMENT, 14 vols.; NEW TESTAMENT, 10 vols.; APOCRYPHA, 1 vol. Subscription price, net, 15s. each.

———— ST. MATTHEW AND ST. MARK, 3 vols. 8vo, 31s. 6d.; ST. LUKE, 2 vols. 8vo, 18s.; ST. JOHN, 2 vols. 8vo, 21s.

Lechler (Prof. G. V., D.D.)—THE APOSTOLIC AND POST-APOSTOLIC TIMES. Their Diversity and Unity in Life and Doctrine. 2 vols. cr. 8vo, 16s.

Lehmann (Pastor)—SCENES FROM THE LIFE OF JESUS. Cr. 8vo, 3s. 6d.

Lewis (Tayler, LL.D.)—THE SIX DAYS OF CREATION. Cr. 8vo, 7s. 6d.

Lichtenberger (F., D.D.)—HISTORY OF GERMAN THEOLOGY IN THE 19TH CENTURY. 8vo, 14s.

Lilley (J. P., M.A.)—THE LORD'S SUPPER: Its Origin, Nature, and Use. Crown 8vo, 5s.

Lisco (F. G.)—PARABLES OF JESUS EXPLAINED. Fcap. 8vo, 5s.

Locke (Clinton, D.D.)—THE AGE OF THE GREAT WESTERN SCHISM. (*Eras of Church History.*) 6s.

Lotze (Hermann)—MICROCOSMUS: An Essay concerning Man and his relation to the World. Cheaper Edition, 2 vols. 8vo (1450 pp.), 24s.

Ludlow (J. M., D.D.)—THE AGE OF THE CRUSADES. (*Eras of Church History.*) 6s.

Luthardt, Kahnis, and Brückner—THE CHURCH. Crown 8vo, 5s.

Luthardt (Prof.)—ST. JOHN THE AUTHOR OF THE FOURTH GOSPEL. 7s. 6d.

———— COMMENTARY ON ST. JOHN'S GOSPEL. 3 vols. 8vo, 31s. 6d.

———— HISTORY OF CHRISTIAN ETHICS. 8vo, 10s. 6d.

———— APOLOGETIC LECTURES ON THE FUNDAMENTAL (7 *Ed.*), SAVING (5 *Ed.*), MORAL TRUTHS OF CHRISTIANITY (4 *Ed.*). 3 vols. cr. 8vo, 6s. each.

Macdonald—INTRODUCTION TO PENTATEUCH. Two vols. 8vo, 21s.

———— THE CREATION AND FALL. 8vo, 12s.

Macgregor (Rev. Jas., D.D.) — THE APOLOGY OF THE CHRISTIAN RELIGION. 8vo, 10s. 6d.

———— THE REVELATION AND THE RECORD: Essays on Matters of Previous Question in the Proof of Christianity. 8vo, 7s. 6d.

———— STUDIES IN THE HISTORY OF NEW TESTAMENT APOLOGETICS. 8vo, 7s. 6d.

Macgregor (Rev. G. H. C., M.A.)—SO GREAT SALVATION. Crown 32mo, 1s.

Macpherson (Rev. John, M.A.)—COMMENTARY ON THE EPISTLE TO THE EPHESIANS. 8vo, 10s. 6d.

———— CHRISTIAN DOGMATICS. Post 8vo, 9s.

McCosh (James), Life of. 8vo, 9s.

McGiffert (Prof. A. C., Ph.D.)—HISTORY OF CHRISTIANITY IN THE APOSTOLIC AGE. (*International Theological Library.*) Post 8vo, 12s.

M'Realsham (E. D.)—Romans Dissected. A Critical Analysis of the Epistle to the Romans. Crown 8vo, 2s.

Mair (A., D.D.)—Studies in the Christian Evidences. Third Edition, Revised and Enlarged, crown 8vo, 6s.

Martensen (Bishop)—Christian Dogmatics. 8vo, 10s. 6d.

———— Christian Ethics. (General — Individual — Social.) Three vols. 8vo, 10s. 6d. each.

Matheson (Geo., D.D.)—Growth of the Spirit of Christianity, from the First Century to the Dawn of the Lutheran Era. Two vols. 8vo, 21s.

Meyer (Dr.) — Critical and Exegetical Commentaries on the New Testament. Twenty vols. 8vo. *Subscription Price,* £5, 5s. *net ; Non-Subscription Price,* 10s. 6d. each volume.
St. Matthew, 2 vols.; Mark and Luke, 2 vols.; St. John, 2 vols.; Acts, 2 vols.; Romans, 2 vols. ; Corinthians, 2 vols.; Galatians, one vol. ; Ephesians and Philemon, one vol. ; Philippians and Colossians, one vol.; Thessalonians (*Dr. Lünemann*), one vol. ; The Pastoral Epistles (*Dr. Huther*), one vol. ; Hebrews (*Dr. Lünemann*), one vol. ; St. James and St. John's Epistles (*Huther*), one vol. ; Peter and Jude (*Dr. Huther*), one vol.

Michie (Charles, M.A.)—Bible Words and Phrases. 18mo, 1s.

Milligan (Prof. W., D.D.)—The Resurrection of the Dead. Second Edition, crown 8vo, 4s. 6d.

Milligan (Prof. W., D.D.) and **Moulton (W. F., D.D.)** — Commentary on the Gospel of St. John. Imp. 8vo, 9s.

Monrad (Dr. D. G.)—The World of Prayer. Crown 8vo, 4s. 6d.

Moore (Prof. G. F., D.D.)—Judges. (*International Critical Commentary.*) Post 8vo, 12s.

Morgan (J., D.D.)—Scripture Testimony to the Holy Spirit. 7s. 6d.

———— Exposition of the First Epistle of John. 8vo, 7s. 6d.

Moulton (W. F., D.D.) and **Geden (A. S., M.A.)**—A Concordance to the Greek Testament. Crown 4to, 26s. net, and 31s. 6d. net.

Muir (Sir W.)—Mohammedan Controversy, Etc. 8vo, 7s. 6d.

Müller (Dr. Julius)—The Christian Doctrine of Sin. 2 vols. 8vo, 21s.

Murphy (Professor)—Commentary on the Psalms. 8vo, 12s.

———— A Critical and Exegetical Commentary on Exodus. 9s.

Naville (Ernest)—The Problem of Evil. Crown 8vo, 4s. 6d.

———— The Christ. Translated by Rev. T. J. Després. Cr. 8vo, 4s. 6d.

———— Modern Physics. Crown 8vo, 5s.

Neander (Dr.)—Church History. Eight vols. 8vo, £2, 2s. net.

Nicoll (W. Robertson, M.A., LL.D.)—The Incarnate Saviour. Cheap Edition, price 3s. 6d.

Novalis—Hymns and Thoughts on Religion. Crown 8vo, 4s.

Oehler (Prof.)—Theology of the Old Testament. 2 vols. 8vo, 21s.

Olshausen (Dr. H.)—Biblical Commentary on the Gospels and Acts. Four vols. 8vo, £2, 2s. *Cheaper Edition,* four vols. crown 8vo, 24s.

———— Romans, one vol. 8vo, 10s. 6d. ; Corinthians, one vol. 8vo, 9s. ; Philippians, Titus, and First Timothy, one vol. 8vo, 10s. 6d.

Oosterzee (Dr. Van)—The Year of Salvation. 2 vols. 8vo, 6s. each.

———— Moses : A Biblical Study. Crown 8vo, 6s.

Orelli (Dr. C. von)—OLD TESTAMENT PROPHECY ; COMMENTARY ON ISAIAH; JEREMIAH ; THE TWELVE MINOR PROPHETS. 4 vols. 8vo, 10s. 6d. each.

Owen (Dr. John)—WORKS. *Best and only Complete Edition.* Edited by Rev. Dr. GOOLD. Twenty-four vols. 8vo, Subscription price, £4, 4s. The '*Hebrews*' may be had separately, in seven vols., £2, 2s. net.

Philippi (F. A.)—COMMENTARY ON THE ROMANS. Two vols. 8vo, 21s.

Piper—LIVES OF LEADERS OF CHURCH UNIVERSAL. Two vols. 8vo, 21s.

Popular Commentary on the New Testament. Edited by PHILIP SCHAFF, D.D. With Illustrations and Maps. Vol. I.—THE SYNOPTICAL GOSPELS. Vol. II.—ST. JOHN'S GOSPEL, AND THE ACTS OF THE APOSTLES. Vol. III.—ROMANS TO PHILEMON. Vol. IV.—HEBREWS TO REVELATION. In four vols. imperial 8vo, 12s. 6d. each.

Plummer (Alfred, D.D.)—ST. LUKE. (*International Critical Commentary.*) Post 8vo, 12s.

Pressensé (Edward de)—THE REDEEMER : Discourses. Crown 8vo, 6s.

Pünjer (Bernhard)—HISTORY OF THE CHRISTIAN PHILOSOPHY OF RELIGION FROM THE REFORMATION TO KANT. 8vo, 16s.

Räbiger (Prof.)—ENCYCLOPÆDIA OF THEOLOGY. Two vols. 8vo, 21s.

Rainy (Principal) — DELIVERY AND DEVELOPMENT OF CHRISTIAN DOCTRINE. 8vo, 10s. 6d.

Reusch (Prof.)—NATURE AND THE BIBLE : Lectures on the Mosaic History of Creation in Relation to Natural Science. Two vols. 8vo, 21s.

Reuss (Professor)—HISTORY OF THE SACRED SCRIPTURES OF THE NEW TESTAMENT. 640 pp. 8vo, 15s.

Riehm (Dr. E.)—MESSIANIC PROPHECY. New Edition. Post 8vo, 7s. 6d.

Ritter (Carl)—COMPARATIVE GEOGRAPHY OF PALESTINE. 4 vols. 8vo, 26s.

Robinson (Rev. S., D.D.)—DISCOURSES ON REDEMPTION. 8vo, 7s. 6d.

Robinson (E., D.D.)—GREEK AND ENG. LEXICON OF THE N. TEST. 8vo, 9s.

Rooke (T. G., B.A.)—INSPIRATION, and other Lectures. 8vo, 7s. 6d.

Ross (C.)—OUR FATHER'S KINGDOM. Crown 8vo, 2s. 6d.

Rothe (Prof.)—SERMONS FOR THE CHRISTIAN YEAR. Cr. 8vo, 4s. 6d.

Saisset—MANUAL OF MODERN PANTHEISM. Two vols. 8vo, 10s. 6d.

Salmond (Prof. S. D. F., D.D.)—THE CHRISTIAN DOCTRINE OF IMMORTALITY. 8vo, 14s.

Sanday (Prof. W., D.D.) and Headlam (A. C., B.D.)—ROMANS. (*International Critical Commentary.*) Post 8vo, 12s.

Sartorius (Dr. E.)—DOCTRINE OF DIVINE LOVE. 8vo, 10s. 6d.

Schaff (Professor)—HISTORY OF THE CHRISTIAN CHURCH. (New Edition, thoroughly Revised and Enlarged.) Six 'Divisions,' in 2 vols. each, extra 8vo.

    1. APOSTOLIC CHRISTIANITY, A.D. 1–100, 2 vols. 21s. 2. ANTE-NICENE, A.D. 100–325, 2 vols., 21s. 3. NICENE AND POST-NICENE, A.D. 325–600, 2 vols., 21s. 4. MEDIÆVAL, A.D. 590–1073, 2 vols., 21s. (*Completion of this Period*, 1073–1517, *in preparation*). 5. THE SWISS REFORMATION, 2 vols., extra demy 8vo, 21s. 6. THE GERMAN REFORMATION, 2 vols., extra demy 8vo, 21s.

Schleiermacher's CHRISTMAS EVE. Crown 8vo, 2s.

Schmid's BIBLICAL THEOLOGY OF THE NEW TESTAMENT. 8vo, 10s. 6d.

Schubert (Prof. H. Von., D.D.)—THE GOSPEL OF ST. PETER. Synoptical Tables. With Translation and Critical Apparatus. 8vo, 1s. 6d. net.

Schultz (Hermann)—OLD TESTAMENT THEOLOGY. Two vols. 18s. net.

Schürer (Prof.)—HISTORY OF THE JEWISH PEOPLE. 5 vols. 8vo, 52/6.

Schwartzkopff (Dr. P.)—THE PROPHECIES OF JESUS CHRIST. Crown 8vo, 5s.

Scott (Jas., M.A., D.D.)—PRINCIPLES OF NEW TESTAMENT QUOTATION ESTABLISHED AND APPLIED TO BIBLICAL CRITICISM. Cr. 8vo, 2nd Edit., 4s.

Sell (K., D.D.)—THE CHURCH IN THE MIRROR OF HISTORY. Cr. 8vo, 3/6.

Shedd—HISTORY OF CHRISTIAN DOCTRINE. Two vols. 8vo, 21s.

——— SERMONS TO THE NATURAL MAN. 8vo, 7s. 6d.

——— SERMONS TO THE SPIRITUAL MAN. 8vo, 7s. 6d.

——— DOGMATIC THEOLOGY. Three vols. ex. 8vo, 37s. 6d.

Simon (Prof.)—THE BIBLE; An Outgrowth of Theocratic Life. Cr. 8vo, 4/6.

——— THE REDEMPTION OF MAN. 8vo, 10s. 6d.

——— RECONCILIATION BY INCARNATION. Post 8vo, 7s. 6d.

Skene-Bickell—THE LORD'S SUPPER & THE PASSOVER RITUAL. 8vo, 5s.

Smeaton (Professor)—DOCTRINE OF THE HOLY SPIRIT. 2nd Ed., 8vo, 9s.

Smith (Prof. H. P., D.D.)—I. AND II. SAMUEL. (*International Critical Commentary.*) Post 8vo, 12s.

Smith (Professor Thos., D.D.)—MEDIÆVAL MISSIONS. Cr. 8vo, 4s. 6d.

Smyth (Newman, D.D.)—CHRISTIAN ETHICS. (*International Theological Library.*) Post 8vo, 10s. 6d.

Somerville (Rev. D., D.D.)—ST. PAUL'S CONCEPTION OF CHRIST. 9s.

Stählin (Leonh.)—KANT, LOTZE, AND RITSCHL. 8vo, 9s.

Stalker (Jas., D.D.)—LIFE OF CHRIST. Large Type Ed., cr. 8vo, 3s. 6d.

——— LIFE OF ST. PAUL. Large Type Edition, crown 8vo, 3s. 6d.

Stanton (V. H., D.D.)—THE JEWISH AND THE CHRISTIAN MESSIAH. A Study in the Earliest History of Christianity. 8vo, 10s. 6d.

Stead (F. H.)—THE KINGDOM OF GOD. 1s. 6d.

Steinmeyer (Dr. F. L.)—THE MIRACLES OF OUR LORD. 8vo, 7s. 6d.

Steinmeyer (Dr. F. L.)—THE HISTORY OF THE PASSION AND RESURRECTION OF OUR LORD, considered in the Light of Modern Criticism. 8vo, 10s. 6d.

Stevens (Prof. G. B., D.D.)—THE THEOLOGY OF THE NEW TESTAMENT. (*International Theological Library.*) Post 8vo.

Stevenson (Mrs.)—THE SYMBOLIC PARABLES. Crown 8vo, 3s. 6d.

Steward (Rev. G.)—MEDIATORIAL SOVEREIGNTY. Two vols. 8vo, 21s.

——— THE ARGUMENT OF THE EPISTLE TO THE HEBREWS. 8vo, 10s. 6d.

Stier (Dr. Rudolph)—ON THE WORDS OF THE LORD JESUS. Eight vols. 8vo, Subscription price of £2, 2s. Separate volumes, price 10s. 6d.

——— THE WORDS OF THE RISEN SAVIOUR, AND COMMENTARY ON THE EPISTLE OF ST. JAMES. 8vo, 10s. 6d.

——— THE WORDS OF THE APOSTLES EXPOUNDED. 8vo, 10s. 6d.

Stirling (Dr. J. Hutchison)—PHILOSOPHY AND THEOLOGY. Post 8vo, 9s.

——— DARWINIANISM : Workmen and Work. Post 8vo, 10s. 6d.

Tholuck (Prof.)—THE EPISTLE TO THE ROMANS. Two vols. fcap. 8vo, 8s.

Thomson (J. E. H., B.D.)—BOOKS WHICH INFLUENCED OUR LORD AND HIS APOSTLES. 8vo, 10s. 6d.

Thomson (Rev. E. A.)—MEMORIALS OF A MINISTRY. Crown 8vo, 5s.

Tophel (Pastor G.)—THE WORK OF THE HOLY SPIRIT. Cr. 8vo, 2s. 6d.

Troup (Rev. G. Elmslie, M.A.)—WORDS TO YOUNG CHRISTIANS : Being Addresses to Young Communicants. On antique laid paper, chaste binding, fcap. 8vo, 4s. 6d.

Uhlhorn (G.)—CHRISTIAN CHARITY IN THE ANCIENT CHURCH. Cr. 8vo, 6s.

Ullmann (Dr. Carl)—REFORMERS BEFORE THE REFORMATION, principally in Germany and the Netherlands. Two vols. 8vo, 21s.

Urwick (W., M.A.)—THE SERVANT OF JEHOVAH : A Commentary upon Isaiah lii. 13–liii. 12; with Dissertations upon Isaiah xl.–lxvi. 8vo, 3s.

Vinet (Life and Writings of). By L. M. LANE. Crown 8vo, 7s. 6d.

Vincent (Prof. M. R., D.D.)—THE AGE OF HILDEBRAND. (*Eras of Church History.*) 6s.

——— PHILIPPIANS AND PHILEMON. (*International Critical Commentary.*) Post 8vo, 8s. 6d.

Walker (James, of Carnwath)—ESSAYS, PAPERS, AND SERMONS. Post 8vo, 6s.

Walker (J., D.D.)—THEOLOGY AND THEOLOGIANS OF SCOTLAND. New Edition, crown 8vo, 3s. 6d.

Warfield (B. B.)—THE RIGHT OF SYSTEMATIC THEOLOGY. Crown 8vo, 2s.

Waterman (L., D.D.)—THE POST-APOSTOLIC AGE. (*Eras of Church History.*) 6s.

Watt (W. A.)—THE THEORY OF CONTRACT IN ITS SOCIAL LIGHT. 8vo, 3s.

Watts (Professor)—THE NEWER CRITICISM AND THE ANALOGY OF THE FAITH. Third Edition, crown 8vo, 5s.

——— THE REIGN OF CAUSALITY : A Vindication of the Scientific Principle of Telic Causal Efficiency. Crown 8vo, 6s.

——— THE NEW APOLOGETIC. Crown 8vo, 6s.

Weir (J. F., M.A.)—THE WAY : THE NATURE AND MEANS OF SALVATION. Ex. crown 8vo, 6s. 6d.

Weiss (Prof.)—BIBLICAL THEOLOGY OF NEW TESTAMENT. 2 vols. 8vo, 21s.

——— LIFE OF CHRIST. Three vols. 8vo, 31s. 6d.

Wells (Prof. C. L.)—THE AGE OF CHARLEMAGNE. (*Eras of the Christian Church.*) 6s.

Wendt (H. H., D.D.)—THE TEACHING OF JESUS. 2 vols. 8vo, 21s.

Wenley (R. M.)—CONTEMPORARY THEOLOGY AND THEISM. Crown 8vo, 4s. 6d.

White (Rev. M.)—SYMBOLICAL NUMBERS OF SCRIPTURE. Cr. 8vo, 4s.

Williams (E. F., D.D.)—CHRISTIAN LIFE IN GERMANY. Crown 8vo, 5s.

Winer (Dr. G. B.)—A TREATISE ON THE GRAMMAR OF NEW TESTAMENT GREEK, regarded as the Basis of New Testament Exegesis. Third Edition, edited by W. F. MOULTON, D.D. Ninth English Edition, 8vo, 15s.

——— THE DOCTRINES AND CONFESSIONS OF CHRISTENDOM. 8vo, 10s. 6d.

Witherow (Prof. T., D.D.)—THE FORM OF THE CHRISTIAN TEMPLE. 8vo, 10/6.

Woods (F. H., B.D.)—THE HOPE OF ISRAEL. Crown 8vo, 3s. 6d.

Workman (Prof. G. C.)—THE TEXT OF JEREMIAH; or, A Critical Investigation of the Greek and Hebrew, etc. Post 8vo, 9s.

Wright (C. H., D.D.)—BIBLICAL ESSAYS. Crown 8vo, 5s.

THE FOREIGN THEOLOGICAL LIBRARY.

The following are the Works from which a Selection of EIGHT VOLUMES for £2, 2s. (or more at the same ratio) may be made. (Non-subscription Price within brackets):—

Baumgarten—The History of the Church in the Apostolic Age. Three Vols. (27s.)
Bleek—Introduction to the New Testament. Two Vols. (21s.)
Cassel—Commentary on Esther. One Vol. (10s. 6d.)
Christlieb—Modern Doubt and Christian Belief. One Vol. (10s. 6d.)
Delitzsch—New Commentary on Genesis. Two Vols. (21s.)
—— Commentary on the Psalms. Three Vols. (31s. 6d.)
—— Commentary on the Proverbs of Solomon. Two Vols. (21s.)
—— Commentary on Song of Solomon and Ecclesiastes. One Vol. (10s. 6d.)
—— Commentary on the Prophecies of Isaiah. *Last Edition.* Two Vols. (21s.)
—— Commentary on Epistle to the Hebrews. Two Vols. (21s.)
—— A System of Biblical Psychology. One Vol. (12s.)
Döllinger—Hippolytus and Callistus; or, The Church of Rome: A.D. 200–250. One Vol. (7s. 6d.)
Dorner—A System of Christian Doctrine. Four Vols. (42s.)
—— History of the Development of the Doctrine of the Person of Christ. Five Vols. (52s. 6d.)
Ebrard—Commentary on the Epistles of St. John. One Vol. (10s. 6d.)
—— The Gospel History. One Vol. (10s. 6d.)   Apologetics. Three Vols. (31s. 6d.)
Ewald—Revelation : Its Nature and Record. One Vol. (10s. 6d.)
—— Old and New Testament Theology. One Vol. (10s. 6d.)
Frank—System of Christian Certainty. One Vol. (10s. 6d.)
Gebhardt—Doctrine of the Apocalypse. One Vol. (10s. 6d.)
Gerlach—Commentary on the Pentateuch. One Vol. (10s. 6d.)
Gieseler—Compendium of Ecclesiastical History: A.D. 451–1409. Three Vols. (31s. 6d.)
Godet—Commentary on St. Luke's Gospel. Two Vols. (21s.)
—— Commentary on St. John's Gospel. Three Vols. (31s. 6d.)
—— Commentary on the Epistle to the Romans. Two Vols. (21s.)
—— Commentary on 1st Corinthians. Two Vols. (21s.)
Goebel—On the Parables. One Vol. (10s. 6d.)
Hagenbach—History of the Reformation. Two Vols. (21s.)
—— History of Christian Doctrines. Three Vols. (31s. 6d.)
Harless—A System of Christian Ethics. One Vol. (10s. 6d.)
Haupt—Commentary on the First Epistle of St. John. One Vol. (10s. 6d.)
Hävernick—General Introduction to the Old Testament. One Vol. (10s. 6d.)
Hengstenberg—Christology of the Old Testament. Four Vols. (42s.)
—— Commentary on the Psalms. Three Vols. (33s.)
—— On the Book of Ecclesiastes, etc. etc. One Vol. (9s.)
—— Commentary on the Gospel of St. John. Two Vols. (21s.)
—— Commentary on Ezekiel. One Vol. (10s. 6d.)
—— Dissertations on the Genuineness of Daniel, etc. One Vol. (12s.)
—— The Kingdom of God under the Old Covenant. Two Vols. (21s.)
Keil—Introduction to the Old Testament. Two Vols. (21s.)
—— Commentary on the Pentateuch. Three Vols. (31s. 6d.)
—— Commentary on Joshua, Judges, and Ruth. One Vol. (10s. 6d.)
—— Commentary on the Books of Samuel. One Vol. (10s. 6d.)
—— Commentary on the Books of Kings. One Vol. (10s. 6d.)
—— Commentary on the Books of Chronicles. One Vol. (10s. 6d.)
—— Commentary on Ezra, Nehemiah, and Esther. One Vol. (10s. 6d.)
—— Commentary on Jeremiah and Lamentations. Two Vols. (21s.)
—— Commentary on Ezekiel. Two Vols. (21s.)   Book of Daniel. One Vol. (10s. 6d.)
—— Commentary on the Minor Prophets. Two Vols. (21s.)
—— Biblical Archæology. Two Vols. (21s.)
Kurtz—History of the Old Covenant; or, Old Testament Dispensation. Three Vols. (31s. 6d.)
Lange—Commentary on the Gospels of St. Matthew and St. Mark. Three Vols. (31s. 6d.)
—— Commentary on the Gospel of St. Luke. Two Vols. (18s.)   St. John. Two Vols. (21s.)
Luthardt—Commentary on the Gospel of St. John. Three Vols. (31s. 6d.)
—— History of Christian Ethics to the Reformation. One Vol. (10s. 6d.)
Macdonald—Introduction to the Pentateuch. Two Vols. (21s.)
—— Christian Ethics. General—Social—Individual. Three Vols. (31s. 6d.)
Martensen—Christian Dogmatics. One Vol. (10s. 6d.)
Müller—The Christian Doctrine of Sin. Two Vols. (21s.)
Murphy—Commentary on the Psalms. *To count as Two Volumes.* One Vol. (12s.)
Neander—General History of the Christian Religion and Church. Vols. I. to VIII. (60s.)
Oehler—Biblical Theology of the Old Testament. Two Vols. (21s.)
Olshausen—Commentary on the Gospels and Acts. Four Vols. (42s.)
—— Commentary on Epistle to the Romans. One Vol. (10s. 6d.)   Corinthians. One Vol. (9s.)
—— Commentary on Philippians, Titus, and 1st Timothy. One Vol. (10s. 6d.)
Orelli—Prophecy regarding Consummation of God's Kingdom. One Vol. (10s. 6d.)
—— Commentary on Isaiah. One Vol. (10s. 6d.)   Jeremiah. One Vol. (10s. 6d.)
Philippi—Commentary on Epistle to Romans. Two Vols. (21s.)
Räbiger—Encyclopædia of Theology. Two Vols. (21s.)
Ritter—Comparative Geography of Palestine. Four Vols. (26s.)
Sartorius—The Doctrine of Divine Love. One Vol. (10s. 6d.)
Schürer—The Jewish People in the Time of Christ. Five Vols. (10s. 6d. each.)
Shedd—History of Christian Doctrine. Two Vols. (21s.)
Steinmeyer—History of the Passion and Resurrection of our Lord. One Vol. (10s. 6d.)
—— The Miracles of our Lord in relation to Modern Criticism. One Vol. (7s. 6d.)
Stier—The Words of the Lord Jesus. Eight Vols. (10s. 6d. per vol.)
—— The Words of the Risen Saviour, and Commentary on Epistle of St. James. One Vol. (10s. 6d.)
—— The Words of the Apostles Expounded. One Vol. (10s. 6d.)
Ullmann—Reformers before the Reformation. Two Vols. (21s.)
Weiss—Biblical Theology of the New Testament. 2 Vols. (21s.)   The Life of Christ. 3 Vols. (31s. 6d.)

THE INTERNATIONAL THEOLOGICAL LIBRARY.

THE following eminent Scholars have contributed, or are engaged upon, the Volumes named :—

An Introduction to the Literature of the Old Testament.	By S. R. DRIVER, D.D., Regius Professor of Hebrew, and Canon of Christ Church, Oxford. [*Seventh Edition.* 12s.
Christian Ethics.	By NEWMAN SMYTH, D.D., Pastor of the First Congregational Church, New Haven, Conn. [*Third Edition.* 10s. 6d.
Apologetics.	By A. B. BRUCE, D.D., Professor of New Testament Exegesis, Free Church College, Glasgow. [*Third Edition.* 10s. 6d.
History of Christian Doctrine.	By G. P. FISHER, D.D., LL.D., Professor of Ecclesiastical History, Yale University, New Haven, Conn. [*Second Edition.* 12s.
A History of Christianity in the Apostolic Age.	By ARTHUR CUSHMAN McGIFFERT, Ph.D., D.D., Professor of Church History, Union Theological Seminary, New York. [12s.
Christian Institutions.	By A. V. G. ALLEN, D.D., Professor of Ecclesiastical History, Episcopal Theological School, Cambridge, Mass. [12s.
The Christian Pastor.	By WASHINGTON GLADDEN, D.D., Pastor of Congregational Church, Columbus, Ohio. [10s. 6d.
Theology of the New Testament.	By GEORGE B. STEVENS, Ph.D., D.D., Professor of Systematic Theology in Yale University, U.S.A. [*Just published.* 12s.
Theology of the Old Testament.	By A. B. DAVIDSON, D.D., LL.D., Professor of Hebrew, New College, Edinburgh.
An Introduction to the Literature of the New Testament.	By S. D. F. SALMOND, D.D., Principal, and Professor of Systematic Theology and New Testament Exegesis, Free Church College, Aberdeen.
Old Testament History.	By H. P. SMITH, D.D., late Professor of Biblical History and Interpretation, Amherst College, U.S.A.
Canon and Text of the New Testament.	By CASPAR RENÉ GREGORY, Ph.D., Professor in the University of Leipzig.
The Latin Church.	By ARCHIBALD ROBERTSON, D.D., Principal of King's College, London.
The Ancient Catholic Church.	By ROBERT RAINY, D.D., Principal of the New College, Edinburgh.
Encyclopædia.	By C. A. BRIGGS, D.D., Professor of Biblical Theology, Union Theological Seminary, New York.
Contemporary History of the Old Testament.	By FRANCIS BROWN, D.D., Professor of Hebrew and Cognate Languages, Union Theological Seminary, New York.
Contemporary History of the New Testament.	By FRANK C. PORTER, Ph.D., Yale University, New Haven, Conn.
Philosophy of Religion.	By ROBERT FLINT, D.D., LL.D., Professor of Divinity in the University of Edinburgh.
The Study of the Old Testament.	By HERBERT E. RYLE, D.D., President of Queens' College, Cambridge.
Rabbinical Literature.	By S. SCHECHTER, M.A., Reader in Talmudic in the University of Cambridge.
The Life of Christ.	By WILLIAM SANDAY, D.D., LL.D., Lady Margaret Professor of Divinity, and Canon of Christ Church, Oxford.
The Christian Preacher.	By JOHN WATSON, D.D. ('IAN MACLAREN'), Sefton Park Presbyterian Church of England, Liverpool.

EDINBURGH: T. & T. CLARK, 38 GEORGE STREET.

THE INTERNATIONAL CRITICAL COMMENTARY.

EIGHT VOLUMES NOW READY, VIZ. :—

Deuteronomy (Dr. Driver), 12s. ; **Judges** (Dr. Moore), 12s. ; **Samuel** (Dr. H. P. Smith), 12s. ; **S. Mark** (Dr. Gould), 10s. 6d. ; **S. Luke** (Dr. Plummer), 12s. ; **Romans** (Dr. Sanday and Mr. Headlam), 12s. ; **Ephesians and Colossians** (Dr. T. K. Abbott), 10s. 6d. ; **Philippians and Philemon** (Dr. Vincent), 8s. 6d.

The following other Volumes are in course of preparation :—

THE OLD TESTAMENT.

Genesis.	T. K. CHEYNE, D.D., Oriel Professor of the Interpretation of Holy Scripture, Oxford.
Exodus.	A. R. S. KENNEDY, D.D., Professor of Hebrew, University of Edinburgh.
Leviticus.	Rev. H. A. WHITE, M.A., Fellow of New College, Oxford, and Theological Tutor in the University of Durham.
Numbers.	G. BUCHANAN GRAY, M.A., Lecturer in Hebrew, Mansfield College, Oxford.
Joshua.	GEORGE ADAM SMITH, D.D., Professor of Hebrew, Free Church College, Glasgow.
Kings.	FRANCIS BROWN, D.D., Professor of Hebrew and Cognate Languages, Union Theological Seminary, New York.
Isaiah.	A. B. DAVIDSON, D.D., LL.D., Professor of Hebrew, Free Church College, Edinburgh.
Jeremiah.	A. F. KIRKPATRICK, D.D., Regius Professor of Hebrew, and Fellow of Trinity College, Cambridge.
Minor Prophets.	W. R. HARPER, Ph.D., President of Chicago University.
Psalms.	C. A. BRIGGS, D.D., Edward Robinson Professor of Biblical Theology, Union Theological Seminary, New York.
Proverbs.	C. H. TOY, D.D., Professor of Hebrew, Harvard University, Cambridge, Massachusets.
Job.	S. R. DRIVER, D.D., Regius Professor of Hebrew, Oxford.
Daniel.	Rev. JOHN P. PETERS, Ph.D., late Professor of Hebrew, P. E. Divinity School, Philadelphia, now Rector of St. Michael's Church, New York City.
Ezra and Nehemiah.	Rev. L. W. BATTEN, Ph.D., Professor of Hebrew, P. E. Divinity School, Philadelphia.
Chronicles.	EDWARD L. CURTIS, D.D., Professor of Hebrew, Yale University, New Haven, Conn.

THE NEW TESTAMENT.

Acts.	FREDERICK H. CHASE, D.D., Christ's College, Cambridge.
Corinthians.	ARCH. ROBERTSON, D.D., Principal of King's College, London.
Galatians.	Rev. ERNEST D. BURTON, A.B., Professor of New Testament Literature, University of Chicago.
The Pastoral Epistles.	Rev. WALTER LOCK, M.A., Dean Ireland's Professor of Exegesis, Oxford.
Hebrews.	T. C. EDWARDS, D.D., Principal of the Theological College, Bala ; late Principal of University College of Wales, Aberystwyth.
James.	Rev. JAMES H. ROPES, A.B., Instructor in New Testament Criticism in Harvard University.
Peter and Jude.	CHARLES BIGG, D.D., Rector of Fenny Compton, Leamington ; Bampton Lecturer, 1886.
Revelation.	Rev. ROBERT H. CHARLES, M.A., Trinity College, Dublin, and Exeter College, Oxford.

Other engagements will be announced shortly.

EDINBURGH: T. & T. CLARK, 38 GEORGE STREET.
LONDON: SIMPKIN, MARSHALL, HAMILTON, KENT, & CO. LTD.